# The Catholic Tradition

REV. CHARLES J. DOLLEN
DR. JAMES K. McGOWAN
DR. JAMES J. MEGIVERN
EDITORS

# The Catholic Tradition

## Personal Ethics

### Volume 2

A Consortium Book

Library of Congress Card Catalog Number: 79-1977
ISBN: 0-8434-0729-8
ISBN: 0-8434-0725-5 series

The publisher gratefully acknowledges permission to quote from the
following copyrighted sources. In cases where those properties contain
scholarly apparatus such as footnotes, such footnotes have been omitted
in the interest of the general reader.

AMERICA PRESS
Vatican II *Declaration on Religious Freedom* edited by Walter M.
Abbott, S.J., ©1966.

ANDREWS AND McMEEL, INC.
Selections from *Sin, Liberty and Law* by Louis Monden, S.J., translated
by Joseph Donceel, S.J. © 1965 Sheed and Ward. Reprinted by permission of Andrews and McMeel, Inc.

BRUCE PUBLISHING COMPANY
Chapter 11 from *The Power and the Wisdom, An Interpretation of the
New Testament* by John L. McKenzie, S.J., ©1965. Reprinted by per-
mission of Bruce Publishing Company.

GEOFFREY CHAPMAN LTD.
Selections from *Christ and the Modern Conscience* by Jacques Leclercq,
translated by Ronald Matthews. © 1962 Geoffrey Chapman, a division
of Cassell Ltd. Reprinted by permission of Geoffrey Chapman, Ltd.

CHARLES E. CURRAN
Chapter 1 from *New Perspectives in Moral Theology* by Charles E.
Curran, Fides Publishers, Inc. Copyright © 1974 by Charles E. Curran.
Reprinted by permission of Charles E. Curran.

DOUBLEDAY & COMPANY, INC.
Selections reprinted from *Toward a New Catholic Morality* by John G.
Milhaven. Copyright © 1970 by John G. Milhaven. Used by permission
of Doubleday & Company, Inc.

# Table of Contents

## THE CATHOLIC TRADITION: Personal Ethics

# Bernard Häring
## 1912-

"*The principle, the norm, the center, and the goal of Christian moral theology is Christ. The law of the Christian is Christ Himself in Person. He alone is our Lord, our Savior. In Him we have life and therefore also the law of our life. . . . The Christian life is following Christ, but not through mere external copying, even though it be in love and obedience. Our life must above all be a life in Christ.*"

*With this beautiful and simple statement, rare in the history of manuals of moral theology, Father Bernard Häring, a German theologian with an international reputation for his sound theological scholarship, introduces his work,* The Law of Christ. *His objective was to describe the perfect ideal of the life in Christ and for Christ. He wanted also to point out the limits of the law beyond which lies the realm of death and loss of the life in Christ.*

*From the structural point of view, Häring goes about his task in a fairly traditional style. His first volume is general moral theology, which treats basic concepts. Volume two, special moral theology, studies the virtues of faith, hope, love and religion. The influences mentioned by Häring in his introduction are Augustine, Cyril of Jerusalem, Thomas Aquinas and Alphonse Liguori, as well as several theologians of modern times.*

*What is unique about Häring's work is not the subject matter or the organization of it, but the perspective through which he approaches moral theology. After a few centuries of a rather legalistic perspective, mention of Christ and love are almost startling. Is it not strange that theologians had wandered so far from the original insights of the Christian message? The law had been so over-emphasized that the simplicity of evangelical love had been forgotten. It is for this reason that the modern generation of moral theologians owes much to Bernard Häring. He sees Christian morality as life flowing from the victory of Christ, as salutary and apostolic, as oriented toward mystical identification of one's whole being in Christ.*

*We have selected, for our reading below, a portion from Häring's first volume, a chapter entitled "The True Basis of Morality." Human freedom, which is the basis, is the capacity to take one's stand in accepting or rejecting God's call. It remains a great mystery, anchored in the more profound mystery of God's own freedom. There are degrees of freedom, limits, and ways to destroy freedom. Häring carefully explores all of these aspects. The discussion of freedom leads into the theme of the knowledge of God, which is the basis of all value. Here, concepts such as man's likeness to God, knowledge of good and moral knowledge are thoroughly clarified.*

*Bernard Häring's work can be seen as a nexus between an era that was dominated by the legal approach to existence and the post-Vatican II era. It really belongs to neither. While showing where we have been and can no longer be, it points toward a future that is necessarily full of risk—for lovers there is no law.*

# THE LAW OF CHRIST

## CHAPTER FOUR

### THE TRUE BASIS OF MORALITY

I n the previous section we surveyed the setting of moral activity. We presented the background of tremendous dimensions which provides the setting for moral decision and personal moral growth and development. Moral responsibility embraces both body and soul. Its roots are sunk deep in every sphere of the social order; its effects are experienced in every social area. Its source and effects can be traced to the past, into the depths of history and the *eschata* of history. Man with full moral responsibility stands in the shadow of the divine majesty through the obligation of divine cult. However, the direct and immediate source of moral responsibility is the free will of man which can be considered morally free and responsible only in the light of man's knowledge of values, his own inner disposition and spirit, his own conscience.

### I. HUMAN FREEDOM AS BASIS OF MORALITY

#### 1. *The Essence of Freedom*

We recognize the true nature of our freedom when we perceive values and experience the challenge of the morally good. Often we are brought to the keenest realization of our freedom by the very revolt of evil which we confidently trust we can resist and master. Freedom is not enunciated in the necessity of the Must, but in the Ought of the good, not in the triumph of sin, but in the temptation to embrace it. Freedom exists only in those profound depths of personality where the convictions are formed and positions taken, accepting the divine summons or revolting against it. In essence freedom is the power to do good. The power to do evil is not of its essence. Freedom is present only where there is the power to overcome evil. Indifference to good or evil is not a quality of liberty as such, but only of the finite and limited liberty of man. The power to do good, however, derives from the likeness of man to God, from the created participation in the divine freedom. When man is infallibly preserved from sin through the action of efficacious grace, he suffers no loss of liberty, but attains a superior power of freedom, which in itself transcends the normal condition of his finite nature.

### a. Human Freedom in the Divine Image

Just as God is the Lord of the entire universe because He created it, so is man the ruler of the universe because God created him in His own likeness and placed him over it. "God created man to his own image: to the image of God he created him: male and female he created them. And God blessed them, saying: 'Increase and multiply and fill the earth, and subdue it, and rule over the fishes of the sea, and the fowls of the air, and all living creatures that move upon the earth.' " (Gn 1:27f.). God is Lord and Creator of the world. He does not spend Himself in creation and governance of the universe, but He celebrates His eternal Sabbath rest, His absolute blessedness apart from the world. In like manner the freedom of man is not spent in the task of ruling the world. If he is not completely absorbed in this mundane effort, if he is not taken up altogether in things of the world, but constantly raises his eyes to the Sabbath joy of God, then his freedom is safeguarded and preserved.

God's liberty is absolutely circumscribed only by His own great glory, for there can be no motive for His free acts outside Himself. Analogously God's creature, man, made in the divine image, is constrained by nothing beyond his own freedom, for nothing altogether extrinsic to himself can determine or force his will.

Just as God transcends the world and yet preserves and governs it immanently, so in an analogous manner the free will of man transcends the composite of soul and body (only analogously, for there is no complete independence), and yet governs the entire body-soul structure with all the human urges and drives through the most intimate coordination with them. Similarly in the pattern of the divine causality, as God is the First Cause and has no cause outside Himself moving Him,

4

so it is with man, though in an analogous and limited manner. Always dependent on God in all his acts, he is still a kind of first principle, a manner of "first cause." "He in himself is the cause that in one instance he becomes grain, in the other chaff."

Freedom is always fresh and new, always a creative beginning. It pertains to its essence that the free act is never univocally predetermined. But the free act itself, though on an entirely distinct level, is the first determining cause of the still undetermined movement of the will. It is really a new beginning, which is truly "creative" in so far as it is posited new and for the first time by the will. But it is not blind and irrational. Rather, as God creates according to the pattern of ideas, so also the creative new beginning in the free act decides according to motives, according to guiding ideas.

### b. Human Freedom, Participation in the Divine

Human freedom is the capacity to take one's stand in accepting or rejecting God's call to us, but only by virtue of a participation in the divine freedom. The free human act produces itself, is a cause of itself (*causa sui*), though always dependently, for it depends on the First Cause. Even though absolutely speaking man himself in his voluntary act is the cause of his sin and the "first cause of the fall from grace," he can be so only by force of the actuation of his freedom to do good through the exercise of the causality which comes from the First Cause, God. Sin as defeat of freedom is a diminution of the sharing of divine freedom and therefore a lessening of human freedom itself. Conversely, the highest participation in the divine freedom is acting entirely under the influence of divine grace.

Altogether incomprehensible, especially to the science which relies solely on principles of natural causality, human liberty remains ever a great mystery, for it rests on the still greater mystery of God's own freedom. Most obscure in this mystery of human freedom is its participation on the one hand in the divine freedom and its profound inviolability on the other. It partakes of God's freedom and yet is so highly esteemed by God Himself and so utterly and inviolably its own that man can say no to God by force of the very freedom God grants him.

5

The grandeur of human freedom is manifested in the most exalted fashion when it surrenders entirely to the guidance of grace and thus becomes capable of saying yes to God, in filial obedient love in and through Christ. The dizzy height of freedom towering over the abyss of evil manifests itself in the terrifying and incomprehensible power of decision against Christ, which expels the Spirit of God, the loving source of liberty itself.

## 2. Degrees of Freedom

The power of freedom is effective on many levels, highly diversified in breadth and depth. Human freedom is greatly restricted in its scope by our biological and spiritual heritage and by our environment through the attraction of motives or ideals and the suggestion of lines of action. It is also circumscribed in many ways by the effects of our previous conduct and former free decisions.

The power of freedom is granted us only in germ. Its seeds implanted in us must grow from within through the development of person into personality. This growth and expansion is through the full exercise of the inherent capacity of the will tending to the good. Freedom in man is the power by which he transcends himself in his own act, attaining thereby—albeit gradually and progressively—a new and higher freedom. But neglect of the practice of true freedom (freedom in omission) or failure to exploit it fully will result in atrophy of liberty. If practiced only in the failure which is sin, it is progressively reduced to impotence for the good and ultimately impotence for true freedom altogether. On this point it is necessary to caution against any delusion arising from the force of passion in doing evil. It is true that freedom, if it is not to become impotent, must press the passions into its service. But the characteristic power of human freedom is to guide and direct them; its deepest impotence is to be overcome by them. Even though the utmost force of passion is manifested in evil, still the power of freedom itself is no greater than its practical capacity to channel the forces of passion into the good.

Freedom can be so far lost that the spirit becomes entirely the slave of base drives, free and responsible in its enslavement only because of prior voluntary decisions made when the capacity to choose the course of good was not yet vitiated. But still we must hold fast to the conviction that, so long as we are pilgrims on earthly sojourn, God will never deny the grace of returning to Him. To everyone still possessed of normal mind and will He graciously grants the power to take the first step toward conversion. But a new guilt is always incurred if the sinner delays his conversion.

Freedom can also attain the stage in which man surrenders entirely to the guidance of the Spirit. "Now the Lord is the spirit; and where the spirit of the Lord is, there is freedom" (2 Cor 3:17). There is no greater freedom than that of the children of God, who have freely risen above the impotence of sin, thrown off the shackles of the slavery of Satan, and voluntarily submitted to the law and yoke of Christ; who have liberated themselves from the selfish quest of self and from the law as a mere instrument of self-righteousness, and instead have placed themselves entirely in the service of the Kingdom of God. They have freed themselves from the universal law as the sole and ultimate norm of morality and without constraint of law have accepted the joyous responsibility of seeking what is most perfect in the situation in which God has placed them; they have cast aside all desire of resisting the guidance of the Holy Spirit and have thus arrived at the very summit of freedom in obedient service to God.

Freedom is both a gift from the divine bounty and a divinely imposed task; it is both gift and burden. It is like a bud with the urge to blossom forth and ripen into rich fruit of virtue. But like the bud it can wither away, fail to blossom and ripen. Then the power of virtue is lost, and freedom becomes impotent. Freedom which makes man responsible for his actions is itself a noble trust committed to man, a tremendous responsibility.

### 3. *Freedom and Law, Freedom and Motive*

God's freedom knows neither law nor limitation outside Himself, but it would be rash to hold that it is in the slightest capricious or arbitrary. It is governed by the inviolable law of the sanctity of the divine essence. God's free will is under the sovereign law of divine love. Similarly human freedom, if it is true freedom in action, is not submission to the coercive pressure of external force, but self-fulfillment through inner love of the good in accordance with the pattern of the divine holiness which is the eternal law (*lex aeterna*) reflected in man's own nature (*lex naturalis*). Obviously God's freedom is infallibly effective in accordance with the law of His sanctity, whereas man on his earthly sojourn is in constant danger of lapsing from the lofty eminence of obedience to law and thereby marring the integrity of his liberty. But he is still free even in his defection from the integrity and ideal of freedom, free in breaking the hedge of freedom which is the law and lapsing into the slavery of license. The law is the warning which safeguards liberty. It grants liberty and imposes a task upon it: law is both gift and summons to duty. The more the Christian grows to maturity in the liberty of God's children, the more does the law of God unfold itself to him as a living safeguard of love. It is the hedge that encircles the golden center of love. Only those who possess the liberty of the children of God have real insight into the true nature of law, which in its depths is loving dialogue with God.

In the divine activity God's creative freedom is in accord with the pattern of his eternal ideas. Therefore human freedom, fashioned in the divine image, is all the greater the more man's activity is motivated by clear and evident ideals. Just as God Himself cannot act outside Himself without the light of His own love, so too man cannot exercise his freedom without motives. And as God in His free creative activity chooses from the infinite treasure of His eternal ideas, so man (analogously) within certain limitations chooses among a diversity of motives. He can elect from among various good motives, preferring one to another. He can choose between the evident good and the enticement of darksome passion, choose the illusory allurement of sheer pleasure and profit or follow the attraction of the morally good motives pleasing to God, often obscured by the vain pleasure of sense.

The crucial point in question regarding liberty is not whether the external act flows freely from the inner source (from the *actus elicitus,* the elicited act), but whether this inner

8

source itself is pre-determined by the free will itself or by something else. The decisive question is this: is freedom unequivocally determined by the motives which press upon it, or does it transcend these very motives and remain free in choosing (though it cannot make any choice without motive)? The will is not necessitated. It determines itself in making its own final or ultimate decision, whether it permits itself to be drawn to the basically good and lofty or abandons itself to the illusive splendor of self—self-glory or self-seeking. Once this final or ultimate decision has been made (i.e., the willed choice of what shall be the ultimate and decisive goal of life), the motives directing one's particular actions still leave room for freedom within their own area and according to their own scope of influence, so that the will is not necessitated by them, but itself selects from among them and directs them in accordance with the ultimate goal (assuming, of course, the limitations imposed by psychological laws).

If a motive thrusts itself upon the spirit of man with such insistence as to create an abnormal psychological tension which diverts the free will from every other possible alternative, then psychic coercion has removed the conditions of freedom. It is quite a different matter if the will with undivided force of freedom is motivated by a clear and lofty incentive. The more profound the motivation, the more potent is the freedom. In the choice and nurture of true ideals lies the final decision of freedom.

### 4. Education to Freedom

From what we have just said, it is evident that any formation in obedience which merely domineers by means of imperatives, without furnishing insights and motivation, breaks the free will, at best "breaks it in," but does not truly educate it. Though liberty is in part a matter of exercise and use (of true freedom), it is still much more a matter of fostering motives with insight and love. This throws light upon the importance of meditation in the spiritual life. Education to obedience springing from the inmost source of liberty must be based on motivation rather than command. Even though at first the mind cannot provide an insight into the inmost nature of the good itself, still there must always be the wholesome motivation of noble authority and the gradual clarification of the intrinsic values and a growing perception of the worth of the commandment.

Genuine formation in obedience is without doubt also education in the law (in the established norm of the good), but it is even more initiation into liberty which goes beyond the universal law, into that liberty which is born of the insight into the good and of love for the good and for that which is always more perfect. Freedom unfolds its capacity as it exercises itself in obedience, but it must be obedience of the spirit. And this is impossible without the true spirit of independence and self-mastery. The spirit of true independence (virtue of freedom) reigns when the Christian acts even without bidding, when he possesses the disposition and will to obey even though there may be no mandate or precept. The spirit of obedience is marked by free initiative and acceptance of responsibility even without command.

### 5. *The Limit and Extent of Liberty*

Man's liberty is relatively narrow in the scope of its activity, though, as explained above, this scope can be significantly and gradually broadened. But it can likewise be restricted and narrowed through our own fault. Scope, impress, limit of freedom are all determined by one's own individual temperament, by the historic heritage, by the moral level of environment, by the surrounding communities. The "destiny" of man sets the bounds of his liberty, but it also determines the tasks and duties and broadens the scope of the free actions. Man must accept his destiny in freedom, bear up with it, and at the same time master it.

Freedom is effective not merely on the immediate level of decision or in actual intention (*intentio actualis*). In every moral act, besides the present actual free decision, in some way the prior decisions, the predeterminations, the prejudices make themselves felt. The virtual intention (*intentio virtualis*) is the prolongation of previous decisions which are still effective in their influence until they are revoked or completely lose their dynamic power. Even in conversion, which is the act of renouncing or repudiating the past and revoking the prior false

10

decisions of the will, they still may exert a very considerable influence as false attitudes or dispositions (examples are the lowering of esteem for true values due to mental dullness or partial blindness in this important area, superficiality in positive value judgments). Only steadfast and determined personal intervention will enable us to deprive these prior decisions of their force and render them impotent.

It is likewise true that previous decisions of our will often exert no influence on subsequent series of acts either because their effectiveness is suspended for the moment, even though the past may not have been actually repudiated or renounced, or—and this is usually the case—because they are not our present concern. However, for this very reason they can reassert themselves when occasion arises, since the disposition and tendency (*habitus*) still persist. The unrevoked prior intention or attitude of mind which does not influence the subsequent acts is a habitual intention (*intentio habitualis*). But should it again become efficacious, it is no longer merely a habitual, but a virtual intention by which we again influence the subsequent acts.

We speak of a presumed intention or readiness of will (*intentio interpretativa*) in those instances of doubt when we have no evidence that the intention was ever actually made, but reasonably presume that it was. From the entire attitude of the individual concerned we have reason to assume that he would have made such an act (the actual intention if the matter had been placed before him for decision, or that he actually did so. An interpretative intention is real and effective in so far as it is rooted in this attitude of the Christian and is expressed in acts corresponding to it.

## 6. *Extent of Responsibility in Free Decision*

Man is directly accountable for the entire object of his free decision, whether it be through positive act or through failure to act. In fact, the consequences of omission can be as important and as far reaching as the effects of the positive acts, or acts of commission. Man is responsible, not merely for what he directly chooses or decides upon, but also for the other objects which are mediately or indirectly within his choice. In this way they fall within the scope of his intention. Responsibility, in fact, extends to much which is not included in his particular intention as means or end (*voluntarium in se* or *voluntarium directum*), but which is foreseen as a mere result of the act intended without being directly intended or sought (*voluntarium in causa* or *indirectum*).

An example: a drinker knows how he will act when he is under the influence of drink. He may indulge in profanity, resort to quarreling or fighting, engage in immoral conversation. Despite his attempt to assure himself as he takes his drinks, "I just want to enjoy a drink or two," he is still the voluntary cause responsible for all the resultant deviations in moral conduct precisely because he voluntarily makes himself their cause. He freely does the act and foresees, in a general way at least, the effects which will ensue. The guilt, however, and it is important not to overlook this point, is not so serious as the guilt of the premeditated offense. One who consciously seeks after a sinful object is far more culpable than one who is guilty as cause. The malice is greater in the former instance because there is a greater freedom of will in the choice of evil.

The mature man must have a keen realization of the profound and far-reaching influence of his moral conduct on his own personality as a whole and on the community, both in the immediate present and in the future. And if he does good or evil with this background of general knowledge, he also assumes the responsibility for his act and its consequences. He must bear the burden of blame for his bartering with evil and is responsible for the evil consequences of his acts, even though he may deplore them. However, the difference between deliberate choice of evil and the conscious but regretful acceptance of it in this form of package deal is quite apparent.

Responsibility for the consequences of such decisions is all the weightier the more certain and immediate is the consequence or effect which is foreseen, though not intended. The certainty is greater if the cause is direct (*causa per se*) than if it is indirect (*causa per accidens*). The effect is more immediate if the cause is a proximate or immediate cause (*causa proxima vel immediata*) than if it is only mediate or remote (*causa mediata vel remota*). There is a vast difference between an act which physically and necessarily produces an effect as its efficient cause and a moral impulse given to the free act of another.

One cannot entirely prevent one's own good or even one's obligatory acts from accidentally (*per accidens*) or remotely (*remote*) producing many evil effects. Some of these are physical, such as suffering and hardship; others are moral, as vexation and scandal to others (actions with double effect). Still there is an obligation in conscience to prevent the evil effects if one can do so without offending against what is right in the particular situation in which one is placed, or against the good which one is obliged to do. If the act as such and immediately (*per se et proxime*) produces an undesired evil effect, then only proportionately serious reasons (fulfillment of an obligation, attainment of a higher necessary good) can justify the act despite the evil effects. But all the circumstances must be seriously pondered. And under no condition may evil effects which in themselves are unlawful as ends of our action, be employed as means even for the attainment of a good end. Nor is it licit to will them or approve of them subsequently in the completion of the action. Moral evil may never be made the direct object of the deliberate free act of our will.

### 7. Diminution and Destruction of Liberty

#### a. Interference with Liberty: Violence

A purely physical intervention proceeding from some external agent can destroy the freedom to perform an external action (*actus imperatus*), but not the liberty of interior decision. Violence or force, in any instance, if it is bound up with the refined cruelty of present-day methods of psychological torture, can constitute a serious temptation and often also contribute toward a notable diminution of inner freedom.

An example of violence is that of the sinful attack on a virtuous girl: by firm exercise of her freedom she can adhere steadfastly to chastity in her mind and heart and also shun every wilful word and deed contrary to the virtue. The result of the violence to which she is shamefully subjected is not really a human act (*actus humanus*) on her part, but passive sufferance. Therefore, it is neither voluntary nor imputable (*actus imputabilis*) except in so far as the inner decision of her will may not have been sufficiently firm and the external resistance may have fallen short of the vigor possible and necessary in the particular circumstances.

### b. Diminution of Freedom: Fear

Fear which arises entirely from without (*metus ab extrinseco*) can weaken or destroy freedom of the will only to the extent that it produces a partial or total paralysis of the powers of the soul (*metus ab intrinseco*). In some instances sheer exterior force or the threat of force can so completely unsettle man inwardly that he is no longer master of his own inner acts and still less of his external actions.

Fear which is overcome by freedom (*metus concomitans*) reveals the power of free will. Fear which precedes decision of will (*metus antecedens*) does not in itself lessen liberty and accountability. Surely it is possible that extreme fear stifle freedom and responsibility temporarily and yet not destroy imputability for the simple reason that guilt may have been incurred through the prior failure to control incipient fear when mind and will were still capable of facing the menace.

The new psychology distinguishes between fear and anxiety: fear knows exactly the reason for fright and is in direct proportion to the cause producing it, neither greater nor less. Consequently, control over it is more readily within man's grasp. But anxiety is the haunting formless fear in which the individual does not know what he fears, but is just afraid. Fear becomes anxiety when one succumbs entirely to it, so that the feeling of anxiety (acute anxiety) is out of all proportion to the cause of fear.

Anyone who violates a commandment binding him in conscience because of fear of temporal loss or of punishment is guilty of sin. Even the menace of torture or death can never justify any act in itself sinful, such as apostasy from the faith or denial of the faith. But if fear arising from anxiety totally or partially unbalances the mind, then freedom is destroyed or diminished and consequently the guilt is entirely absent or is diminished. Fear of a great evil or loss out of all proportion to the gravity of the law itself excuses from any positive law, for such laws do not bind so strictly as to require their observance even at a great loss or under great difficulty.

What is true of fear holds also for the other passions—sadness, joy, anger. But the passion which is controlled and channeled properly by the free will increases the force of the free action.

### c. Diminution of Freedom: Unbridled Concupiscence

In so far as inordinate concupiscence precedes the free decision of the will (*concupiscentia antecedens*), it can diminish liberty, but it is a constant challenge to the full assertion of freedom and the mastery of passion. When passion disturbs the mind (above all, through the imagination) to the extent that the use of reason is entirely lost, it also destroys freedom altogether. But passion to which the will has freely consented (*concupiscentia consequens*) strengthens the voluntariness of the action through its organic drive. Because the degree of freedom at the moment of decision is above all the determining factor in the gravity of sin, the sins of weakness committed under spell and lure of passion are not so grave as sins of malice to which the will freely consents with cold and dispassionate calculation. We must differentiate between the force of will as such (*voluntarium*) and the power of free decision (*liberum*), which stand in inverse relationship to each other under the abnormal conditions referred to. Morover, in drawing the line between sins of malice and sins of weakness, the distinction of motives is highly significant, for the motive largely determines the merit or demerit of the act.

The impulses of passion and concupiscence which precede the free decision of the will are devoid of all moral guilt. But there may be a degree of culpability, for the very passion in evil concupiscence is often the effect of previous sinful conduct. Similarly evil impulses are frequently voluntary in their source or cause. In the language of the schools, impulses which have not been brought under the discipline of reason and free will are "non-deliberate impulses" (*motus primo primi*). Disordered impulses which are not fully deliberate because distraction or confusion of mind disturbs the attention or because they lack the full and complete approval of the will (*motus secundo primi*) can never be more than venial sin. For every grave sin is a perfectly free act. Only the deliberate evil concupiscence and disordered passion (*motus secundi*) which the free will fully approves are mortal sins, always assuming that the object is a matter of moment.

### d. Diminution or Loss of Freedom through Ignorance

If there is no conscious advertence to law or value on the part of the mind, there can be no question of violation of law. Quite often, however, lack of advertence and ignorance is the fault of the free will in so far as there was some realization of the obligation to be more attentive to duty. Thus, for example, a physician or a priest who has seriously neglected to continue his professional studies, cannot be excused on the ground of ignorance if he blunders in the performance of his tasks. In the language of the law, culpably serious neglect of the necessary effort to inform oneself regarding it is called crass or supine ignorance (*ignorantia crassa seu supina*). Ignorance arising from direct and deliberate refusal to inform oneself is called pretended ignorance (*ignorantia affectata*). Most particularly this latter type of ignorance does not diminish accountability, but rather displays the enormity of the irresponsibility.

### e. Diminution of Freedom through Inveterate Habits

A good habit (*habitus*), as consequence of the repetition of many prompt and ready acts which say yes to the morally good, augments the power of freedom. An evil habit, as expression and result of a multitude of voluntary evil acts, bears within itself the weight of these previous free decisions, with responsibility for all their after-effects and manifestations until the habit is entirely repudiated. Should it still recur in individual unworthy acts, despite the basic good resolutions to the contrary, the resultant evil acts are less culpable because the evil habit has lessened the individual's freedom.

Example: so long as one who is in the habit of swearing or cursing or indulging in profanity does not in any way give up his sin by true repentance for dishonoring the divine name or bestir himself to counteract the habit, all his acts of profanity

16

constitute a kind of unity. They flow like a current from his evil freedom. In fact, by the very lack of effort to combat the vice, the man takes a position, voluntarily and permanently, which imparts its evil character to all his individual acts of profanity. But should he repent of his sins and resolve to fight against them, the individual evil words themselves, which at any time may crop up despite his most resolute good intentions, are basically removed from the current of freedom, at least to the extent of the genuineness of his sorrow and desire to rid himself of the bad habit. Through sorrow the individual acts of profanity which still occur are torn from the evil root of voluntary culpability and no longer partake of sin, in the sense of conscious and actually willed offense, though perchance there is some culpability in the remissness of effort in the struggle which the conquest of bad habits requires.

### f. Loss of Freedom through Hypnosis and Narcotics

Anyone who voluntarily submits to hypnosis subjects his use of freedom to the hypnotist's influence as long as the spell of hypnotic dependence lasts and deprives himself of the power of insight into values and the ability to make decisions, which are the bases of freedom. Acts performed in this condition in which liberty is diminished or destroyed are morally accountable in virtue of the free cause which was responsible for the loss of liberty. It is beneath the dignity of man to surrender to the dictation of any hypnotist who may misuse or abuse him or lead him into morally evil ways.

The persistent use of narcotics readily produces addiction or the drug habit. The addict deprives himself of his freedom directly and immediately only in the sphere of the abnormal craving for the drug. But as the craving and dependence become more insistent and insatiable, the loss of will power and eventual total loss of freedom in this sphere will gradually affect the entire domain of free decision. If, despite his better knowledge and the freedom still in his possession, the addict refuses to take the necessary therapeutic and other measures to cure his habit, he incurs additional guilt and is accountable for the persistence of the abuse and the progressive deterioration of his will power. All the evil effects in any way foreseen as resulting from such impaired freedom of will, including the corresponding wrong attitudes and evil actions, are radically voluntary. They are voluntary indirectly and in cause.

### g. Loss of Freedom through Suggestion: Mass Suggestion

It is a serious duty to resist the insidious influence of evil suggestion, either by actively fighting against it or by publicly exposing it or at least by attempting to escape from it by flight. Certain types of individual are endowed with such power of suggestion that weaker men fall irresistibly under their spell, so that escape from the evil is possible only through flight or extreme reserve, if this power of suggestion is turned to vile purposes. Friendship or marriage between immoral and skeptical men or women with great suggestive power and weak and susceptible individuals must result in a far-reaching surrender of moral freedom on the part of the latter.

In our time propaganda by means of mass suggestion or mass hypnosis is one of the greatest hazards to our freedom. Its effect is not only acute and deep, but extends to the broad masses like an epidemic. It may affect the groups massed in assemblies, the workers in industry, the members of legislative bodies, men in the armed forces, in fact, an entire people. The result is such that men of weak will are almost totally defenseless against the contagion, and even morally mature men and women may be perceptibly hampered in the free and independent exercise of their moral responsibility. Pestilential outbursts of fanatic nationalism and hatred for other nations and races, the rash of superstition, anti-Semitism, kangaroo and "lynch" justice, must be studied and to a great degree appraised in the light of mass psychology and mass hypnotism.

Though there are cases on record in which criminal elements cynically exploited the extreme caducity of certain men and by the vilest calculation achieved their base ends, it often happens that the leaders and spokesmen of causes are themselves the prey. Caught in the net of psychic illusions, irresistible mass movements, propaganda of hate, they become victims of the very forces they exploit and direct. But those who succumb to the violent force of mass suggestion are no worse off than the chronic victims of the moral deception and perversion of mass thinking. The evils are equally grave. The development of true moral freedom is nothing less than the gradual emancipation of self and the human person from the fraud and delusion of the herd.

Existentialism in serious minds touches a nerve in its analysis of "coming to oneself," "coming to the truth." It focuses attention on a very essential point, even though it largely fails to grasp the real meaning of the antithesis between community and impersonal man, between the value of community and the value of man as a mere individual.

The supreme hazard of being caught up with the herd and being led by the unproved ideals of the mob demands constant self-examination: do I permit myself to be influenced by the notion that "men think thus"; "men act thus," or do I decide on the basis of moral principles, which I have made my most sacred possession? To regain our moral independence, we must escape from the masses and the cultural mass production with its outpouring of syndicated news and reports, its daily and weekly press, its pamphlets, magazines, books, movies, broadcasts, telecasts, its multiple appeal to indulgence and even sin. This moral independence demands that we throw off the serfdom of "impersonal man." And no means is more suited to this effort toward moral freedom than the manful intervention for the cause of the true faith and sound morals. No means is more effective than bold engagement for the good when the masses withhold their applause. The strangle hold of the masses on our freedom cannot be broken without the support of the true community of the good, the community of faith and love, which is the Church, and the invigoration of the natural communities. The evils of an unspiritual climate of thought and opinion in which freedom is imperiled are most effectively combatted by the concerted apostolic effort of the community of the good with all its force of counterattack. Encouraging examples are evident all about us: one instance is the "circles of young families" formed for mutual encouragement in the maintenance of the Christian ideal of marriage in the pagan surroundings of our time.

### h. Restriction of Freedom through Psychic Defect or Illness

Some mental abnormality is permanent and due to structural deviations of the brain or to physiological malfunctions traceable to embryonic life or to infancy. Such abnormalities are all classified as mental deficiency or amentia. They may range in severity from mild feeble-mindedness to imbecility and idiocy.

The psychoses are severe mental illnesses in which the subject has little or no insight into his affliction and from which issue extremely aberrant thought and behavior. The term *psychosis* is usually restricted to severe illnesses of psychogenic origin (such as schizophrenia, manic-depressive psychosis, paranoia, and involutional melancholia), but it may at times be extended to include illnesses due to impairment of brain tissue function (such as general paresis and the alcoholic psychosis). The psychoses tend to pervade the total personality and generally mean extremely poor contact with reality. There is generally serious intellectual impairment or deterioration, and the subject is often dangerous to himself and to society. The psychotic almost always requires hospitalization.

Certain personality types display symptoms and traits that can be likened to those of schizophrenia or the manic-depressive psychosis. This is not to say that persons with such symptoms or traits tend to become schizophrenic or manic-depressive. They may be and usually are quite normal individuals who are simply characterized by one or the other pattern of traits. Persons of schizoid type are shy, close-mouthed, incapable of overt emotional display, and not particularly interested in social or group activity. Some are hostile and easily given to suspicion and jealousy. Others are apathetic, passive, and unresponsive. The cycloid type of person is boisterous, emotionally unstable, has marked swings in mood between elation and depression, is interested in social events, and is in general outgoing in behavior. Such a person tends to be generous with help and with gifts. But he will wish—and even demand—a return in kind for his generosity.

Mental deficiency and the psychoses may and often do entirely exclude moral responsibility in those afflicted. It is nevertheless the duty of society to hinder these unfortunates from performing evil actions as far as possible. Above all, it is the duty of society to bestow loving care upon them in the effort to provide necessary scientific treatment for their afflictions, provided there is still hope for a cure. If relatives, despite ample financial resources, fail to furnish the necessary medical assistance for the mentally retarded and disturbed as long as there is reasonable hope, they sin gravely against love and piety.

The psychoses are to be differentiated from the psychoneuroses. In the latter form of mental illness, character and personality are basically intact. The subject is able to live in society and maintains fairly good contact with the real world of persons and events. He can usually perceive the deviation from the normal pattern of behavior in his fancies and urges or at least can be made to realize it by others. He is still in possession of a wholesome sphere of knowledge of values and a sound area of freedom available in his struggle to master mental suffering or at least to bear up with it in Christian patience.

Some authorities think there is a previous basis for all psychic disorders rooted in personality structure or physical constitution. We cannot hold that the disorder itself is innate, but that there is an inborn predisposition to any of a wide variety of mental and emotional deviations. It has become increasingly evident to students of psychotherapy and psychiatric medicine that in these matters the determining factors are not merely somatobiological. Total environment, especially in early childhood, is of supreme importance in the whole process of ideational and affective development. Heredity, physical constitution, health or sickness, social and economic status, interpersonal relationships, educational and cultural patterns, and last, but not least, the moral-religious training together with its discipline of personal responsibility and self-determination are decisive factors in the development or the prevention of serious neurotic traits or out-and-out psychotic aberrations.

Becoming a neurotic is far more than suffering a simple weakening of nerves. It is rather induced by an extremely unfavorable milieu, which has a gradual disorganizing effect on behavior. Characteristic in the origin of neurosis is a weakness in coping with reality and a more or less unconscious effort to escape responsibility. It often arises from a subconscious attempt to find an escape from a difficult situation in life through various possible reactions (for example, anxiety, hysteria, phobias, obsessions and compulsions, depression) instead of employing the forces of mind and will to master it. The morbid reactions of the nervous system which formerly were simply called nervousness often have a psychogenic origin. Mutual interaction of the psychical and the corporeal clearly revealed in current studies in neurosis, together with the sharp stress laid on psychic origins of illness in modern medicine, serve to teach us, among other things, how profoundly not only health but also freedom depends on the spiritual attitude of man himself and his interpersonal relationships. This points up our moral obligation, not only to have a rational concern for our health, but also to gain the right attitudes of mind and heart toward conscience and its obligations in order to prevent or to offset the restrictions which neurosis imposes on freedom.

Those who have charge of the mentally ill and those around and about them must do their part through kindly understanding and through patient and sympathetic realization of their needs in order to help them come to a wholesome insight into their own condition and to unhampered use of their freedom and, if necessary, to assist them in obtaining therapeutic care.

The organ neurosis reaction is the development of any one of a number of diverse physical symptoms (cardiovascular, intestinal, urinogenital) interfering with specific organic functions; it is appropriately termed psychosomatic. Other neurotic reactions, on the other hand, like the obsessive-compulsive reaction or phobias, produce painful psychic disturbances. On the basis of the psychic area in which the obsessive-compulsive symptoms are evidenced, we distinguish obsessive images and compulsive urges. Basically they are the same kind of reaction, i.e., they are involuntary and compelling. The same may be said of phobias. Because of their domination of consciousness, obsessions lead to indecision, hesitation, and uncertainty, while resistance to compulsive acts may give rise to severe anxiety. This results in what is sometimes called abulia, or lack of volition, but it should not be confused with the abulia or generic irresoluteness of simple neurasthenia (chronic fatigue). The obsessive-compulsive person may not readily do anything evil despite images and urges, but his affliction leads him to fail to do much good.

One who is tortured by psychic compulsion bears some resemblance to certain cases of psychosis. But unlike the latter, he has a real perception of the irrationality or immorality of his fancies, impulses, restraints, or anxiety complexes, and the very realization causes him acute suffering. At times persons of culture and lofty moral character suffer from psychic compulsions. In fact, psychoneurotic traits in any sphere are not at all incompatible with lofty cultural (especially artistic) and moral endowments. At times they seem to be simply the counterpart of these gifts, the reverse side of a precious coin.

Compulsive ideas or impulses do not manifest themselves exclusively in the area of the ethical. Of frequent occurrence are phobias concerning disease in all conceivable forms. The compulsive ideas may be concerned with personal cleanliness, with endless self-analysis. In religious natures there is a predilection for fancies and impulses diametrically opposed to the religious attitude and moral earnestness. Galling persistence of blasphemous thoughts in the minds of those who love nothing so much as to honor God is a clear instance of the image compulsion.

As in many ills of a psychic nature, so particularly in cases of psychic compulsion, calm perception of the nature of the illness, the detection of the hidden origin and cause, and resignation to the will of God are the first steps toward recovery. Convulsive attacks on these defects and fretful wrath over them are likely to create fixation of ideas and only to aggravate the evil. Far more prudent is it to go about one's daily tasks, disregarding the troubles with the gentle humor of the Christian who may heartily laugh at all that is not sinful. Impulses that contravene Christian morals may never be deliberately approved. However, the opposite extreme is no less to be eschewed; to defend oneself by all sorts of assurances against temptation can only lead to secondary compulsive acts and to a general aggravation of the evil. There is scarcely any danger of moral deviation when the individual's conduct is objectively lawful (simple rejection of sin, cheerfulness, tranquil resolution not to yield to impulse, buoyant use of energies for the good in other areas).

Another well-known type of neurosis is hysteria. This term, however, is very inclusive in scope and for that reason difficult to define or even adequately describe. In conversion hysteria, psychological disturbances are "converted" into physical complaints, the physical symptoms replacing in this manner the emotionally charged ideas and ensuing inner conflicts. The symptoms may involve practically any organ or function of the body. Among the more frequent symptom categories are the loss of sensory function (anesthesias, blindness, deafness), the loss of motor function (paralysis), and autonomic disturbances (tachycardia, shortness of breath, constipation, nausea). The individual suffering from conversion hysteria is usually rather childish in personality and desirous of gaining attention. He is talkative, sociable, and inclined to dramatize himself (noticeable in the character of his complaints). His numerous physical complaints appear, disappear, and shift to other forms without any demonstrable organic basis. He is not, however, a malingerer or faker, as he does feel the symptoms, although he is unaware of their basis and meaning. His symptoms may definitely serve the purpose of helping him to escape some uncomfortable or disagreeable situation or to keep him from doing something he feels he should not do, but has an urge to do. He himself is not conscious of any such motivation.

Other hysterical symptoms (now referred to as dissociation symptoms) take the form of amnesia, fugue states, multiple personality, or other trance states. These symptoms are functional, not organic. They unconsciously serve the purpose of escaping an intolerable situation or conflict.

Obviously hysteria in all its forms implies a typical loss of freedom and of the conscious mastery of life. The hysterical person can hardly be held responsible for his behavior, influenced as it is by unconscious desires. But the failure to struggle against infantile self-will and selfishness must bear some of the burden of blame for his condition.

Among personality disorders the most noteworthy is the so-called psychopathic personality, today usually referred to in official circles as the sociopathic personality. Included under this term are those cases involving antisocial or asocial behavior, deviant morality (especially sexual), and addiction to drugs or alcohol. Psychopathic persons invariably return to their disturbing behavior and constantly distress their families and society, but seldom if ever themselves. Their deviant behavior usually starts in childhood and is now believed to be due predominantly or even exclusively to familial and social factors prejudicing adequate moral development. They are often intellectually normal and perfectly logical and reasonable in conversation, but they behave according to impulse, quite often of an aggressive type. They say what they do not mean; or if they mean it, they immediately forget it. Once psychopathic behavior is well established, neither praise nor punishment works as a corrective. Drug or alcoholic addiction is distinctive by reason of its compulsiveness, but this is more often due to long-standing abuse of drug or intoxicant. Sometimes addictive abuse of drugs or alcohol is merely a symptom of deeper disturbances of a neurotic character. Today there is more hope for helping psychopaths (and particularly drug and alcohol addicts), provided they can be made to want help. Unlike neurotics, the psychopath seldom wants help and scarcely listens to suggestion.

In serious cases of neurosis and personality disorders, the sick man must consult a specialist in the field of psychopathology. The treatment of psychic aberrations and mental disorders which under certain conditions gravely endanger moral freedom is a much more pressing obligation than the care for mere bodily health. Even though the major part of mankind is not seriously affected by mental disorder, nevertheless most men show some symptoms or traits which can develop into neurosis or into some great handicap to the practice of virtue. This is a serious matter for men who become slaves of passion and do not exercise themselves in the discipline of will power or fail to meet the test of severe trials of life in the spirit of faith. Each individual can profit from a realization of his own frailties. True humility not only gives him an insight into his weakness, but to a degree indicates its origin as well (for example, organic deficiency or profound failures and disappointments in life have a correspondingly deteriorating effect on the mind).

Every defect and every mental illness which hampers moral freedom is a cross. To bear it patiently makes us like to Christ in His passion. But both the individual who is afflicted and those connected with him must do all they can to safeguard the liberty imperiled by his condition and attempt to extend the scope of his moral freedom ever more widely.

### i. The Church's Doctrine on Human Liberty

The Church has defined as a dogma of faith that the children of Adam even after the fall are still in possession of moral freedom of choice. This means simply—neither more nor less—that the normal human being, at least in the decisive stages of his moral life, has at his disposal the measure of freedom of will necessary to decide for or against God, with such validity and earnestness that by God's own sanction eternal happiness or eternal loss depends on his free choice. As far as each particular action is concerned, however, we are often perplexed. Does it or does it not have this measure of freedom? It is impossible to form a clear and certain judgment on the moral maturity of many individuals of extremely elemental mentality or of the mentally ill or feeble-minded persons: are they sufficiently free to make a deliberate decision, such as is required for mortal sin? In other words, is the restricted scope of their free will such that they are still able to take a deliberate position in opposition to God, a position which God will judge with such stern disapproval as to respond to it by eternal rejection? Ultimately, only God can judge the individual. Our study and knowledge of psychology can and should serve to teach us to be mild and cautious in our judgment of our neighbor. It should help us to do all we can by way of understanding and correcting ourselves and also others. We must make every effort to broaden the scope of moral freedom through control or elimination of the psychic disorders that hamper it. In the fundamental problem of the nature and degree of freedom essential for moral responsibility, the Church, not experimental psychology, has the authority to make the final decision.

We learn about the transcendent splendor and mystery of our liberty only through revelation: it is the exaltation of our freedom to a supernatural likeness to God in the liberty of His children. It is the divine dowry of Christ's own obedience unto death on the cross and the incipient revelation of Christ risen in His glory. It is the power to follow Christ, which is perfected and preserved in filial obedience to God, whose message of command to His children is expressed only through His deeds and gifts of love.

The freedom of the children of God is His noblest gift and therefore it is also our most sacred obligation and bond of love.

## II. KNOWLEDGE OF GOD AS BASIS OF VALUE

### 1. Our Likensss to God through Moral Knowledge

That man is created in the "image and likeness of God" implies not only that his liberty is patterned on the divine, that it is participation in the divine freedom, but also that man's knowledge is like to God's and partakes of its splendor. Indeed, God's freedom is not blind, but essentially lucid and splendid. According to the measure in which man shares this infinite lucidity and splendor of divine knowledge, in the measure of his enlightenment by the divine knowing, can he be like to God through participation in His freedom. Man's likeness to God manifests itself in every conception of truth and every act of knowing, for there can be no truth except through participation in the eternal truth. A mere theoretic grasp of contingent realities, which is not directed to any action, is on the lowest rung of similarity to God. Next follows the knowledge of practical truth with power, a "power-conscious knowing" [hence patterned on God's creative mandate: "have dominion!" (Gn 1:26)]. Higher is the philosophical knowledge of essences which with true insight into supreme causes and principles points to the ultimate source of all things, God, and shows how they all lead to God. Essentially the loftiest level of divine likeness in our knowledge is attained only through love. The summit is knowledge penetrated with love, engendering love, made dynamic in love. Such in its innermost reality is God's knowledge, for God is love! The second person in the most

Holy Trinity is "not just any word, but the Word breathing forth love." We can enunciate nothing more pertinent on the essence of the Word of God than this: the Word in eternal and necessary *élan vital* breathes forth the Spirit of love in union with the Father.

Moral religious knowledge, salutary knowledge or "science of salvation," therefore, reaches a singular depth of assimilation to God and participation in God. This cannot be said of the most exalted scientific understanding of the profane sciences unless their essential relation to God shines forth from them and awakens love for God. As a matter of fact, a simple peasant mother with her loving knowledge of God and of good has a much nobler cultural formation (in confirmity with the image of God) than a "learned" sceptic. Moral-religious knowledge elevates man in the hierarchy of the divine likeness in proportion to the degree with which it is animated by the spirit of love and inspires us to love. The most brilliant theoretic moral knowledge is not on the same high level as the simple understanding of a saint who may be altogether illiterate.

## 2. *Knowledge of Good the Basis of Moral Freedom*

In God, the Word is the second person, Love is the third. This means that the Holy Spirit, the personal love, proceeds from the Father and the Son. Here we have the divine pattern showing that the free acts (moral obedience and love) must have their essential source in knowledge. The free decision of our will in the image of God is in proportion to our knowledge in the image of God. Our decision can reach no further than the light of the knowledge which is in the divine image. Where understanding is absent, there freedom is absent, there responsibility is lacking. The more comprehensive and profound the understanding the greater the responsibility before God. Thus the Lord says: "If I had not come and spoken to them, they would have no sin. But now they have no excuse for their sin" (Jn 15: 22ff.). "If you were blind, you would not have sin. But now that you say, 'We see,' your sin remains" (Jn 9:41).

As long as we recognize the good, we must live according to it. Otherwise the light could be lost through our fault and we would not be capable of doing good any longer: "Walk while you have the light, that darkness may not overtake you" (Jn 12:35). All knowledge of God and the good is an appeal to us to choose God and His law. A clear and practical knowledge places our decision in an altogether different light than does mere conceptual or speculative knowledge. (It is immensely important for the preacher and teacher of the divine word to realize this.) But the eternal "Word of the Father, breathing forth love" transcends this distinction of practical and speculative. He is indeed the eternal Concept, but also the living person, infinite knowing. Since we are all created in the Word and after the pattern of the Word, no one may make the excuse that he has acquired only a theoretic understanding of the good.

There can be no knowledge of God and the good which is not in some degree dynamic, moving us to love in the divine image, since there can be no normal man who does not feel in his inmost likeness to God the dynamic force of the known good, impelling him to action.

To frustrate the theoretic knowledge of the good by making it sterile and void of all fruit is a fault fraught with the direst consequences, which profoundly deforms the divine image in man. But the very possibility that man possessed of the knowledge of good can fail to make the decision for good or to do the good action, reveals most clearly, despite all resemblance to God, his created dissimilarity.

### 3. *Goodness of Person Preliminary to True Moral Knowledge*

Even though in the Holy Trinity the Word is the second and Love is the third person, nevertheless in the intimate divine life (*perichoresis*) which is the Trinity, love is not in any way just a term or conclusion. It is also the source and center of the *perichoresis*. In love, from love, and to love, the Father speaks His consubstantial Word. Accordingly there must also be a mutual relation of moral knowledge and moral decision (attitude) in man. "Will and knowledge can be conceived only in the mutual interrelationship of priority, not as unilinear relationship of direction." Only in so far as knowledge of good is sustained by the goodness of the subject, infused or acquired, can it provide the impulse to the good and the highest perfection of virtue. Through the power of grace infused by God this impulse ceaselessly carries the subject beyond the status of moral perfection already attained. From the psychological point of view, we can say that moral knowledge is not a torch which merely sheds light without heat or warmth. Indeed, it must first glow with warmth before it can rightly and thoroughly shed its light. Often, however, the circle of light is cast much farther than the warmth of its glow.

That moral-religious attitude and conduct serve as the basis for the ethico-religious knowledge and understanding is evidently set in the clearest light in the doctrine of the primacy of love over knowledge in the Augustinian-Franciscan theology. But Thomas, though he holds the primacy of the intellect, is far from ignoring the mutual interdependence of the two. The noted Thomist, the philosopher Maritain, says on this point: "Here (that is, in the moral knowledge and specifically in prudence) Saint Thomas has correctness of understanding depend on the uprightness of the will and this indeed by reason of the existentiality, no longer speculative, but practical, of the moral judgment. The practical judgment can be right only if actually here and now the dynamism of my willing is right and strives for the true goods of human life. It is plain, therefore, that practical wisdom, prudence, is indivisibly a moral and at the same time an intellectual virtue."

In the Sacred Scripture, especially in Saint John, there is the clearest evidence, not only that the basis of moral decision is in knowledge, but also reciprocally that the basis of knowledge is in love. Perhaps the clearest and profoundest passages are those in which the Lord calls the promised Holy Spirit the "Spirit of Truth" (Jn 14:17; 15:26). Only through the "Spirit of Truth," only when they are filled with charity in the Holy Spirit, will the disciples know the truth fully. "Let the anointing which you have received from him, dwell in you, and you have no need that any one teach you. But as his anointing teaches you concerning all things, and is true and is no lie, even as it has taught you, abide in him" (1 Jn 2:27). "But you have an anointing from the Holy One and you know all things" (1 Jn 2:20). Through the anointing of the Holy Spirit, that is, through love, we are confirmed in the truth. "He who does not love does not know God; for God is love" (1 Jn 4:8; cf. Jn 8:47; 18:37).

The more love grows in us, the more will God manifest Himself to us, the more shall we also understand the morally good. Knowledge of God and moral knowledge are intimately bound together. "He who loves me will be loved by my Father, and I will love him and manifest myself to him" (Jn 14:21). Profound authentic understanding of God and the moral good is possible only for one who possesses love and manifests it practically in his conduct. One who constantly neglects good and turns to evil deeds will grow vile and sinister. "He who says that he is in the light, and hates his brother, is in the darkness still. He who loves his brother abides in the light" (1 Jn 2:9f.).

An understanding of values is in itself a treasure of moral values. To welcome the light of truth beckoning us is surely a morally worthy act, a profound moral decision. To accept the truth and not shun the burden and hardship of its claims is itself a great good.

Knowledge of values (here we do not have in mind purely speculative or theoretical knowledge of the good!) expresses and reveals the whole moral value of the person. Not only in our morally good actions (Jn 14:21) is our virtue manifest. Even the clear perception and depth of moral understanding reveals the good in us, manifests our love for God. Who does not keep the commandments does not love God. But it is also true that one who breaks the commandments can lay no claim to "knowing" God. "He who says that he is in the light, and hates his brother, is in the darkness still" (1 Jn 2:9). (Obviously the word *light* means more than the simple light of reason; it means the total splendor of grace proceeding from the light of knowledge in the Word.) A life of sin is unthinkable in one who actually "knows" God, and the good is incompatible with this "knowledge." "No one who sins has seen him, or has known him" (1 Jn 3:6). Thus the observance of the commandments is not merely a sign that we love God, but also that we "know" Him. "And by this we can be sure that we know him, if we keep his commandments. He who says that he knows him, and does not keep his commandments, is a liar and the truth is not in him" (1 Jn 2:3f.).

Are the statements contradictory? On the one hand, we say we cannot love what we do not know. We cannot do the good before we know it. On the other hand, we cannot know what we do not already love. Surely it is true that we must have some knowledge in order to do good, otherwise our neglect of it would not be culpable. But to know the good as it should be known implies that one is already good. "He who knows God listens to us" (1 Jn 4:6). A study of the diversity and degrees of moral knowledge should clear up any difficulty arising from such paradoxical statements. To these we now turn our attention.

### 4. *The Species of Moral Knowledge*

#### a. Knowledge of Law and Experience of Value

There is a profound difference between theoretically clear conceptual knowledge and the concrete and practical perception of the good one has experienced. The most radical difference in moral knowledge is between mere legal knowledge that something must be done or avoided and the insight into the value itself which is the basis of obligation. The science of law provides a strict norm and determines the limits for action in general or gives an imperative for particular action. In one way or other one who knows the law must possess the basic realization that the "ought" is good. Otherwise there would be no moral knowledge at all. But this reference to the good is, in the first place, only in the background. Secondly, it is not a clear and evident intuition of the good or the experience of it from within, but only a kind of extrinsic knowledge. There is another entirely essential distinction in the science of the law. The imperative character of law may be viewed primarily from the standpoint of sanction (reward or punishment) or under the aspect of recognition of the lawmaker's authority which is recognized as good. In this latter case there is an approach to the awareness of value.

Knowledge of value (as distinct from knowledge or science of law) on its part again comprises a diversity of species and degrees: there is a simple and basic abstract intuition, conceptual understanding of something as good and perception of the intrinsic reason why it is good. This knowledge, however, suffers from a certain frigidity. It arouses no personal enthusiasm, lacks concreteness, color, warmth, unless it is bound up with direct appreciation of values. Then there is the practical perception of value: value is plainly discerned in its clarity and splendor and its concrete worth and claim to our acceptance. Next we note what we may call a sense of value: one experiences the value not merely in the full radiance of its beauty and exaltation, but also with ardent devotion to it. In fact, the sense of value attains perfection only in the total response to its word of love, only when the attitude of the one who perceives it measures up to the essential attraction of the good, in so far as this is possible. For ultimately the essence of the good is its appeal to love. Finally, there is the knowledge of value arising from a kind of intimate conaturality with the good. Not only does one see and experience value concretely in particular situations, but one possesses a bond and contact with it, an actual and most intimate affinity with it which transcends every particular instance and situation. This exalted knowledge of value is altogether within the reach of virtuous men who do not have the capacity to explain its object in conceptual and philosophical terms.

It is precisely these two latter kinds of value-experience which justify the assertion of Scheler: "There are more men who grasp God familiarly through love than there are men who familiarly conceptualize Him." But the sense and the knowledge of values as just explained should not be construed as being opposed to the conceptual grasp or science of values, nor should it be explained as irreconcilable with them. Precisely the authentic sense and knowledge of values provide the basis for a flawless conception of value, always assuming the maturity of reasoning power with adequate capacity for abstractive thought.

Whereas capacity for abstraction or conceptualization has its limits, concrete perception and sense and knowledge of value are capable of ever greater development in depth according to the total moral worth of the person. And this is not an endowment limited to privileged individuals, though we do say that the morally perverted or even the morally immature individual lacks moral endowment. But the reason is that such an individual here and now is no longer capable or is not yet capable of any noble moral conduct.

Whereas a knowledge of the law, in fact, even some perception of value is also within the reach of one who is morally very immature, authentic vital experience of value demands a far greater moral sensibility. *"Conditio sine qua non* of the perfect experience of value is the endowment of a clear intuition. But this is not sufficient guaranty to preserve it; an inner competence of the subject must be added in order to make possible the acceptance of value."

We must make a clear distinction between knowledge and appreciation, between possessing knowledge of value and assuming a position toward it. We must distinguish between the appeal and summons in the awareness of value which is in the intellect and the response which is in the will. However, the sense of value and the knowledge of value, as we have used the term, strictly and typically, are characterized by an inner presence and participation of a loving will.

Saint John uses the term *knowing* in its religious sense. In this "knowing" there is a loving will supporting the "knowledge," and therefore the right response of will to God's appeal is assured. "He who knows God listens to us" (1 Jn 4:6). On the contrary, one who does not have love, who is not entirely and utterly devoted to the good, cannot have any such knowledge of it. "He who does not love does not know God" (1Jn 4:8). In this sense the Socratic aphorism that it is sufficient to know the good in order to do it, is justified. But to arrive at this knowledge there must be some antecedent good acts based on a less intimate esteem for the good, a point which seems to have escaped Socrates.

### b. Basic Value, Type of Value, Particular Values

All particular values and all types of value rest in basic value: in the "good" (ultimately in God, the fulness of all good). But it does not follow that knowledge of basic value always guarantees the right understanding of all types of value and all particular values. Obviously a perfect and comprehensive grasp of the basic value of the "good" would include within it the full knowledge of all the values contained in the concept.

34

However, one may possess a general knowledge of the good with a vital awareness of good and evil, together with some understanding of significant types of value, and still have only a meager knowledge and appreciation of the value of certain virtues. There are many people, for example, who understand and appreciate the virtue of justice. And they also have a knowledge and a sense of the evil of injustice. With this sense of virtue and the inner conviction of its value, they earnestly strive to promote justice. But the inner dignity and beauty of chastity and particularly of virginal chastity escapes them altogether. For them it is an alien value. But this does not imply that they are ignorant of the precept of chastity and could not fulfill it!

The fact is that the value of many virtues is more difficult to attain because they are so exalted; we might say that they are qualitatively finer and loftier. Such are unselfish kindness, simple humility, purity. It is well to bear in mind also that many a one is quite aware of the worth of chastity, and not only because of extrinsic knowledge through precept, through warning against violation of the sixth and ninth commandments. And yet under stress of temptation and its enticement and lure he no longer realizes that now and for him this value of chastity is at stake. Such is the power of temptation to deceive and blind men, especially if they fail to pray and struggle nobly against it. For man also has the power to resist temptation. Though we cannot enter into a detailed explanation of the conditions and circumstances under which temptations have this blinding effect, the underlying basis is evident: in the deeper level of one's character there is a basically defective moral attitude.

Corresponding to the three objects of moral knowledge (basic value, type of value, particular value) are three species of blindness to value: comprehensive blindness to value, partial blindness to value, and blindness in the application to value. The first of these, comprehensive blindness to value, is found in various degrees of obscurity in various individuals. There may be an incapacity for vital perception and appreciation, for clear intuition, for right realization of the basic value, the "good," or even for the proper acceptation of legal obligation. But incapacity for knowledge of the precept of the good is never absolute as long as moral freedom and responsibility are still present.

Partial blindness to value has as its object a particular type of value or perhaps even a group of these. The loftier types of value are most likely to be affected where there is no profound and ceaseless effort to attain the good. But again we must insist that even the lack of such vital effort does not necessarily exclude the very basic knowledge of precept necessary for an incipient fulfillment of good.

As to the third kind of blindness, it is concerned with the application of moral principles to concrete instances: one recognizes moral value in general, but fails to discern the particular instance in the light of the general moral principle which should apply. More or less unconsciously one shies away from those values which might pain or grieve. The danger of blindness to value, particularly in the application of principles, is not so great if we ourselves are not directly concerned. One is not so likely to err regarding the obligations which bind others. Obscurity more readily blinds one to a realization of his own duty, for the element of personal interest very conveniently destroys true objectivity.

Blindness to value usually assumes one of two possible forms which correspond to the diversity of its source: hostility and insensibility. Hostile to value is the malicious man who has set for himself an ultimate goal which is irreconcilable with the good as such, especially, however, with certain specific or particular values in virtue. Perhaps he can still discern the values, but in the depth of his soul he does not care to notice them. They are an accusation against his false attitude, a disparagement of his autonomous self-glorification. This is the aspect of value he actually perceives, whereas the true dignity of the value itself is something alien to him. The proud man is actually hostile to value. And the summit of such pride is diabolical malice. Satan has knowledge of values. But he is totally hostile to them. He does not penetrate into value itself, but looks only to the hostile aspect turned to him. This attitude of hostility toward value gradually makes a complete fraud of man as he develops a mastery in the vile art of obscuring and scorning disagreeable values, even though he cannot totally disavow them. Still the very hatred of the good shows that one cannot altogether evade the verdict of the good.

One who is insensible to value is not thereby necessarily hostile to an equal degree or in the same manner. A common type of insensibility toward value is the "Don Juan" voluptuary or bon vivant. Totally bent on enjoyment, he has no desire to "harm" any one, though he plays fast and loose with all the virtues where enjoyment is concerned. The source of this insensibility is not so much pride as self-indulgence and lust.

When the blindness is only partial, the attitude of hostility or insensibility is directed, not against the good as such, but only against that realm of values which is in opposition to the still potent pride or lust. But it is not incompatible with an incipient will to do good.

The ultimate root of all man's moral blindness is sin, although not every sin invariably leads to moral blindness in its evil domain. Only the sin which is not erased by repentance has this dire consequence, for it gains the mastery over the acts of man and over his personality as well. In our teaching on conscience we shall probe more deeply into much of this, in so far as conscience is connected with the dynamic of the ontic unity of knowing and willing. If the movement of the will does not follow the knowledge of the intellect, it will recoil against the intellect. Then the unity for which nature clamors will be forced into a reverse, with inevitable darkening of the mind through malice of will.

Only too often knowledge outdistances moral performance. Unless humility bridges this gap which imperils unity, a deceptive pride will assume control of our powers and totally destroy the inner harmony. Thus defect of obedience in the face of the challenge of the good will conspire with defect of humility to effect moral blindness. Psychologically the blinding force of pride or indulgence has its source in the normal ontic tendency toward unity in knowing and willing. Both the dynamic of conscience with its tendency to good in the case of the obedient will and the blinding power of sin in the case of persistent disobedience spring from the same source. Merely partial blindness in application to particular instances has its special source in the striving of the "I," at once proudly passionate and yet in some way attached to the moral, in the endeavor to erase the moral conflict. On the one hand frivolous hostility or indifference to value is absent. The basic position in favor of the good or at least in fear of evil still remains. On the other hand, "there is no intimate resolution or decision to renounce whatever is pleasant or agreeable even though it is bound up with moral evil." It is possible that actually the will is inclined to acknowledge value, but still on a deeper, more or less unconscious, level an obstacle exists and a deviation occurs. This is due to the fact that one seeks the good in a general way indeed, but not at the price of every sacrifice.

Blindness to value ceases to exist only after a profound and universal orientation toward the good replaces it; this means serious and total conversion to God. Unless we are ready to deny that the person must and can convert, we must concede that the person is responsible for this sort of blindness to value even though the forces that blind operate mainly on the level of the unconscious. He is aware of the existence of these forces, for he can discern the false tendencies. As to the particular act arising from this attitude influenced by the blindness to value, it is not here and now a responsible act of the human agent, but it is in some manner the effect of a prior responsible free decision.

Conversion does not bear with it the perfection of an immediate intimate sense of value or even the perfect "knowing" of the good in the sense of the text of Saint John. For this, love must first develop and exercise itself in the good. For such growth and self-exercise simple insight into values or the right application of the knowledge of precept to one's own case is sufficient.

The blindness to value due to a will which blanches in fear of moral conflict and will not hear of it is called, in the language of the Schools, *ignorantia affectata,* pretended ignorance. It is a deliberate not wanting to know. But this ignorance embraces very diverse degrees of knowledge or lack of it and, consequently, of responsibility. In one instance it can arise rather from a genuine fear of the menace of conflict with moral principles, the while one cannot muster the courage to break away from the occasion of sin and hazard to salvation, from objects one wishes were still (and in consequence of the wish, also believes they are) morally permissible. But this type of pretended ignorance may also be caused by a calculating will seeking the excuse of ignorance before the lawgiver with his sanction of punishment. Though these two kinds of ignorance are quite different and also admit of many intermediate variations and shades, it is this latter calculating type which is the usual concern of jurists when they deal with ignorance.

## 5. Depth of Value Knowledge

We must distinguish a twofold depth of moral knowledge: the first is on the level of individual value; the second, on that of the person, already discussed in the preceding paragraphs. As the mere novice in moral effort does not possess the same depth of will as the saint, so they are unequal in moral knowledge. (Obviously the comparison is far from perfect.) On the part of the subject, the depth essentially depends on the radical nature of the "basic intention." If the good does not derive from the universal resolve to do the good always and under all circumstances, the essential depth is lacking. And this absence of depth is associated with a parallel deficiency in knowledge as long as particular values and whole types of value are excluded from the recognized fundamental values.

From the standpoint of value, the saint who does not merely perceive the particular value in its own dignity and in the moral seriousness of its demand of his acceptance, but who also knows all moral values in the splendor of the divine sanctity, is on a much profounder level than the man of stern moral fiber who is not a saint. Even an irreligious man can see and sense the value of justice, but he does not perceive the profound interior depth which belongs to the value of justice: it is founded in the depths of the divine justice and holiness and reaches the heights of the divine attributes. There is also a profound diversity between the man of faith who does no more than hold fast to faith—firmly but coldly—and the saint whose faith is vitalized in love, and who sees in every moral value the splendor of sanctity which is God, the Lawgiver, the source of all good.

We may not conclude from all this, however, that slighting of particular values can ever be justified. Just as the values are resplendent in the light of the divine holiness as a harmonious whole, in unity and multiple diversity, so the genuineness and depth of man's knowledge of values is preserved and safe-guarded only through the insight into and earnest acceptance of each particular value. How superficial are we if we fail to cultivate the spirit of love and warm appreciation for the particular value entrusted to us! If, instead, we do no more than formally direct our acts to the will of God! (As for example: "Objectively I am indifferent in the matter, but since it is the will of God. . . .") Surely all things center not only in the will of God, but also in the eternal intelligence of the divine essence Each particular value has its corresponding task in the creative manifestation of the one infinitely simple all-holy essence of God.

Mere knowledge of law, mere legal science, is obviously superficial. But when the holy Legislator is seen in His law, the knowledge of law rises inestimably above the mere sense of legal values. It has a profound assurance that makes it superior even to the intimate sense of values which perceives God only as ultimate source of all good.

### 6. Sources of Moral Knowledge

### a. Objective Sources

The objective sources are community and divine revelation. It is the great service of community to propose moral ideals to the developing personality through doctrine, precept, and example. Particularly significant and important is the service of a superior association, of the community, of the people, of the cultural circle, especially of the holy Catholic Church. She leads us to virtue through her teaching and precepts, which she presents to us in the living example of her saints. All this is of inestimable value for the moral orientation of the individual. But the quality of this service is very diverse according to the times, for there are periods of lofty moral achievement, with their noble heroes and saints, and periods of moral decline and decadence. The moral man as a rule owes his inner formation in the good to the family in which he was born and raised.

The good has been revealed to us by God naturally in the order of creation, from which we can learn the hierarchy of natural values and the design of the good. But because of original sin our minds were darkened. We no longer saw the light which "shines in the darkness" (Jn 1:5). Then God in His mercy gave us the Law and the Prophets and finally His only begotten Son as teacher.

In the order of His creation and more particularly in His Covenant with the Chosen People, God gave man more than arid legal knowledge, more than the dead letter of Law. He taught us through the works of His love. The Covenant with the Chosen People was made the foundation and motive of the law. It was a covenant and alliance of love. (Indeed, motivation in the order of value transmutes science of law to science of value.) Still more gloriously did God exalt this divine instruction and orientation through Christ, who teaches His precepts with words of infinite tenderness, with words filled with impressive and loving earnestness, and not least through acts of His love. Christ gave us a new commandment, the commandment of love. He presented it to us as He Himself lived it, so that we can penetrate into the profound depths of its value and meaning.

Christ is the universal teacher of moral as well as of religious knowledge. "One is your Master" (Mt 23:10). "I am the way, and the truth, and the life" (Jn 14:6). "I have given you an example, that as I have done to you, so you also should do" (Jn 13:15). "Have this mind in you which was also in Christ Jesus" (Phil 2:5).

It is our duty to study incessantly in the school of the Master. And basic to that study is meditation, which is therefore essential for every true Christian. But meditation is far more than mere acquisition of abstractive or theoretical knowledge. Only through the love of our hearts, that is, in loving meditation, are we actually formed in the knowledge of the school of Christ. Just as the Master teaches the good in His love, so we can learn from Him only through the "anointing of the Spirit" and "in the Spirit of truth," who is Love.

To go to the school of the Master means above all to seek to enter into the mind and heart of Christ. Imitation of Christ is obviously not a mere copying of His acts, unique and inimitable as they often are, not a mere mechanical fulfillment of His words and law. Only if we are united to the Person of

Christ in love, through profound submission of heart, will we become docile disciples of Christ with true perception of values and right application of them to ourselves.

Not merely the historic Christ as He is depicted in the Gospels is our teacher, but the whole Christ, the historic and the mystical Christ, who lives on in His Church. Through the Church in every age He makes known to us our personal tasks and places before us concrete and varied illustrations of His own example in the lives of the great saints.

In the ultimate analysis, if we are to arrive at a clear understanding of the true import of community, authority, law, and example of Christ for our moral development, we must reflect again on the various steps or degrees of knowing, from simple knowledge of law to the lofty spiritual "knowing" of the good which we have just discussed. How can beginners in the moral life or souls blinded by the obscurity of sin find an opening to the good? Or how can they be brought to enlightenment if there is no brother to admonish them, no superior to direct them, no authority to lay down laws and norms for their conduct? How can we enter the intimate sanctuary of the good unless the word and example of Christ and His saints clearly and plainly point the way. The school of Christ is adapted to the novice in virtue, and equally as well to the more advanced, since Christ employs all motives, all forms of teaching, so that even the dullest of minds can harken to it with some understanding and the most intellectual does not exhaust it. Christ is not just one teacher among many. He teaches us as the eternal Truth, and not merely externally. He teaches us as the "true light that enlightens every man" (Jn 1:9). "He awakeneth my ear, that I may hear him as a master" (Is 50:4). He has given us the "Spirit of truth" through whom alone we become docile disciples of the eternal Truth.

### b. Subjective Sources

Our knowledge of values is based essentially and primarily on our affinity for the good, which is a kind of second nature (*connaturalitas*). We are good in the depth of our being and created for the good. Only because "our eye is made for the light" can it see the light of goodness. Only because we are created for love by Eternal Love itself are we challenged by the force of love in the good and inflamed by it. This natural affinity of ours for the good (ultimately for God) can be disturbed by habits of sin, so that we become partially blind spiritually, but the seed of the good is not destroyed. It still remains in our nature, and the warmth of divine love like rays from the sun can quicken it with life. The heavenly physician offers the remedy and makes possible the beginning of recovery from the blindness of sin through the warm love of His heart. The great spiritual preventives and remedies for moral blindness are: vigilance and mortification of the disordered appetites, humility and purity, prompt repentance after every fall, conversion and earnest penance after the failures of an evil life.

The motivating power of our moral knowledge is the firm and inviolable resolution to submit to God in all matters, cost what it may. Where moral obedience has attained self-mastery by shuffling off the caprice of contingency and relativity, where it rests and relies on an absolutely good interior disposition, a true knowledge of law will develop. There will be a conscious appreciation of fundamental value rightly directed as source of this knowledge of law, which will enter all realms of virtue and attain the surest and clearest awareness of value on that summit of true knowledge mentioned by Saint John when he spoke of the understanding of divine things. This inner dynamism of moral knowledge can be developed by obedience only when it is animated by a love transforming the servile obedience under law into filial obedience in liberty under God. The freedom of the children of God can exist only where the child lovingly harkens in every command to the loving voice of God. Loving obedience, obedient love in the school of the divine Master, is attended by zeal and vigilance, on the strength of which one is not merely aware of the good in general, but also harkens to the direct invitation of the good appealing to the person in each and every situation, even when it summons to arduous and painful tasks.

Only the accomplishment of the good gives us that intimate conaturality with the good, from which we are able to grasp it with true interiority and "know" it. "He who does the truth comes to the light" (Jn 3:21). This passage surely does not primarily mean the light of evidence, but that light which "has come into the world" (Jn 3:19). To come to Christ, the "light" of eternal truth, also means to arrive at a profound understanding of the good.

One of the principal sources of moral knowledge has already been mentioned, prayer. Meditative prayer is nothing more than instruction in the school of the Saviour. Prayer of petition must incessantly beseech God for the "anointing of the Spirit," for "the Spirit of the truth," without which we can never become docile disciples of Christ.

We add by way of practical comment for confession: although it is true that the penitent is obliged to confess only what he recognized as sinful at the actual moment when the sin was committed, still we must also realize how wholesome is the attitude of those Christians who, after their conversion, when their eyes are opened, react with horror to their past acts and accuse themselves of many faults which they had previously committed without any thought of sin. Since these material faults are fruits of an evil tree, planted and nurtured in the state of fallen liberty, it is spiritually profitable to expose in confession the tree with all its fruits. However, it surely would be sufficient in itself to make known one's evil state and those evil fruits of conscience of which one was actually guilty.

# Jacques Leclercq
## 1891-

*"Each man is my brother. Each man is my friend." Why?*
*Why must I see my brother in every man? Why must I look*
*upon another as friend?*

*Christianity has long taught the sonship of all mankind in*
*God the Father and a universal brotherhood founded on Jesus*
*Christ. The secularism of the twentieth century has rejected*
*this teaching and chosen rather to create an atmosphere that*
*declares the other to be enemy or someone to be used. The*
*tension between these two world views, brotherhood and*
*enemy, has forced Christianity to take a new look at its basic*
*moral teachings. If the claim of brotherly love is to be valid, the*
*time has come to review that claim, to understand once again*
*what is meant by it, and to seek new ways to express it in a*
*world that insists on war and enmity.*

*Professor Jacques Leclerq, through his teaching and writing,*
*has made a significant contribution to the recent process within*
*the Catholic world of reworking basic moral ideas and of relating*
*them to the needs of modern man. For many years he has*
*taught moral and social philosophy at the University of Louvain,*
*Belgium. His writings include a five volume study of natural*
*law, an introduction to sociology and several books on ethics.*

Christ and the Modern Conscience, *from which the reading*
*below is taken, is an effort to understand Christian moral*

*thinking in the light of contemporary problems and to develop a response to these problems by way of the Christian tradition. Leclerq discusses various ethical theories such as eudaimonism (happiness), stoicism, and Christian ethics. He writes simply and clearly, and draws his examples from the world of the average person of today.*

*Our selection deals with the concept of altruism. Why must I see my brother in every man and why must I respect him, are the questions with which Leclerq introduces the topic. One might quickly respond that God is the basis for treating everyone as brother. But such a response, without adequate critique in the light of the development of ethics does not suffice. Leclerq examines the concepts of equality and ethics for the elite as distinct from ethics for the majority. He then presents three forms of altruism: respect-altruism, which is based on the fundamental equality of men; assistance-altruism, which builds on the concept of mankind engaged in the common task of self-realization; and social sense-altruism, which defines human relationships according to the needs of the society in which one dwells. Each of these forms has strengths and weaknesses and each must cope with specific problems. It is the wise man, says Leclerq in his conclusion, who discovers how to blend all three forms into a unity, thus collaborating with his fellowman in a truly efficacious manner.*

# CHRIST AND THE
# MODERN CONSCIENCE

### III. THE DUTY OF ALTRUISM

To conclude this chapter, we must try to clarify the notion of the duty of altruism, altruism on behalf of others and not of ourselves. I shall inquire in the next chapter how altruism assumes a place in the exigencies of my personal development. But altruism is not really itself, it is not really altruism, unless it really has others as its object, and it has not if I practise it for my own sake.

The question therefore is why regard for others *qua* others is incumbent on me. That refers to any others, whoever they may be; the question is why I must see my brother in every man, and why my brother compels my respect for him. This question goes far beyond that of the human community; those who are determined at any price to link it up with social life must engage in veritable intellectual acrobatics to see a virtual, implicit or possible society implied in every man they meet. It is clear that the notion of society, in the sense of organized society which it bears in sociological literature, is much narrower than that of humanity.

It seems easy to resolve this question of mutual aid through the intermediacy of God. We have just seen that the religious basis is the only one that appears sound. Even so, there is some clarification to be done, for since God is the basis of everything, he is in one way the basis of nothing, that is to say that in order to know whether God is the basis of any particular value, we must know whether this value is binding on the mind. God is the basis of everything that is binding on the mind, because a value is only binding on the mind because God has made it so. But how are we to know that God has made it so except by discovering that it is binding on the mind?

Fourier used to say: 'Passions come from God; we must therefore abandon ourselves to them.' It is true that if I pursue my good, it is because God has put it in me; but that gives me no indication of the nature of my good. We must therefore examine the question of altruism closely so as to determine what is its place in human condition as a whole, what arguments can provide it with a valid justification, and what are its limits.

Respect-altruism is in a different position from assistance-altruism, particularly when assistance-altruism goes to the extent of sacrificing the self. Respect-altruism is based on equality: Nietzsche allows it between equals. But equality cannot provide a basis for mutual aid. The fact that somebody is my equal cannot oblige me to jump into the water to rescue him.

## 1. *Respect-altruism and equality*

It seems that it is a self-evident fact for human beings that equals should respect each other. When Kant makes the primary expression of the categorical imperative: 'Always act on a principle such that you would be willing to see it become a universal rule', he was only translating into what he thought was philosophical language the universal formula: 'Do unto others as you would they should do unto you.'

For it is a universal maxim. We meet with it everywhere, constantly repeated, constantly violated and constantly recalled. The justifications advanced for it are as often as not unconvincing, because the rule can only be fully justified if we go beyond the human. As long as man remains centred on himself, others can only be thought of as instruments. Kant was impregnated with the Christian tradition. Since he had lost his faith, he believed he was thinking independently, with no *a priori* assumptions, but the things he accepted as self-evident were those that came to him from his environment. If a thinker deliberately throws over the idea of an Absolute existing outside of man, he lapses into incoherence, as we have seen.

The precept for respect-altruism is to be found in commutative justice. Since men have all the same rights, we should respect those of others for the same reason that we expect ours to be respected. The precept for commutative justice is 'Give and take'.

At first sight this appears simple. Respect for the life and property of others, the duty of telling the truth, respect for marital rights (moral philosophers class adultery as theft) can all be justified in this way.

It is all simple, indeed, as long as we are dealing with the usual type of case, where two equal rights are in conflict: I should pay the just price for an article. But this very equality leads to a breach of material equality when a man defies law and order and when two unequal rights are in conflict.

The first case is not too difficult; it is the case of legitimate defence. Another man defies law and order. He treats me as an inferior by, for example, molesting my life or property for his personal advantage, and I have then the right to defend my position as an equal. The case of legitimate defence which is most often cited is that of the defence of one's life. It is also the simplest case, because the two values confronted in it are the same; on both sides alike, the right to life is at stake.

A more difficult case is that of conflict between two unequal rights. There is a hierarchy of goods; one man's right to an inferior good cannot prevail over another man's right to a superior good. In virtue of this principle, Catholic moral philosophers teach that a man can violate the right to property in order to save his life, because the right to life is a right superior to the right to property. They also teach that a man can conceal the truth in certain cases, when higher interests are involved. They justify this last rule in more than one way, but they are all agreed on the fundamental idea.

Nevertheless, the cases we have just cited are almost the only ones theologians allow. At first sight, this seems surprising, for there are many other cases of conflicts of rights, particularly where property is concerned. On one hand it is laid down that property as a whole is put at the disposal of men as a whole, that property is thus designed to be common, and that its owners are caretakers for the community. But on the other hand, when an owner fails in his duty of stewardship and does not help others as he ought to, these others are not allowed the right to restore order in the use of the property by taking what ought to have been given them.

Let us imagine the case of a poor man with a talented son, who is capable of making the best of a good education and of occupying an important place in society. The social order is such that this child cannot become the man he might because his parents are poor. Their neighbour is a rich man who makes a bad use of his property, and who could help the poor man, but does not do so. Why cannot the poor man appropriate some of the resources of his rich neighbour, if he can do so without being noticed and so avoid social conflict? The moral philosophers oblige the poor man to submit to the 'established disorder'.

The argument they put forward is, moreover, as often as not an indirect argument. They appeal to the need for social order. If everyone could right his own wrongs, there would be bound to be abuses, because most people have strong feelings and are not intelligent enough to be able to pass an equitable judgment on their own case. The philosophers therefore call on men to respect the established order, even if this order is a disorder.

It will be seen that the considerations which prompt these solutions are by no means those of the rights which are in conflict. Casuistry is anyway a not very logical science. Cases are resolved in accordance with an overall view into which there enter the most varied practical considerations, such as the social order or the fear of abuses. What is more, philosophers are subject without realizing it to the influence of their environment. The ethics of the good man, which is inspired by current ways of thinking, often comes into their thinking, justified by remarks which look like general principles, such as 'We mustn't make morality too hard for ordinary people', or 'We must make allowances for use and custom'.

Inspired as they thus are by varied considerations, casuistrical systems are not usually intellectually satisfactory. They raise a certain number of questions in which we shall have to try and clarify the principles involved. One which concerns the object of this chapter is how far ethics should make allowances for the customs of the community and the conditions of life in common. Another, which we shall examine in the next chapter, is how far a man should make up his mind in accordance with his personal judgment and, should occasion arise, assume the right to be an exception to the rule.

But all these questions raise that of the unity of ethics. In order to clear the ground, we will start by trying to clear up the question of ethics for an elite and ethics for the majority.

## 2. *Elite-ethics and majority-ethics*

We have seen that wise men are non-conformists, individualists, and in a manner of speaking, aristocrats: they tend everywhere to shy away from the masses. The wise men's ethics thus stands in contrast to that of the masses.

The thinker who expresses this in the plainest terms is Nietzsche, and he did a service to thought by raising the problem in such an outspoken way that it is now impossible to evade it. At first sight, his conception seems to be in contradiction with the traditional conception, and with the Christian conception in particular, and he puts it forward as such. The traditional conception is that of an ethics which is the same for everyone. Duty is duty and sin is sin. What is a duty or a sin for one man is so for all.

All the same, certain passages in the Gospels strike a more relativist note. An example is the parable of the talents, which declares expressly that duty is not the same for all and that he who has received more must give back more. We meet this idea in varying forms in every ethical theory. It appears in such proverbs as 'Noblesse oblige', and wherever ethics assumes a social aspect, we find a popular ethics and an ethics for the elite, obligations for the masses and obligations for the elite.

This double ethics emerges as soon as an attempt is made at a social organization of ethics. In his Republic, Plato pictures an ethics for the ruling class of philosophers and another for the warrior class, while he exempts the working class from a moral rule, since they should not think but should confine themselves to doing what they are told.

We talked earlier of dualist ethics and of the double ethics that the Cathari prescribed for the perfect and for believers respectively. In Buddhism we find a not dissimilar arrangement, an ethics for the pious devotee, the *upasaka,* who pledges himself to avoid the five fundamental sins, and an ethics for the monk, who commits himself to a higher degree of perfection.

It is true that these freely accepted rules are not accepted as moral rules by those who link ethics and duty, in accordance with the outlook that has prevailed since Kant. But if they do not form part of ethics, what are they? What is more, duty and moral aspirations are inextricably interwoven.

The most thorough examination of the question is to be found in Catholic moral theology, whose finely shaded system makes it possible to understand the problem's delicacy.

Moral philosophers have distinguished sin from imperfection. Sin is a transgression of the moral rule, which is the same for all. The impression given is that of an absolute uniformity. When the sinful character of theft is determined, an attempt is made to specify what a theft consists in and how big it must be to be gravely or slightly sinful. Imperfection is not contrary to the law, but it is better to do what is perfect.

So far, every obligation is common to everyone. But a man may commit himself to the way of perfection, and undertake obligations which are not applicable to everyone. The question has been systematically discussed in connection with religious vows, but it applies to all Christians. A man who engages in a profession contracts obligations which are not those of the common man. When a man accepts a post as minister or president of a republic, he is accepting responsibilities which it would be sinful to try and evade later. The head of a business has responsibilities which go beyond those of his employees or workmen, and a man is at the top of the social scale has duties, in particular that of setting a good example, which do not concern those at the bottom of the scale. We find here, in a much more finely shaded form, the conceptions of Plato in the Republic.

When we read the lives of saints, we see that they regard themselves as sinners on account of acts which are not considered sins according to the general rule. It is the same with many of the people who hold positions of authority, though they do not always formulate their feeling, for lack of the appropriate training. All this results in an ethics of many levels, very different from the undifferentiated ethics that seems to emerge from the manuals.

# Jacques Leclercq

What is more, in the Gospels, there is a manifest difference in the Saviour's attitude according to those he is talking to. To the crowd, his attitude is one of mercifulness; he knows that men are weak, and he grants forgiveness at the least sign of good will. But at the same time he preaches an uncompromising ideal of purity, renunciation and love, an ideal which he may be said to launch at the crowd, with a 'he that has ears to hear, let him hear . . .' He calls for an unreserved generosity from those who present themselves to him as disciples. All these elements make Christian ethics an extremely finely shaded and varied one, which allows for every situation in a manner suited to its real importance.

But this being so, can we say that ethics is the same for everyone? Here we are once more confronted with the twofold idea of code morality and wisdom morality.

Code of morality is an ethics inspired by social considerations and wisdom morality one inspired by individual considerations.

The man who teaches code morality is not concerned with himself, but with the people, and he is not concerned with perfection, but with the virtues to be required of the masses.

The most advanced of code moralities is that which developed, first among the Jews and then in the Catholic Church, and we have seen why. In the Catholic Church, it was elaborated with the idea of mercifulness, so as to try and make the conditions of salvation as little of a burden as possible. Hence certain attitudes which I noted earlier, that of not putting forward an inapplicable ethics, for instance, and that of allowing for human weakness. The problem of code morality is to raise the masses to the highest moral level accessible to them. That is a social consideration.

How it works out can be seen as soon as a community is formed and a rule has to be adopted for a body of men. In the Catholic Church, the religious orders constitute an unrivalled criterion in this domain. Their sole objective is perfection. Nevertheless, they demand no more than a perfection which has been carefully calculated on the basis of what can be expected from ordinary men. When an order is launched, its founders concern themselves to make it 'viable', that is to discover a rule of life applicable to a certain number of people.

In contrast, wisdom morality is little concerned whether those who will follow it are many or few. Jesus seems convinced that his disciples would always be a minority—'the harvest is plentiful enough, but the labourers are few'—and we have seen the individualist character of those who teach wisdom morality. The moral teacher is concerned with the good, the One and reduction to the One, with perfection or renunciation. He does not ask himself whether many people will follow in his footsteps. That does not interest him, and if the question is put to him, he will readily agree that 'the labourers will be few'. That is not an objection for him. So much the worse for men if they do not understand.

The conflict between the two kinds of ethics is eternal. The parish priest who has a logically perfect ethics put up to him will reply: 'It's useless to preach that to my people.' He needs an ethics he can teach with some chance of success, and it is the same with everyone who has a social responsibility to shoulder. But that is of no interest to those who are concerned with wisdom morality. The question about the Sermon on the Mount or Kipling's *If* is not whether many people will put them into practice, but whether they are true or whether they are beautiful.

When men organize an ethics for a people, social sense, that is to say concern for men in a body, causes them to concentrate on what is visible. Now what is visible is outward phenomena. When we adopt a collective standpoint, intentions and individual conditions fall into the background. What is common is physical attitudes.

People actuated by social considerations find it tedious and embarrassing when questions of intention are brought up. In the army, soldiers are expected to be in line and in a factory, workers are expected to clock in punctually. Those who put forward individual excuses for exemption from the rule are a nuisance. The ideal that comes naturally to every man with social responsbilities is the ideal of the anthill: perfect conformity, working for the common good. When moral teachers have social interests, they want a virtuous anthill, but it is an anthill all the same. They apply themselves to working out prescriptions for virtue. What matters most is the form of prayer and the act of devotion which they try to persuade the community to use, not spontaneous, free and personal prayer, which can only be the act of a minority. They lay down acts of charity and forms of alms or of mutual aid to be recommended to everyone, and they attach more importance to these than to developing a feeling of love for one's neighbour, the manifestations of which have a personal character. The man actuated by social considerations has the impression that everything that is inward, that is feeling or that is intention, is of its nature vague. He seeks to draw up a code to which the whole community can be subjected, with rules of sobriety, decorum, godliness and kindness which will ensure a common life conforming to the moral rule.

This code morality, which tallies in its main lines with the ethics of the good man, often becomes a crushing burden for some people and extremely easy for others. If, for example, a moral rule is laid down on the subject of theft which takes into consideration solely the value of the object stolen, the rule will be far less severe for a rich man, who has no temptation to steal, than it will be for a poor man. The gravity of theft depends also on the mutual positions of the thief and his victim, the motives of the theft, the means of the victim and those of the thief, and the use the thief plans to make of what he has stolen. Discerning casuists try to take all this into account, but the spontaneous tendency of the man who is concerned with the good moral order of the community is simply to try and make sure that people do not steal. The man who does not steal will pass for upright, and nobody will worry whether he has any merit.

Christ set himself against this way of looking at things in the story of the widow's mite. He praised the poor woman more than all the rich for her alms-giving, though it was far more modest than theirs, for 'the others all made an offering to God out of what they had to spare; she, with so little to give, put in her whole livelihood'. This remark of Jesus is characteristic of wisdom morality, but it always seems more or less paradoxical, because for most people there is no other morality than code morality, and this is essentially quantitative.

The good man of code morality can thus easily be a conventional egoist, devoid of generosity, but observing the rules of good breeding, leading an orderly life, displaying few passions, but giving no more evidence of a passion for good than many other people. The man who gives his goods to the poor is not the good man of code morality. Such a man inquires what he *ought* to give to be right with the moral law. On the other hand, if the man who has given all his goods to the poor should display occasional ill-humour, the good man of code morality will upbraid him. If a rich man says that he hardly sees he has any merit for giving what he has been told he *ought* to give, because he can do so without depriving himself of anything, the partisans of code morality will tell him he is over-scrupulous; once a man has done his duty, they will say, there is no further problem . . . But the implication of this statement is that duty is the same for everyone. . . . The man of wisdom morality will tell the rich man: 'Perhaps your duty goes further' . . .

Code morality is thus often easy for the mediocre and stifling for strong personalities. The result is a sharp reaction against it by all those who have a feeling for moral purity. The attitude of Christ is very characteristic. He never talks of social rules of ethics except to say that we must transcend them.

In contrast to code morality, wisdom morality is an ethics for the elite, for those who have a concern for the moral. Concern for the moral, as we have seen, is concern for the good, the absolute, the individual and the One.

Wisdom morality looks on life as a whole. It is not out for a recipe which will ensure that a man is 'in order' and specify the conditions on which he can be certain of having a good conscience, leaving him free thereafter to pursue his own interests. Wisdom morality is out for unity in life, and since man is manifold, unity in life means order and harmony. The important thing in these circumstances is not the value of each part considered in itself, but the harmony of the whole. Life is a concert, and all its notes must contribute to the total effect.

Individual acts thus assume a very different aspect according to the place they occupy in the whole, according to the spotlight on them. To give a pound, a hundred pounds or ten thousand pounds to the poor can never have the same value for two men. One must be congratulated, while the other must be told: 'That's not enough': the widow's mite again.

But in this case, duty assumes an extremely subjective aspect. My duty is to do what fits in with the harmony of my life. Now the harmony of my life is my perfection. My duty is thus to achieve my perfection, or to do what I can to attain to it, and in practice, my perfection consists in doing what I can to attain to my perfection.

The word perfection has thus two senses here. In the first sense, perfection is what I should be able to achieve in theory, that is to say, it consists in the complete development of everything I have in me. But in practice, this perfection is beyond my reach, because I am the victim of a series of pernicious tendencies which I also have in me, and which are the result, either of my character or of my past life. The perfection I can attain today is thus inferior to the perfection which is deduced from taking account of my qualities alone. And my perfection today is to achieve the perfection of which I am capable now, with the collection of qualities and defects that are in me.

What is the position of this ethics in relation to code morality?

To start with, perfection can be a source of obligations. Here we have the principle *'noblesse oblige'*, and this manifests itself on the psychological plane by the diversity of vocations. A man's vocation corresponds to the lines along which he must realize his own perfection, and the man with a moral sense sees in his vocation a source of obligations. It is a source of obligations, because he is anxious to pursue the reduction to the One which is the prime objective of his life. Whereas on the level of code morality, the problem of vocation arises only in the form of a call to which a man is free not to respond, since duty is merely to do what everyone ought to do.

On the level of wisdom morality, everything which allows me to realize the objective of my life is a source of obligations. This is a strictly personal point of view. I do not have to worry about what others do. As in the parable of the talents, I only have to worry about what I have received.

But though perfection may be a source of obligations, it is also a source of freedom from them. In proportion as a man accedes to a higher level of life, he is freed from obligations which are necessary on a lower level. In workshops and offices, the men who are at the top of the hierarchy are freed from the obligation to clock in on time; the man who devotes himself completely to the service of his neighbour or who uses his property only to make his fellow-man happy need not worry about what he is bound to do. Duty disappears, as it were, in the superabundance of good.

It is possible, all the same, that a man may have to submit to a rule out of social discipline, though it has no more object as far as he is concerned. A man who does his job conscientiously, and whom there would be no reason to hold to fixed hours of work if only he were concerned, must sometimes consent to put up with the general rule, because if he were dispensed from it, others, who do not deserve it, would demand the same concession. Cases of this kind are common: they explain why, even in monasteries, fixed hours for prayer or common rules for mortification are laid down. Whatever the degree of perfection the wise man has attained, he must still accept social discipline as long as he is living with his fellow-man.

This is what Nietzsche did not see. His superman was supposed to shake himself free from all obligations because he acknowledged nothing above himself. But if man is a creature, he must take into consideration the social order of which his fellow-men form part; he must accept the common life which forms part of the law of man, and the discipline which is a consequence of it.

This allows us to clarify the position of social ethics. There are elements of truth to be found even in the ethics of honour and even in the confusion between ethics and morals.

It is true that every state of life makes its own demands, and that these accord a particular importance to certain virtues; it is true that physical courage is particularly important for the soldier and respect for his word for a tradesman. A properly interpreted ethics of honour, which confines itself to emphasizing the virtues specially necessary in a given environment, without prejudice to the body of rules which govern life, results in a professional or class morality which takes differences into account, but produces conflict. There are legitimate differences between different social circles, and one question for practical ethics is, which are legitimate differences which should be taken into account, and which constitute abuses which we should not tolerate.

In the same way, to a lesser degree, morals can affect ethics, in the sense that acts and words sometimes bear the meaning that men attribute to them, for example when it is a question of rules of good manners or commercial practices.

But ethics would go astray if it had no other rule than normal practice, because this reflects an average morality which keeps man at a somewhat low moral level. For example, it is normal practice to mislead men to some extent, but not to exceed certain limits, and to pursue our own interests to some extent, but not to go too far to avoid injuring others beyond a certain point. As we have seen, when a man confines himself to code morality, he can easily lapse into a condescending attitude towards normal practice which kills moral fervour.

And yet it is true that certain acts draw their meaning from normal practice. We should take this into account, but we cannot do it without danger unless casuistry is inspired by a concern for wisdom morality which orientates life.

Again, a man who has adopted an attitude of wisdom morality should refrain from following certain practices, because the very fact of his drawing his inspiration from wisdom morality is contrary to them. The first sign of wisdom morality in a man is that when he is confronted with a particular practice he asks what is its value. The man who has committed himself to code morality never raises this question; he confines himself to asking exactly what he ought to do according to the established rules. Now custom assumes that men are mediocre, and the social environment reacts against anyone who adopts a personal attitude. The man who pursues wisdom morality is thus departing from custom; he is a non-conformist. We find this phrase cropping up on every page.

Customs correspond to normal virtue. The man who seeks wisdom seeks something quite different from virtue which is normal. He seeks virtue in itself and for itself. Other men vaguely realize that he is not like them and look for an attitude on his part that will cut across the normal. They look for a certain disinterestedness, for example, and they will be more than a little shocked if they see that he values money and creature comforts as much as they do, though they do not feel they are doing any wrong.

On the other hand, if the wise man interferes with their habits or their prejudices, they regard him as unmannerly or tactless. It is customary in fashionable society to say only pleasant things. The wise man, for his part, is seeking the truth, and if he is surrounded by people like himself, friends or disciples, they practice brotherly admonition, because they all desire wisdom. If he leaves this circle and practices brotherly admonition, he is not understood, because those to whom he is speaking are satisfied with themselves, want a pleasant life and have no desire to be admonished out of their failings. They will not even allow anyone to accuse them of failings. On the other hand, people attach particular importance to the wise man's judgment, because they count on him to tell the truth. Thus they will not agree either to the wise man telling them unpleasant truths, nor to his paying empty compliments. He is often reduced to holding his tongue. If, in order to conform to custom, he pays the compliments everyone does, people are astonished as if it were a weakness. They do not regard the paying of compliments as a weakness in others. On the contrary, it is a virtue to be amiable; but there are certain virtues that become weaknesses for the wise man.

Thus, as soon as we go into the question of relations between men, we come up against problems which we cannot solve if they are considered in isolation. Only wisdom morality, the morality of the orientation of life, can provide the solution.

### 3. The basis of the three forms of altruism.

We are now in a position to determine the extent to which concern for others modifies individual morality, whether it is a question of human contacts in the broadest sense or of social collaboration in the more restricted sense. There are three aspects to the question: respect-altruism, assistance-altruism, and social sense-altruism.

First for *respect-altruism*.

It is based, as we have seen, on the fundamental equality of men. Men apprehend this fundamental equality as a self-evident truth, though they apprehend it somewhat vaguely, because it is contradicted by innumerable inequalities of every kind, and because it only manifests itself decisively in terms of the future life. A clear idea of commutative justice seems to call for synthesis of our ideas, linked with the notion of God as a sovereign master. Before him, human inequalities lose their importance, and men rediscover their fundamental equality in reduction to the One or possession of God, which is their common end.

The problem of respect-altruism is thus that of allowing every man to fulfil his destiny. Any infraction of commutative justice thus amounts to depriving another man of a means of action to which he is entitled.

But this identical right of men to fulfil their destiny is expressed through varying vocations. Everyone has the same right to achieve his perfection, but this right assumes different forms.

Aristotle believed certain men to be slaves by nature, and Nietzsche revived this idea in connection with the herd-man. But though slavery may be contrary to the rights of man, because it puts one man at the service of another without taking his own aspirations into account, it is also true that some men have a vocation to be masters and others to be subordinates. Ford notes in his autobiography that it is difficult to find workmen who will agree to shoulder responsibility, even if they are offered extra pay. Many people fear responsibilities more than they want powers of initiative. If one set of men is cut out to be masters and the other to be subordinates, one set of men is also cut out to be teachers and the other to be disciples. There are some men who like to propound ideas, and others who are afraid to do so, and who are only interested in reporting what the first class have said. The second class is far the most numerous.

Consequently, real reciprocity between men in material things is rarely possible. The example that comes naturally to the mind when commutative justice is discussed is the commercial example of the exchange of goods, for there it is a question of material values. But as soon as it is a question of human relations, we come across moral values with no material equivalence. The love of a woman for a man is never the same as the love of a man for a woman, and the relationship of the employer to a workman has no equivalence in material terms to the relationship of the workman with the employer. It is the same with the relationships between parents and children, masters and servants, rulers and ruled. Their duties are different, though the fundamental duty remains the same, that of respecting the personality of others.

If one man must take orders from another, it is still in order to achieve his destiny. He from whom the other takes orders must allow him to achieve his destiny, his personal destiny. The inferior must only subordinate his destiny to that of his superior in so far as the achievement of his own destiny lies in this subordination. We are thus back at the principle of an equal right for men to achieve destinies which differ among themselves according to their situation in the world.

We now come to *assistance altruism.*

This also corresponds, as we have seen, to something that is self-evident to men. This self-evidence has always been unmistakable on the level of patriotism, whether the object of the sentiment was the clan or the tribe of primitive peoples, the city-state of antiquity, the modern nation, or any other form of human community. But in the past, it was impossible for the sense of human solidarity to extend beyond the limited communities in which men became aware of their common destiny. Only a few wise men extended their thinking to the whole human race, generally in connection with the pantheistic conception of a spark of the divine existing in every human being.

The development of the idea of civilization has led modern western thought to see human collaboration in a completely new light. For the idea of civilization makes the basis of human life the duty of collaborating in a collective task, which can only be achieved by the co-ordination of activities.

On one hand, men can improve their living conditions through this organized mutual aid, and if they can, they should. This is a self-evident truth which is not disputed.

On the other hand, human living conditions can be improved indefinitely, not only on the level of particular societies, but on that of the entire human race. The human race is seen as a single whole. The work of progress is a collective task of a universal character. When a scientist makes a discovery, he does not make it for his country, but for humanity; when a cure for a disease is found, it would seem cruel to reserve it to the country to which its discoverer belongs.

Men should thus devote themselves to the collective work of the progress of the human race. All ethics is dominated by this prospect, and the duty of mutual aid is first and foremost this duty of collective mutual aid, which is social in the sense that it is concerned with the entire human community, and not in the sense that it is concerned with a particular society. Whether humanity as a whole forms or does not form an organized community, man's life is dominated by the necessity of this mutual aid.

On the other hand, this collective mutual aid does not stand in the way of individual mutual aid. The notion that the whole human race is engaged in a collective task only accentuates the idea that men are all brothers and that they must feel about one another as brothers. This trend of thinking is producing a growing reaction, whose development can be followed for two or three centuries past, against differences and inequalities between classes, races, colours and nations, and even between sexes and ages.

As we have already seen, the arguments advanced to justify altruism are a farrago. When we try and sort these ideas out, it becomes apparent that this duty of mutual aid can only be accounted for by making it dependent on a mission which man has received, and that man cannot receive a mission unless there is someone to entrust him with it.

We are still up against the same dilemma. In the first place, man's end may lie within himself; in this case he cannot be obliged to subordinate himself to anything whatever, he need not accept any discipline and can have no other objective than to assert himself. Under these conditions, he will only take others into consideration in so far as he thinks it in his own interest. Or secondly, man may himself be subordinate. In this case, he must agree to identify himself with an order of which he is not the author and to perform the task which falls to him in this order.

If there is an order which compels man's recognition, he cannot attain his complete fulfilment if he fights against this order. Kant's line of argument comes to mind at once: this fulfilment of man is not always achieved on earth, and we must therefore admit the existence of another world where justice is done. Kant's only mistake was to advance this argument as apodeictic, whereas it entails no more than a presumption, and it remains to be seen whether we can reach the conclusion that things are so by other means.

If the existence of a creator God is admitted, the human situation appears to be as follows; man has been put on earth to give glory to God and to serve him, which is the same thing, or to perform the task to which God has called him. This task is to subjugate the world to his reason and to achieve a collective life where all men are perfectly developed and devote their lives to the divine praise. This divine praise can be thought of on the lines of a work of art and of certain mass demonstrations where poetry, music and dancing blend to express man's highest sentiments in a completely harmonious way.

We are here on the level of a prophetic vision picturing a perfect age from which the human race is so far away that we cannot even visualize the contingency of attaining it. Nevertheless, this end where we do not expect to arrive is the goal towards which we must strive. But if he is to organize his action, man must assign himself other and nearer goals.

The starting-point of humanity is that man finds himself on earth with an intelligence capable of progressively coming to understand the world and turning this to account. But at the moment when he appeared on the earth, man understood almost nothing and was almost incapable of using his intelligence. Hundreds of centuries had to pass before he could even begin to harness nature to his service. Then the development accelerated, one discovery leading to another till finally the idea emerged that the mission of man was to transform the natural conditions of the world so as to be able to live more and more by his reason.

Primitive man is subject to nature. Civilization frees man from nature or, to be more accurate, subjects nature to man and makes it an instrument in his hands. Civilization frees man successively from all the servitudes of nature, from hunger, dark, cold, distance and gravity, and it postpones the moment of death. It allows man to develop training and education, and permits him to stamp out moral infirmities such as drunkenness and debauchery, laziness and instability. But though civilization can do all this, it does it only in the course of a turbulent evolution, with trends in every direction, advances and relapses, progress in one direction being often neutralized by a new obstacle to progress. We develop hygiene and discover cures for a hundred and one diseases, but there is a parallel increase in nervous disorders . . . We fight alcoholism, and the use of drugs spreads . . . Nevertheless, man *can* progress; he therefore must. Is he doing so? That is a question of fact that is outside our present scope.

But we should realize the profound transformation of thought brought about by this discovery of the possibility of progress.

The ancients argued in terms of a static humanity. When Plato or Aristotle, or St Thomas in the Middle Ages, considered human problems and social organization, they never anticipated that the conditions of man's life might change. They took the state which civilization had then reached and sought the formula for optimum communal organization, taking into account existing conditions. From time to time a discovery would change certain conditions. It was then integrated into life, and the philosophers resumed their speculations taking into account the new position. But they did not anticipate the possibility of further changes, still less propose that men should actually seek change. The utopian novels, which put forward the picture of an ideal humanity, all picture it in the form of a return to a primitive life on the simplest possible lines.

A reversal of that trend of thought has occurred in the last two centuries, under the influence of technological progress. This reversal did not happen all at once, but little by little, and it is still far from being at an end. Even in our days, we still find champions of the old-time 'sheepfolds', who rail against progress. But their number is diminishing as it grows clearer that the whole progress of man is bound up with the progress of his knowledge, and that this is dependent on the forms of material and moral progress, moral progress governing all the others because it points the way for action.

The progress of civilization is necessary, were it only to allow men to eat their fill. Up to now, the men who have eaten their fill have never been more than a minority of the human race. Providing an adequate diet for the whole of mankind is even today an objective which has still to be realized. Now in our days, the achievement of this objective depends solely on moral conditions, that is to say on the spirit of mutual aid, of disinterested mutual aid, among men, for technological civilization has reached a point where it would present no physical problem to feeding the whole human race. Not only is it easy to produce the necessary foodstuffs; it is just as easy to transport them. What is not easy is to make men accept the necessary conditions; to get the underfed people, for example, to change certain habits of life to which they are accustomed, and to get the rich people to sacrifice a part, even though it were an infinitesimal part, of their well-being.

When we compare a point like this with the ideal picture of a happy humanity which we outlined earlier, we realize that prophetic visions of the end before us are utopian, that is to say they portray an ideal we know we shall never attain. But if we start to think about it, we shall see that the chief obstacle is a moral one; it lies above all in the pride and egoism through which men evade their duty of mutual aid.

In any case, the concrete objective we must pursue lies along the lines of a threefold material, intellectual and moral progress, one stimulating the other or the others, with a view to achieving ever improved living conditions.

Here is an example which will bring out the interdependence of all the forms of progress. Progress in medicine is bound up with progress in the specialized industries which permits the manufacture of ever more perfected instruments, and with progress in chemistry, which is itself bound up with industrial progress. These various forms of progress enable doctors to remedy physical deficiencies which themselves lead to disturbances formerly attributed to moral causes. It is thus possible, through scientific progress, to make men more balanced, calmer, more stable in character, and consequently more efficient workers. This improved balance then provides the individual with a new starting point for his personal progress. It has always been true that certain privileged circles have a higher average moral standard than those outside them. Scientific progress provides a means of extending to the masses what was once reserved for a privileged few.

These implications of collective progress are commanding more and more attention as the effects make themselves felt. The whole of Western social thinking is now focused in this direction; so is that of the Communist world, and the Far East is offering no resistance to the doctrine. Inadequate moral dispositions are now the only obstacles to its achievement. But the problem I am concerned with here is that of the basis we must attribute to this duty in order to embody it in a tenable synthesis.

The question is why man *should* devote himself to a progress of the human race from which he is unlikely to profit himself; why, that is to say, he should exert himself in order that the men of the future should enjoy better living conditions. The old conception was only concerned with organizing a happy community for the men living then. Nobody worried about working towards progress down the centuries. Today humanity is moving forward in a sort of apocalyptic dream, shot with nightmares, no doubt, but focused on the prospects held out by realization of the possibility of continuous progress. The question is therefore not merely why men now living should combine to organize the best possible communal life, but why they should subordinate their action to a progress of which generations still unborn will be the beneficiaries.

The question is different too from that of old-style patriotism. The starting point of this was the consciousness of a security which could not be assured without the protection of the community. It is enough to read Homer, and see how Troy was treated after its defeat, to understand that, under those conditions, only the city-state could guarantee a truly human life. It is therefore easy to see why the permanence and prosperity of the city should be looked on as the supreme blessing, to which citizens must be ready to sacrifice everything. It was against this primitive background that there developed the tradition of patriotism, in whose name men are still repeating the same slogans, without bothering whether they still hold good. *Pro aris et focis,* we read on some war memorials: 'They fell for their altars and their homes' . . . In reality, in modern wars, neither altars nor homes were concerned.

In any case, the contemporary idea of civilization is very different. All humanity is engaged in a common task, which will go on indefinitely down the years. Everyone must take his place in this endless chain, and he must not ask whether he will benefit himself from the progress towards which he is lending a hand.

Men thus have the mission of bringing into being a more and more humane humanity or of bringing out more and more the specifically human character of man. But—we must repeat the question—how can man have such a mission if no one has entrusted it to him? If there exists no higher being having power over man, logic lies in the Nietzschean conception of the superman, or in eudaimonism.

When we talked earlier of the 'moral shock', we noted its individual character, and indeed this moral shock results from the intuition of the nobility of the individual person. The moral philosopher, as we have seen, is sensible of this value; that is why he is a non-conformist, and his spontaneous tendency does not go along with the modern conception of the primacy of civilization or collective life. On the other hand, there is a certain number of elements in Christianity which look like a prefiguration of contemporary thinking.

All the same, at first sight the trend of modern thinking does not seem to have developed in sympathy with Christianity, still less under the inspiration of it. The development of technological civilization and the trend of thinking linked with it originated in great part, and may even be said to have originated as a whole, apart from the Christian tradition, and even in opposition to it. Nevertheless, this development occurred in a part of the world which had been subject to Christian influence. Could that be an accident? It is true that, at first sight also, this trend of thought seems to grow stronger as the Christian tradition grows weaker. We may ask ourselves how far this appearance corresponds to reality, and also how far it corresponds to transitory historical circumstances and how far to the nature of Christianity.

The second question is the only one that concerns us here. There is much that we could say about the question of facts. What concerns us here, however, is man's duty, not what he does. Our interest is in the conception of duty which emerges from Christianity; we do not need to inquire whether Christians are faithful to their calling.

Now the starting point of the 'good news' that Christ came to preach is that God loves men, that he loves them all alike, that he was them to be happy, and they must all work together, animated by his spirit, to establish on earth conditions of virtue which will give them happiness beyond compare. The instrument of this happiness is love between men, and this love, as we know, is the love of God himself, which lives in his disciples.

The Church of Christ is the community of the faithful in whose souls Christ lives through grace, and this community is destined to spread to the whole world. All men are summoned to enter it, and Christ enjoins his disciples to preach to every nation. The universal character of Christianity goes back to its beginnings. We find nothing like it in any other religion. Here, it is the founder himself who, right back at the foundation of his Church, manifested his will that it should spread throughout the earth. This universal character did not emerge later on, under the influence of circumstances and success. It was deliberately willed at a moment when the Church did not yet even exist; it forms an integral part of the basic conception of Christianity. We have seen earlier that certain thinkers, almost everywhere, have hit on this idea of a human brotherhood in an incidental way. But no other doctrine identifies itself with this idea in anything like the same fashion.

This does not mean that Christ expects that all men will be converted. Whether they are in fact converted is one thing, whether they are called is another. All are called, and that is what is important doctrinally.

The Church forms a body, the body of Christ. That is to say that, since Christ lives and acts in Christians, these form together the body through which he acts in the world. This life of Christ in them, the same life of the same Christ in all the millions of Christians, gives the Church a real unity incomparably more solid than that of human societies. Society has often been compared to a body, and the sociological thinkers of our time have revived the expressions of antiquity and tried to justify them. But the social reality of the Church is of quite another kind, and not even the strictest definition will deprive the unity of the Church's body of its solidity.

Christians must thus carry out a common task, which is the building of the Kingdom of God. The building of the Kingdom of God is the growth of Christ in the world. It is beyond the individual; the Christian must dedicate himself completely to this work. It matters little whether this growth of Christ comes to pass in his time or in the course of centuries. It matters little whether this or that individual will benefit perceptibly from the conditions of life it will establish among men. The fulfilment of the Christian vocation lies in action in the service of the Kingdom.

This is quite different from the principle of mutual aid which is roughed out in more or less pantheistic doctrines, in Lao-tse, in Epictetus and in Hinduism. According to this, man has in him a spark of divinity, which he meets with in other men, in every man, so that for every man, other men are other selves. This conception has nothing to do with the idea of the Kingdom of God and of a duty to work together at a common task which is God's task, and even less with the idea that this task of the Kingdom should be the central object of the care or of the duty of man.

We need not inquire here through what tragic misunderstandings the idea arose in certain circles that Christianity was opposed to material satisfactions and even to earthly satisfactions in the most general sense. No doubt, like every religion, Christianity calls on men not to set their hearts on material goods, but to seek spiritual values first, and the Christian is told to be wary of comfort. But when Christ wants to express the signs by which his disciples will be recognized, the examples that come to his lips are that they will feed the hungry, take in the homeless and clothe the naked. When this is linked with the universal vocation of Christianity and the conditions of our times, it leads straight to aid to under-developed countries and the universal solidarity of the human race.

It is true that in one way the object of Christianity is confined to Christians. Its primary aim is to summon men to the Christian life, and the human community which is the result is a community of Christians. The modern conception of human solidarity, which covers all men irrespective of their faith, might be described as a de-Christianized Christian conception. But though Christ may not speak of a task of civilization to be undertaken over and above the propagation of the faith, which is the direct and primary object of his message, he does teach his disciples that they are 'the salt of the earth' and 'the light of the world', and this means that the Kingdom of God, in so far as it unites all the Christians on earth, should extend its activities to all humanity. In the present position of the human race, this conception summons Christians to make themselves the agents of any mutual aid calculated to improve the living condition of the human race.

It remains for us to clarify the idea of *social sense-altruism*. The question is an easy one after what we have just seen. By society is here meant organized life in common. It is organization which characterizes society in the strict sense, whereas the duty of respect-altruism like that of assistance-altruism extends to all men, organized or not, to each man in particular and to all in general, to the whole and to the individual members of it.

The duty of taking into account the demands of social life fits into this general obligation, and becomes of secondary importance for the man who has grasped his duty to humanity as a whole. But common membership of a society, like common membership of a family, gives birth to a collection of sentiments which convince members of either that they are confronted with a sacred reality, superior to the individual. Hence the extravagances of every form of patriotism.

These extravagances do not mean that it is not true that man must accept the fact of living in society and accept the conditions of social life. These imply a certain discipline, that is to say they imply that the members of a society must be ready to forgo certain elements of their personal fulfilment for the good of the whole. This discipline ranges from the most commonplace acts, such as the observance of polite usages and sartorial conventions, to the gravest acts, such as the devotion of a man's life to the service of the community, the surrender of his worldly possessions and even, in certain extreme cases, the sacrifice of his life.

The sacrifices a man must accept out of a spirit of social collaboration can be reduced to two types, those which are inspired by the needs of co-ordination and those which are a consequence of human weakness.

The needs of co-ordination oblige men to comply with rules of life in common without which collective action would be impossible. A business cannot function unless its staff complies with a time-table which may not perhaps suit everyone in terms of his personal tastes, but which is necessitated by work in common. In the same way, in a modern town, street traffic cannot be easy and safe unless drivers comply with regulations.

Other forms of rules are dictated by human weakness. In so far as men are unreliable, they must not be trusted. Hence the forms of supervision and the regulations whose object is to validate legal instruments. A man who is getting married must comply with formalities, as must a man who is entering into an important commercial contract, and these formalities would be unnecessary if men were all really trustworthy. Those for whom these formalities are unnecessary must submit to them all the same, because the common good requires that they should be applied without any discrimination between persons.

Social life is thus continually prescribing attitudes which ethics requires man to respect. Ethics calls on a man to be a good citizen, and it is at this point that organized social life comes into ethics.

Reduction to the One, the final object of moral life, thus entails acceptance of the human situation, which is to be engaged in a common task expressing the will of God for man. The genuine completely developed wise man is thus eminently social, non-conformist as he is. He is social because he realizes that he will only achieve the reduction to the One which is the object of his aspirations if he accepts the human order. All the same, he remains a non-conformist, for he passes judgment on this human order and appraises it in terms of the reduction to the One which he is pursuing and which he would like other men to be following with him. This position makes him extremely different from the instinctive and impersonal masses, who conform without any constraint to the usages of their environment.

The perfect wise man is thus at once social and a nonconformist; he collaborates in the common task of men and remains independent. And it is in so far as his whole life is unified in the One, that the collaboration he brings his fellowmen is really efficacious.

# Jacques Maritain
## 1882-1973

*Jacques Maritain is clearly one of the most brilliant and influential intellectuals of the twentieth century. His entire life was dedicated to a careful, meditative search for absolute and eternal truth. The fruit of this search, lucidly expressed in more than fifty books, has played a significant role in shaping Christian, and especially Catholic, views of the modern world's most important problems. Born in Paris, November 18, 1882, Jacques Maritain grew up in a liberal Protestant atmosphere. He pursued his studies at the Sorbonne. While a student there, he met and married Raissa Oumancoff, a young woman of Russian Jewish origin, who was searching as seriously as was Maritain for meaning in life. In 1906, the Maritains became Catholics.*

*Maritain turned his attention to a thorough study of Thomas Aquinas, the great thirteenth century thinker. What he found in the Thomistic system of thought shaped the remainder of his life. He was convinced that his task was to use the principles of Aquinas in his effort to resolve the questions of art, science and society in the twentieth century. From 1913 through to 1960, Maritain taught philosophy at universities such as Louvain, Oxford, Chicago, Columbia and Princeton. After the death of his wife in 1960, he retired to Toulouse, where he lived with the community of the Little Brothers of Jesus. He died there April 28, 1973.*

*This great intellectual's lifelong dedication to teaching and writing bore fruit. He must be recognized as one of the major personalities who prepared the Church for the Second Vatican Council. The ideas and positions developed by the Council owe much to Maritain's philosophy. At the close of the Council, Pope Paul VI, who referred to Maritain as his teacher, embraced him in St. Peter's Square.*

*The reading below is taken from* Moral Philosophy, *which is an historical and critical survey of the great ethical systems known to mankind. Maritain takes us through the ethical theories of the two most influential of the Greek philosophers, Plato and Aristotle. The ethical systems and terminologies on which our twentieth century are established owe much to these two men. Several centuries before the Christian era, they had raised and theorized on the questions of man's purpose, happiness, virtue and vice, habit, the good, value, the golden mean and freedom. Christian ethics is a blend of Plato and Aristotle with the Judaeo-Christian biblical tradition. Maritain shows how Christianity and Greek philosophy shaped one another and made available to mankind a new, revealed ethic. In the concluding portion of the reading, Maritain introduces us to three great intellectual shocks that have shaken the confidence of contemporary man, viz., Darwinism, Marxism and the discoveries of Freud. The Christian of today, in order to create an ethic capable of sustaining the pressures of modern life, must have the openness to absorb these shocks and work the insights developed by them into a new Christian vision.*

# MORAL PHILOSOPHY

## *The Idea of the Good*

L et us try to characterize, by indicating in rough outline the traits which seem most significant to us, the contributions which moral philosophy has received from Plato, or at least has incorporated into its heritage as bearing the mark of Platonism.

The ethics of Plato, like that of Socrates, is an ethics of happiness. But the happiness of man is only a participation in a transcendent Absolute, whose reality is independent of us and of human life: the Good, which is identical with the One, and "beyond essence"; subsistent Good, the Idea of the Good, which, despite this term "Ideal" which we are indeed obliged to apply to it by reason of Platonic dialectic, is superior to all intelligibility and to being itself, since in the last analysis, for Plato, being cannot be freed from the multiplicity inherent in mutual relations among intelligible types or essences. In the perspective of Platonism carried to its logical extreme, God—who, like the Sun, illumines and vivifies all that is below him and who is cause of the order and harmony of the cosmos and of the soul—is beyond Intellect just as he is beyond Essence, and is finally attained in some degree only by a kind of mystical death of the intellect, swallowed up in the Good under the impulse of the supreme Eros. The end which the initiate aims at above all in his moral activity (and which only the philosopher, or the sage, can attain) is therefore to free himself from the prison of the body and to purify himself by asceticism and love, turning toward the interior in order to bring out the divine resemblance which is instinct in the soul, a divine thing, and to contemplate the divine, to "escape from here to the beyond", to achieve "assimilation to God" by means of a death that wisdom brings about and that is incomparably more perfect and more liberating than physical death, and that alone enables physical death to *succeed*, by triumphing over transmigration.

Here again, analysis of the moral thought of the philosopher reveals five themes or typical characteristics. The first theme is that of the Good. The Good is now disengaged, in the fullness of its meaning, more decisively and more forcefully than with Socrates. At the summit of beings and of eternal archetypes, beyond the shadows of becoming, it is the light which nourishes the eternal contemplation of the Gods, whom Plato in the *Laws* regards as the souls which control the revolution of the Firmament. All that which we call good is so only by participation in this subsistent Good, which is at the same time the sovereign metaphysical Good of the universe, and the ideal moral good of human life, for the most fundamental tendency of Platonic ethics seems to be not, doubtless, to suspend the moral from the supramoral as Christianity was to do—that is, as a matter of principle and universally—but to do so at least *for the sage* (and for him alone). It is from a supra-morality concerned with the conditions and laws of ascetic and mystical progress toward the Transcendent (and from which are derived the moral virtues in him whom wisdom puts in harmony with divine measures) that the sage descends to the world of men to teach them morality and to make them practise it (if they were not so mad) in governing their political life. The good does not belong to the empirical world, or belongs to it only as a reflection. And our knowledge of the subsistent Good is rather divination than knowledge, because it is beyond everything, even, as we remarked above, beyond being.

In relation to this transcendent Good, happiness in this conception appears as a never-ending ascent, a progress in participation which never arrives at its ultimate limit. And this very fact, this transcendence of the Good in relation to Happiness—carrying Plato, or the internal logic of Platonism, beyond Hellenic thought—marks a distinction between the Good and Happiness which in general the moral philosophy of the Greeks never made explicit. It is as if the trans-natural or trans-philosophical desire which lies within us were awakened in philosophy itself in order to make it aspire, not, surely enough, to the intuitive vision of the separate Good (which would be to superimpose on Platonism a Christian interpretation, which is not at all appropriate to it), but to an endless ascent toward such a unity—regarded as unattainable—with that separate Good. But this is only a virtuality of Platonic thought. In fact Plato, in the *Phaedrus*, makes happiness consist in fixation in an end and a state of achieved perfection— but far from the supreme unity, in direct contemplation of the Ideas or separate Forms, a happiness like that of the gods, souls unencumbered by the body.

### The Transcendence of the End

2. The second theme is that of the End. The End of human life is now absolutely transcendent. This transcendence of the Good and of the End was doubtless already suggested in certain virtualities of Socratic thought; nevertheless the opposition between Socrates and Plato on this point seems to me quite clear. Whereas for Socrates, in the last analysis, the end of human activity, though implicitly superhuman, is inherent in human activity, which if it is good makes us happy by the same token, whereas for him morality is the art of being happy through right living, for Plato, on the contrary, morality is the art of preparing oneself for a felicity which transcends human life, since, beginning with earthly existence, and continuing afterward, the true life is beyond life, the true happiness is beyond happiness.

### Supra-empirical Happiness

3. The third theme is that of Happiness. Happiness is not only internal, but it loses all empirical character. Happy is the just man who is being tortured—this extreme consequence of Socratic logic shatters the unstable structure of Socratic happiness. In reality it is above all a paradoxical challenge and refers to a hoped-for felicity, to a supreme *élan* of separation and passing beyond. But Plato cherished this assertion and put all his fervor into it, because in the ethical order as in the metaphysical order his thought is entirely dominated by the idea of participation. For him it is not a matter of obtaining a beatitude to be purchased here below through suffering. It is a matter of participating here below in a beatitude which transcends all earthly

conditions; it is quite necessary, then, that the just man who is tortured *be* really happy, but that itself is only possible because the immortal in us constitutes our own reality, and because the true happiness is not happiness—whence the sarcasms of Aristotle directed against the sublimity of Plato.

Let us look again at a few of the celebrated passages of the *Gorgias*: "Then happiest of all is he who has no evil in his soul, since we have shown that to have it there is the greatest of all evils. . . . In second place, no doubt . . . would be the one who was admonished, and rebuked, and punished. . . . And worst, then, is the life of him who has injustice, and is not delivered from it." ". . . Then it would seem that he who wishes to be happy should pursue and practise self-control, and flee from license, every one of us as fast as his feet will take him, and contrive if possible to have no need at all of chastisement; but if he does require it, either he himself or any of those connected with him, be it individual or state, he must submit to justice and endure correction, if he is going to be happy." "Callicles, I deny that to have one's face slapped wrongfully is the vilest thing that can befall a man, nor yet to have his purse cut or his body. I say it is more of a disgrace, and worse, to strike or cut me or my belongings wrongfully; and that robbing, aye and kidnapping . . . doing me and my belongings any wrong whatever, is worse and more disgraceful, to the doer than to me who suffer it." ". . . Doing wrong must be avoided with more care than suffering it. . . . And let any one despise you as a fool and cover you with abuse if he will, yes, by Heaven, and cheerfully take from him that blow of infamy; for you will suffer no harm from it if you really are an upright man and true (*kalos-kagathos*), pursuing virtue."

In the *Republic*, Plato writes in the same vein: "And he who lives well is blessed and happy, and he who lives ill the reverse of happy. . . . Then the just is happy, and the unjust miserable." "Need we hire a herald, or shall I announce, that the son of Ariston . . . has decided that the best and justest is also the happiest, and that this is he who is the most royal man and king over himself; and that the worst and most unjust man is also the most miserable, and that this is he who being the greatest tyrant of himself is also the greatest tyrant of his State?"

All this remains strictly true even if, in picturing to oneself the just man falsely accused, one imagines him as "scourged, racked, bound . . . his eyes put out; and at last, after suffering every kind of evil, . . . impaled". There is joy only in the pious and just life.

4. Plato does not only affirm that it is *a worse evil* to commit injustice than to suffer it,—humanity pays little heed to this axiom in practice, but it is quite true that it is fixed in its conscience "with arguments of steel and adamant". Plato also holds that one is *happier*, and that one experiences more joy when one suffers injustice than when one commits it. On the near as well as on the far side of the grave justice is sanctioned by happiness.

Not only the doctrine of the immortality of the soul, but the whole metaphysical idealism of Plato is involved here. The End of human life is to be attained beyond the grave, and it is to be attained beyond that grave which is the body, beginning here below, supra-humanly and mystically, at the summit of the spiritual life, by a divine liberation. The End of human life is expressly, absolutely supra-human, and the contemplation of the Forms in which the separate Good shines forth. And the art of conduct, at this heroic moment when Platonic thought first affirms its most radical exigencies, is less the art of conducting one's life than the art of quitting it in order to experience ecstasy in the light of the intelligible Sun.

I am well aware of the fact, moreover, that the heroic moment I just spoke of is not the only moment of Platonic thought. There is the movement of return: the sage, delivered, returns among men to fulfill his mission of leading them to virtue while guiding the legislation and the government of the City by his advice—or better still—by taking the reins in his own hands.

## The Morality of Value and Participation

5. The fourth theme is that of value. For Plato as for Socrates, and still more systematically, virtue is knowledge and moral fault is ignorance. But on another point there is radical opposition between Socrates and Plato: no morality in the ancient world was further removed from utilitarianism than the morality of Plato. Socrates recognized virtue in terms of what is

expedient, advantageous. For Plato virtue is worthwhile without regard to utility, worthwhile in itself. It bears its value within itself, its measure of goodness is judged by its relation to the absolute, it is intrinsically lovable, it is beautiful. The *kaloskagathos* acquires a metaphysically founded ethical significance within the treasury of philosophy.

And so another central notion is disengaged from the shadows and appears in broad daylight, the notion of value, or *moral value.* This term is modern (and employed by moderns in senses that are often debatable), but the idea is as old as the world. For the ancients it was enveloped in the classical idea of virtue, since virtue is a stable disposition through which we live *rightly*: a *good* life is a life which occupies a determined place in the scale of values.

### Value and End

6. It is well to dwell on these considerations for a moment, in order to bring out a point of central importance for what follows. This point concerns a concept which is quite primary—the concept of the good.

The concept of the good has two typical implications. Let us observe the way people employ it: we see it cleft in twain so to speak (this is the result of its essential analogicity) following two quite distinct lines of signification, oriented in two different directions.

On the one hand the good is a synonym of *end.* Here we have the direction of "final causality". The good, by the very fact of being good, is the goal toward which we aim. And all the rest—that is to say, the whole order of means—is good only in relation to that end, or insofar as it is such as to lead toward that end.

If the philosopher engaged in the domain of moral philosophy—the term "moral philosopher" seems grammatically doubtful to me, let us say rather the ethician—if the ethician considers things solely in this perspective, human acts will appear to him morally good as means, and solely as *means* leading to the end, that is to the ultimate good or sovereign good of human life. Their moral quality will be regarded as consisting entirely and exclusively in their function as *means* ordered to that end.

Such will be the standard by which the morality of human acts will have to be measured, and will have to be determined and justified before the tribunal of reason. These remarks are valid for the moral utilitarian, they are valid also for the kind of super-utilitarian represented by a religious morality which would define good actions solely and exclusively as actions which lead to the ultimate eternal end.

7. On the other hand the good is a synonym of *value*. Here we have the direction of "formal causality". If the good appears to us as good, it is because it appears to us as a certain fullness of being, a certain intrinsic qualitative achievement whose property is to be lovable or desirable: that which is good is worthy of love, worth being loved and desired, has a value in itself and for itself. And in truth, this aspect is the primordial aspect of the good; it is by means of it that the good must be primordially described (we should say "defined" if a primary notion could be defined in the strict sense of the word).

If the ethician considers things in this perspective, human acts will no longer appear to him morally good only as means to the end, the ultimate end of human life. Their moral quality will be conceived as an intrinsic value which, by itself and for itself, independently of any consideration of the end, demands approval or disapproval by the conscience. Such was clearly the point of view of Plato.

In fact, in the common judgment of men, is it not in this fashion that good and bad actions are held to be such? I mean, immediately, in themselves, and not as mere means to an end (even the ultimate end). Let us consider some obvious examples, say a coward, an egotist or a debauchee of some kind: if he hears tell of a courageous exploit, or of a life of devotion to others, or of a life of purity, he will know at once and hasten to declare that these kinds of things are good and beautiful. All of us, just by being, all of us know from the beginning, at first glance, that it is a fine thing to tell the truth without fear, or to risk one's life to save a man in danger of death or to care for the lepers, and that it is bad to betray a friend or to let oneself be bought by a suborner. And at that moment we do not ask ourselves whether the act is or is not a means of attaining what we regard as the true end of human life: our judgment is purely and simply a judgment of value; the idea of the supreme Good of man, and of the relation of a given act to that Good, remains foreign to it. This kind of immediate judgment, arising from spontaneous knowledge, moral intuition or moral sense, by whatever name we call it, poses a problem for the philosopher—it is a factual datum whose existence he ought to recognize, not conceal. The discussion of this problem is not within the scope of the present volume. For the moment I wish only to point out that one of the tasks of the ethicist is to try to explain this kind of intuition, after he has applied himself to showing how value, the intrinsic moral quality of human acts, is measured and determined—and reflexively justified—by reason.

Let us remark here in passing that while noting the essential importance of the good *as end*, it was upon this aspect of the good *as value* that Thomas Aquinas was especially to insist in his ethics. For him a human action is good because it conforms to reason. And it is because it is good, because in the first place it has in itself a positive moral *value*, that it is in consequence of such a nature as to lead us toward our final *end*.

## The Primacy of Value

8. But let us return to our reflections on the moral philoophy of Plato. What I should like to note is that precisely because the End of human life is, for this philosophy, transcendent and supra-human, it is very difficult to find a common measure between that End and the means which lead toward it, in other words to see how that End could be the measure of our acts as means leading toward it.

Let us place ourselves in the perspective of a non-transcendent or intra-human conception of the end, like that of Socrates: the end is a happiness within our reach—virtue, or wisdom, or power and liberty of spirit. And now suppose that I am inclined to anger—I choose this example because it was the case with Socrates himself, according to Porphyry. It is easy to understand that abandoning oneself to an access of fury against others is not a proper means of arriving at happiness: we lose peace of soul, we call forth the resentment of others, we make a lot of enemies for ourselves. Anger, then, is not a virtue.

But let us place ourselves in the perspective of a transcendent or supra-human conception of Happiness or of the End, like that of Plato, for whom Happiness was the state of the soul which has arrived, here below and then beyond the tomb, at the contemplation of incorporeal reality and the separate Forms. Now I ask: why is patience with others a more suitable means than anger for arriving at that end? Suppose I do not know at first that anger is not good; suppose that the only way I can measure my acts is by their proportion to my ultimate End—what kind of relation can I perceive between the Subsistent Good, transcendent, absolute, ineffable, and my movement of anger or my act of patience? Could I not just as well think that in giving free reign to my anger I shall be co-operating with the effort of nature to expel stupidity and meanness from its bosom; that I shall be avoiding tension or repression and consequently be better preparing myself for union with the divine? I am without a guide and without a compass. The Absolute is too high to serve as a standard for measuring these poor things which are my acts. If the End is transcendent, if it transcends man and the human life, it transcends also the moral measurement and regulation of human acts.

In such a perspective, consequently, moral values will not be reduced to the simple condition of *means* in relation to the end; it is in *themselves* that they will be primarily considered and determined. Thus Plato will define virtue as the order, the harmony and the health of the soul. Virtue makes the soul beautiful, it is a participation, on the level of human activity, in the subsistent absolute Good and Beautiful.

9. It is on values in themselves that the accent is placed in the ethics of Plato: an ethic of values, with the intrinsic dignity which inheres in them, rather than an ethic of the final End. This ethic has so to speak an aesthetic character, because nowhere more than in beauty does value appear purely and simply in and for itself, independent of any relation of means to end. Justice is not good because it serves some end, it is purely and simply good, it puts the soul in accord with the standards proper to a rational society, it renders the soul healthy and beautiful. Let us say that with Plato philosophical thought made the discovery,

begun by Socrates, of the *bonum honestum,* of the good-and-beautiful, of the good-in-itself; it became conscious of this aspect of the good in a fully explicit way. I know very well that there is no incompatibility between End and Value. What I should like to emphasize for the moment is that the ethic of Plato disengages and underlines, brings the notion of value into relief with an exceptional force and puts it in first place, particularly in regard to the manner in which the morality of human acts is measured or determined.

It is true that when it comes to application Plato's answers too often remain metaphorical and insufficiently precise. He sees quite clearly that every morally good or "virtuous" action possesses an internal value, by reason of which it merits in itself the approbation or disapprobation of the mind. But because of that aesthetic character and that predominance of the beautiful that we noticed above in his moral philosophy, and because in general, as Aristotle and St. Thomas were to observe, his thought operated less in terms of analysis and scientific demonstration than in terms of perception and symbolism proper to poetic knowledge, he had difficulty, in particular cases, in rationally justifying a given value or a given canon or moral conduct, and in offering us a scientific analysis of various virtues. He left us the list of the four great fundamental moral virtues which was to become classic (the cardinal virtues: practical Wisdom or Prudence, Courage, Justice and Temperance). But in order to indicate the nature of these virtues he has recourse to comparisons (with the typical functions of the harmonious City) rather than to definitions.

## The Platonic Utopia

10. Dependence and independence with regard to popular norms—that is the fifth characteristic we should like to examine. We remarked in speaking of Socrates that in fact the ethicist depends in large measure on the values and norms commonly recognized in his milieu and time. This remark is applicable in a general way to all philosophers, whatever their moral system may be. Plato is one of those rare philosophers who is to a certain extent an exception. He transcends the mentality of his times when he derides the division of humanity into Greeks and

barbarians. He transcends it too, and above all, when he proposes an idea—of the sage fleeing toward the eternal regions—which, in fact, carried the sage beyond and above the city.

But he is caught short immediately by the Greek conviction of the absolute, insurpassable importance of the political order and of the city; and from then on only one way remains to reinstate the sage in the city which he transcends: to crown him, to make him the sovereign of the city. Thus the kingly quality of the sage is a rigorous logical necessity of Platonic thought.

On many other scores Plato, too, depends on the common conscience of his time—he received from it the fundamental notion of the *kalo-kagathia*, likewise the conviction to which I just alluded, that political activity is the highest form of human activity (after his unhappy experiments with tyrants, whose mentor he wished to be, he applied himself to making of the Academy a school for statesmen as well as a school of wisdom); he draws upon the notion of civilization elaborated by the Greece of his time, and upon the aberrant ideal it formulated of a heroic masculine society closed in upon itself; he partakes of the ideas of the reactionary aristocracy with which he had family ties, and he has just that *bit too much* pessimism about human nature which marks those who weep for a long past.

Finally, if his morality is so inseparably linked to his politics that it can be characterized as a morality of the conscience itself centered on the city and committed to the city, and if he did not perceive (any more than Aristotle did after him) that in every human being, and not only in the sage, there are calls, values and possessions which transcend the temporal city, it is because for him as for Aristotle man is not fully man except as he is a member of the city (at once citizen and non-slave). In short, Plato accepts without question the conception of the City (regarded as a sacred and supreme monad, let us say the hieropolitical conception of the city) which was characteristic of antiquity. But he submits that conception to the inflexible logic of a reason so passionately desirous of perfection and absoluteness that he transforms it into a utopia in which he is not afraid to reverse the scale of accepted values, to fly in the face of and scandalize the popular conscience, either by installing the community of women in his city or by driving out Homer and the poets after having politely crowned them.

11. To tell the truth, he knew very well, in writing the *Republic* and the *Laws,* that he was too right for anyone to listen to him. And I do not think we ought to embark upon a consideration of the great themes of his philosophy without taking into account the transcendent and extraordinarily refined irony with which he abandons himself all the more freely to the most extreme exigencies of his logic, and is all the more at ease in really believing in them (on the level of pure reason) for the fact that he himself laughs at them on the sly when he thinks of men and what they are.

But what he is quite sure of, in any case, is that if the task consists of obliging men to lead a good life and to be *virtuous,* or irreproachably men, that task can only be accomplished by the city, and only if the city itself is founded and organized on the basis of the science of the supreme verities or upon wisdom. ". . . There might be a reform of the State if only one change were made, which is not a slight or easy though still a possible one. . . . Until philosophers are kings, or the kings and princes of this world have the spirit and power of philosophy, and political greatness and wisdom meet in one . . . cities will never have rest from their evils—no, nor the human race, as I believe." It is for the sake of the virtuous life, to be established here below, that the absolutism of the city is imposed. And looking forward to such an Establishment of moral perfection, it is a small thing to be forced by the rigors of dialectics to sacrifice to the political all those things, interests, possessions, family, which pertain to the private domain of the individual.

I used the term "hieropolitical" above, in speaking of the conception of the city formulated by the ancients. One must be careful not to use the word "totalitarian" here, the more so for having discerned the true nature of the abject totalitarianism whose visage our age has been privileged to see. Greece did not know the totalitarianism of a State which holds itself to be the arbiter of good and evil and which laughs at truth because it is itself the insane god of an immanentist world and ideology; its idolatrous cult of the City was a cult of the City which kept faith with transcendental values and subordinated itself to them.

Nothing is clearer in the case of Plato. If the Republic must be ruled by philosophers, it is because the Republic itself is measured by wisdom, and because the intemporal truth of the world of Ideas reigns above it. The absolutism of the Platonic city is a kind of theocratic absolutism: the autocracy of wisdom, through law. The philosopher-king is a kind of hierarch who governs a politico-religious society in the name of the eternal Laws.

This city, which imposes adherence to the three articles of its philosophical credo (Gods exist, the universe is morally governed by them, no offering or incantation can seduce them or cause them to betray justice) on pain of punishment by five years' imprisonment, and even, for heretics who are second offenders, on pain of death, is not without some resemblance to the Geneva of John Calvin. A deceptive resemblance however, for its is in nowise a city-church—nothing is more foreign to Greek thought than the concept of a church (the first suggestion of which is found not in any Hellenic notion but in the Hebraic notion of *Qahal*). The Platonic city is strictly temporal and rational. It is at the same time something temporal and rational and something divine; and therein lies the deepest source of utopia and at the same time of serene pride. It is a matter of founding the virtuous life for humanity, of leading man to his perfection through man himself, elevated to the state of a political body in which, as servitor and organ of the gods, he is rendered divine because he participates in the wisdom and sovereignty which emanate from the One and the Good. Plato is the greatest of the Theocrats who in the name of Reason have wanted to force men to be good.

12. It was a vain attempt. And the tyrants will never listen to the philosopher, nor will the people ever crown him. After all, why should Plato be astonished at this? If a rigorous logical necessity of his philosophy is met head on among men by a pure impossibility, is this not simply a confirmation for him of the fact that this world is not the world of truth, but of shadows on the wall and of illusion? "Now human affairs," Plato says in the *Laws*, "are hardly worth considering in earnest, and yet we must be in earnest about them—a sad necessity constrains us. . . . Man . . . is made to be the plaything of God, and this, truly considered, is the best of him. . . ."

It is by his failure, indeed, that Plato offers us his most precious lesson. For he was too great not to perceive this failure with complete awareness, and to disengage its full significance. "If, as everyone seems to agree, the *Republic* was completed around 375, that is, before the last two voyages to Sicily and the definitive failure of his attempts to install philosophy on the throne of Syracuse, it was already before this major setback that Plato foresaw, as though determed *a priori,* the necessary failure of the philosopher. Taking up once again, and this time at his own expense, the sarcasms of Callicles (in the *Gorgias*), he shows us this great soul, too pure, thrown defenceless into a world given over to injustice, too corrupt to trust him: he is sure to perish, profitless if he takes it into his head to want to reform the State; and the philosopher gives up this useless ambition, and, withdrawing into himself, he turns to 'the city which is within him', πρὸς τὴν ἐν αὐτῶ πολιτείαν, profound and admirable phrase, the last word (if there is ever a last word), bitter and resigned, of the great wisdom of Plato.

"When he wrote the *Gorgias* he had perhaps not yet reached this point, perhaps not yet renounced that will to power which had animated his youthful ambitions (is there not some self-satisfaction in the fiery, life-like portrait he draws of Callicles, that amoral but effusive politician?). Now, the step has been taken: he knows that the philosopher, led essentially by his ideal of inner perfection, is beaten at the start. He will always be a failure among men: a stranger to political, everyday life, his thoughts absorbed by this sublime object, he will cut the figure of a fool, like Thales falling into the well as he looked at the stars, of an impotent; and yet only he is free. . . .

"Now Plato sees clearly into himself: his teaching aims to make *a* man, at the most a little group of men, joined in a school, forming a closed sect, a cultural islet, healthy in the midst of a decayed society. The Sage—for Platonism heads already into a personalist type of wisdom—will spend his life 'occupied with his own affairs', τὰ αὐτοῦ πράττων.

"Thus, Platonic thought, prompted at the start by the desire to restore the totalitarian ethics of the ancient City, comes in the last analysis to transcend definitively the compass of the ancient City and to lay the foundations of what will remain the personal achievements of the classic philosopher."

## CHAPTER 3

### THE DISCOVERY OF ETHICS

#### ARISTOTLE

*The Good and Happiness identified*

1. The fundamental question, for Aristotle, is again that of the *supreme good* or sovereign good of man, and that supreme good is, again, *happiness.* It is a question of "living in a blissful and beautiful manner". Happiness, *eudaemonia,* consists in the perfect fulfillment of human nature. We must understand this word nature, not in an empirical sense but in a metaphysical sense, and as a synonym of essence—was not Aristotle the father of the concept of essence? Each being possesses an intelligible structure which constitutes it in its species, and tendencies and inclinations which, unlike the accidental variations found in individuals, emanate necessarily from that typical structure itself. (It will be seen that in the course of time the maxim "follow nature" is given directly opposite meanings, depending on whether the word nature is taken in an empirical sense, as designating only what exists in fact, or in a metaphysical sense, as designating an essence, a locus of intelligible necessities . . .)

Εὐδαιμονία is the state of a man in whom human nature and its essential aspirations have attained their complete fulfillment, and attained it in conformity with the true hierarchy of ends proper to that nature. "Not to have organized one's life with a view to some end is the mark of much folly." In order to determine what happiness is, it is necessary to find out what the ends of our nature are (what is "the meaning of life", the first question to awaken moral anguish in us), and to discover what kind of good above all others man is made for, the good which is uniquely appropriate to a rational being and through which he achieves the fulfillment of his nature.

In order to avoid any misunderstanding it is important to make the following points clear: (1) Aristotle does not tell us that we *ought* to tend toward happiness—the aspiration toward happiness is a fact of nature. It exists in man necesssarily. Aristotle tries to discern or determine *what happiness really consists in*, this happiness toward which we necessarily aspire. (2) This determination of what happiness consists in is the proper task of moral philosophy. But men did not wait for the reflections of moral philosophy and the theories of ethicists in order to begin living and acting. They must, then, have a way of their own—a spontaneous or "pre-philosophical" way—of knowing what is really the meaning of life and what the true supreme good consists in (whether or not the idea of happiness occurs to them explicitly at this point). I mention this problem; it is not within the scope of the present volume. (3) Whether this knowledge be acquired in a practical and spontaneous way or in a speculative and philosophical way, in any case, as soon as we know what the supreme good truly consists in, we know also that we *ought* to tend toward that true good; we are obliged to do so by conscience, not by virtue of some philosophical demonstration, but by virtue of a "first principle" known in an immediate way by each person and self-evident to what Aristotle calls the "intuitive reason" or "the immediate intelligence of principles": one must do good and avoid evil.

When the philosopher has determined what *is the true* supreme good of man, he has by the same token indicated the first choice which every man is obliged by conscience to make.

2. We can now outline with some precision the positions Aristotle takes with regard to the basic issues we were able to discern in studying the thought of Socrates and Plato.

First of all, it is clear that the concept of the Good, and that of the supreme or sovereign Good, is as central for Aristotle as for Socrates and Plato and Greek philosophy in general. The observations we have just made only confirm this fact. It is to be noted here that if Aristotle identifies the Sovereign Good with Happiness, it is not that for him the Good is eclipsed by Happiness. For him as for Socrates, the Good remains the Good. It retains its own meaning even though identified with Happiness. It even retains a certain priority over Happiness, for the concept of the Good is in itself a more primitive or primordial concept than that of Happiness—but this priority remains purely implicit in Aristotle's thought.

The fact that Aristotle neglected to elucidate and explain this point in his moral philosophy gives rise, as we shall see, to the kind of amphibology which his system does not succeed in avoiding.

### The End—the Aristotelian Sovereign Good

3. In his ethics as in his metaphysics and his philosophy of nature, Aristotle attributes an absolutely major role to finality. All things are, as it were, suspended from the Final Cause. Thus for him the primary aspect of the Good is its aspect as End. And the first question for moral philosophy is the question of the Sovereign Good. This theme was to become classic for centuries in the occidental philosophical tradition, up to the Kantian revolution.

But as for the manner in which he conceives the End of human life, or the sovereign Good, Aristotle takes his place midway between Socrates and Plato.

In contrast to Plato, the ethics of *eudaemonia* deliberately steps down from the sublime heights of Platonic morality. The supreme good pertains to human life, becomes immanent in that life. It is a happiness which exists here below, a terrestrial happiness. This does not mean that Aristotle failed to recognize its necessary relation to that which is superior to man. He made wisdom, whose object is divine, the principal ingredient of that happiness. He has a theory of good fortune, and, more important, a theory of inspiration, in which he sees a superhuman element intervening in human affairs. We must not forget that, for him, to propose to man only that which is human is to do him disservice, for by virtue of the most excellent part of himself, which is the intellect, man is called to something better than a purely human life. In the *Eudemian Ethics,* whose doctrine we hold to be authentically Aristotelian, we find such a passage as this: "As in the universe, so in the soul, God moves all things. The principle of reasoning is not reasoning, but something better. Now what could be better than even the knowledge of the intellect, if not God? Not virtue, for virtue is an instrument of the intellect. . . ."

In contrast to Socrates, he holds that the practice of virtue does not result in the immediate possession of happiness. The art of living rightly is not the art of being happy through virtue, or of realizing that virtue equals happiness. It is the art of ordering one's life in such a way as to attain the supreme end: happiness—in this earthly life no doubt, in this perishable body, in the midst of the city of men (and not beyond the grave, beyond the prison of this body, by means of a kind of death begun here below, as Plato conceived it)—but not immediately either, as Socrates envisaged, as if happiness were the reverse side of the virtuous act itself. A well-ordered life attains happiness at the end of a long term, after long exercise, at a ripe age, when the hair is beginning to turn silver. Yes, God knows, that is so! Such a view does not arouse great enthusiasm, perhaps—the man who is starving does not like much to wait—but it is eminently reasonable.

4. And now, of what is happiness composed? What are its essential elements? Three things are the principal constituents of happiness: wisdom, virtue, pleasure. For the perfect and happy life is "the most beautiful and best of things, and also that which gives the greatest joy".

There is an order among the three elements of happiness, a hierarchy of importance. The first place belongs to wisdom, the possession by the mind, however precarious in the case of man, of contemplated truth. Wisdom is essentially contemplative, it is an immanent activity, an activity of repose and fruition. And contemplation is superior to action. The perfect life is above all theoretical, it is the life of knowledge achieved in unity.

In second place comes virtue. The life according to virtue is obviously an integral part of the full accomplishment of human nature.

Pleasure takes third place, and occurs as a surplus, so to speak. It exists as a necessary result. By virtue of a general rule, it is added to the act, as bloom is to youth. And man cannot live without a certain measure of joy or delectation. That kind of interior contentment or that feeling of expansiveness which, in the most profound sense of the word, we call pleasure is the natural recompense of a virtuous life.

But that is not all. The three sorts of good we have just spoken of exist within the soul. There are still other kinds of good, exterior to the soul, which are included in the notion of happiness, if not as integral components at least as indispensable conditions: friendship—a man without friends is not a happy

man; health; the possession of material goods (a certain abundance is necessary to the external manifestation of virtue—
poverty does not permit munificence, and we may add that
poverty is a terrible obstacle to virtue itself); and finally, Aristotle
was too much of a realist to be unaware that chance, with its
favorable coincidences, the free gifts of good fortune, plays an
indispensable role in the happiness of the human being.

The Aristotelian conception of happiness, or of *eudaemonia,* is definitely not hedonistic, since pleasure occupies the
third rank in its hierarchy of goods. Rather, it takes the supreme
good as it was conceived by Plato and renders it immanent,
secularizes it in an eminently humanistic, noble and reasonable
way. Like man himself, the happiness of man is complex. It is a
compound, made of matter and spirit, of sense and intelligence,
of animal conditioning and rational, even super-rational freedom,
all of this crowned, and guided, by wisdom and contemplation.

In Aristotle's moral philosophy everything is measured in
relation to this complex totality: the best and most beautiful life,
the accomplished fullness of human nature, happiness—consisting
in the true order of the parts which compose it. It is the end
toward which we tend insofar as we are not foolish, insofar as
we do not make a mess of the art of living. Herein lies the source
of a nuance peculiar to the conception of moral obligation and
moral fault which is to be found, if not in the religious thought
of the Greeks (witness the great tragedians), at least in their
philosophical thought. The idea of duty, as conceived by the
Greek philosophers, has less affinity with the idea of a sacred
imperative than with that of a masterful ordering of means,
something which is required of man in order to attain his end,
and something which is recognized by every reasonable and cultivated spirit anxious to assume his true happiness. Their idea of
moral fault is most closely akin to the idea of a badly conducted
or senseless action which mars the beauty of life and leads away
from happiness. The notion of culpability, rendering man unworthy of existence and bringing down upon him the wrath of
the gods, this notion which was so strong in Aeschylus, is now
greatly attenuated. As for the concept of the norm, if it still
plays an essential role, it also has lost the sacred character it
possessed in the beginning. It designates less a divine command-

ment than a rule of conduct required by the order of nature and of the cosmos. In short, it is not the Kantian *"ought"* that we find here, but *"such is the way to happiness"*. It is significant that for antiquity the vocabulary of ethics and that of art remained substantially identical. The artist possesses his virtue just as the prudent man possesses his. The word "sin" is applied as readily to a grammatical or musical error as to a fault against justice or temperance.

*The search for an equilibrium between Finality and Value—the primacy of Finality*

5. Aristotelian ethics consists of the search for a doctrinal and systematic equilibrium between these two major considerations: that of the End, and that of Values.

Far from neglecting the consideration of values, it deliberately emphasizes their importance: the concept of virtue has a central place in this ethics. One of the great tasks successfully performed by Aristotle was to establish rationally the philosophical theory of virtue: what is the ontological "stuff" of virtue? Virtue is by nature that kind of quality which he calls a *habitus*, a ἕξις; and moral virtue is a ἕξις or stable disposition which fortifies and perfects the powers of the soul in respect to the *right use* of freedom. Now as we have remarked before, the concept of virtue is by its nature inseparable from the concept of value.

But for Aristotle, what dominates the whole field of ethics, and the way in which specific virtues are to be determined, is the consideration of the ultimate End, the primacy of the Supreme Good, or the happy life. At this point he turns away from the positions of Plato to come back to those of Socrates, not, to be sure, with the perspective and to the advantage of that utilitarianism to which Socrates was constrained to limit himself for want of the necessary means to go beyond it, but with the perspective and to the advantage of eudemonism. I mean that in the eyes of Aristotle the good of the virtues is at the same time *bonum honestum* (good worthy in its own right) or good in itself and through itself, and the *means* of arriving at Happiness.

Value and finality—how are these two fundamental aspects of ethics harmonized? Let us recall the famous theory which makes moral virtue consist in a *mean*, a midpoint (μεσότης) be-

96

tween an excess and a deficiency. In each case moral good or moral rectitude is defined by the fact that it strikes the *right note,* a correct, exact and appropriate consonance which is produced by reason. The fundamental notion of the *measurement* or the regulation of our acts by reason makes its appearance here, a notion which was to have a bright future, for it was to become the keystone of moral philosophy in the Christian tradition. Now if my interpretation is correct, we must say that for Aristotle a morally good act is an act which has not only been worked over, brewed, prepared, adjusted, harmonized, concocted, digested, formed, measured by reason—but, more precisely, which has been measured by reason in its very capacity of tending directly toward the ultimate end of human existence, toward Happiness, toward "the good and beautiful life, if one hesitates through a kind of fear to call it by its true name, the blissful life."

On the one hand, then, in virtue of being measured by reason, the moral act attains its peculiar configuration, its beauty, its brilliance, the plenitude proper to a human act. It is invested with a quality which makes it good in itself and for itself (*bonum honestum,* good as right). Here the role of *Value* is emphasized.

But on the other hand, it is as *means* to the Happy Life that the moral act is formed and determined, measured by reason. It is in function of its tending directly toward the ultimate End that reason measures the moral act. Here the role of the *End* is emphasized.

It is thus that Aristotle reconciles the claims of Finality and those of Value in ethical theory.

6. But in actual fact, and in a definitive way, the consideration of the ultimate End, or Happiness, plays the major role and carries all before it, since it is by virtue of tending directly toward true happiness that reason regulates human acts. Finality is not only predominant in the order of action, but it is the supreme criterion even in the order of specification, even in the determination of the moral goodness of human conduct. And the result is that the "absolute" or "categorical" character of the moral imperative or of the *bonum honestum* is in some sort relegated to the background. Thence a trace, in spite of all, and more than a trace, of utilitarianism.

All this amounts to saying that the equilibrium sought by Aristotle was not decisively attained. I fear, moreover, that a kind of vicious circle is implied in his procedure: the fact is that virtue appears herein as essentially a *means* toward the good and beautiful life, the blessed life; and yet virtue is also an *integral part* of that blessed life, since without virtue there is no good and beautiful life—the means to the end (virtue) thus enters into the very notion and constitutive of the end to which it is directed.

Aristotle discovered the right road, but his solution remained imperfect, enveloped in insurmountable difficulties.

When, with the advent of Christianity, the ultimate, the absolute End, and the Beatitude with which it is connected, were to become even more transcendent and supra-human than with Plato, the norm in relation to which reason measures human acts, that norm which must be proportionate with man (as was Aristotelian happiness), was no longer to be supreme Happiness itself—it is too transcendent to serve as a norm for measuring human acts. Beatitude is in fact the end to be attained in the order of action by the righteous human life, but it is not, in the order of specification, the criterion of moral goodness. That criterion (at least in the perspective of nature, which is the basic perspective of the philosopher) was to be the ensemble of primary rules known to us without reasoning (though reflexively justifiable in reason) by virtue of the essential inclinations of our nature, in other words *natural law*, along with all the rules which can be inferred from its principles. At that point the concept of natural law already brought to light, but in a different perspective by the Stoics, was to take its true place in the structure of ethics. And the notion of the *accomplishment of the natural law* was to replace that of *Happiness* as the objective specifying standard in function of which reason measures human acts.

The vicious circle which I just pointed out in speaking of Aristotle no longer exists. For natural law enables us to see what the virtues must be, but the concept of virtue or the virtuous life in no way enters into the notion of the natural law itself. The equilibrium sought by Aristotle is finally attained.

The chart to be found on page 99 indicates in a diagrammatical way the various positions we have mentioned up to now, and at the same time the kind of trajectory described by the idea of happiness.

Happiness was at first identified with virtue. Then it left this earthly sphere for the transcendent world of subsistent Ideas. In the third stage it came back to earth and to human life. In the fourth stage it is to have its seat in the celestial homeland, as absolutely perfect Happiness, or Beatitude, toward which man tends by the very fact of tending toward his ultimate End, God loved for Himself and above all else.

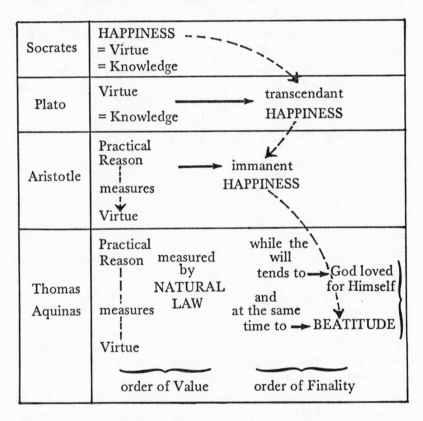

*Ethics and the common Conscience—the theory of the Virtues*

7. In the case of Aristotle as in that of Socrates, and even more definitely than in the case of Plato, we can verify the fact that ethical theory works on the basis of moral structures already in existence in the human community and is most often occupied

with justifying the scale of values and the rules of conduct accepted by common conscience in a given cultural atmosphere and period. At this stage of our enquiry, the period in question is the fourth century B.C., and it is well known that even slavery, which was one of the foundations of that society, was regarded by the Philosopher as grounded in reason and required by nature.

Aristotle was fully conscious of the general fact we have just mentioned. The experience of men plays a fundamental role in his ethics. He refers to it constantly. The conduct of the prudent man, the opinion of the elders and their experience of life, the customs of various cities were, for him, indispensable data for the very construction of moral philosophy. But he uses all this human experience in order to disengage by induction the rational principles with which it is pregnant. Thence the considerable amount of space he devotes to empirical description, the abundant and richly detailed psychological descriptions we find in so many chapters of the *Nicomachean Ethics* and the *Eudemian Ethics*.

On the other hand, Aristotle was in a position to propose a teleological justification of values and moral rules, in function of the last end, because, as we have seen, that last end found itself humanized in his system, brought back to the level of terrestrial existence and terrestrial standards. Since in the internal hierarchy of earthly happiness theoretical activity or contemplation holds the most exalted place ("Perhaps he thought," Aristotle wrote concerning Anaxagoras, "that he who leads a life without afflictions and free from all injustice, and who in addition is engaged in some divine contemplation, is, insofar as man can be, blessed"), it is in relation to this contemplative wisdom that our various choices and the exercises of the virtues must be ordered. "Whatever choice, then, or the possession of whatever natural goods— bodily welfare, riches, friends, or whatever else—is most apt to lead to the contemplation of God, that choice or that possession will be the best. There we have the most noble criterion. . . ." In order to attain to the sovereign good man must, on the one hand, regulate by reason (which is "royal" or "political", not "despotic" government) the lower functions, especially the passions, and, on the other hand, develop the powers of the spirit, and the superior life of the νοῦς.

8. It is here, and still in reference to the good and beautiful life not to be missed, that the theory of virtue as the *golden mean* between opposed vices finds its place—not the golden mean of mediocrity, but the golden mean of eminence, the summit between two contrary depressions, according to that observation so true that it has become trite. It has often been remarked, along the same line, that what Aristotle called prudence is not fear of risk or precautionary timidity; its function is rather to make man master of himself and superior to events, and ready freely to take the risks required by justice, by the dignity of a rational being, and by magnanimity.

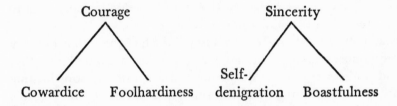

The mean which constitutes virtue is an indivisible thing—it is just a point, the just point; it is what corresponds in the moral order to having a "good ear", to musical or poetic exactitude. The two opposed extremes—by excess or by defect—meet at the summit and fade away, disappear when they come in contact with each other in virtue. To take up a remark of André Gide's, about himself, each virtue could say: extremes touch *me*; and they die of it.

We find the Aristotelian list of the moral virtues and the contrary vices by excess or defect in the *Nicomachean Ethics,* Book II, chapters 6 and 7, and in the *Eudemian Ethics,* Book II, chapter 3 (1220 b 36-1221 a 12). It should be noted that there is no word in the language for the extreme opposed by defect to envy, and so this vice remains unnamed, although it is a very real thing, as we see in the case of those who do not suffer at all by reason of the prosperity of the unworthy, but who "accept everything, as a glutton swallows no matter what, while those in whom exists the opposed vice are impatient, through envy, at the good of others". There we have an example of Aristotle's method. In this whole analysis of the moral virtues and opposed vices, he relies on the common conscience and refers constantly to the moral judgments men make in the ordinary course of life. But he has disengaged therefrom a universal law, to wit, virtue consists in the proper mean. And armed with this instrument, he corrects common experience and supplies examples of what it fails to notice when "the other extreme, as if it did not exist, escapes our knowledge, remaining unperceived because of its rarity".

*Freedom*

9. Virtue is not knowledge. In Aristotle's moral philosophy a fundamental characteristic of the ethical theories of antiquity, especially in the heroic age of Greek philosophy, becomes clearly apparent: I am thinking here of the "cosmic" or "ontological" character of this moral philosophy, of the fact that ethical theory presupposes a system of metaphysics and of natural philosophy, and that no ethics can do without prerequisite notions bearing upon the world, man and the supreme realities, in other words, that the universe of freedom (the moral universe) is founded upon the universe of nature.

The ethician must know that there are natures or essences, that there is a human nature, that what pertains to spirit and to reason in man is superior to what is irrational in him. He must be aware of the existence of free will.

This privilege of the being gifted with reason—freedom of choice—is particularly emphasized by Aristotle.

It is a question which caused Plato serious difficulties. He believed in freedom, and had no inclination to contest its existence. But the theory of *virtue as knowledge*, the idea that all sin is ignorance and that it is sufficient to know the good in order to do it, was in reality incompatible with the existence of free will. Plato tried hard to find a way out, for the difficulty was not insurmountable. He sought refuge in a theory of supra-temporal freedom which is not without analogy with that which Kant was to propose—such theories in fact eliminate freedom.

Aristotle, on the contrary, held on to the reality of free will at no matter what cost. This is one of the points at which the existential value of his doctrine, which it is fashionable these days to call into question (and in fact he shows many deficiencies in this regard), appears most clearly. As Hamelin has clearly shown, he was so profoundly conscious of freedom that, rather than compromise its existence, he did not hesitate to scandalize the logicians by enunciating his famous theory (so admirable, and so true) of the indetermination of the truth of propositions relating to future contingents.

Of the contradictory propositions relating to a future contingent, he teaches in *On Interpretation,* one will be true when the time in question comes to pass, and the other will by the same stroke be false; but neither can be determined today as true or false, since the truth comprised by these propositions is as indeterminate as the event to which they relate, which itself will not be determined until it takes place. "A sea-fight must either take place to-morrow or not, but it is not necessary that it should take place to-morrow, neither is it necessary that it should not take place, yet it is necessary that it either should or should not take place to-morrow. Since propositions correspond with facts, it is evident that when in future events there is a real alternative, and a potentiality in contrary directions, the corresponding affirmation and denial have the same character."

Similarly, which of the two contradictory propositions is true and which is false remains undetermined until the future moment in question has become present. If this were not the case everything would occur by necessity, and there would be neither contingency nor liberty. "There would be no need to deliberate or to take trouble, on the supposition that if we should adopt a certain course, a certain result would follow, while, if we did not, the result would not follow." A thousand years in advance a prediction concerning the result in question would have had to be necessarily true and its contradiction necessarily false, so that the event itself would arrive necessarily on the date indicated.

10. Since he fully recognized the reality of free will it is not surprising that Aristotle treats of the idea that virtue is knowledge without mincing words. "In regard to virtue," he says, "not to know *what* it is, but to know *whence* it comes (or how to acquire it), that is what is most precious. For we do not want to know what courage is, but to be courageous, nor what justice is, but

to be just, in the same way that we want to be in good health rather than to know what kind of thing health is."

He even added that to know is of little use for virtue, or even of no use at all. "As condition for the possession of virtues, knowledge has little or no weight at all."

This memorable disillusioned maxim is evidence that Aristotle was possessed of a more profound human experience and a clearer view of moral problems than Plato, or even than those modern little Platonists who no longer believe in the Ideas and install themselves comfortably in the shadows of the cave, but who believe in "scientific" ethics, and think that it is the business of the empirical sciences to lay the foundations of the good life for humanity—just wait a little while until biology, psychology and sociology have completed their discoveries and men will put into practice the laws of good conduct (it will be a long wait, for it is the nature of these sciences to substitute one new approach for another and one new theory for another indefinitely).

### The Sage and the City

11. When Aristotle writes that he who escapes social life is either a beast or a god, he certainly intends to reject any kind of solitary life, even that eremitical life so widespread in India and so honored by Christianity, which without doubt does not cut all the bonds linking man and society but where—as far as the essential thing that is the spiritual order is concerned—the "delivered" or "perfect" one is entirely sufficient unto himself and has no need of others. The sage of Aristotle lives no more apart from the city than the sage of Plato.

But there is a profound difference between the two. Carried toward the beyond and the contemplation of separate Ideas, Plato's sage transcended by his own motion, as Sage, the common life of the citizen, and if at the same time it was absolutely necessary for him to bear witness to the ineluctable political vocation of the human being, he could do this only as a prince, as king of the city, wielding political power by a kind of divine right. The sage of Aristotle, on the other hand, is not called to govern the city by virtue of his wisdom, and has neither the mission nor the desire to assume political authority. He is in the city, he does not rule it. And doubtless the immanent activity of con-

templation depends to such an extent on what is divine in us
that a purely contemplative life "would be too high for man".
Life according to the intellect is divine in comparison with human life. But the fact is that if the philosopher participates in a
super-human divine life, he is not a god for all that. Because the
life he leads is principally, but not purely, contemplative; he
remains a man, and thus a member of the city.

It is quite remarkable that when, in the *Politics*, Aristotle
speaks of the too superior man whom the city must either exile
or make king (and to tell the truth how could the ostracism of
such a man be tolerabel in a perfect city? "On the other hand,
he ought not to be a subject—that would be as if mankind should
claim to rule over Zeus"; the city should therefore take advantage of its good fortune and take him as its king)—Aristotle is
not thinking here of the sage, or the philosopher, but of the hero
of action, the man who is "deemed a God among men" because
he possesses preeminently the virtues of command and political
genius. (One thinks of Alexander; many centuries later did not
Hegel regard Napoleon as "God revealed"?)

Thus the vocation for wisdom and the vocation for political
power are separated. And henceforth the question presents itself
of knowing whether the philosopher or the statesman leads the
most enviable life. Let us say that each excels in his own order,
but to be loyal to Aristotle's principles on the superiority of the
contemplative life, let us say that the order in which the philosopher excels is higher than that in which the statesman excels.

The fact remains that neither is the philosopher a pure
contemplative nor the statesman a pure man of action. The philosopher devotes himself especially but not exclusively to contemplation; he participates in the political life of the city. The
statesman devotes himself especially but not exclusively to action; his very virtues require that he participate in some measure
in the leisure of contemplation. For he must be wise, even if he
is not dedicated to wisdom (this is why he needs the philosopher
more than the ordinary citizen does).

The heroic life is therefore at once contemplative and active;
and it is normal that all of human life should be drawn to it. This
is why, in the perfect city, something of this life—at once contemplative and active—would be the portion of every citizen; to

one degree or another, in one form or another, he would have access to contemplative activity concentrated within itself and to practical activity turned outward: since these two activities, each in its own place, are integral parts of happiness.

12. The city of Aristotle holds to justice. The "happy city" is the one which "acts rightly", and "neither individual nor state can do right actions without virtue and wisdom". There will be no good life for the city without "courage, justice and wisdom". Political philosophy was to remain attached to this theme of moral rightness and justice as inherent in the common good of the city until the time of Machiavelli.

But Aristotle's city is at the same time—for the individuals who make it up—a good which is purely and simply supreme; the notion of the person has not emerged; and there is no suggestion that the human person—who is a part of the city and must work for its common good, and if necessary give his life for it—might nevertheless transcend the political order of the city according as he is himself directed to supra-temporal goods.

In saying that the good of all, or of political society, is more divine than the good of the individual, Aristotle, like all classical Greek thought, directs the individual in all of his aspects to this more divine good—which St. Thomas was careful not to do (though he liked to repeat Aristotle's phrase, but as a formula to be interpreted freely according to the needs of each particular case). "If all communities aim at some good, the city-state or political community, which is the highest of all, and which embraces all the rest, aims at good in a greater degree than any other, and at the highest good."

It follows that for Aristotle the ruling, supreme science in the order of practical knowledge is politics; it is to it that all ethics is directed.

On this point St. Thomas Aquinas, while striving to keep using Aristotelian language, adds in his commentary on the *Nicomachean Ethics* that if political science is termed the ruling science, "this is not true absolutely speaking", but only in a certain aspect. As a matter of fact, as he teaches elsewhere, the end which comes under the consideration of politics is an ultimate end in a given order only (in the order of temporal civilization); if it is a question of the absolute ultimate end of human life, in other words of "the ultimate end of the whole universe", "it is the *scientia divina* which considers it, and it is she who is the ruling science in every respect". Here we find ourselves far removed from the perspective of Aristotle himself. In his perspective the ultimate end was temporal: earthly happiness; and man achieved it in and by the city, directing himself to the good of the city as far as all that is in him is concerned.

If, on the other hand, we take the point of view indicated by St. Thomas, it will appear that a reinterpretation—actually a serious recasting—is in order of the division of ethics, classic in the peripatetic school, into "monastic" (concerned with the life of the individual), "economic" (concerned with the life of domestic society) and "political" (concerned with the life of civil society)—with politics having primacy over the two other parts of moral knowledge. For if the ethics of the individual person remain directed to the ethics of the city, or to politics, in this sense that not only in his political activity, but in his private activity itself and his virtues as a private person the individual must take into consideration the common good of the city and direct himself to this end, nevertheless this end is supreme only *secundum quid* or in a given order. It is to the separate common Good, to God Who infinitely transcends the cosmos and human society, that the activity and the virtues of the individual are directed, as to their purely and simply ultimate end. And in this light, which is primordial, the ethics of the individual identifies itself with an ethics of the common good which Aristotle did not and could not know, and which is above politics as the heavens are above the earth, and which one might call the ethics of the kingdom of God. There the supreme common good of the society of men en route toward their final end is identical with the most personal supreme good of the individual person en route toward his final end: God to be possessed by the vision of His essence; which will be the beatitude of all and which will also be the beatitude of each.

13. I just said that Aristotle could not know such an ethics of transcendent common good: it belongs to the supernatural order, and depends on the revelation progressively made to the prophets of Israel and consummated in the Gospel. But what Aristotle might have known, and did not, is the fact that in the

natural order itself the "monastic", as far as it considers the purely and simply final end of human life, identifies itself with a
supra-political ethics. For even in the purely natural order (where
there is no question of beatific vision) it is not the earthly city
but God Who is the absolute final end of man as of the whole
universe. And even in the purely natural order there is for human
persons, members of the city, a common good which is superior
to that of the city, that is the common good of minds, the supra-
temporal order of goods, of truths and of intangible laws which
reveal themselves to the intellect—and which human life could
not do without. The common good of the earthly city itself
demands that the city recognize this supra-political common
good, and that the persons who are members of the city direct
themselves to it, thus transcending the political order of the city
by what is eternal in man and in the things to which he is attached.
One might say that it took the fracas of revelation and the scandal of grace coming to complete nature to make philosophy see
these supreme data of the natural order, which it had been looking at all along, without realizing it.

It is the same here as with the creation, or the immortality
of the soul, or the *Esse per se subsistens* and its knowledge of the
world. If Aristotle did not know these things, if in his political
philosophy he thought that the city was for individuals a purely
and simply supreme good, and that there is no way in which the
person transcends the city, it is not that his principles obliged
him to think so, but rather that he did not follow his principles
far enough. What he did not know how to bring out or see explicitly, he held implicitly. We said above that the Greek conception
of the city was hieropolitical and not totalitarian. This is especially true of Aristotle's political philosophy; the spirit of this
philosophy is profoundly opposed to totalitarianism. And to tell
the truth it was at the price of a latent contradiction that Aristotle did not bring out the truths we insited on above, which his
own principles called for.

If the city is committed to justice, it is because without
justice there is no "good life" or happiness; doubtless yes, but
why is there no happiness or "good life" for the city without
justice, if not because the city must recognize laws which matter
more than its own advantage or even its own existence? For

there are instances where the city, like the individual, can serve justice only to its own detriment. To say that the city is committed to justice is to say that it is not a purely and simply supreme good.

And what does all Aristotle's teaching on contemplation mean, if not that there are for man goods of another, and better, order than that of political life? In pursuing these goods the individual serves the common good of the earthly city, to be sure—in fact the city needs the impetus given it by those who live according to the intellect, and the wisdom which comes down from their contemplation and incorporates itself in the common heritage; but it is not *for* love of the common good of the earthly city that the individual pursues these goods; it is for love of these goods themselves.

If it is true that "the activity of reason, which is contemplative . . . seems to aim at no end beyond itself, and to have its pleasure proper to itself . . . and the self-sufficiency, leisureliness, untrammelled state" characteristic of perfect happiness; and if it is true that "we must not follow those who advise us, being men, to think of human things, and, being mortal, of mortal things", but must on the contrary "so far as we can, make ourselves immortal, and strain every nerve to live in accordance with the best in us; for even if it be small in bulk, much more does it in power and worth surpass everything"—then it must be said that there are goods and activities for man which depend on an order superior to that of political life; and that with respect to all that which in man concerns these goods and activities, the person emerges above the mortal city, and passes beyond its good, "more divine" as it may be.

## The Paradox of Aristotelian Ethics

14. I should like to point out, in conclusion, what one may call the paradox of Aristotelian ethics. There is no moral system more thoroughly and authentically humanistic. And there is no moral system more disappointing for man. At this point it is permissible to speak of the defeats which Aristotelian ethics cannot avoid.

*The first Defeat*

15. The sovereign good, Happiness, has been brought back to earth, humanized, adapted to the structure and to the essential aspirations of our nature. Yes, but it involves so many ingredients and so many conditions which are hardly attainable—even for a small number of individuals, for a limited aristocracy of philosophers.

It goes without saying that Aristotle had no such consequence in mind. His intentions were generous. He remarked, for example, that "if the beautiful life" consisted "in the gifts of good fortune or of nature, it would be something that not many could hope for and that neither their precautions nor their efforts would permit them to attain; but that if it depended on the individual and on the character of his personal acts, then the sovereign good" would be "at the same time more generally possessed and more divine—more generally possessed because accessible to a greater number, more divine because happiness is then the prize offered to those who impress a certain character on their person and on their acts".

And yet in fact, given the structure of Hellenic society (approved by Aristotle), the philosophical contemplation of truth and of things divine is rendered possible for free men only thanks to slavery and the servile labor of the greatest number; and even then, even at this price, such contemplation, which is the principal ingredient of the good and beautiful life, can only be the privilege of a very limited number of sages among these free citizens.

What is more, those who achieve happiness must also possess the virtues, lead a virtuous life. And they must not only lead a virtuous life but also a life crowned by pleasure. They must know the joys of culture and of art and all the beauty of the world, and not be exempt from an appreciable enjoyment of the corporal pleasures.

And they must have friends whose very presence will intensify their effort toward virtue, and whose society will add charm to existence.

And they must have money, enough worldly possessions to profit by their freedom. And good health is also necessary, in order that the higher activity and peace of the spirit not be troubled or destroyed by bodily ills. And they must not be the victims of misfortune—chance, finally, plays its role. A certain measure of good fortune is required.

There we have the happiness of man. Who, then, as things really go, is capable of attaining the sovereign good, that sovereign good the thirst for which is the source and the fundamental motivation of our whole moral life? It is understandable that Aristotle should ask himself sometimes if, "supposing the choice were offered us, not to have been born would not be the most desirable" thing.

Our whole moral life, all our effort and striving toward rightness and virtue, are suspended from an End which, in fact, eludes us, vanishes within our grasp.

This is the first defeat suffered by Aristotelian ethics.

### The second Defeat

16. A second defeat is involved, which derives from the eudemonist conception itself. Aristotle, in agreement with Socrates and all the Greeks, identifies the sovereign Good and Happiness. Now Happiness is, so to speak, the subjective side of the Good; in the concept of Happiness the notion of Good refers back to the subject. If there is no good which is desired and loved more than Happiness, it is inevitable that Happiness should be desired and loved for the sake of the subject it beatifies.

There are many things, according to Aristotle's conception of happiness, which man loves and desires for their own sake and for their intrinsic goodness—in a way which transcends his own interest, even when his own interest is involved: contemplated truth, wisdom, virtue, all that which depends on the beautiful-and-good (*bonum honestum*). It even happens that he loves them more than his own life. But from the moment that they are included in the overall idea of Happines, subordinated to that idea, and desired as ingredients of Happiness, from the moment that Happiness takes precedence and becomes purely and simply the supreme End, this whole which is Happiness and which is desired and loved as such can only be desired and loved for the sake of the subject whom it perfects. Even in the case of the philosophic contemplation of truth and of things divine, it would be for the good of my own intellect that I loved them if I loved them only as an ingredient of my happiness. Implicitly, the ethics of Happiness was an ethics of the Good. But this fact remains implicit, veiled. He never makes explicit and precise the distinction between the Good and Happiness which, as a matter of fact, his own metaphysical system requires (since for him it is the Thought of Thought attracting to itself the whole universe which constitutes the absolute End, and thus the supreme Good-in-itself), and which is in a very real way operative in his own ethical judgments and in his moral system. As a result, because this distinction between the Good and Happiness is nowhere clearly elucidated in his moral system, Aristotle leaves us in a state of ambiguity. In spite of everything, in the last analysis his moral teaching leaves us enclosed in love of ourselves. It is *my* good that I love and will in willing and loving Happiness as the supreme Good supremely loved, that is to say the Good taken subjectively, the Good as a perfection of the subject and a resonance in the subject or as a fulfillment of human life. It is a good which I will *propter me*, for my own sake, for love of myself. It is impossible for Aristotelian ethics to escape from the embrace of the Self, from a kind of transcendental egoism. Within the moral perspective of Happiness as the supreme Good, I cannot deliver myself, I can never be delivered of myself, I can never be freed from my egoistical love of myself. And yet in the end it is just such a deliverance that we long for.

*The ineffectiveness of the appeal made to Man by the End proposed*

17. The two defeats we have just pointed out indicate the practical, existential weakness of Aristotelian ethics. By a curious paradox, it happens that all its principles are true (in particular, the very principle of eudemonism is true, in the sense that Happiness is the last *subjective* End of human life, or the last end *relative to the human subject*; Aristotle's error was in not going *further*—and could he, with only the weapons of philosophical reason?). All the principles of Aristotle's ethics are true, all its themes are carefully adjusted to what is most human in man. And yet they remain ineffective in fact, they do not come to grips with existence, they do not succeed in taking hold of the

internal dynamism of the human will. They ought to have a decisive and imperious appeal for man—they do not at all.

This is the case above all because Happiness as ultimate subjective End did not lead the Philosopher to discover a supreme Good which is loved more than Happiness, a Good worth more than Happiness and for the love of which our Happiness itself is loved. Thus the supreme Good was identified with Happiness. The last End relative to the human subject, the last End as *my* fulfillment or my supreme perfection, or as End in which *my* nature and *my* being are realized, the last End taken subjectively, blocked Aristotle's vision of the last End *in and for itself*, which at the same time he implicitly recognized. It did not totally replace (as was to happen with the Epicureans) but left in shadow the supreme Good to which I and my Happiness are ordered. From this moment the supreme End, remaining essentially human, also remains involved in human complexity. It is proportioned to man and commensurate with man, that is to say with the deception inherent in the human condition, the precariousness and the falsity of human goods. It is the sum and the summit of a collection of goods each of which is uncertain and menaced—a fragile and fleeting supreme End, deprived of all power of *decisive attraction*.

True as they are (but incomplete), the true principles of Aristotle's moral philosophy do not penetrate the concrete existential reality of the human being. They are incapable of stirring his aspirations and his profoundest hopes, which go beyond rational and reasonable happiness, incapable of probing the recesses of his ego and the world of the irrational with its impulses toward death and the void. In a word, what is infinite in man has been forgotten. The *vanitas vanitatum* of the Preacher is the reverse side of Aristotelian eudemonism.

The moral philosophy of Aristotle, which is the truest and the most authentic, the most honest of purely philosophical ethical theories, lacks effectiveness and existential bearing because it is a system of means suspended from an End which does not possess the value of an End *practically* absolute, nor the value of an End *practically* accessible, nor the value of an End *practically* constraining.

Aristotle was right to seek in happiness—I use the word in its most indeterminate sense, the happiness toward which we tend not by choice but by necessity of nature—the point of departure of ethics. But when it comes to the point of arrival, and the determination of what the true happiness of man consists in, the happiness toward which we must tend by free choice, then he sees neither that this true happiness is in fact something beyond purely human happiness, nor that it is itself ordered to a Good which is better and loved more than any happiness. The supreme good which he proposes to us is incapable of a decisive hold on existence.

Aristotelian ethics is *par excellence* the natural (purely natural) ethics and the philosophical (purely philosophical) ethics. And in what concerns the real direction of human conduct it runs aground in inefficacy.

II

THE IRRUPTION OF THE JUDEO-CHRISTIAN REVELATION

5. These very general observations have been by way of preface to the remarks we should like to make concerning the effects produced in the realm of moral philosophy by the irruption in the world of the Judeo-Christian revelation and the impact of Christianity on the tradition of Greek philosophy.

Whether one believes in this revelation oneself, or considers it strictly from without and from a historical point of view, one is obliged to note that in fact the impact in question produced a kind of transmutation of ethical values—a unique phenomenon in the history of humanity, as a matter of fact—and that as a consequence it profoundly transformed the perspectives of moral philosophy.

Such a transfiguration was due to the influence of a religious factor, exterior to philosophy as such—let us say, to speak in terms of its rational formulation, a theological factor—upon a philosophical discipline. In our opinion, that influence was manifested primarily in the way we are now going to try to define—be it understood that these incursions into the theological and religious domain are directed by a philosophical interest, and have as object to mark certain repercussions which occurred in the domain of moral philosophy itself.

*"To-day thou shalt be with me in Paradise"—The Absolute*
*Ultimate End and the Subjective Ultimate End*

*Beatitude*

6. It came as a strange novelty to learn that the final End of human life—not only as supreme Value good in itself and for itself, but as the supreme Object the possession of which constitutes human happiness—is God Himself, the infinite Good, self-subsistent Being. God in His intimate life, the uncreated Glory itself is the end in which our appetite for happiness will be satisfied beyond measure. In this view the transcendence of the final End is affirmed in an incomparably more decisive way than it was by Plato: the infinite transcendence—with which we are called to unite—of a personal God who created the world out of nothing, whom no concept can circumscribe and whom no creature can comprehend, infinite Self, supremely perfect, independent and free, and who is the boundless ocean of being, of intellection, of love and of goodness.

By the same stroke the notion of happiness was transfigured. Happiness is now Beatitude, absolute happiness, absolutely saturating; "Eye hath not seen, nor ear heard, neither have entered into the heart of man, the things which God hath prepared for them that love him."

That it is possible for man to attain absolute happiness is not a datum of reason or of philosophy, but of Christian faith. Reason by itself, if we consider not the infinite power of God, of course, but the human condition, would have ample grounds to make us doubt the possibility. The most unhappy of animals necessarily desires happiness, and that is no doubt why it is so unhappy. We are starving for happiness, we make of the *pursuit of happiness* one of our fundamental rights, we seek happiness in everything that is perishable, in the love of a woman or in the conquest of power, and it is almost impossible for us to believe that we can be perfectly, totally, absolutely happy; our experience of life affords too much evidence to the contrary. There are two things in which our nature has not the strength to believe:

death, which we see, and perfect happiness, which we do not see. *Verily I say unto you, to-day shalt thou be with me in paradise.* That is an astonishing announcement. Faith, not reason, is the source of it. Men seek beatitude, without believing in it. Christians believe in it, through faith.

In that beatitude, the object of Christian faith, we find, moreover, a supreme verification of the law mentioned above—namely, that joy or delectation is a kind of savor issuing from the possession of a substantial good, and always remains distinct from that possession, but is the more closely bound up with it the higher nature of the substantial good in question. The essence of beatitude—the possession of the supreme substantial good—is the vision of God: the supreme joy which derives from it is in itself distinct from that vision, but is so nearly identical with it that we can hardly distinguish the joy from the vision.

### Absolute Ultimate End and Subjective Ultimate End in the Natural Order and in the Supernatural Order

7. It would be well to pause a moment here to take note of two things. In the first place, as we just pointed out, for Christian faith man is called to an absolutely saturating happiness, and it is the possession or intuitive vision of God Himself which constitutes that happiness; it is the immediate and transforming union with the ultimate End of all creation—to which, unless it is raised by grace, a created nature can only tend or aspire from afar, in fact, from infinitely far—it is the direct union with the absolute ultimate End, good in and for itself, which constitutes the subjective ultimate End of the human being, his final fulfillment, his perfect and eternal happiness.

But in the second place, Christian faith holds at the same time that this beatitude is of a supernatural order; it is a gift of grace, the gift of grace *par excellence*; it does not arise from nature.

If, therefore, man had not been raised to the state of grace, if God had left him in the purely natural order and with only the resources of his own nature, there would be no question for him either of attaining beatitude or of immediately possessing God as object of his perfect happiness. The happiness toward which he would tend, and which would be the subjective ultimate End of human life, or the end relative to the human subject, would be anything one wished, I mean anything philosophy and theology can more or less plausibly conceive, but it would not be God possessed. God would remain the absolute ultimate End, good in and for itself, to be loved above all else, for man as for every creature; but the possession of God would not be his subjective ultimate End, his ultimate end in the line of the subject. Between the absolute ultimate End, the transcendent Good which must be loved above all things, and the subjective ultimate End or the happiness of the human being, there would be in such a case an infinite distance, an infinite abyss. At this point we see clearly and explicitly that distinction between the Good and Happiness which Aristotle missed.

The astonishing tidings brought by Christianity were that in fact, and by the free and gratuitous superabundance of divine generosity, the separation, the cleavage of which we have just spoken between the absolute ultimate End and the subjective ultimate End does not exist for man. The subjective ultimate End or the beatitude of man consists in an immediate and indissoluble union with the absolute ultimate End (to which, as the theologians will put it, man is rendered proportionate through grace and the *lumen gloriae*). But in this very union, this kind of coincidence, the distinction between the subjective End or beatitude of man and God Himself or the absolute ultimate End obviously continues to exist, the distinction between the supernatural plenitude in which the human subject is fulfilled, with the endless joy that goes with that fulfillment, and the divine Essence, the subsistent Good, the vision of which beatifies the human subject. And it is for love of the subsistent Good, loved more than all things, more than the human subject itself and more than his own happiness, it is for love of the absolute ultimate End that man desires the beatitude in which his own being is divinely perfect.

Because the notion of the Good in itself and for itself is no longer related only to the *bonum honestum* (God as right) in the moral order—or, in the metaphysical order, to the supra-personal Idea of the Good, or to the Thought which thinks itself at the summit of the world—but has its supreme archetype in a subsistent Good which is a living Personality—three Persons in a single nature, one of whom has been incarnated, moral reflection now understands definitively and explicitly that the Good is something other than Happiness, and that the first demand and the first condition of moral rectitude is to love the Good more than Happiness.

## Absolute Happiness is desired for love of the Good subsisting of itself

8. In the perspective of Christian ethics three things are to be distinguished: in the first place, the absolute ultimate End. God in His infinite goodness and lovability is the absolute ultimate End, and it is in the vision of God, or the possession of the absolute ultimate End, that beatitude, or the subjective ultimate End of the human being, consists.

In the second place, the subjective ultimate End, in its essential constitutent element: that is to say, the vision of God, through which the human being, supernaturally fulfilled, enters into the divine plenitude in knowing God through His essence.

In the third place, the subjective ultimate end in its flowering, in its super-effluence: that is to say, the perfect satisfaction of all the aspirations of the soul in the love of God possessed, the joy or delectation which is a participation in the joy of God itself—as it is said in Matthew, *intra in gaudium Domini tui.*

These three things are distinct from one another. The desire of the second is inseparable from the love of the first; and the desire of the third is inseparable from the desire of the second. But the desire of the second and the desire of the third are for love of the first. Beatitude is loved, but God is loved more; and beatitude, precisely because it is union with the supreme Good subsisting in itself, can only be really and truly loved if it is loved in and for the love of the subsistent Good, supremely loved for itself. The love which the human being naturally has for himself is not abolished, certainly, but it loses first place, it is chased from the primary and royal seat; the absolutely primary love, the love which is above and beyond all others, can and must be torn away from the self and directed toward the uncreated Personality with whom the human person is in a direct relation over and above all the things of this world. The absolutely primary love can and must be fixed in Him whose good we then wish more than our own good—and that is possible, and even, in one sense, easy, since according to Christian faith He is our friend, in the supernatural order of charity.

Thus the egocentricity in which Aristotelian eudemonism remained in fact enclosed is definitely overcome. At the very moment that beatitude is promised to man, he is offered the possibility of finally being delivered from himself and from the devouring egoism which perverts his love of himself.

My happiness, which I naturally and necessarily desire, which I cannot help desiring, and which finally consists in the vision of God, has now been subordinated to something better, subordinated to God—and this is implied, as we remarked above, in the very essence of that happiness, since it consists in the possession of God, who is infinitely better than my happiness. According to a precious saying of Cajetan, *"volo Deum mihi, non propter me"*; Christian hope makes me wish that God be *mine*, but it is not *for me* or by reason of myself, it is not for love of myself that I wish God to be mine; it is for God and for love of God, for I love God more than myself and more than my happiness.

Christian morality is a morality of beatitude, but first and foremost it is a morality of the divine Good supremely loved.

9. The thologians are perfectly clear on all this. But popular preaching is often inclined to put the emphasis above all, if not even, exclusively on the joys of the reward and the pains of punishment. These are truths which immediately stir our natural appetite for happiness and our natural fear of suffering. And even if one insists only on them, one can always hope that once the sinner is turned toward the subsistent Good from motives in which love of self hold first place, the living faith will thereafter make him spontaneously subordinate his own interest to God loved first.

After all, one lends only to the rich. And the preachers of the Gospel feel themselves excused in advance if, in the arguments by which they push us toward salvation, they employ without too much scruple a kind of eudemonism, even hedonism, at least ambiguous in character, in the service of the God of love.

It is for the philosophical intelligence—not to speak of the pseudo-philosophical opinions current in popular thought, and

sometimes in textbooks of ethics or the history of philosophy—
that the final result of this emphasis is dangerous and can be the
occasion for serious misconceptions. Even a philosopher like
Kant, following a great many others, could imagine that traditional Christian morality (until revised by Pure Reason) was a
morality of sublimated egotisitic happiness and personal interest,
in which it is for love of itself and of eternal pleasure, to which
all else is subordinated, that the soul loves the Author of all good
and strives to practise his precepts, which in reality is to be conceive of Christianity after the model of the idolatrous cults it
overthrew.

## The Supernatural Order and the Grace of Virtues and Gifts— Divine Charity and Friendship

### Theological Virtues and moral Virtues

10. With Christianity a new order in being is made manifest
to the human mind—essentially distinct from the order of nature
and at the same time perfecting that order—the order of grace
and of supernatural realities. This word "supernatural" signifies
for Christianity a participation in that which is actually divine,
in the intimate life itself of God—something, as we have already
noted, which is beyond the possibilities of any created nature
through its own capacities, and which is not *owed* to nature, but
depends on free and gratuitious divine communication.

From this moment the very concept of nature undergoes a
change, opens out, so to speak. Nature is not closed in upon itself, impenetrable by a superior order. It blossoms in grace, is
"perfected" or fulfilled by grace, which is not simply added to
it like an ornamental facade, but which penetrates its most intimate depths, and which, at the same time that it elevates nature
to a life and an activity of another order, of which nature is not
capable by itself, heightens it in its own order and in the domain
of its own proper activities.

Several remarks may be tendered on this subject. The first
concerns the three virtues to which Christianity has given absolutely first rank, and which are called the three *theological* virtues.
They do not figure in the Aristotelian list of virtues. It was St.
Paul who named them, and who, in a singular reversal of values,
gave precedence over the powerful cardinal virtues to interior

120

dispositions—adherence of the intellect to an object which is not seen, confidence in one more powerful than oneself, love—which in the purely human order were too humble to constitute virtues, but which in the divine order, and because they are directed toward God Himself, are henceforward recognized to be the virtues *par excellence*: "And now abideth faith, hope and charity, these three: but the greatest of these is charity."

The object of the theological virtues is the transcendent God, the divine Good with which they united the human soul. They are a gift of grace. In opposition to them, the term "moral" virtues will be reserved for the virtues enumerated by the philosophers, in the sense that the latter have to do with simply human order. Unlike moral virtues, the theological virtues do not consist in a mean between excess and defect; no excess is possible in the exercise of these virtues—one never believes too much in God, one never puts too much hope in Him, one never loves Him too much. For Christian ethics the theological virtues are superior to the moral virtues. The latter are still required, but they are no longer supreme. The supreme virtues are of a supra-moral order, and the highest of them, on which the perfection of human life depends, is charity.

In order to clarify the distinction between the narrow sense ("moral virtues") and the broad sense ("the moral life", "moral science") of the word "moral", we may arrange the notions with which we have just been dealing in the following table:

| Supra-moral or theological virtues and rules (proportioned to the divine life) | The moral life (or the ways in which man makes use of his freedom)—the object of moral science |
| --- | --- |
| Moral virtues and rules (proportioned to human life) | |

The theological virtues are not the only supernatural energies the notion of which Christianity introduced into our knowledge of the moral life of man. Divine grace, according to the teaching of the Fathers and the theologians, also produces super-natural or "infused" moral virtues in the soul, which are of a higher order than the natural moral virtues or those acquired through the exercise of the will, and which have to do with the life men lead among themselves as members of the city of God and "fellow-citizens with the saints". And the term "gift" is especially reserved for still other capacities that the soul receives through grace and which are the gifts of the Spirit enumerated by Isaiah: they bring the theological virtues to an experimental stage, so to speak, and, like a keyboard in us, touched by divine inspiration, they permit man while he is still here below to have a foretaste of the eternal Life, in other words, contemplative expe-rience through union of love. (This is especially true of the gift of wisdom, the highest of the gifts.) With respect to this con-templative experience of divine things, the moral virtues have only the rank of means for Christian ethics. St. Thomas Aquinas says that the virtue of Prudence "is the service of Wisdom, intro-ductory to it, and preparing the way for it, like a gate-keeper in the service of the king".

It is thus that Christianity has suspended the moral from the supra-moral in the moral life of man.

### Friendship's Love between God and Man

11. All this shook the foundations of the purely philosoph-ical theory of the virtues elaborated by the moralists of antiquity, and singularly transformed it. And all this depended—this is our second remark—on a fundamental change in the notion of the relations between man and God. A *friendship* properly so called, and in the strongest, the most extravagant sense of the word, *a love as between friends* is possible between man and God, and this love between friends—charity, the gift of grace, the highest of the theological virtues—is, over and above the moral virtues, the keystone of the whole edifice of morality. Such a teaching, brought to the ancient world by the evangelic message, was in-deed a scandal for philosophy.

How, asked Aristotle, could any kind of friendship worthy of the name exist between Jupiter and man? And in the purely natural order it is quite true that divine transcendence excludes a friendship properly so called between God and man, because

122

all friendship presupposes a certain equality. It is normal for man to love the First Cause. But he loves God in fear and trembling, as his sovereign, not as his friend. If he loved Him as his friend, it would be because God also loved him in the same way, for love between friends is a mutual love. And how (continuing in the perspective of the purely natural order) could God love man as being His friend, or "another Himself"? If man is loved by God, it is in quite a different way, in the sense that God wishes him well, as He does all that exists, but without having any community of life and interest in common with him, and remaining enclosed in his transcendence.

We find a similar position maintained by the orthodox Moslem theologians, who thought that love from person to person being a passion, and among the most extravagant, it cannot exist in God, and who condemned the mystic at Hallaj to be crucified because he believed in such a love between God and man.

And an analogous position is also to be found in Spinoza, in his great arrogant notion of *amor intellectualis Dei*, of the perfect love with which the sage loves the God immanent in the world without any hope or desire of being loved in return.

As far as Aristotle is concerned, "it would be ridiculous," he says, "to reproach God because the love we receive from him in return is not equal to the love we give him, just as it would be ridiculous for the subject to make a similar reproach to his prince. For it is the role of the prince to receive love, not to give it, or at least to love only in a different way." Here it is philosophical wisdom itself which loses its head, for even in the purely natural order, and even in a love which is not between friends but between sovereign and subject, how could we give more than we received, and love God more than He loves us?

For Christianity, in any case, grace, by raising man to the supernatural order, makes him partake of the very life and goods of God, and by the same token produces that community of life and of goods, and that kind of equality, however scandalous in the eyes of pure philosophy, which are the conditions of friendship properly so called. God is no longer enclosed in His transcendence, He communicates it. Between God and man, as between friends, there can be love from person to person, with all its extravagance, love as between father and son, love as between husband and wife, the love of total giving hailed by the Song of Songs, and to which God was the first to surrender Himself, when He was incarnated. And the mystics will be able to say in this sense that God, because He thus wished it, needed our love as the friend needs the love of his friend, who is "another self". The great news, which is identical with that which promises us absolutely flawless happiness, or beatitude, is that God yearns toward us with love, and that He wishes to be loved by us as His friends.

This news was already contained in the Old Testament. "I love those who love me." It was fully manifested in the Gospel. "He who loves me will be loved by my Father, and I will love him." "Henceforth I call you not servants . . . *but* I have called you friends." And St. Thomas was to define the virtue of charity as the friendship created by grace between man and God therefore involving mutual love from person to person, and founded on God's communication to man of His own life and finally of His own beatitude.

This charity-love goes out to God first and foremost, and by the same token it goes out to all those who are called to be His friends, it goes out to all men. Love of God and fraternal love are one indivisible charity. And it is on this charity that Christianity makes the whole moral life of the human being depend. The whole law is contained in the precept to love God with our whole soul, and in the precept to love all men as our brothers, and these two form one single precept.

## The reversal of Values—the call of the Ultimate End

12. A corollary to all the preceding remarks is the absolute primacy accorded by Christianity to charity-love in the scale of values relating to human life and conduct.

Without it, wisdom and virtue are empty and without value for eternal life. Our good acts are definitely good only by virtue of the charity which animates them. And if it is there it makes up for all the mistakes resulting from our weakness. As St. John of the Cross was to put it, "in the evening of this life it is on love that we shall be judged".

Thus, in the last analysis, mercy fulfills justice; the mercy of God comes to man's rescue while he is bound to the precepts of the law. God forgives, something the God of the Platonic Republic did not do. And He does not assign to the earthly city the task of forcing men to be good, and irreproachably men; He leaves it to His grace, to His own kingdom, which is universal and above all earthly cities, to work within them to make them His sons and make them good through the very exercise of their most intimate freedom, through the love of charity which animates their acts and which is the form of their virtue, and which also compensates for their weaknesses. As we have already noted, the Christian saint is not a superman formed by human agency, a Hercules of moral virtue like the Stoic sage; he is a friend of God who draws his life from supernatural charity and is formed by the divine hand, and who throws human weakness open to the divine plenitude descending into him. The vain-glory of Man is dethroned, and humility, wherein lives the force of God, is exalted.

This reversal of values in relation to the perfection of human life, henceforth conceived as the perfection of charity whose working in the soul no obstacle can stop or restrain, is tied up with a similar reversal regarding wisdom and contemplation. Supreme wisdom and supreme contemplation are no longer the summit of human Science and philosophy, but the abyss in man of the gift of the uncreated Spirit which makes him experience, in faith and through Charity and the union of love, what no effort of the human intelligence can comprehend, and the things of God known as unknown. The very notion of contemplation changes in meaning, because from now on it designates an experience in which love instructs the intelligence, and a veiled communion with subsistent Truth, Life and Goodness, a communion which is the work of charity under the very touch of God. Christian contemplation exists not "for the perfection of him who contemplates, and does not terminate in the intellect, like the contemplation of the philosophers. It exists for the love of Him who is contemplated and does not terminate in the intellect, for the sake of knowing, but passes into the heart, for the sake of loving," because it proceeds itself from love. And for the same reason it does not terminate in a "theoretical" accomplishment for superabounds in action.

And all are called to such contemplation, from near or from afar, because it does not depend on nature, or on the knowledge of man, but on grace and divine gift—just as all are called to perfection. "Be ye therefore perfect, even as your Father in heaven is perfect", is a precept addressed to all, as indicating the end toward which each one should tend according to his ability and his condition. The great novelty introduced by Christianity is this appeal to all, to free men and slaves, to the ignorant and the cultivated, adolescents and old men, a call to a perfection which no effort of natue can attain but which is given by grace and consists in love, and from which therefore no one is excluded except by his own refusal.

The same thing is true regarding final Beatitude, the possession of the ultimate End through vision. It is promised to all, if only they really wish it. Impossible to attain through the capacities of nature alone, it offers itself as incomparably more attainable than earthly happiness and Aristotelian eudemonia, for which there is no Penitent Thief.

Thus the moral ideal of Christianity, and the ultimate End it proposes, finally possess that effectiveness of appeal to the human being and his thirst for happiness (now transfigured) which was lacking in the rational ethics of Aristotle, and to which Stoic and Epicurean ethics sacrificed everything, but only to be disappointed in the end. This moral ideal of Christianity is not an easy one; and if one considers only the capacities of human nature, and its infirmities, its propensity to evil, it would seem even more impossible to realize than the Stoic or Epicurean ideal. The fact is that Christianity has only raised the level of human civilizations at the price of bringing about trouble and division in them at the same time, as a result of the yes or no it requires of the heart. It has not an end to wars. It has activated history—it has not subjugated it (God Himself does not do that). It has evangelized the earth—it has not subdued it. Not only contrary efforts and the rebellions of nature, but the action of humanity's own deficiencies upon the divine leaven itself, when the forces of man have undertaken to serve Christ with their own means, have brought it about that Christianity has increased suffering in our species, at the same time that it brought about all real moral progress and every real increase of goodness. But the evangelic hope has left its mark forever in the depths of humanity. Saintliness has transfigured the heart of man, not only among the saints, but among all the sinners whom a ray of it has touched. And in revealing to us that God is love and makes us His sons through grace, that the ultimate fulfillment toward which our poor life proceeds is to possess Him through vision, Christianity, without giving way to any illusions about the potentialities of nature or underestimating its dignity either, has succeeded in assuring the decisive effectiveness of the appeal to the human soul of the ultimate end which is proposed to it—and this is the crucial freedom for ethics.

## Philosophy put to the test

13. Where the New Law has been received, the various factors of which we have spoken in the preceding pages have been integrated into the common consciousness and the rule of common morality, which form the proper subject of the moralist's reflection. And thereby moral philosophy is placed in an embarrassing position. If the moral philosopher recognizes these factors, he makes a place in his philosophy for things which depend on religious faith, not on philosophy. If he fails to recognize them, he is leaving out things which form an integral part of that human reality which he intends precisely to elucidate on the level of reflection, and so he causes moral philosophy to quit the soil of existence and fly off into the void.

In actual fact, not to speak of certain authors of textbooks of Christian philosophy who have naively taken the tack, as vain from the point of view of the faith as from that of reason, of making moral philosophy a kind of decalcomania or counterfeit of moral theology, we have seen the philosophers engage first in an attempt at *separation,* seeking with Descartes a more or less Stoic natural morality which Science would establish to ensure happiness in the life here below, while Faith would in addition provide man conceived along the lines of this kind of Christian naturalism with eternal delights for life in the hereafter. Or, like Sponiza, they made of ethics a world apart, reserved for the rationalist sage. Or they followed the theoreticians of natural religion, and reduced all the data issuing from Christian revelation, and even God Himself, to the measure of deist philosophy and its enterprise of rational eviction. Later, with Kant, and particularly with Hegel, in their desire to construct an ethics capable of integrating all values, and the most vital ones, recognized by the common consciousness, the philosophers were to engage in an enterprise of *absorption* and *substitution* of vastly more profound significance, in which philosophy would explicitly assume the whole burden which theology regarded as its own, and finally, in the name of the God of history, would take charge of destinies and salvation of the human race.

### III

#### REVEALED ETHICS

*The Tables of Moses and the Gospel—Moral Law divinely promulgated*

14. There exists for man a *natural* knowledge of moral rules —natural, though more or less perfect and developed—a knowledge which presents itself in two quite different modes: in the first place, what can be called a *natural-spontaneous* knowledge of moral rules, which is at work, without words, in the conscience of everyone and which expresses itself socially—at a level which is no longer the level of natural law itself—in the customs and taboos of primitive tribes, then in the laws and customs of political societies. In the second place there is what can be called a *natural-reflexive* knowledge of moral rules, which is the concern of philosophers (it constitutes the object of our present historical analysis). Religious belief, moreover, has always influenced the social expression of the natural-spontaneous knowledge of moral rules, and in an especially direct way in primitive civilizations and in the great ancient civilizations, in which religion was closely incorporated with the social group as one of the organs proper to it.

When Christianity spread in the ancient world, it brought with it—along with the idea of the distinction between the things that are God's—what may be called a *revealed knowledge* of moral rules—which did not render the efforts of philosophical reason superfluous in this domain, but relegated them to second place, and, if I may say so, remarkably signified the task to which the great ethical systems of antiquity had dedicated themselves in their search for the moral ideal to propose to men. This was a change of incalculable significance.

God, the ultimate absolute End, He who Is and whose Name is above all names, God the creator and savior, the personal and infinitely transcendent God of the Judeo-Christian tradition, God Himself speaks and instructs men in His precepts, declares to them what are the right ways in human life.

Through Moses He gave them the Decalogue. Through Christ He gave them the New Law.

The rules of human life are taught from on high. The knowledge of them is brought to us by faith, not by reason. It is a revealed knowledge, even the knowledge of the moral rules which are otherwise naturally knowable by the human intelligence and are, in a more or less obscure, imperfect or warped way, spontaneously perceived by human intelligence (the precepts of the Decalogue are essentially a revealed formulation of the principles of natural law).

Humanity finds itself in the presence of a *revealed ethics*, an essentially religious ethics. It is given to man with the absolute, unquestionable, infallible authority which belongs to the Word of God. Let us recall the thunder and lightning, and the voice of the trumpet, and the flames and the smoking mountain, which made the people tremble and kept them at a distance; and the glory which hindered the children of Israel from fixing their gaze on the face of Moses, because of the brightness of his countenance. Such was the attire in which the Table of the Law were given to men, and the revealed Ethics enthroned before them.

The moral order in consequence will acquire a fixity, a solidity a rigor; it will deliver itself in unconditional commandments and in absolute requirement which did not appear in any of the ethical theories elaborated by the reason of the philosophers of classical antiquity. It was under the influence of the Judeo-Christian revelation that these properties of the moral law were inscribed in common consciousness.

The New Law, Thomas Aquinas explains, is less severe than the Old Law, because the Old Law imposed on man a far greater number of external actions and obligations. But the New Law carries its precepts and prohibitions into the very intimacy of the heart, the internal acts and movements of the soul; and in this sense Augustine could say that the New Law is easy for him who loves, but hard for him who does not.

In any case, the Old Law and the New Law have both given a sacred significance, immediately referred to God and the Sanctity of His Justice, to the notion of the precept, as to that of sin and of duty; and this significance was even more profound and more exacting in the New Law.

As a result of the impact of Christianity, the sense of transgression and of obligation were thus to take on a new character, both in common consciousness and in ethical theory.

The sense of transgression and the sense of obligation are both natural to us. They derive from the natural functioning of the practical intellect in each of us (whatever the adventitious part played by the constraints of the group or by social taboos in their development). Yet Greek reason, in its philosophical elucidations, except perhaps in the case of the Stoics, had a rather lowered notion of moral obligation and moral fault, which it considered on a level close to that of art. The Judeo-Christian revelation, on the contrary, raised them to the supra-rational level of divine injunction obeyed or transgressed, and reinforced and magnified them by giving them a sacred status much more profound and purer (because related to a transcendent God, and disengaged from the particularisms of the human group) than the sacro-social regimes of the primitive and ancient religions had been able to do.

Sin is henceforth an offense to God—and according to the Christian faith it is responsible for the death of the Son of God on the cross.

Duty is henceforth a requirement in us emanating from the Creator whom heaven and earth obey, and from the Father whom we love if we do His will.

As for the notion of moral rule or of moral law, it will continue to bear the mark imprinted on it at Sinai, the character of commandment laid down by the hand of God in the radiance of His glory, even if, with the Gospel, it was to be interiorized. The tables of the Decalogue have had the same importance in the history of moral ideas as the words repeated by Moses, "*I am who is*," or, according to modern exegesis, "I am who I am," have had in the history of speculative reason. The rules of human conduct no longer have to be discovered by the gropings of the tribe's collective conscience or by the philosophic reason. They are made manifest by God Himself, in a code or morality fixed from on high.

### A reinforcement which may regenerate Moral Philosophy or endanger it

15. Here again it is well to remark on the fact that God is more interested in the salvation of the human race than in the labor of philosophers. No doubt revealed ethics offers invaluable assistance to moral philosophy, if the latter knows how to profit from it; in particular, it was no small matter for philosophy to see the unwritten law written and formulated by its Author. But philosophy does not always know how to profit by divine occasions; they put a purely rational discipline in an embarrassing position, concerned as it is on its own account with primary realities and supreme Laws. If it is not tempted to reject that which it has not itself discovered, and which escapes the grasp of pure reason, philosophy is tempted to bring divine revelation down to its own level, use it to increase its own store by denaturing it in order to bring it within the grasp of pure reason.

The historian of culture has no trouble observing that this divine reinforcement, and, if I may put it so, this sacred aggravation of human morality, have been an immensely valuable help to humanity in its forward movement. But he is also aware that in order correctly to understand the contribution made by the Decalogue and revealed ethics to the moral life of humanity, one condition is necessary: namely, that one also understand that such a reinforcement and such an absolutization of the moral rule must be nurtured in the climate of the supernatural reality of grace given to men, and of the redemptive Mercy in which the Justice of the Author of the Law is consummated, and in the climate of the primary precept—the love above all else of Him who is love itself and who wishes to give Himself, to make the human creature partake of His own life.

If we secularize the Tables of the Law, if we transfer the features of the morality of the Ten Commandments to the natural moral law as it derives from reason alone, and is supposed to operate in the order and climate of pure nature, from which all that pertains to the faith and to grace has been eliminated, then we debase and degrade revealed ethics, the morality of the Ten Commandments, and at the same time we deform and harden, perhaps not in its content but in its attitude, the countenance of natural morality—I mean the spontaneous ethics of the conscience which is guided by the inclinations of nature and the reflective ethics of philosophical reason. We arm natural morality with a thunder which properly belongs only to revealed ethics.

Let us think about the natural rule of morality, that rule of which St. Paul spoke *apropos* of the pagans, whose conscience, with its reproaches and incitements, witnesses that they bear in themselves their own law; one may compare it, in its natural manner and bearing, to a child of man, a young hunter armed with his bow, who trudges along as best he can in the forest. He has a good eye, he aims straight, but his equipment is humble and primitive. He has a long way to go to become an expert hunter in the years to come. And now suppose that we conceive of this natural rule of morality after the model of revealed ethics. Here is our same apprentice hunter transformed into a king seated on his throne, a crown on his head and a scepter in hand—and giving stern looks, because he is, after all, only a child of the woods.

The last three centuries have been rich in examples of social formations in which the inherited rules of revealed ethics were still to be found in force, but in which the context normally furnished by the order of grace had been lost from sight, and in which a kind of natural religion or decorative Christianity, maintained as a moralizing agency, protected and sheltered earthly interests which were very sure of themselves. If people who shared in this way of thinking were not much interested in God, except as a guardian of order, they nevertheless believed firmly in a code of moral austerity filled with commandments all the more unconditional, with prohibitions all the more rigorous, and with condemnations all the more severely applied because the code was primarily concerned with external acts and aimed above all at the conservation of the structures of the social group. This was a case of a deconsecrated and secularized sacred morality. It was not a Christian morality, which is suspended from the theological order and from love, which knows pardon and pity, and which is attuned to contemplation, and to what St. Paul calls "the goodness and love of God our Savior toward man". Nor was it natural morality, which has its source in our essential inclinations and in reason, and which shares the human mood and the seeking attitude of authentic reason, an attitude in which there is indulgence, curiosity, sympathy, always a little hesitation and a little irony, and always a desire to understand and clarify.

But it is in the realm of philosophy, with Kant and Kantian ethics, that we find the most significant example of the way in which the influence of Christianity and of revealed ethics can impair a reason which in other respects repudiates the most essential content of Christianity. It is always dangerous to be half Christian. The impact of Christianity quickens reason (without rendering it infallible) when reason nourished itself on the substance of Christianity. When reason fattens itself on the left-overs of Christianity, the impact of Christianity warps it. The sacralization of the moral life becomes a dangerous blessing when we cease to understand what that sacralization means. Then what was a supernatural reinforcement and a sacred promulgation of the moral law, becomes a hardening and arrogance against nature in an ethics which only retains the imprint of the Tables of the Law in order to make of them the Tables of Pure Reason.

Another historical accident, another misconception for which revealed ethics offered an occasion to human reason, and for which certain theologians this time bore primary responsibility, can also be pointed out. I allude here to the line of thinkers (the teachers of Islam above all, but also, on the Christian side, Scotus and Occam in the Middle Ages, Descartes in modern times) who, struck more or less consciously by the grand image of the revelation of the Decalogue amid the lightning and thunder of Omnipotence, believed that the moral law, and finally even the distinction between good and evil, depended not at all on divine Wisdom and Reason, the foundation of eternal necessities, but uniquely and exclusively on the pure Will or the pure All-Powerfulness of God, and on an arbitrary decision of His sovereign Freedom. A kind of divine despotism thus became the source of the moral law, decreed and imposed without reason by the celestial High Command. It seems probable to me that this way of looking at things, which St. Thomas Aquinas considered blasphemy, but which was not without its effect here and there on popular consciousness, or popular ignorance, exercised a serious influence on Kant, and played a double role in his thought. On the one hand, I believe, it made him reject, as subjecting the spirit of man to a despotic heteronomy, any idea of making the authority of the moral law depend on the Creator of nature. On the other hand, it made him transfer this same despotic sovereignty to the pure practical Reason, itself identified with the autonomous Will of Man, taken in its supra-empirical dignity.

## CHAPTER 15

### BRIEF REMARKS IN CONCLUSION

*The method followed in this book*

1. May I be permitted to confess that the composing of this large work has brought the author, in addition, a satisfaction of a subjective order? It was, at a time of life when the soul turns towards the higher regions, a way for me to pay my respects to, and thus take leave of, the philosophers—in particular the modern philosophers, whose historical work it was once claimed I purely and simply rejected. I believed on the contrary that I have given due credit to them, and that I have, at least after my early years, shown them the sort of intellectual friendship which is proper among seekers and disputants each attached to his own vision. How better to honor them than by taking their effort seriously; by trying to understand and penetrate their movement of thought; by applying oneself to disengage their central intuitions, and the advances one owes to them; finally, by criticizing them, where they are in error, without indulgence or caution (what philosopher ever asked for indulgence?) but with more attention doubtless and more true respect than they ordinarily show one another. However, I will not be sorry to shake them off.

But let us leave that. The real purpose of my book has nothing to do with the subjective satisfaction mentioned above. As I indicated in the Preface, what I proposed to do was to employ an historical and critical analysis of sufficient depth as an instrument of exploration of the field of moral philosophy. The unfolding of the ethical theories that can be considered the most significant, the apperceptions from which they have sprung, the errors from which they have suffered, thus enable one to have a better awareness of the problematic proper to moral philosophy. And many essential truths are at the same stroke gathered in along the way, in a manner that is non-systematic but perhaps more stimulating for the mind, because they emerge from the long reflection that is pursued from age to age, with its advances and its failures, and from the successive occasions that it offers for discussion. I think that in a general way such a procedure, turning to account, under a resolutely critical light, a heritage of time-honored labors and disputes, could be carried out with advantage by the disciples of the *philosophia perennis* in the most varied fields.

2. It was, I believe, particularly necessary to have recourse to this historico-critical method in the field of moral philosophy, so as to rediscover in a sufficiently concrete and comprehensive manner its place and function among the philosophical disciplines, and at the same time to recognize its essential distinction from anthropology, on the one hand, and moral theology, on the other, with both of which it is however closely associated.

In the course of our long study we have thus seen take shape little by little the basic notions that must be regarded as the primary notions of moral philosophy, and with which the various thinkers we have considered have all had to do in some way, sending them back and forth, so to speak, from one to the other, to play with them in different ways. "When you play tennis," Pascal said, "you both play with the same ball, but one places it better."

We have likewise seen take shape the principal problems to which the ethician must apply himself, the first of which has to do with the very nature of moral philosophy, its practical and normative (in a sense not at all Kantian) function, its essentially reflexive character, its dependence with regard to certain great metaphysical truths and its dependence with regard to experience, the relations it maintains with the religious experience of mankind and with the theological data concerning the existential condition of man. We have met on our way many other fundamental problems, in particular the problem of natural law and the problem of the relationship between ethics and supra-ethics.

I shall not undertake to enumerate here all the primary notions and all the basic problems to which I have just alluded. Indeed, our whole second volume, given over to the doctrinal examination of the great problems, must constitute the normal conclusion to the long historico-critical introduction that has been the object of the present volume.

### On some possible renewals

3. I should like to propose now some remarks of a quite different order. The first have to do with the great challenges to accepted ideas that took place in the course of the nineteenth century, and from which the coarsest materialist metaphysics or anti-metaphysics at first tried to claim the profit. I am thinking of the three great intellectual shocks that shook the confidence of man in himself, and which in reality could be salutary and powerfully assist moral philosophy if we knew how to understand things as they should be understood, and if modern man, instead of abdicating under humiliation, stood erect again in the two conjoined virtues of humility and magnanimity.

The first great disturbance was produced by Darwinism, with the theory of the animal origin of man. Such a shock can have a double result: a result ruinous for moral life, and which dehumanizes man, if one believes that man is only an evolved monkey; one has then the materialist ethic of the struggle for life.

But the same shock can have a salutary result if one understand things in another way, if one understand that the matter out of which man is made is an animal matter, but an animal matter informed by a spiritual soul, so that there is biological continuity in the sense of the natural sciences between the universe of the animal and the universe of man, but irreducible metaphysical discontinuity. The scientific concept of evolution is then likely to lead us to a better appreciation of the vicissitudes and the progress of human history, and to an ethic more conscious of the material roots of the rational animal, of the depths of the dynamism of the irrational element in him, but also of the deeper depths of the dynamism of the spirit in him that makes his grandeur.

4. A second shock was that of Marxism, with its insistence on the economic substructure of our moral ideas and of our rules

of moral behavior. Here again a double result is possible. The result is ruinous for human life if one fancies that all that is not the economic factor is only an epiphenomenal superstructure; one moves then towards a materialist ethic—either towards a materialist ethic suspended from the myth of technocracy organizing human life on the basis of pure productivity; or towards a materialist ethic such as the Marxist ethic, suspended from the myth of revolution and from that of the self-creation of man manifested by the titanic struggle of the working class freeing itself through violence from a condition presumed to be irremediably servile, and by the final coming of a universal communist society.

The result can be salutary if the shock in question forces us to be aware of the interdependence and interaction, interpreted in an Aristotelian sense, of economic factors and moral or spiritual factors. Ethics becomes then more conscious of the concrete situation of man, and of the meeting of structures and conditionings dependent upon material causality with what, in the order of formal causality, constitutes morality. A new field of exploration is opened up for ethics, a field independent in itself of the Marxist theory, which however supplied the impulse for this new problematic.

5. The third shock finally was that of the discoveries of Freud, bringing to light the autonomous life and the swarming activity of the unconscious, and the ruses by which it seeks to take control of human conduct.

The result is ruinous for human life if man is looked upon as a creation of mere infra-rational tendencies, of libido and of the unconscious of instinct, without reason being thought to possess any vitality and energy of its own or to exercise any control other than a purely extrinsic one over the forces in conflict in the determinism of nature, and without one's according any reality to the universe of liberty which is the very universe of morality.

The result is salutary if the shock in question leads us to recognize the immense universe of instincts and tendencies at the point of which reason and liberty work. Then ethics becomes more conscious of the concrete situation (no longer social, but psychological) of man, and of the meeting of the precombined structures and disguises of the unconscious with moral conscience. Thence an ethic more truly human, in this sense that it will know better what is human, and in this sense that it will care with more pity for man and his wounds.

The great problem of the relations between the conscious and the unconscious will be one of its principal concerns. It will be a question of establishing a normal relation between the dreaming and sleeping part of man and the waking part. It can happen that the waking part may exercise no rule, no control, or a pseudo-control only, over the dreaming part. Man is then the plaything of unconscious tendencies, which a banal process of lying rationalization will endeavor only to justify.

It can also happen, on the contrary, that the waking part may mistrust the dreaming part, hold it in contempt, and fear it, to such a degree that it may wish at any price to become conscious of all that takes place in us, to light up forcibly all the innermost recesses and to put conscious reason and deliberate will at the origin of all the movements of the soul. It is to be feared that this second method succeeds mainly in developing neuroses and in bringing about the victory of the disguises and ruses of the unconscious.

In other words, a despotic regime with regard to the unconscious is no better than a anarchic regime. What should be sought is—to use one of Aristotle's words—a *politic* control, that is, a control exercising an authority that would be without violence and based on friendship, taming to the spirit the vital spontaneities, in short, supposing a certain confidence in the sleeping part of man and a progressive purification of it. Such a purification is not brought about by trying to make this unconscious emerge from sleep, but by being at once attentive to this sleep and respectful of it, and by recognizing with an entirely frank and pure glance, without fright and without connivance, all that emerges from this sleeping part.

What would also be required, and first of all, is to recognize the existence in man of another unconscious than the animal unconscious of instinct, desires and images, repressed tendencies and traumatic memories, which asks only to be closed up in itself as an inferno of the soul. This other unconscious is the unconscious or pre-conscious of the spirit, which is not separated from the world of conscious activity and the works of reason, but on the contrary is their living source. It is on the activating motions —when man does not betray them—and the radiance of this spiritual unconscious on the whole soul, that depends above all the long work through which the instinctive spontaneities can be, as I said above, *tamed* to the spirit.

### *Man and the Human Condition—a problem preliminary to any moral systematization*

6. The considerations that follow do not have to do with doctrines and systems, they bear on human conduct itself and on the most general options with which our attitude in life is linked. These considerations are connected however in an indirect way with the philosophical positions examined in the present work; every great moral system, indeed, is in reality an effort to ask man, in one manner or another and to one degree or another, to go beyond his natural condition in some way. But either these same great philosophical doctrines refuse to acknowledge the effort in question, or else they leave in a wholly implicit state the problem it envelops. To my mind, on the contrary, it is important to disengage the problem explicitly. One sees then that it concerns the moral life of each one of us in such a fundamental way, and involves so profoundly the individual subjectivity, that it depends, to tell the truth, on a sort of metaphysics of conduct which precedes moral theories and systematizations. If one tries to examine it in itself, reducing things to the essential, one is led, it seems to me, to distinguish the four different attitudes I am about to discuss, of which the first two, more or less outlined, in fact, in the lives of certain among us, but impossible to carry through, are too irrational to correspond to any definite doctrine; and of which the last two correspond, one to the thought of India, the other, inchoatively, to the Western philosophical tradition, and, under its perfected and really effective form, to Christian thought.

The fact is, I believe, that in the background of all our moral difficulties there is a fundmental problem which is ineluctably posed for each of us, and which in practice is never fully resolved, except in those who have entered into the ways of perfection:

the problem of the relation of man to the human condition, or of his attitude in the face of the human condition.

This condition is that of a spirit united in substance with flesh and engaged in the universe of matter. It is an unhappy condition. In itself it is such a miserable condition that man has always dreamed of a golden age when he was more or less freed of it, and so miserable that on the plane of revelation, the Christian religion teaches that mankind was created, with the grace of Adam, in a superior condition in which it was free of sin, of pain, of servitude and of death, and from which it fell through its own fault. The Judeo-Christian tradition also teaches that after the end of history and in a new world the human condition will be supernaturally transfigured. Those who believe neither in the state of innocence nor in original sin put the golden age at the end of history, not at the beginning, and fancy that man will attain it in the last stage of his terrestrial adventure, through his own liberating effort, thanks to science and to radical social transformations; others, who want no part of consoling illusions, try to escape the spectacle of this planet by surrendering to some powerful passion which distracts them day after day from themselves and from the world, or by the ardor of a despairing pity which in a way appeases their hearts while it corrodes them little by little.

Indeed, the tragic perplexity in which we are placed consists in the fact that we can neither refuse the human condition nor accept it purely and simply. I will explain later on in what sense I understand the expression "to accept *purely and simply* the human condition". As to refusing the human condition, it is clear that it is a question there only of a moral disposition. Such a refusal belongs to the world of dream; but man nourishes himself on dreams, and a dream which has its roots in the depths of the individual psychology of the subject can determine his fundamental attitude in life.

## The temptation to refuse the Human Condition

7. It is solely in the perspective of nature that we shall consider things in this and the three following sections. We have just noted that the human condition is an unhappy condition. The state of intermediary species is in general a state little to be envied;

and it is in a paradoxically eminent manner that the human species, at once flesh and spirit, is an intermediary species. The heavens tell of the glory of God, but the earth that He has made is dreadful to man. A "vale of tears", yes, and this is not a mere poetic image.

It is not a question here of any sort of Manichaesism. It is quite true that the material universe abounds in wonders and is resplendent with an inexhaustible beauty that makes apparent the mark of the Spirit Who created it; it is quite true that despite the cruelty and voracity which inhabit it the world of nature is penetrated with the goodness and the generosity of being, and embraces finally all things in the imperturbable peace of its great laws, and of its great rational necessities which superbly ignore us; it is quite true that in man himself the world of the senses, whatever bitterness it may harbor, is made first and above all to enchant us with its sweetnesses and its joys; it is quite true that human nature is good in its essence, and that for every living being, eminently for man, to live is a marvellous gift. And yet, for all that, a spirit whose operations have need of matter surmounts matter only at a formidable price and by running immense risks, and is most often scoffed at by it. The spirit is immortal, and matter imposes the law of death on the body animated by it. Man has more grandeur than the Milky Way; but how easy evil is for him, how inevitable (if one considers the species collectively) it is, in a being in which sense and instinct, and the animal unconscious, ask only to elude or to twist the judgment of the mind. As for suffering, it is already a frightful thing to see an animal suffer, but the suffering of beasts is of small account in comparison with the suffering that pierces a flesh united to spirit, or spirit itself.

8. Thus we can understand that the temptation to refuse the human condition has a greater chance of worming its way into us when man has in one manner or another become better aware of the natural exigencies of the spirit in him—of that spirit which is his soul, and which reveals itself to him in the highest powers of the soul. Such a temptation does not exist in the primitives. We may believe that in the collective history of mankind it is largely this temptation which, at work in us without our being aware of it, makes the very progress through which

civilization advances go side by side with delusions which impair it or degradations which corrupt it.

To refuse—in one's innermost heart—the human condition, is either to dream of leaving our limits and to wish to enjoy a total liberty in which our nature would expand through its own powers; or else to play the pure spirit (what I once called the sin of angelism); or else to curse and try to disown all that presents an obstacle to the life of the intellect, and to live in a state of interior revolt against the fact that one is a man; or else to flee by no matter what frenzy, even if it be in the folly of the flesh, this situation of a reason everywhere at loggerheads with matter which is a permanent challenge to the demands of the spirit in us. It is hardly surprising that those who devote themselves to the life of the intelligence, the poet in particular, and the philosopher, are more or less exposed to this temptation. The ancient sages of Greece succumbed to it when they said that the best thing for man is not to have been born.

In the life of an individual the most frequent occasion for this temptation—which does not justify it for all that—is that the man who endeavors, as Aristotle said, "to live according to the intellect", is more conscious than those who live "according to the human" of everything we said above concerning the misery of the human condition. Often even the man dedicated to meditation forgets that the spirit finds, through the senses, the source of its life in the very matter that torments it; he forgets too that the evils that matter causes are made transitory to a certain extent by matter itself, since it is a root principle of change.

But above all, if he pays attention to the lessons of history and to the long cry of the poor and the abandoned, he understands that naked suffering, horror, anguish without consolation —all this is the true background of the world for us, however generous nature may be, and however admirable the victories won by human generations to make things less hostile to man and the structures of his own life more worthy of him, through the progress of civilization, of art and of knowledge. It may be that for a long while we almost lose sight of this background of the world. But every now and then it reappears to us.

The man who has passed the threshold of the life according to the intellect understands all that is offensive and humiliating—

for that spirit in which his specific difference itself and his dignity consist—in the radical contingency linked with matter and the dependence with regard to matter which constitute the metaphysical infirmity of our existence. In the eyes of material nature is a man worthy any more than the sound of the brook? To pursue its work there the spirit struggles ceaselessly against the fortuitous and the useless; its very movement depends not only on the absolute values in which it has its proper object, it depends also on chance, on good and bad encounters; it advances from generation to generation enduring a perpetual agony, only to have in the end what it has produced here on earth fall—I mean with regard to men, and unless it is divinely protected—under the law of decay and futility which is the law of matter, and only to have what is immortal in itself be received by our species only at the cost of equivocations and misunderstandings that are perpetuated throughout time.

The fact remains that all that must be accepted. Even when they do not repeat in their own way, and however pitifully, the story of Faust, there is no sadder and more fruitless distress than the distress of men who under the pretext of wanting to live according to the intellect allow themselves to be carried away by the temptation to refuse the human condition. They are vanquished beforehand, and their defeat aggravates their subjection.

*The temptation to accept purely and simply the Human Condition*

9. Would the solution therefore be to accept *purely and simply* the human condition?—This pure and simple acceptance would be just as costly, and is no less impossible. It would be a betrayal of human nature not to recognize the demands, which are consubstantial to it, of the superhuman in man, and this nature's need of the progressive movement of the spirit, with its torments and its dangers, in other words, its need of perpetually going beyond the presently given moment of our condition on earth. And if we want to go beyond it, it is because to that extent we do not accept it without reserve.

It is fitting moreover to see the whole import of the expressions one uses. To accept the human condition is to accept—with all that life offers of the good and the beautiful and the pure, and with all the grandeurs of the spirit, and with "the call of the hero"—the radical contingency, the failures, the servitudes, the immense part of sorrow (as regards nature) of inevitable useless-ness of our existence, sickness, death, the different kinds of tyranny and hypocrisy which prey on social life, the stench of gangrene and the stench of money, the power of stupidity and of the lie. But if it is a question for a man of accepting *purely and simply* the human condition, why then, after all, in accepting all the evil of suffering that our nature entails, should he not accept at the same stroke all the evil of sin to which it is inclined? He has been made as he is, with the weaknesses of his flesh and the covetousness that is in him, with the longing for pleasure and power and the rage of desires, of that obsessing desire especially which does not come from him but from his species, to which his individual person matters little but which has need of his chromosomes in order to perpetuate itself. All that also is part of the human condition. To accept *purely and simply* (if that were possible) the human condition, means to accept it in its entirety, with the misery of sin as well as with the misery of suffering.

This cannot be, moreover, without a fundamental contra-diction and without additional torments. For the social groups—horde or society—and the state of culture without which the human species cannot endure on earth require rules and taboos guaranteed by terrifying sanctions; and it is essential to the human condition that the sense of moral obligation, and of the distinc-tion between good and evil, which exists naturally in the soul of each one of us (and which is in itself contradictory to the accep-tance of moral evil as supposedly required by our nature), exert itself at least under the wholly exteriorized form of obedience to tribal prohibitions, and according as good and evil appear only as what is permitted or forbidden by the social group. To accept *purely and simply* the human condition is therefore an intrinsi-cally contradictory moral disposition (although more or less outlined in fact in a great number of human beings)—a disposition to accept not only subjection to Sin as well as subjection to Suf-fering, but also subjection to the law of Fear, which forbids certain definite faults as infractions of the general conduct and the rules of the closed society.

Supposing that it could be fully carried out, such an acceptance of the human condition would make man live on the edge of animality; it is, as we have noted, as impossible in reality as the refusal of the human condition, because to accept fully subjection to moral evil, in whatever manner one conceives it, is not possible for the human being. What we are calling *pure and simple* acceptance of the human condition is only a limit to which, even in its most primitive representative, our species have never attained. Indeed, it is in more or less approaching this limit that many among us seem to accept purely and simply the human condition. They accept it *almost* purely and simply. They not only have the code of their gang, their class or their accustomed social group (which implies already, though under a very inferior form, the prohibition of wrongdoing), they have also an outline at least, and often a great deal more than an outline, of authentic moral life, by reason of which they do not love the evil that they do. But even if their conscience has in other respects firm convictions, there are a certain number of domains—notably the domain of sex, and, in certain periods, that of "honor" (duel), and that of war—in which to act without taking account of the moral law seems normal in their eyes: it's the human condition that requires it, they believe that at this point it imposes another code on them. Perhaps however they will repent one day of the actions thus committed in contempt of the moral law (not to speak of many others among us who violate the law only in the pangs of remorse). To do evil and to repent of the evil that one does is the minimum of what the human being is capable of to testify that it is impossible to give in completely to the temptation to accept *purely and simply* the human condition.

*To answer to Indian spirituality*

10. What is asked of man is neither to accept purely and simply nor to refuse the human condition—it is to transcend it. Here too however two very different ways can be envisaged. It can be a question of transcending the human condition in a manner which implies a certain refusal of it (because in this case it is through his own forces that man has to transcend his condition, he must then engage himself in an effort against the grain of nature); or it can be a question of transcending the human

145

condition while consenting to it (because in this case a "new nature" has been grafted on human nature, and permits man to transcend his condition by going, not against the grain of nature, but higher than nature). The first way corresponds to what we shall call, to be brief, the Hindu-Buddhist solution; the second, to what we shall call the Gospel solution.

By abolising, by means of a sovereign concentration of the intellect and the will, every particular form and representation, the wisdom of India adheres, through the void, to an absolute which is the Self in its pure metaphysical act of existing—experience conceived as leading at the same stroke either to the Transcendence of Being (Atman) or to total indetermination (nirvana). All the forms of illusion in the midst of which our life is spent have disappeared, everything is denied and annihilated, there remains only the Self in contact with itself.

It is clear that to attain such an end (not to speak even of the "powers" for which one is supposed to search without pause), is to transcend the human condition by dint of spiritual energy. But it is also clear that it is to transcend it by the means of refusal. The living delivered one gains a sort of interior omnipotence by falling back upon himself and separating himself from everything human; he enters into a solitariness incomparably more profound than the solitude of the hermit, for it is his soul itself which has broken with men and all the miseries of their terrestrial existence. To pass beyond illusion, and to deliver oneself from transmigration, or at least from all the sorrow that it carries with it and perpetuates, is at the same stroke to deliver oneself from the human condition. The refusal of this condition is there but a means of transcending it, it is not an act of revolt against it, a pure and simple refusal. It remains however essential to the spirituality of India. That is why, even when the sage, as in the Buddhism of the Great Vehicle (Mahayana), spreads his pity over men, it is as it were through the condescension of a being who no longer belongs to their species, and whose heart—by the very exigency of solitariness in nirvana—is not wounded by their troubles and does not enter into participation with them.

How can we not see in the implicit refusal of the human condition of which I have just spoken one of the weak points of the spirituality of India? If one considers in itself (independently of the graces which in fact can supervene in a soul of good will) this effort to escape the state in which we are naturally placed by our coming into the world, it manifests, along with an exceptional courage, an exceptional pride of spirit. Moreover such a refusal is in reality doomed, whatever victories it may bring, to a final defeat. Courage and pride are precisely two of the most profound features of the human condition. The Hindu or Buddhist sage quits the human condition only by showing in spite of himself his belonging to it—I mean, by the very negations to which he is led and all the apparatus of exercises and techniques he needs, and by the kind of never-ending *tour de force* by means of which he comes to transcend this condition. And the living delivered one still has to die like the others; he is not delivered from that which is the most tragically human in the human condition.

*The Gospel answer*

11. What of the Christian or Gospel solution? It takes us beyond pure philosophy and pure reason, and yet, by a strange paradox, it is in it and in the mystery that it proposes to us that an authentically rational attitude toward the human conditon becomes possible for man.

I said above that every great moral system is in reality an effort to ask man, in one manner or another and to one degree or another, to go beyond his natural condition in some way. These systems in fact (let us mention here only those which have been examined in the present work) ask man—while he rejects moral evil but accepts the suffering to which the human condition is exposed—to go beyond the human condition: either, as with Plato, Aristotle, the Stoics, Epicurus, Kant, Sartre or Bergson, by attaching himself to a good superior to human life, or to a happiness in which human life is achieved rationally, or to virtue, or to pleasure decanted to the point of indifference, or to duty, or to liberty, or to the sovereign love to which the great mystics call us; or, as with Hegel, Marx, Comte or Dewey, by deifying nature. But even in those cases where the effort to go beyond the human condition is the most authentic, there is no question, except in Bergson (and, in the name of faith, in Kierkegaard) of truly transcending it. And the attempt to go beyond the human condition by the sole means of man remains in the last analysis doomed either to futility or to illusion. It is only with Christianity that the effort to go beyond the human condition comes to real fruition.

It is superfluous to remark that I am not speaking here of the average behavior of the mass of people of Christian denomination. I am speaking of the exigencies of Christianity such as they are proposed to every one—and almost completely realized only in saints.

The question for the Christian is to transcend the human condition but by the grace of God—not, as for the Indian sage, by a supreme concentration on oneself—and in consenting at the same time to this condition, in accepting it as to all that pertains to moral evil and sin. Rupture with the human condition as to sin, acceptance of the human condition as to the radical contingency and as to the suffering as well as to the joys that it entails: that is demanded by reason, but is decidedly possible only by the configuration of grace to Him Who is sanctity itself because He is the Word incarnate. At the same stroke, the acceptance of the human conditon ceases to be simple submission to necessity; it becomes active consent, and consent through love.

That in a certain measure every soul inhabited by the gifts of grace, and in a full measure the saint, the one who has entered into what we called in a previous chapter the regime of supra-ethics, transcends the human condition—this is obvious to anyone who holds that grace is a participation in the divine life itself. It is the other aspect of the Gospel solution, the simultaneous acceptance (except as to sin) of the human condition that it is important for us to insist on here.

In the human condition thus transcended and accepted at the same time, everything, to tell the truth, remains the same and everything is transfigured. If grace makes man participate in the divine life and if it superelevates his nature in its own order, nevertheless it is a nature still wounded which is thus superelevated, it is a man still devoured by weakness who shares in eternal life and in God's friendship. The human condition has not changed. It has not changed because the Word of God assumed it such as it was and such as it will remain as long as history endures. In taking upon Himself all the sins of the world, He who was without sin also took upon Himself all the languors of the world, and all the suffering that afflicts the human race, and all the humiliation of its dependence with regard to the contingent and the fortuitous. What matter henceforth the contingency and the metaphysical futility to which our existence is subjected, since the most insignificant of our acts, if it is vivified by charity, has an external value, and since the Son of God has accepted to undergo Himself the servitudes of our condition?

During His hidden life He was a poor village workman, and His activity as preacher and miracle-worker took place in an historical milieu which made weigh on Him all its circumstances of time and place and all its hazards. He willed to die as the most unfortunate of men died in His time. His passion was an atrocious condensation of all the agony and abjection attached to the human condition since the Fall.

Consequently, when what I called just now the true background of the world—the world of naked suffering, of horror, of anguish without consolation—reveals itself to the Christian and takes possession of him, this matter of accepting (as to the evil of suffering) the human condition takes on an entirely new sense for him, comes to enter into the redemptive work of the Cross, and to participate in the annihilations of Him Whom he loves. No wonder the saints are desirous of suffering. Suffering, because it is for them a signature of their love, and cooperation in the work of their Beloved, has become for them the most precious of goods here on earth.

There they are, then, the saints, who by an apparent contradition give thanks to God for all the goods He heaps upon them and for all the protections, consolations and joys He dispenses to them, and give thanks to Him at the same time for all the evils and afflictions He sends them. We who are wicked, do we give a stone to our children when they ask us for bread? And yet thanks be to God when He gives us bread, and thanks be to Him when He gives us a stone and worse than a stone. The evil of suffering, while remaining what it is, and while being fully experienced as such, is transvalued now in a superior good, one perfectly invisible besides, unless there appear for an instant some sign of the more than human peace that inhabits the tortured soul.

12. The unbeliever sees here only a ghastly facility that religion allows itself, playing on two boards at the same time. The believer sees here the supreme grandeur of a mystery accessible to faith alone, and which can—in faith—be attained in some fashion and stammered by the intelligence, but which remains in itself as incomprehensible as God Himself.

It is doubtless for the philosopher that this mystery is the most incomprehensible, because the philosopher knows too well that essences do not change, and that in the ordinary course of things, suffering, unless the one that it visits undertakes bravely to surmount it, degrades and humiliates the human being. He would be a fool however if he did not bow before the testimony of the saints. But in his perspective as a philosopher the best he can say is that God's love is as transcendent as His being, which is as no thing is; and that it is more difficult still for the heart of man to apprehend the transcendence of Love subsisting by itself than it is for the human intelligence to apprehend the transcendence of Being subsisting by Itself. "Believe that God loves you *in a way that you cannot imagine*," said Dostoevski.

And here again can the philosopher refrain from asking some questions?

He is astonished by another apparent contradiction in the behavior of the saints. They desire suffering as the most precious of goods here below. After all, that's their affair, or rather an affair between God and them. But what about the others, those whom they love, and who comprise all men? Do they not desire for them also this most precious of goods here on earth? Yet this is not what they do, they spend their time trying to lessen the suffering of men and to cure them of their wounds. The answer, to the extent that one can catch a glimpse of it, concerns the very structure of the spirit.

In itself suffering is an evil, and will always remain an evil. How then could one wish it for those one loves? The simple knowledge possessed by the Christian (and so frequently recalled to his attention by the commonplaces of pious literature) that suffering unites the soul inhabited by charity to the sacrifice of the Cross, superimposes on suffering, ideally and theoretically, a quality thanks to which this knowledge helps one to accept suffering; it cannot make it be loved or desire, it does not transvalue it. If there is real and practical transvaluation, it can only be in the fire of the actual and absolutely incommunicable love between the self of a man and the divine Self; and that remains a closed secret, valid only for the individual subjectivity. Thus the saints would keep for themselves alone what they consider to be the most precious of goods here on earth. Singular egoists! They want suffering for themselves, they do not want it for others. Jesus wept over the dead Lazarus, and over the sorrow of Martha and Mary.

But the philosopher has still other questions. What strikes him above all in the human conditon is not the suffering of the saints, it is the suffering of the mass of men, the suffering they have not willed, the suffering that falls on them like a beast. How could he resign himself to the suffering of men?

He knows that the struggle against suffering is one of the aspects of the effort through which humanity goes forward, and that in this struggle the work of reason and the ferment of the Gospel, the progress of science and the progress of social justice, and the progress of the still so rudimentary knowledge that man has of himself, enable us constantly to gain ground. He is not tempted to adore the Great Being, but he renders thanks to the men—to the innumerable workers known and unknown who throughout the course of an immense history, by dint of inventive genius and sacrifice of self, have applied themselves and will always apply themselves to making the earth more habitable. But the philosopher also knows that as one gains ground in the struggle against suffering, new causes of suffering begin to abound so that man, despite all his progress, will never have done with suffering just as he will never have done with sickness. Modern man suffers in other ways than the cave man. On the whole, one can wonder whether he suffers less; one can wonder whether all the victories gained in the struggle against suffering do not result in maintaining, by compensating the progress in suffering, a kind of middle level at which life as a whole is almost tolerable. However this may be, there will always remain enough suffering to put the heart and the intelligence in anguish.

Thus the answers that the philosopher gives himself in thinking about the suffering of men are valid but insufficient. There is another answer still, one that not only concerns terrestrial history but also and above all eternal life. It was given in the Sermon on the Mount.

If there is in humanity an immense mass of suffering which is not redemptive like that of Christ and His saints, it is in order that it may be redeemed, and that everywhere at least where human liberty does not intrude its refusal, those who have wept in our valleys may be consoled forever.

# Louis Monden
## 1911-

Has mankind become so cold that it has lost all sensitivity toward what is right and wrong? Has the very concept of sin been voided? Has the law of the jungle conquered the modern city? Such questions reveal a common mood among many Christians that the awareness of sin has disappeared and that the Christian moral sense has been seriously dulled. Yet it must be recognized that alongside the anarchy, disorder and terrorism that seems so prevalent in the world, positive attitudes of social justice, of tolerance and of concern for the under-privileged have been strengthening.

Louis Monden, the author of Sin, Liberty and Law, proposes that the sense of sin has not vanished but has simply undergone a considerable change, a change that is a phenomenon, not of decay, but of maturation, a change that is one aspect of man's growing towards a new adulthood. In pursuing this theme, Monden makes full use of the findings of modern personalist philosophies, depth psychology and sociology. Monden's formation in philosophy and theology at the University of Louvain, Belgium, as well as his years as a university professor and counsellor, have equipped him to approach the question of sin responsibly and to offer a positive, relevant interpretation of Christian morality.

At the very outset, Monden recognizes the confusion and ambiguity that hovers around words such as guilt, sin, duty, contrition and conscience. These words can no longer be treated as though they were endowed with clearly defined, unchangeable meanings. Each word has many and quite different meanings. In an effort to give direction to our understanding of these terms, Monden presents three fundamental levels of ethical conduct (instinct, moral, Christian-religious); the terms of the ethical vocabulary take on a wholly different meaning according to the level on which a person dwells. This insight alone can be of great service to the person who is trying better to understand human conduct. The three levels naturally permeate one another, for man's psychological life is never exclusively instinctual, intellectual or religious. All three represent a threat and a promise for an authentic sense of sin. The individual ultimately decides through the power of choice.

Monden cautions the reader that moral adulthood does not coincide with physical adulthood. Tragically, moral infantilism may accompany a high degree of intellectual development or cultural refinement.

Among the present-day problems which must be met by moral theologians, Monden considers freedom and determinism, freedom and law, and moral effort and religious salvation. The manner in which these three problems are resolved will determine greatly the degree of ethical maturity than an individual may hope to achieve.

The reader who has tended to back away from serious reflection of ethical concepts will find Sin, Liberty and Law an enriching and liberating experience. Its flexible handling of ethical terms invites one to explore new dimensions of human relationships and to mature fearlessly as a moral person.

# SIN, LIBERTY AND LAW

## CHAPTER 1

### THE MEANING OF THE WORDS

In recent years the question of theological language has become one of the main problems—perhaps *the* main problem—of theological methodology. First, much attention is given to the search for the most appropriate categories into which to translate God's message. Theologians weigh the advantages and disadvantages of a less technical terminology, one not bound to certain philosophical schools, likewise of a wider use of images and concepts belonging to the Bible. Next there is felt a growing need, whatever the terminology used, to determine precisely the logical status of these terms, clearly to distinguish their several *levels of signification* and to define exactly the linguistic field within which they can meaningfully be used.

There is no domain of thought where such work is more indispensable than that of Christian moral theology. For until recently the practice prevailed of treating concepts such as guilt, sin, duty, contrition, conscience as if they were univocal terms, endowed with a clearly defined, unchangeable meaning. Most of our contemporaries continue to do so, and even in present-day theological publications this vague and confusing use of language is frequent. Yet philosophical analysis, especially phenomenology and linguistic philosophy, using the discoveries of psychology and sociology, has reached the conclusion that each one of these terms covers many and quite different meanings, irreducible to each other, which should be clearly distinguished if one is not to introduce insidious ambiguities into theological discussion, with the danger that there will be no real meeting of minds, since the same words are employed on totally different levels of signification and within quite different domains of application.

# THE CATHOLIC TRADITION: Personal Ethics

We might use the word "ethics"—somewhat arbitrarily, to be sure, but we cannot do without some well-defined terminology—for the whole of man's modes of being and of behaving in their undivided totality. The ethical conduct of man may then be considered on *three fundamental levels,* whereby the selfsame terms of the ethical vocabulary receive a wholly different meaning.

## The Level of Instinct

When an animal's drive fails to reach its goal, because of the resistance of things or the competition of another animal or a human sanction, that drive may give rise to behavior which—especially in domesticated animals, whose reflexes are heavily conditioned by human contact—strongly resembles the conduct of a human being who feels or is guilty. In man too there is an experience of guilt and a sense of duty which, although strongly influenced by the intellect and rationalized with higher motives, stands essentially upon *the level of instinct.*

The *law* which directs this instinctive ethics comes not from within but from without, from the pressure of reality, and especially of society, which, by means of prohibitions and "taboos," builds a dam against the impulses of individual instinctivity. Although this pressure is introjected by the individual and turns into instinctive self-control, into a feeling of *obligation,* that "ought" is always felt as something alien to the person, even as something hostile to his instinctive impulses. Hence it is experienced with an ambivalence of rebellious resistence, neutralized by fear of sanctions or of failure and by the impression that the pressure is irresistible. That ambivalent feeling, which is not experienced as lucid insight but undergone as an instinctive warning, is, on this level, called *conscience.*

*Guilt* and *sin* of this kind consist in the material transgression of some prohibition or taboo. Whether the intention was good or not, the purpose wrong or nonexistent, the action performed freely or without freedom—all this has no bearing on guilt. The sin consists in the material fact of "transgression"; this or that action, this or that object, is *ipso facto* sinful. The ensuing reaction is equally instinctive, although it may be rationalized with all kinds of moral considerations. It is a blind *feeling,* rather than a consciousness *of guilt;* it derives from the awareness not of having acted badly, irrationally, against one's conscience, but of having acted wrongly, faultily, against some order. It is an almost physical occult sense that one has strayed beyond a safe boundary and is now threatened with the vengeance of the mysterious power that guards it; a feeling of anxiety which makes one cower instinctively in expectation of the coming punishment and experience something almost like relief when it finally does come.

*Contrition* for sin too is, on this level, not an awareness of one's wickedness and a desire for amendment, i.e. for becoming one's good self again, but simply the instinctive urge to escape the consequences of the transgression. On this level contrition looks mostly for formulas, rites of reconciliation and magic gestures by means of which the angered powers may be placated, the transgression undone, the punishment avoided and the safety of legal limits regained. *Confession* of the fault, expression of a *firm resolve* to stay henceforth within the limits of the law, all this belongs to the conjuring rites. Both are sincerely meant, not however in the sense of a personal decision, but as an instinctive anxiety reflex: "I'll never dare do such a thing again, too bad I ever ran that risk."

## The Moral Level

We shall use the word "moral" here not in the general meaning of ethical conduct, but in the specific sense of the element in this ethical conduct which belongs to the level of the conscious and free self-realization of the human person. Hence "moral" refers to the most human aspect of the ethical. It is present where man, having reached adult conscious insight, fully realizes the conditions of his free and authentic self-development as a spirit in the world, in communion with his fellow men and in union with the absolute Spirit, God.

On this level the *law* is no longer a pressure from without. It is based ultimately on man's essential dependence on God. In practice it is experienced as autonomous, with an autonomy that does not reject every kind of dependence but emphasizes the fact that even man's profound dependence on God can manifest itself only through the structure and the growth of his own nature as a source of moral obligation. What man experiences as law is nothing but his own essential growth as a proffered possibility and as a task to be fulfilled; it is the direction towards total self-development which corresponds most closely to the structure of the inner self, put before the free act as an absolute demand. This absolute demand is moral *obligation:* man's freedom owes it to itself to be faithful to its authentic self-development. And *conscience* is the deepest self-consciousness of man, insofar as it acts as a power of discrimination deciding in every choice what will promote authentic self-realization and what will stand in its way. That conscience is not infallible, because it depends on the information it receives about a moral problem in a definite situation; hence it can err in good faith owing to insufficient data or the incorrect judgment of some situation. Yet the voice of conscience, even when erring in good faith, must unconditionally be obeyed.

There is moral *guilt* where the free will acts against conscience. It never consists in the matter of the action taken objectively. Only the free choice and the wrong direction taken by the will must be considered. Moral guilt is always freely chosen infidelity to authentic self-realization and the free yielding to a pseudo-value. The objectively wrong action which conscience considers good is not morally guilty. The objectively good action which conscience, in good faith, deems wrong is morally guilty. Likewise *punishment* for such an action is no longer feared from without, as the vengeance of a mysterious offended power. The guilty deed punishes itself, because it is a self-inflicted wound, a matter of growing in the wrong direction. Considered from without, the sinful course may look like the free unfolding of life and of one's own sovereign vitality; in fact it always means a denying of oneself, the teeming within one's soul of spiritual weeds or cancerous growths.

Hence on the level of morality *contrition* will always be the inner acknowledgement of an action as self-negation, the uttering of a verdict of guilty over one's own deviations, not as a resigned recording of some failure but as an active will to correct the deviation and as a steady *resolve* to restore and to make up for the missed occasions of self-development by a more vigorous moral growth in the future. The *confession* of one's guilt adds nothing to the value of the inner self-judgment. It may be one of the many means used for recovery, because it places one's self-condemnation and steady resolve in the concrete framework of one's moral development within a human community.

## The Christian-Religious Level

The moral self-unfolding of man mentioned in the previous paragraph takes place mainly through the development of his personality in an adult, loving self-donation to others. On the moral level, however, ethical conduct does not find its norms directly in this self-donation, but in the degree of authenticity of human self-realization as expressed in that self-donation. Hence when that natural self-unfolding is raised to a totally new level of value, as it is gratuitously assumed into a divine intimacy of love, this intimacy itself must become the only norm of the new ethical conduct of the human partner in his dialog with God.

The *law* which guides this meeting with God is no longer the growth of one's own being, but the proffered invitation to rise above that level towards a new meeting in love, an invitation which is at once possibility, question, offer, and, in its own way, exigency for total donation. At first it looks as if the autonomy of self-decision has been given up once more for a law forced upon man from without. In fact there is no coercion from without, no giving up of one's own self-development, but a yielding in love to a God who is *intimior intimo meo* ("closer to me than I am to myself"), so that letting oneself go in this love entails a higher and deeper self-realization, a real divinization of man.

Whereas the outer pressure of taboo upon instinct entailed an inframoral heteronomy of the law, the heteronomy of the divine invitation to love is the basis of a supramoral ethics. This is true also of the *obligation* imposed by that law: moral duty is not suppressed by it, but assumed in a totally new "ought" which is even further removed from all coercion than moral obligation and might be called a "vocation" rather than

159

an "obligation." The specific forms of this "ought" considerably transcend the moral forms; they lie in the domain of what might be designated as "counsel" or "beatitude." *Conscience* on this level will be love itself as a power of discriminating what can promote from what will hinder its growth. It is no longer a natural or rational insight—although moral insight continues to act in the religious conscience—but an affinity with the beloved, a communion in feeling and in thinking, a "connaturality" with him.

Here *guilt* and *sin* are less than ever a material action, nor are they even the impairing of one's own power of growth. They consist in saying No to love. Sin becomes man himself in a relation of refusal to God's love. Hence, on this religious level, a merely material transgression can never be a sin. A moral fault can, but owing to the religious relation it acquires a new dimension, because refusing to be oneself turns into refusing to be for the Other. Over and above the moral fault there is a specific religious refusal, a violation of divine love in itself, a kind of guilt which is now in the fullest meaning of that word a "sin." The *punishment* for that sin, too, is not a threat impending from without but the enduring invitation of love itself as the torment of him who rejects it.

On this level *contrition* too becomes a function of love: it is the awareness of our unfaithfulness to love, joined to our conviction that this love surpasses every infidelity, that "God is greater than our heart." Religious contrition is therefore infinitely more than a search for security from the avenging wrath of an offended power; much more, too, than self-condemnation and a will for restoration. It is an appeal to the *mercy* of the beloved, a certitude that love will accept the guilt which we confidently offer and turn it into a new increase of the love relationship. It is our boldness in converting the fault into a trustful offering of love. The answer to this contrition—for on this level of the meeting of persons a response always comes— is *forgiveness*. A word devoid of meaning on the instinctive and the ethical levels, on the religious level it means the creative restoration of love through the integration of the fault within its growth. It is not a gradual reparation which remedies the fault, but the resumption of the love relationship, the reawakening of love itself, out of the meeting of mercy and repentance. And precisely because this meeting is granted by God in a fully gratuitous manner, love can be restored more wonderfully than ever in one creative moment of mercy. The *confession* of the fault is the sign, the opening word of the dialog in which the encounter takes place. And penance or *reparation* is the making real, on the level of moral growth, of what has already become a reality on the religious level in the one creative moment of love.

The distinction between the three levels of the ethical might become clearer from a consideration of how one and the same concrete situation can be experienced on each of them.

A young mother has given birth to a deformed baby. All her instinctive love and possessiveness surges in rebellion. *Instinct* says: "It is better not to let this child live. It can grow up only for a life which will be a hell, it will not know one moment of happiness." "Happiness" is understood here on the instinctive level as health, beauty, success, acceptance, the possibility of realizing one's plans. Underneath the instinctive compassion for the child the voice of self-pity too may be heard: fear of all the selfless love which such a child will demand, of the innumerable humiliations which may be expected. Against the impulse of instinct the only barrier is the law: it is forbidden, I may not do it, they don't allow this, I will be punished for doing it. If, at a given moment, the pressure of instinct prevails and the action is performed against the pressure of external law, then everything will depend on the reaction of society. If the courts and public opinion are in the main hostile, the young mother breaks down under her feeling of guilt. On the other hand, should public opinion show itself favorably disposed (and public opinion too will almost unavoidably move on the level of instinct in its judgment above love and happiness) and force the law to approve—or, at least, to acquit—then all feeling of guilt is gone. The brakes are off; "Now it is allowed." One is even proud of having had the courage to force the external law to open this gate, of having breached the wall of social pressure by the sheer force of the maternal drive. In all this there is not the slightest element of moral judgment.

It is quite a different matter if the mother wishes to make her decision on the *moral level.* In that case, independently of any concern for legislation or eventual consequences, she will ask herself: "Have I a right to interfere with this life which has been entrusted to me? I am responsible for the meaning which this young life will one day possess. Have I ever any right to say that a human life has no meaning?" Her idea of human happiness, too, will no longer be merely instinctive, corresponding to the public norms of wealth, success and social acceptance. She will have to ask, "What are the ingredients of real happiness? How can we explain the fact that people who seem to have none of the things instinct considers essential for happiness call themselves happy, and others who seem to have all these things in abundance commit suicide? Might not the meaning of human life depend mainly on the meaning one gives to it—on the meaning which, from the start, the love of the parents bestows on it? Is the action instinct trying to force on me a real gesture of mercy, or is it an attempt against what is authentically human? Only the answer to this last question can be decisive, and if the young mother goes against it she will keep on feeling guilty even if all the courts acquit her and public opinion hails her as a heroine.

Finally, the young mother who is a Christian, who from the very start puts herself on the *religious level,* will not even have to deliberate. From the beginning of her pregnancy she has felt that the new life growing within her was a mandate and an invitation of God's love. Neither wealth nor success nor complete self-fulfillment is for her the meaning of human existence or the norm of happiness. To her every life means an invitation to grow in loving intimacy with God, and every human being, in the shelter of that depth of love, can find the strength to fulfill his own task and vocation in love and happiness. She knows that as a mother she is called to love that child too, with all her resources for sacrifice and suffering, in such a way that she may teach him to accept his painful yet beautiful destiny, and make him capable of authentic love and real human and divine happiness. For her the rejection of that mandate, however burdensome and difficult it may look, would be to reject God's invitation, to doubt the love which beckons and run away from the suffering involved in the task which is set before her.

For the sake of clarity we have made a very sharp distinction between the three levels of signification of the ethical vocabulary. This does not, however, mean that they are hermetically sealed off from each other. All three are forms of human experience, and no one of them is ever totally free of resonances and influences emanating from the other two. Man's psychological life is never exclusively spiritual or exclusively instinctual. The religious element is never independent of intellect or instinct. The lower level will always be implicitly present and active in the higher. The higher level will always rest on all the lower levels as a substratum, assuming them into itself and imparting a new and higher meaning to them. The growth of human psychic life will always proceed from instinct to spiritual self-development and culminate in religious self-donation. This is true not only of every individual but also of the moral development of humanity as a whole.

In *individual existence* the child appears at first as a bundle of instincts seeking gratification. The clash of these instincts with a refractory reality, especially their meeting with a partly acquiescing, partly restricting, directing, punishing attitude on the part of the parents, evokes in the child the first feelings of duty and of guilt, still entirely on the level of taboo. This does not mean that the child as yet possesses no spiritual experience, but that the spiritual element is still no more than implicit, manifesting itself only in projections within instinctive activities. Even when, around the age of four, external parental authority is introjected within the psyche of the child himself, becoming thus, as it were, an endopsychic counterpart of instinct, that "superego," as depth psychology calls it, is not yet a spiritual consciousness, directing in full clarity the impulses of instinct towards human self-realization. It remains a collection of taboo commands and taboo prohibitions, which is only gradually taken over by a developing consciousness and transformed into a personal "conscience." The "age of reason," which traditional moral doctrine places around seven years, appears in this respect to be a very arbitrary boundary line, although we must grant that the first flashes of spiritual self-possession do indeed occur around that time. They enable the child to put some conscious order into the domain of his instincts, at least if the problems encountered remain within the dimensions of the child's own world.

The growth towards maturity will depend precisely on the gradual self-conquest of consciousness and on the capacity for integrating the instinctive impulses ever more harmoniously within that conscious self-development. We do not mean that man gradually breaks away from his instinctivity into undiluted spirituality. Such "angelism" fails to take into account the unity of the human body-soul composite. Man continues to carry within him not only his instinctivity but also his whole past, with all the experiences, reflexes and habitual automatisms, with all the feelings of guilt and anxiety and coercion which the child has experienced within the world of taboo.

We may try to picture the development towards ideal moral maturity in a hypothetical case: that of a child in whom the world of taboo morality is a perfect prefiguration, within infantile dimensions, of the moral norm of life which conscious self-development will later propose as an ideal. There would be a real analogy between the child's morality and that of the adult: the growing self-consciousness would consist in a gradual and harmonious personalization, not so much of the impersonal as of the prepersonal infantile elements. The habits, reflexes and automatisms, in such a hypothetical case, constitute a safe, harmonious, instinctive substructure for the morality of the adult. There would be no discordance between the warning signal of instinctive feelings of duty or guilt arising from the unconscious past and the consciously recognized duty or guilt. It is obvious that the superego will not have this prefigurative harmony in everybody and that in cases where early education has had a less favorable outcome the integration of the superego within the conscious moral personality will take place much less smoothly. There is even some danger that the integration may be so much hampered that the adult never quite proceeds beyond the childish taboo conscience but bogs down in a morality which is for the most part instinctive, one which he will endeavor to rationalize with the full resources of his intellect and his culture.

The *religious reality* of God's grace can likewise be present in the baptized child from the very beginning as a new essential relation to God, not detached from the natural existence either of the spirit or of the instincts. The role of grace is to leaven and to raise this whole reality, "integrating" or harmoniously assuming it in its turn within the divine dialog. In this process divine grace itself will be influenced by the course of natural growth. In the small child the world of faith will take shape only within the child's world of image and under the form of projections. Religious conduct and religious feelings of guilt will long remain only implicit within the taboo morality of the superego. Even the seemingly adult religious ideology of asceticism, penance, self-donation and sacrifice may be alloyed by a number of infantile taboo elements. Furthermore, the religious relation may come into conflict with a too anthropomorphic ethic which is able to conceive the meeting with God only in terms of a personal conquest and in which a natural adult pride refuses a supernatural self-donation. When the religious relation enters a human life only in the adult years, as in a "conversion," the conflict with the residue of taboo morality and the purely natural ethical attitude of the past will be more acute and the slow integration of life within the sphere of grace will take place even more laboriously and more gradually.

*Moral adulthood* does not, therefore, simply coincide with bodily or even with spiritual adulthood. In a person adult in years, moral infantilism may accompany a high degree of intellectual development, cultural refinement, a deep psychological insight and a wealth of human experience. Moral adulthood, in its turn, does not necessarily go along with *religious-ethical adulthood:* a person who is highly developed morally may remain undeveloped religiously or may cling to infantile forms of religiosity.

*Mankind* likewise grows into adulthood. In mankind too there has probably been a very gradual growth from a largely implicit moral choice caught up in taboos to a clarified moral insight. The Christian awareness of sin as well has undergone a divine preparation, through the slow breaking away of the

165

religious conscience from the taboo and magical implications in which it was at first confined—as shown in the Bible stories —until Christ, in the fullness of time, could propose the mature purity of this religious awareness of sin. It is the confluence of moral insight developed to adult lucidity in Greek thought with the religious conscience as fully revealed within the Christian religion which has given Western ethics its specific character. Even sociologically, the "guilt cultures" of the West (where the ethical norm consists in the self-experienced personal value) are often contrasted with the "shame cultures" of other places (in which the norm of ethical action consists in social acceptance).

Further development of these historical considerations is not within the scope of this book.

### PRESENT-DAY PROBLEMS

An awareness of the complexity of our ethical activity presents modern moral theology with a number of problems, among which we would like to consider three in particular.

A *first series* of questions refers to the *relation between freedom and determinism* in the actual ethical activity of the average human being. Even if one does not deny human freedom in theory, the question arises as to what extent the average person in fact escapes mere taboo morality. Is not the pressure of biological heredity, of social influences, of unconscious inhibitions and complexes such that, for most people, the possibility of a real moral judgment is excluded? Furthermore, is it possible for a man to measure the real freedom in human actions—either in his own or in those of others—to isolate it in the network of determinisms in which they are, often unconsciously, caught? This involves all kinds of vexing practical problems—e.g., what is the real meaning of the notion of "mortal sin," and how does it remain possible to know what one must mention in confession as "mortal sin"? On the religious level the whole question arises of the relation between psychic health, maturity, and holiness.

A *second series* of questions refers to the relation between the inner spontaneity of *freedom* and the *law* imposed from without. Is there really a double morality, as taught by Bergson? Or does a reciprocal relation exist between them in which each is a prolongation of the other? Can the inner, spontaneous spiritual growth of man be formulated in a permanent, unchangeable natural law? Or is human nature an evolving structure developing historically in given situations, one which cannot be caught in rigid formulas, so that the individual moral judgment can, in the last analysis, be made only with reference to a concrete situation? Which shall we choose: an *ethics based on the natural law* or a *situational ethics*? And what is the relation between the religious law of love and the inner law of human growth and the external law imposed by society? Is it, as Hesnard claims, unavoidable that under the cloak of an evangelical law of love Christian ethics in fact always falls back to the level of an inframoral taboo ethics?

Finally, a *third series* of questions concerns the true relation between *moral effort* and *religious salvation* from evil. Do these two factors normally go together or are they to a large extent independent of each other? Is moral rectitude a help or rather a hindrance to the religious awareness of sin? Will one who is morally blameless unavoidably degenerate into a religious pharisee? And must we, then—in some kind of *"sin mystique"*—consider moral guilt as an almost indispensable condition for being received into grace and admitted to salvation?

The next three chapters are an effort to answer these three series of questions. Each time we shall try first to state the problem in as clear-cut and concrete a manner as possible; next we shall gather the data for a theoretical solution; finally we shall indicate a few orientations for a pastoral theology inspired by these principles.

\* \* \* \* \*

### ELEMENTS OF A SOLUTION

Taking into consideration both the warnings of ecclesiastical authority and the valuable elements contained in the new trends, the question must now be asked and answered: What is the value, what are the limits of the law, and what is, for the Christian conscience, the relation of freedom to the law?

## Value and Limits of the Law

In order to understand the relation between love, freedom and law, it seems necessary to keep before one's eyes the *different levels,* mentioned in our first chapter, on which these words can be understood. This has been too frequently overlooked both by those who appeal to the law and by those who oppose the law in the name of "love" and "freedom."

## 1. Natural Law and Positive Law on the Moral Level

It is true that on the level of *instinct*—that is, as long as the law is experienced as a coercion merely imposed from without—mature freedom and external law confront each other as *irreconcilable* elements without anything in common. It is only on the *moral* level that the question of the relation between law and freedom takes on a meaning—at least, if the concept of law keeps a meaning acceptable on that level. What might that meaning be?

For a philosophy inspired by Christianity freedom cannot be reduced to a mere creative arbitrariness. This philosophy conceives man's deepest nature as a relation to God; the fact of being a creature, of existing by and in relation to Another, must affect man's whole unfolding self-realization. Although human freedom does indeed really create value out of itself, it is never only a freedom "from" every coercion, but is always also a freedom "towards" an intended fullness of possible self-realization. That fullness is not prefigured as an abstract scheme, a blueprint to be reproduced, but as a *dynamically inviting possibility,* a concrete project to be carried out in the midst of a concrete situation in which man's "self" presents its demands to an "ego" consciously realizing itself. "Become what thou art" is, on the moral level, the fundamental law by which the authenticity or unauthenticity of a human development, and of the separate actions in which that development takes shape, can be measured.

That inner law of growth has traditionally borne the name "natural law." Hence in its classical meaning the term "natural law" has no connection with the physical or biological concept of "nature," formerly in frequent use in the positive sciences and in ethics, with which it is often wrongly identified even nowadays (for instance, in the treatment of sexual problems). Thus some actions are supposed to be "according to" or "against" nature. But an action which is biologically "according to" nature may very well be morally in conflict with the "natural law." Hence the fact that the notion of "nature" is outmoded in the positive sciences cannot be used as an argument against the natural law in the moral sense, since it has no connection whatsoever with it.

Nor is the natural law in its classical meaning the collection of abstract principles or formulations to which textbook morality has often reduced it, under the influence of the seventeenth- and eighteenth-century theories of natural right. Historically the appeal to the natural law has arisen precisely from the resistance of personal conscience to the arbitrariness of written laws; it appealed to an *unwritten law,* an inborn knowledge of what man ought to do and ought not to do in order to be and to become authentically himself. Among the great classical authors that meaning of the natural law has been maintained in all its integrity.

Thus we find, for example, in Thomas Aquinas the following description: "The rational creature is subject in a more perfect manner than the others to divine providence, insofar namely as it shares this providence and becomes providence for itself and for others. Hence it shares the eternal law and possesses a natural inclination towards its authentic act and finality. It is precisely this sharing of the eternal law in the rational creature which is called natural law."

Hence in its original meaning the natural law is a *dynamic existing reality,* an ordering of man towards his self-perfection and his self-realization, through all the concrete situations of his life and in intersubjective dialog with his fellow man and with God. Although for us the expression may have too static a resonance, the reality it embraces can be integrated without any difficulty in a dynamic picture of the world and still keep its full meaning. For it is precisely man's becoming which is prefigured in it. The norm of man's action is not so much what he is as what he is to become.

The dynamic character of the natural law does *not in the least* mean a variability in that law in the sense that it might be *arbitrarily modified* under the influence of individual or collective feeling. It is precisely the law of evolution, as it appears, for instance, in Teilhard's vision, that an increasing complexity of structures goes along with an increasing interiorization of consciousness, and that this development does not proceed in a steady way but shows, at definite thresholds, sudden total modifications of aspect, situation or disposition.

Besides wholly new phenomena, running in the line of evolution, *regressions too* and ossifications may occur, which can be judged as such and distinguished from the progressive phenomena only by referring them to the general law of development. It is possible that in evolving humanity some implications of the natural law may rise to full consciousness only gradually, or that moral intuition in its full purity may detach itself only in a very gradual way from certain representations or projections in which it was caught. It is even possible that, on reaching certain thresholds, the growing moral awareness may show wholly new aspects and forms. Yet not every subjective modification in the moral sentiments of individuals or of groups lies in the line of authentic evolution. And it is precisely the awareness of what developing man ought to become, hence the inner and dynamic natural law, which *allows* us to *distinguish* authentic developments from regressions and decay.

Thus it is possible that reverence for life may demand certain things which formerly did not emerge so clearly into consciousness. To mention only one example, we may begin to feel that the death penalty is in conflict with our growing reverence for man, hence that it is immoral. But it is impossible that mankind should authentically evolve in the direction of a morality which would destroy or weaken the reverence for life. Again, it is a fact that married love has only in a very gradual manner manifested the fullness of its demands in the mind and conscience of man. It is possible that our insight into the structure of sexuality is still very imperfect and that a growing awareness may, in the future, demand much more from the authentic experience of sexual love. But it is not possible that man should authentically evolve towards a morality of free love, because that would go against the grain of a humanity which is developing towards an ever more intensive amorization.

In the final analysis the natural law does not find its norm in the actual sentiments of humanity, but that very law constitutes *the norm of authenticity* of the evolving sentiments of humanity.

In a human community the natural law should not only be active as a norm deep within every human soul. It must be made *communicable,* available as a principle of education and of community organization. For that purpose it must be laid down in *fixed formulas* and coined into generally valid rules of conduct and even into detailed applications. As soon, however, as it is channelled into maxims and formulas, the lifelikeness of the inner natural law and its organic connection with the situation becomes ossified into an abstraction. It turns into a prescription, a recipe, and it loses all contact with ever changing reality. It must inevitably express itself in the language of a determined cultural milieu, in the concepts of a determined sphere of thought; often it will be interpreted out of very limited philosophical insight. As a result, all these formulations at once acquire a certain *coefficient of relativity.*

Yet this too does not mean that the natural law is arbitrarily changeable. It is precisely the dynamic authenticity of the inner natural law which serves as norm for every change in its expression. It is forever in a process of purification from all the images in which a certain time or a certain culture threaten to imprison it, expressing its changeless authenticity in the language and conceptual forms of a new time, a new culture, a new attitude towards life.

The more the basic finality towards human self-realization tries to translate itself into the *small decisions* of life, the greater the extent to which it becomes contaminated by all kinds of factors bound to that particular time, the wider, too, the *margin of imperfection* in its formulation and the greater the danger of misunderstanding and faulty interpretation. This was already fully acknowledged by classical moral doctrine and expressed, for instance, by Aquinas in the famous distinction between primary and secondary prescriptions of the natural law, where he remarks that in the practical judgment the danger of error increases as one goes down into more detailed applications *"quanto magis ad propria descenditur, tanto magis invenitur defectus"* ("the more we descend to particulars, the more we encounter defects").

The *ten commandments* are mainly a practical formulation of a number of basic assertions of the natural law. A simple comparison, however, between the original formulation, as presented in Exodus (20. 1-17), with some modern catechism formulations shows to what extent, in the course of the history of salvation, the formulas have been detached from all kinds of primitive religious conceptions and antiquated social structures. And it is quite evident that this purification continues, as shown by the whole evolution of the Christian attitude towards abuses of the Holy Name, and from the often painful casuistry into which a formula such as "thou shalt not lie" has led the conceptualistic philosophy of "truth" of textbook teaching.

Not all concrete decisions in minor matters can find their norm in the natural law in such a way that only one manner of acting, one manner of tackling a certain situation, is possible. Frequently there are several ways to reach a certain end. But in a community these differences in conduct between individuals, even though each is good in itself and in accordance with the natural law, can become very harmful to the common good. Hence the need for authority to make a choice within that community between these several possibilities and to impose one of them in the form of a law universally valid for the community.

Such a law, by its very definition, is not self-evident. It is established only by the will of the legislator. That is why we call it a *positive law*. Its necessity does not derive from what it prescribes, but from the need for harmonizing the spontaneous decisions of individuals with the general welfare. Hence the positive law is a real restriction of man's free activity, but a restriction which ultimately promotes and serves that freedom.

That law too—although it unavoidably involves a certain amount of arbitrariness—is *not merely arbitrary*. It should be dictated to the legislator by his concern for the general welfare, while respecting the legitimate freedom of individual conscience.

Such a law is *by definition changeable* since it is to a great extent determined by the concrete, changing demands of a situation. It allows of exceptions in the form of dispensations foreseen by authority itself or of motives which excuse the subject from obeying it. Even while authority continues to uphold it, it may wholly lose its obligatory character because most evidently it no longer corresponds to the given situation and is injurious to the common welfare; or it is an attempt to promote the common welfare at the cost of a manifestly unreasonable and useless limitation of individual freedom; or even because it conflicts with the absolute demands of the natural law.

The virtue which maintains the superiority of the unwritten inner natural law within the application of the positive law has since time immemorial been called *"epikeia" (aequitas),* the virtue of equity. Under the influence of Suarez that notion, too, came to be conceived so narrowly that it was reduced to the idea of an objective *principle of interpretation* of the law, some kind of intra-legal correction of the imperfection or rigidity of the written text of the law. However, according to the conception of classical antiquity, taken over by medieval theology and based on religious principles, *epikeia* was infinitely more: it was a real virtue, hence a *disposition of the soul,* a noble inclination of the heart; it was the decision always to make the juridical serve justice, to keep the law in the service of conscience; and wherever required, to give unconditional priority to the eternal law of nature written in man's heart over every positive text of the law. It is an encouraging fact that present-day moral theology is going back to the original meaning of the word.

## 2. The Christian Law of Life and Laws of the Church

All that has been said up to now applies to the moral level. But the Christian lives on a religious-ethical level, and the question must be asked to what extent the meaning of the law is maintained or superseded on that level.

In our first chapter we said that the religious-ethical level is characterized by the fact that it no longer lies within the range of the development of one's own being, but depends entirely on a new, creative communication of God, inviting man to a dialog of love whose intimacy is outside the sphere of human initiative. Hence that invitation can be accepted by man only if it creatively infuses in him the power to respond to it. For "who among men knows the things of man save the spirit of a man which is in him? Even so, the things of God no one knows but the Spirit of God." (1 Cor. 2.11) When, therefore, we are admitted to intimacy with God, this is possible only because "we have received not the spirit of the world, but the spirit that is from God, that we may know the things that have been given us by God" (1 Cor. 2.12).

It is for this reason that we term "infused" the divine virtues of faith, hope and charity which God's spirit evokes in us, through which we listen to God's word with a new power of hearing in this wholly new supernatural manner; through which we advance towards him in a new way and meet his love with a new heart. As in the natural trend of our being towards its own self-development an objective law of growth is expressed and described, this supernatural shaping of our course through faith, hope and love will develop some kind of *natural law of the supernatural,* an inner *law of growth of the Holy Spirit,* imprinted in us by his influence and by his call to us. We really are, as St. Paul says, "a letter of Christ, composed by us, written not with ink but with the Spirit of the living God, not on tablets of stone but on fleshly tablets of the heart" (2 Cor. 3.3). The norm for Christian life is no longer mere human self-development but "the charity of God poured forth in our hearts by the Holy Spirit who has been given to us" (Rom. 5.5; 8.11).

What is the relation between this inner law of grace and the moral law of nature? The former does not supersede the latter but *raises* and *completes* it. Our self-development on the natural plane becomes a task and a vocation through God's loving invitation; it becomes the topic of conversation in our dialog of love with him. Because they have been taken up into the finality of faith, hope and love, all the moral virtues acquire a dimension of grace; they share the divine, "infused" nature of the theological virtues.

This, however, involves a threat to the natural law much more grave than any posed by the imperfections and weaknesses in us which are merely human. For God's grace not only opens hitherto unsuspected prospects to our existence. It also reveals to us the depth of our dereliction, the fact that we are held in an unavoidable solidarity with sinful mankind, and that we cannot escape from this bondage through our natural powers; only grace can deliver us. The natural law as well is assumed within the tension wrought in us by the opposing forces of grace and sin, original sin and the redemption, concupiscence and the urgings of the spirit.

A comparison of the law of grace briefly described here with the interpretation offered by *Hesnard* of the morality of the Christian religion not only shows clearly that he has not the slightest inkling of the authentic Christian awareness of sin, it also discloses the true bearing of the *a priori* assumption which he regards as obvious, and from which his misrepresentation follows of necessity: his rejection of all transcendence which is not that of the group over the individual and of all experience outside the ambit of perception on a merely psychological level. Whatever stands outside of, or higher than, this is lumped together under the term "myth" and rejected in its totality. Hence he sees the choice between an infantile taboo-attitude and a morality of concrete action of merely social inspiration as a *dilemma*. It does not so much as dawn on him that there might be a *third possibility:* man's ordination towards the infinite love of a God who leans over him, inviting him. In his world closed to the sacred, in which only the profane is real, there is no room for that deepest morality of love, and he can only caricature that loving invitation into some kind of sacralized taboo attempting to exercise its influence on even the innermost feelings and desires. He is even led into distorting into a menacing taboo prohibition the words of Christ concerning the internal sins in which the Christian discovers the deepest appeal to the totality of his loving self-donation. And his primary assumption so wholly blinds him to the nature of the saint's awareness of sin, the result of a consuming love of God, that he is forced to interpret it as an extreme neurotic repression of all sound instinctivity. That is why Hesnard's interpretation will sound as mistaken to the Christian who authentically experiences his inner shaping by grace as the reproach that he lets himself be tyrannized by the whims of his wife sounds to a man really in love.

As the natural law must express itself within the concrete community of men in moral rules and principles, so too the inner law of the Holy Spirit must assume a *tangible shape* within the community of the Church. For God's invitation not only takes hold of man at the highest point of his spirit but encompasses him in the full dimensions of his humanity; it is addressed to him both in the sensory aspect of his being as a spirit in matter and in the relational aspect of his being as a man among men. The dialog of love between God and man will not only be carried on through an inner attraction; God's salvific utterance will be heard within the human community in signs perceptible by the senses; the prophetic words of men he has inspired, his saving intervention through the events in a chosen people's history—all this reaching a climax in the full utterance of his incarnate Word, who came down into our human history and lives on perpetually within the new people of God, his everlasting Church. That Church is the bearer of the fullness of revelation, bringing it down through history to an ever more conscious and rich unfolding, thus gradually preparing humanity for the final achievement of history in Christ's return, when he will give everything into the hands of his Father, so that God may be all in all.

The whole history of salvation is structured *sacramentally*. What manifests itself so clearly in Christ's incarnation and redemption will become the law of God's saving self-communication in its totality: the outer aspect will always be both the *revealing sign* and the *mediating instrument* of the invisible working of grace. Within the Church as the great original sacrament God will speak to us in a plurality of sacramental signs, in the preaching of his word, in the inspiration of Holy Scripture, in the infallible utterances of the Church's magisterium.

The ethical demands which God's invitation presents for our human response will share this *sacramental structure*.

These demands first found expression in the law of the Old Covenant, were uttered more fully in the message of the prophets; thus began the gradual development which would lead to the Beatitudes, to Christ's fulfilling of the law and his formulation of his new commandment. Whereas the natural law is formulated by human society, laid down and applied in prescriptions under man's own responsibility, in the *verbalization* and the shaping of the inner law of grace the initiative is with God, who guarantees the divine validity and authenticity of his demands through the inspiration of his prophets and sacred writers and the human-divine sacramentality of his own Word.

This also applies to some extent to the *further explicitation* of the Christian demands of grace within the *Church,* since she listens to learn the demands of God's love with the continual assistance and at the continual urging of the Spirit. In every believer the inner law of the Spirit is at work like a kind of connaturality with the God who speaks to him through Christ, like a kind of *power of discrimination,* a spiritual sense of touch, capable of discerning what is and what is not an authentic verbalization of God's invitation. But in the individual that power of discrimination remains fallible. Only in the sense of faith of the Church as a hierarchic community does the connaturality with the God who speaks issue in infallible certitude. The pronouncements of the Church's magisterium are the authentic testimony of this sense of faith. It is only by heeding the sense of faith of the Church that the magisterium discovers the basis for its pronouncements, and it is only in this authoritative pronouncement that the Church's sense of faith comes to the full awareness of its certitude. At certain *privileged moments* and within strictly defined limits the Church's pronouncements concerning Christian moral activity become *infallibly assured* of their divine authenticity. Within these limits the decisions of the Church participate in the absolute character of God's own speaking and possess a certitude no human formulation of the natural law can ever claim for itself. Against such pronouncements, every assault of autonomous reason, every appeal to a personal charismatic intuition of the demands of grace, becomes senseless within the Christian perspective.

If, in this connection, there can be a "development" of morality, this can take place only in the same sense and within the same limits as hold for the development of dogma. As for dogma itself, every modification through additions or enrichment from without is excluded. The development can only consist in the *explicitation* of a fullness which was present from the beginning and which gradually reveals its implications and virtualities more fully with the evolving existence of mankind. Development also occurs in the sense of a gradually clearer *distinction* between the core of the evangelical and ecclesial messages and the *presentation* or formulation of them, which may be influenced by time and circumstances.

The assistance of the Spirit in his Church does not end with the infallibly guaranteed utterances of the magisterium. It is constantly at work throughout all time in the moral thinking and feeling of Christendom as a whole, as it takes shape in what is called the Church's *tradition*. Hence, as for the content of the faith, so also with regard to moral issues, there are concentric circles of a gradually decreasing certitude which the sense of faith and the thinking of individuals will take into account. When, for instance, on points which are not explicitly mentioned in the Gospels or defined by the Church's pronouncements, the Church's sense of faith has nevertheless spoken out with perfect unanimity over the centuries, would not the rejection of such an opinion on the sole grounds of some personal feeling or some personal argument be an obvious sign that one was taking oneself too seriously? Only in a respectful listening to tradition and a reverent inquiry into the Church's sense of faith, as it lived in the past, is there hope that, when new problems arise, we may be able to sift, in the traditional conceptions, what belongs to the content of revelation from that which is of the times, and thus promote rather than hinder an authentic development of Christian ethics.

Yet a clear distinction must be made between tradition in the sense intended above and the so-called *traditional concepts* of *moral theology*. Like dogmatic theology, moral theology is in the first place a science which constructs its positions under the guidance of faith, yet on *its own responsibility*. Hence the opinions of the moralists offer no other guarantee in the domain of faith than the degree of certainty of intelligently inquiring scholars working under the guidance of their own experience of the faith and trying to keep attuned to the sense of faith of the whole Church. That is why, although their investigations offer welcome material and useful tools for the development of the moral insight of the faith, the path over which the Church's sense of faith reaches its certitudes is not necessarily marked out by their scientific conclusions, and it is not bound by them.

Besides the embodiment of the inner demands of God's grace in a Christian moral law, the Church also needs a general organization of the individual efforts and free initiatives of the children of God for the common good. Hence the Church too will have a complete system of *positive law,* always influenced by the working of God's grace but lacking any divine guarantee—essentially subject, therefore, to the relativity characterizing all human legislation and to the same limitations. The prescriptions of the Church, too, may turn out to be arbitrary, or lag behind the life of the Church, or give rise to grievous abuses. The normal needs for reform in the Church, felt so strongly, for instance, on the occasion of the present Council, will usually operate more specifically on the level of positive legislation, where the Church enjoys no divine guarantee.

The foregoing considerations with regard to the law may have shown one thing very clearly: that it does not make sense to talk in a general way (as happens too often) about the relation between "the" Christian conscience and "the" law. That relation varies very considerably, not only according to the level of law and the kind of law in question, but also according to whether the Christian conscience confronting the law is mature and adult.

## 1. The Adult Christian Conscience

We should perhaps begin with the attitude of the *adult* Christian conscience before the law in its several aspects. The first thing to be said is that *in principle* there can be no opposition between an adult conscience and the law, hence that an opposition *in principle* to the law cannot be a fundamental attitude of the Christian conscience. For maturity of conscience

179

means the conscious welcoming of the direction of one's own development and God's invitation within his Church. It implies a free decision to become fully what one is through one's human abilities and the divine calling. But the law's only aim is to express and clarify the implications of that direction and that calling. Hence in principle the adult person will acknowledge and welcome in the law the imperative of his own striving towards human and Christian adulthood, even though he may be clearly aware of the imperfections in its formulation and thus of the corrections he must introduce into it. To be in principle hostile and opposed to every law may safely be considered an infallible sign of immaturity.

*Ideal spiritual adulthood* of the conscience would consist in this: that the compass of love would point the direction so unfalteringly that the *external law* is no longer needed. In such a man the law has been so fully assimilated, its deepest inspiration is so much a matter of personal experience, that it has become a conscious instinct and an infallible power of discrimination. This power would automatically sift in the law what is an authentic expression of the person's own growth imperative and of the divine calling from what is unadapted, only human and imperfect, which is to be eliminated if he is to remain or become fully himself in loving self-donation.

Something like this adulthood may undoubtedly be seen, if not at the start, at least in the autumn of some saintly lives. In them the "Love and do as you will" of Augustine finds the fullness of its meaning.

But such a maturity of love is rather rare and cannot be considered the usual situation of the average Christian conscience. To say nothing of all the opportunities of growth we have neglected in our own past through weakness and cowardice, the education of most of us as human beings and as Christians has been far from perfect, and a vast number of potentialities have never been developed in us. Authentic adulthood involves also the humble *acknowledgement* of what has *remained infantile* in ourselves, of our bondage to our own past, of all the subjective projections which color and distort our picture of objective reality. Moreover, the adult Christian knows that deeper even than these personal failures and immaturities is *concupiscence,* the lasting repercussion in him, even after the grace of baptism, of the situation of original sin in which he is caught as a child of man and from which he must allow himself to be ever more perfectly saved. He is all too often made painfully aware of how far short his own spiritual stature falls of the full adult stature of Christ and how awfully little the human race, whose life he shares, thinks and reacts in a Christian way.

When he faces a decision of conscience, the adult Christian will not evade his responsibility by depending blindly on the letter of the law. But he will *listen* with gratitude to what the law can provide as a correction of his own views and as a safeguard against the deforming influence of his drives and prejudices. And more than any law he will take the *Person of Christ* as his norm, adopt him as a model and as the test of authenticity.

In the inner law of nature, in the inner demands of God's spirit, in the pronouncements and gestures of the Church, as guaranteed by God, he will unconditionally rediscover the imperative of his own conscience, for he knows that true love cannot contradict itself. Yet as the applications of the law of nature or of grace which he meets in his life become further removed from the very first principles, the influences of the concrete *factors which make up his situation* and of the insight of the person living in that situation keep increasing. This is especially true when it must be decided whether some positive law obliges in a specific instance.

Within these limits—and although the term has acquired a bad reputation because of the abuses to which it has led—we must clearly affirm with the great classical authors that Catholic morality is, in fact, a *situation ethics.* Once a man has sufficiently formed his conscience by attending to the law of nature and of grace, by purifying his intention and gathering solid information, there comes a moment when God's personal invitation in the concrete situation is something no mere legality can wholly discern.

The final act in which the will to action faces the object in its irreducible concreteness, with all its aspects of pondering, deliberating, and finally deciding, belongs to the essentially practical virtue of prudence.

Textbook morality of the last centuries was obviously so wary of the dangers involved in the personal, prudential character of the ultimate decision of conscience, that it endeavored to foresee all possible situations and to spell out in advance the application of the law for each one of these "cases." Such *casuistry* necessarily remains in the realm of theory and abstraction, never getting beyond objective, anonymous and impersonal data. But in the situation I am myself at stake, in a unique pattern of subjective conditions and objective data which cannot be foreseen or described. Every priest has had this brought home to him by his own bewilderment when hearing his first confessions; for years he has studied "cases," now he faces "situations." Even the best pastoral theology cannot bridge that gap. Ultimately the decision comes from the personal conscience. That conscience must be followed and respected, even when, after honestly inquiring and examining the law—in good faith—it errs in its judgment.

\* \* \* \* \*

## b. The Adolescent

A very important, indeed a critical, moment in the education towards religious maturity occurs in the *years of adolescence*. Important because the basic attitudes into which the emerging personality settles during these years will constitute the basis of his adult conception of life. Critical because, between the onset of adulthood in the physical and psychological domain and the spiritual unfolding of the personality, occurs a *psychological vacuum* of quite some duration, in which the growing youth is no longer enough of a child to accept the attitude of authority, and not yet enough of an adult to arrange his life wholly on his own responsibility. The fact that nowadays physiological puberty occurs about one full year earlier than it did two generations ago, whereas spiritual and characterological adulthood occurs not earlier but somewhat later than formerly, renders the problem posited by that vacuum even more acute. Unsolved problems and conflict situations of the first years of life, which scarcely manifested themselves in any perceptible way during the so-called latency period of childhood, now surge ahead with renewed violence; they increase the confusion of the adolescent and make him more difficult for his educators to understand.

However much the adolescent may seem to wish to shake off every influence of his educators, the fact is that he is never so liable to be *really influenced* as during these years, and that influence will be decisive for the positions he will adopt as an adult. More, however, than advice or instruction, the *personality of the educator* will influence him. For he is looking for somebody towards whom he may lift himself up in admiration, a model for the molding of his growing personality, a rock of certitude in the whirlpool of his moods, doubts and questions. If the educator is, so to speak, on the same wavelength as the young man, he can enter into a dialog with him, challenge him to become an adult at those moments when, in discouragement, he feels like letting himself slip back into childhood; let him see, as in a mirror, the authenticity or unauthenticity of his efforts to become a man (or a woman), encourage him and stimulate him, by just being there, in every authentic self-affirmation.

If the educator wants to succeed in his task, he should be especially careful not to take some things too literally, but to search for their meaning within the context of the global psychology of youth. How can he help the young person to become himself if he sees unbridled arrogance in a rebelliousness which is often only a desperate resistance to a helpless sense of constriction; if, behind the most emphatic black-or-white assertions, he is not aware of the request for clarification, not presented as a request, lest the youth's uncertainty be shown up; if, in the criticisms levelled against our Mother the Church, he does not see the boy's clumsy effort to free himself in a symbolic way of his own mother image; if, in youthful idealism, he cannot distinguish between a real urge for self-donation and a flight from reality? Treating symptoms is generally fatal at that age; only *understanding in depth* can really help. This is perhaps most true for sexual problems, which seem to dominate everything in the young man's field of attention and which often occupy the attention of educators too exclusively. One often gathers from young people and their educators the impression that at that age everything depends on sexuality, whereas, on the contrary, sexuality at that age more than ever, depends on all the rest. For like all other phenomena, or more perhaps than all others, the sexual conduct of the young man is a symbol and a symptom. One can learn all about his deepest affective problems from the manner in which he discovers sexuality and integrates it, or fails to integrate it, in his growing personality. And generally it is only by putting order into his affectivity that he will be able to become a real adult in the sexual domain.

Hence everything is deforming at that age which has the aim of maintaining the growing consciousness on a *childish level* or *pushes it back* towards childish forms of experience: nagging investigation of the youth's intimate life; compulsion in the reception of the sacraments; moral sermonizing; submerging the individual in mere herd discipline; anxiety-generating over-emphasis on the dangers of life, especially the dangers of sex and human love; the quantitative multiplication of prayers, instructions in morals, and what are thought of as character-forming readings; the artificial kindling of youthful idealism in a way that is quite out of touch with the possibilities offered by reality, and so on. But equally deforming is all that which, under the pretext of encouraging autonomy, is in fact an *encouragement of narcissistic needs* at the expense of more oblative values: playing with the young people in an infantilizing way (generally the result of some kind of nostalgia for youth on the part of the educator, who thus fulfills the unfulfilled aspirations of his own youth); that naive "understanding" (received by the young people themselves with a pitying smile) of those adults who shout approval of all these youths ever think of; the harmful encouragement given to the shallow aspirations of youth at the expense of the deeper needs. All that really educates, on the contrary, which goes down to the *sources* of the young person's being and takes hold of the deepest cravings for maturity, assisting its development by helping the dream to ripen into action; good will into resolution; spontaneity into creativity; recklessness into courage; the yearning for tenderness into the commitment of love; self-affirmation into self-donation; sincerity of feeling into honesty of life—and whatever invites the young person to pay for this growth the full, undiminished price.

### c. The Adult

What can be done for the re-education of adults in the sphere of moral decision? The discussion of problems of conscience and the clarification of ideas about law and conscience which take place in sermons, discussion groups, centers for religious formation, and so on, can undoubtedly contribute greatly to the maturation of consciences. Yet no automatic results may be expected from *intellectual instruction*. It would be a great pity if the universal mania for instruction should also spread to the field of formation of conscience. The difficulties which inhibit an adult decision of conscience are in part, but not exclusively or even predominantly, of an intellectual nature, and a theoretical realization of the irrationality of anxieties, doubts and inhibitions is not enough to remove them. One does not render a man autonomous by telling him that he ought to be, however forcefully and emphatically one may tell him so and whatever the strength of the arguments employed.

# Piet J. Schoonenberg
## 1911-

*The scientific theory of evolution has challenged the world
of religion to re-evaluate its concepts of God, human, universe,
good and evil. Many persons not adequately introduced to
scientific and/or theological thinking, and even some who were,
for too long assumed either that traditional religious beliefs had
to be protected against modern science or that science had
finally destroyed religion. Neither attitude contributed much to
the progress of mankind.*

*Happily a sufficient number of intellectuals in the twentieth
century had the capacity to approach the science-religion
dilemma with a vision that superceded both science and religion.
They realized that the magnificent discovery of the theory of
evolution offered to theologians at a moment when theological
speculation was wandering through a rather arid desert, the
opportunity to come alive again with a freshness and vigor that
would enable them to construct for modern man a theological
structure capable of absorbing the tremendous advances made
by science. Their spirit of openness and dialogue has made it
possible for Christian thinking to be relevant to the contemporary
world.*

*Man and Sin, the book from which the following selection
is taken, is a product of this spirit. It was written by Fr. Piet
Schoonenberg, Professor of Dogmatic Theology at the Catholic*

*University of Nijmegen, Holland. In it, he re-examines the phenomenon of sin by bringing together his understanding of modern world as shaped by the concept of evolution and his knowledge of the biblical sources for the Christian meaning of sin.*

*The outcome of Schoonenberg's study is an evolutionary picture of the world in which sin and redemption occupy a prominent place. He summarizes that picture as follows: "The whole evolution of creation is crowned by a historical ascent of mankind, crowned in its turn by Christ's presence, which keeps growing too towards his manifestation in the parousia, the beginning of 'God all in all.' That ascent is crossed by a similar ascent of sin, but God brings about the triumph of the ascent in Christ." (from the Epilogue) The book is an elaboration of this powerful insight.*

*As a simple fact, it is not permissible for mankind to treat itself and its relationship to God as revealed through history as a pile of data. Existence is alive, dynamic, evolving, and will not tolerate being fit into neat little compartments.* Man and Sin *makes a significant contribution to ethical thinking, for it establishes a solid foundation on which modern man can adequately evaluate his actions and make the mature decisions that will bring him a step closer to his evolutionary perfection.*

# MAN AND SIN

## CHAPTER 1

### THE ESSENCE OF SIN

### I. The Vocabulary of Holy Scripture

The most usual Hebrew word used for "sinning" is "hātā' ", which is rendered in the Septuagint by ἁ μαρτά νω, a Greek word which is also used to translate its Hebrew synonyms. The Hebrew bible shows a preference for the use of this word, and the Septuagint pushed that preference even further in its translation. Hence it is important to circumscribe accurately its meaning. Originally both the Hebrew and the Greek verb meant to "miss". We can miss our goal or the right path. In this pre-moral meaning the term "hātā' " occurs often enough in the bible to keep that meaning alive for the Israelites. (See Judges xx. 16; Job xvi. 24; Ps. xxv. 8; Isa. lxv. 20.) Most frequently by far that "missing" is used in a moral sense, as in English the prefix "mis" appears in words having an exclusively moral meaning, such as "misbehaviour", "misconduct", "misdemeanour", "misdeed". That "hātā' " really means "to sin" is evident from the fact that man sins "against Yahweh". Even outside the religious sphere the first person of that Hebrew verb often means that one has misbehaved against the person to whom the expression refers. (Gen. xx. 9; Judges xi. 27; I Sam. xxvi. 21; 2 Kings xviii. 14.) But we find these words "I have misbehaved" used especially as a confession before Yahweh, as an admission by man that he was wrong before God, who is right. Thus spoke Pharaoh Akan of Egypt (Exod. ix. 17; x. 10, 16), after he had appropriated something from Agi against Yahweh's orders (Joshua vii. 20); Saul when he committed the same disobedience (I Sam. xv. 24, 30); David when he sinned with Uriah's wife (2 Sam. xii. 13; cf Ps. li. 6), or when he sinned (we do not quite see why) by holding the census. (2 Sam. xxiv. 10, 17.)

Thus, in the books of the Old Testament, the verbs "hātā' "
and "ἁμαρτάνω" acquire the meaning of a misdeed against Yahweh. This entails an inner injustice or guilt, and a rebellion or
offence against God. Both elements are signified respectively by
the Hebrew words "āwŏn" and "pesa' ", which are often joined
to "hātā' " as parallel expressions: "keeping steadfast love for
thousands, forgiving *iniquity and transgression and sin,* but who
will by no means clear the guilty, visiting the iniquity of the
fathers upon the children and the children's children, to the third
and fourth generation". (Exod. xxiv. 7; see also Job xiii. 23; xiv.
16. f.; Ps. xxxii. I f.; Isa. xliii. 24 f.; Ezek. xxi. 29; Dan. ix. 24.)
The word "āwŏn" points to a twisted situation, to something
amiss. It is used preferably for the guilt which is borne as a burden, which may be carried away, taken away, expiated. (Gen. iv.
13; Exod. xxviii. 38; Lev. xvi. 22; Ezek. iv. 4-6; Isa. liii. 4, II; cf
John i. 29.) On the other hand, later Judaism tends in the extra-
canonical books to conceive rather juridically the guilt of sinners
before God. "Iniquity" appears in the documents from Qumran
as the wickedness of the latter times, a notion which we shall
meet again in the New Testament. As against that which is amiss
in the sinner himself, "pesa'" points even more directly to the
rebellion or offence against God. Athough that word easily has
a juridical sound, it refers in the first instance to hostility, resistance, rebelliousness, even among men. (Cf Gen. xxxi. 36; 1. 17;
I Sam. xxiv. 12.) In a directly religious sense "pesa' " does not
occur in Genesis, but we meet it in the bible starting at Exodus
(xxiii. 21). This word is used especially for the sin of Israel as a
whole, for the obstinacy, infidelity, apostasy of the people whom
Yahweh has selected as his own. In that sense "pesa' " occurs
frequently in the prophets. (Hos. vii. 13; viii. I; xiv. 10; Mic. i. 5;
iii. 8; vii. 18; Jer. ii. 8, 29; iii. 13; v. 6; xxxiii. 8; Isa. xliii. 27;
xlvi. 8; xlviii. 8; liii. 12; lix. 13; Ezek. ii. 3; xviii. 31; xx. 38.)
That unfaithfulness and rebellion against the God of the Covenant
is expressed with even more feeling by the Hebrew word "kā'as",
which expressed how Yahweh's jealousy and wrath are provoked
(hence the Septuagint translation παροργίζω and παραζηλῶ).
It is rendered in our language by "hurt the feelings of", "embitter", "challenge", "provoke". (Judges ii. 12; I Kings xiv. 9 f.;
xvi. 33; Deut. iv. 25; ix. 18; xxxii. 21; Jer. xi. 17; xxxii. 29, 32;

Ezek. viii. 17.) Almost synonymous is the Hebrew word "na'as" (Septuagint: παροξύνω), which is rendered by "scorn", "revile", "disdain", "spurn", "embitter". (Num. xiv. II; xvi. 30; Deut. xxxi. 20; Isa. i. 4; v. 24; Ps. lxxiv. 10, 18.) The notion of sin as an offence against God derives from these words, although the Latin expressions under which "na'as" entered our theology— "offendere", "offensa", "offensio"—occur seldom in the Vulgate.

Turning now towards the New Testament, we obviously expect to see the innermost aspect of sin emphasized. True, the juridical terminology of late Judaism has not disappeared. Surprisingly enough, we meet it again in the best-known Christian prayer for forgiveness, the Our Father: "et dimitte nobis debita nostra, sicut et nos dimittimus debitoribus nostris". (Matt. vi. 12.) But the word "debt" (ὀφείλημα, debitum is used here only for something which we owe God, while the corresponding terms "forgive" and "forgiveness" (ἀφίημι, ἄφεσις; remittere, remissio, to be translated as "remitting" or cancelling") are gradually replaced, outside the Synoptic Gospels, by terms which do not derive from the juridical sphere, thus emphasizing better the inner nature of forgiveness, hence of sin itself. This meaning is evident from the other terms which designate sin in the books of the New Testament. Among them the least striking is the word ἁμάρτημα, which occurs generally in the plural (cf Mark iii. 28; I Cor. vi. 18; Rom. iii. 25) and which, when used in the singular, refers to a very special sin, the "eternal sin" against the Holy Spirit. (Mark iii. 29.) It is even more evident with ἁμαρτία. That word occurs often in the plural, being always plural in the Apocalypse, preferably in fixed formulas such as "the confession of sins" (Mark. i. 5; Matt. iii. 6; I John i. 9; Jas. v. 16), "remission of sins" (Mark i. 4; Luke iii. 3; Matt. xii. 31; John xx. 23; Acts ii. 38; Col. i. 14; Jas. v. 15; I John i. 9; ii. 12), "Christ saves us from sin" or "died for our sins" (Matt. i. 21; I Cor. xv. 3; Gal. i. 4; I Pet. iii. 18; I John ii. 2; iii. 5; iv. 10; Rev. i. 5), and in quotations from the Old Testament (Rom. iv. 7 f.; xi. 27; I Pet. ii. 22, 24). This plural designates several sinful actions. For that purpose the New Testament uses other words such as "misstep" (παράπτωμα) or "transgression (παράβασις). The former occurs mostly in the plural. (Mark xi. 25 f.; Matt. vi. 14 f.; 2 Cor. v. 19;

Gal. vi. I; Rom. iv. 25; Col. ii. 13; Eph. i. 7; ii. I.) We meet παρά-
παράβασις exclusively in Paul and in the Epistle to the Hebrews;
it designates sin as a transgression of the Law. (Gal. iii. 19; Rom.
ii. 23; iv. 15; v. 14; I Tim. ii. 14; Heb. ii. 2; ix. 15.)

The singular ἡ ἁμαρτία, "the sin", acquires an increasingly
special meaning, as the tradition of the New Testament pro-
gresses. "The sin" is seen as belonging more to the inner man
than "the sins" or "the transgressions"; it becomes also a power
which rules over the whole of mankind. We see this first with
Paul, especially in those epistles in which he insists most upon
the truth that only our faith in Christ saves us from sin, in the
Epistles to the Galatians and to the Romans. In Ecclesiasticus
(xxvii. 10) sin has been personified once as lying in ambush; in
the above mentioned epistles of Paul that personification returns
constantly, not only does sin ensnare but it also rules: "But the
scripture consigned all things to sin, that what was promised to
faith in Jesus Christ might be given to those who believe", the
Apostle says in the Epistle to the Galatians (iii. 22) in order to
describe the situation of unredeemed humanity. "Scripture" here
means the operation of God, as revealed in Scripture. (Cf Rom.
xi. 32.) Thus, sin has won a ruling position, as further elaborated
in Romans. It has entered the world" (Rom. v. 12); we might
say sin has appeared upon the stage of the world. There "it has
ruled". (v. 21; cf vi. 14.) Men are "slaves of sin" (vi. 6, 17, 20),
"sold out to sin" (vii. 14), or redeemed from sin (vi. 22). Sin
pays its salary (vi. 23), and has its law, "the law of sin dwelling
in my limbs" (vii. 23; viii. 2). It lives in man (vii. 7, 20); that is
why our concrete human nature is "the flesh of sin" (viii. 3)
and why the body of unredeemed man is "the body of sin" (vi.
6), even as the body of him who has been saved is "a member of
Christ" (I Cor. vi. 15). In man sin dies or relives. (Rom. vii. 8 f.)
In the Gospel and the first Epistle of John ἡ ἁμαρτία "the sin"
is described, with less imagery, but even more emphatically, as a
situation in man and in mankind. If out of the relatively many
passages in which the singular form "sin" occurs in these two
writings of John (13 and 11 times respectively), we pick out the
most striking, "the sin" appears almost always as a lasting inner
disposition. Only once do we meet "being a slave of sin". (John
viii. 34.) On the other hand, for John even more than for Paul,

the devil is the ruler over and the firstborn of sinning humanity. Everywhere else John sees sin less as lording it over man than as residing in man, as a situation of man: "You will die in your sin" (John viii. 21); "your sin remains" (John ix. 41). Sin and being born of God are diametrically opposed. (I John iii. 8 f.) Not only individual man but also "the world" too is in sin: the Lamb of God "takes away the sin of the world". (John i. 19.) What kind of situation in man and mankind "the sin" constitutes is most clearly explained by the fact that John identifies the sin with ἡ ἀνομία. (I John iii. 4.)

This word deserves special attention. Ἀνομία contains the root "νόμος", law. Hence it is generally translated as "violation of the law", "denial of the law", "illegality", "transgression of the law", and similar expressions. But the meaning of a word is determined not only by its etymology but also by its use. In classical Greek ἀνομία possesses indeed the etymological meaning of "transgression of the law", hence of "disorder", "anarchy", but it is remarkable that this connection with "law" disappears in the biblical context. The many Hebrew words for "sin", of which we have discussed a few, are translated by the Septuagint with ἀμαρτία and ἀνομία, whereby the latter word becomes practically synonymous with the former. Therefore, it means "sin" without any further reference to the law. In the New Testament, too, we find this general meaning, namely in quotations from the Old Testament, in which the plural form occurs most frequently. (Rom. iv. 7; Ps. xxxii, I; Heb. i. 9; Ps. xlv. 8; Heb. x. 17; Jer. xxxi. 34.) But the singular form also shows the same development which we have met in ἀμαρτία; moreover, it acquires also a decided eschatological accent. This is already true in an apocryphal writing, the Testament of the Twelve Patriarchs, and especially in the Qumran documents. Ἀνομία is the injustice or the wickedness in which the children of Belial, the followers of Satan, have hardened themselves at the end of the times and from which the sons of justice must keep away. That "iniquity" or "wickedness" is never contrasted with the law, but with God's salvific will, designated as "truth". Likewise in the writings of the New Testament ἀνομία has the character of the inner hardening which will befall humanity at the end of time. Here also, as previously, the text does not refer to the Law, it refers to Christ's coming in judgement. In the Synoptic Gospels we meet ἀνομία only in four passages of Matthew. On the day of judgement Christ will say, "I never knew you; depart from me you evildoers!" (Matt. vii. 23.) Likewise on that day, "The Son of man will send his angels and they will gather out of his kingdom all causes of sin and all evildoers." (Matt. xiii. 41.) When Jesus tells the Pharisees in his famous denunciation, "So you also outwardly appear righteous to men, but within you are full of hypocrisy and iniquity" (Matt. xxiii. 28), the word stands in an eschatological perspective, as evidenced by the context, "You serpents, you brood of vipers, how are you to escape being sentenced to hell?" (xxiii. 33.) Finally the end of time is manifestly described in Jesus' word, "And because wickedness is multiplied, most men's love will grow cold." (Matt. xxiv. 12.) With Paul the meaning of an expression as "from iniquity to iniquity" (Rom. vi. 19) is not so manifest at first sight, but in other passages, where the Apostle himself uses the word ἀνομία, we find this same meaning again. We find the whole opposition as presented in the Qumran documents transposed upon a Christian level, where Paul writes:

> Do not be mismated with unbelievers. For what partnership have righteousness and iniquity? Or what fellowship has light with darkness? What accord has Christ with Belial? Or what has a believer in common with an unbeliever? What agreement has the temple of God with idols? [2 Cor. vi. 14 f.]

We discover the eschatological background where Paul speaks of "the apparition of the glory of our great God and Saviour Jesus Christ, who gave himself for us to redeem us from all iniquity and to purify for himself a people of his own who are zealous for good deeds". (Titus ii. 13 f.) The ἀνομία is most manifestly described as impenitence at the end of times when it is connected with the Antichrist, "the unjust" (ὁ ἄνομος), who manifests himself as the fulfilment of the "mystery of iniquity", which is already at work now. (2 Thess. ii. 7 f.) Out of the whole context of later Jewish and of New Testament literature we must also understand ἀνομία in the only passage in which it occurs in John, where sin is identified with it. "Whoever commits sin, commits also ἀνομία ; and sin is the ἀνομία." (I John iii. 4.) Here, as in the texts which we have just mentioned, there is no reference to the Law, so that etymological translations, such as "lawlessness", lack any foundation. A few commentators suppose that John wished to remind his readers that transgressing the Law is a sin even for Christians, an idea which we find also in the gospels (cf Matt. v. 17-19; Luke xvi. 17), but of which we discover no inkling here. To convey this meaning he ought to have said "lawlessness is sin", using an order of words which is the opposite of the one he did use. From these considerations it follows already that ἀνομία should preferably be rendered as "iniquity" or "wickedness", with the whole content which that notion posses in the texts just mentioned. Then John's saying acquires a meaning which fits its context perfectly. As hope in Christ manifests itself in being pure (I John iii. 3), as remaining in Chirst shows itself in not sinning (iii. 6), as being just expresses itself in practising justice (iii. 7), as being born out of God entails that one does not sin, nay that one cannot sin (ii. 9), so on the other hand "He who commits sin is of the devil; for the devil has sinned from the beginning. The reason the Son of God appeared was to destroy the works of the devil." (iii. 8.) John also says the same thing in the text under consideration (iii. 4): just as our good works are manifestations of our living out of God, of our justice as brought about by him, so every sin is a manifestation of the iniquity or wickedness which came from Satan at the beginning and which will persist until the end.

## 2. Sin is against God himself

From the way the bible uses all the abovementioned words, it is quite evident that sin is against God himself. For the Greeks sinning means going against an essential law of nature, which the Stoics connected with God. But the Greek gods themselves are archetypes or basic laws rather than rulers. In Israel, Yahweh is the Lord, not by ruling arbitrarily, but through a loving Covenant with his people. In that covenant the Law has a place. The Old Testament knows only the Law which comes from God. All its ritual, civil or moral laws are supposed to have been given by God into the hands of Moses; that is why they are mentioned in the story of the desert wanderings. A few passages show that sometimes an appeal was made to natural custom: "such a thing is not done in Israel" (Gen. xxxiv. 7; 2 Sam. xiii. 12), but as the people realize more fully that they are Yahweh's people, their laws become Yahweh's laws. The Pentateuch is the record of this process. In it God gives the Law together with the Covenant.

For Pharisaism the Law will come to stand outside the personal relation between God and man, but this is not true at all for the prophets. It is not even true for the books of the Law, as evident, for instance, from the story of the concluding of the Covenant on Mount Sinai. In the apparition which preceds the granting of the Law Yahweh says, "Now therefore, if you will obey my voice and keep my covenant, you shall be my own possession among all peoples; for all the earth is mine." (Exod. xix. 5.) When, after that apparition, the Covenant is stated [confirmed] by sprinkling blood on the altar and the people, the Commandments of God are read from the book of the Covenant. That book of the Law is so important for the Jewish conception of the Covenant that in Hebrews ix. 19 f. the book rather than the altar is sprinkled with the blood of the Covenant, as if it were the representative of God. The heart of the Law, the Ten Commandments, is interrupted several times when God introduces himself to his people. He does so not by calling himself simply "God", but "Yahweh, your God" (five times in Exod. xx. 2-12). Thus, within the most legalistic sections of the Old Testament, we may already see sin as an infraction of the Law of the covenant, hence as a revolt against the God who wants to be Israel's God.

Especially in the prophets sin is an aversion from and unfaithfulness to Yahweh himself; hence it is placed in the heart rather than in the wrong deed. We see that aversion, that rebelliousness, that lack of faith which precede the act of transgressing the Law already in the story of the sin in paradise, where it is presented as the wish of possessing autonomously the knowledge of good and of evil, of being independently the Law unto oneself (Gen. iii. 4-6). Isaiah points to such a false autonomy in his people when he says, "Woe to those who call evil good and good evil, who put darkness for light and light for darkness, who put bitter for sweet and sweet for bitter!" (Isa. v. 20.) The unwillingness to submit to God is several times represented as an unbending hard neck, as stiff-neckedness, as stubbornness. (Exod. xxxii. 9;

xxxiii. 3, 5; xxxiv. 9; Deut. ix. 13; x. 16; xxxi. 27; 2 Kings xvii.
14; 2 Chron. xxx. 8; Neh. ix. 16 f.; Isa. xlviii. 4; Jer. viii. 26;
xvii. 23; xix. 15; Baruch ii. 30.) This unbending neck, which one
single time is connected with the "unwillingness of the shoul-
ders" (Neh. ix. 29), refers to the rejection of the "yoke" of
Yahweh's Commandments. A more interior conception of the
sinful attitude puts it in the heart. Before the exit from Egypt
"Pharaoh's heart was hardened". (Exod. iv. 21; vii. 3, 13; ix. 12;
x. 20, 27; xi. 10; xiv. 8.) But Israel's heart also gets hardened
against Yahweh; likewise that of the individual sinner. (Isa. lxiii.
17; Ezek. ii. 4; Job. xli. 15.) When man repents he should tear
up that hardened heart, rather than his garments. (Joel ii. 13.)
That heart should be "crushed" (Ps. li. 19) and that "crushing",
in its several Latin translations (contritio, attritio, compunctio)
has become the scholastic term for "contrition". The sinful heart
is unclean and alien to the people of Yahweh; it is uncircumcised
and it must be circumcised. (Lev. xxvi. 41; Jer. iv. 4; ix. 25.)
It is a heart of stone, and the miracle of the messianic message
will consist in this: Yahweh will replace that heart of stone by a
"heart of flesh". (Ezek. xi. 19; xxxvi. 26.) The *Miserere* affirms
that this gift of a new heart must be called a creation. (Ps. li. 12.)
The stiff neck and the hardened or uncircumcised heart are the
most telling expressions known to the Old Testament for a sinful
disposition; sometimes it combines both. (Deut. x. 16; 2 Chron.
xxxvi. 13.) After Christ, Stephen will again use the language of
the prophets, when he addresses his fellow Jews: "You stiff-
necked people, uncircumcised in heart and ears, you always resist the Holy Spirit. As your fathers did, so do you." (Acts vii. 51.)

In all these expressions sin is gradually placed more in the
core of the person; likewise it is considered more and more as a
turning away from the divine person who wishes to meet us, as
a breaking of the Covenant with Yahweh. As such, sin finds its
most complete form in idolatry. This is the first sin forbidden
by Yahweh in the Ten Commandments (Exod. xx. 3; Deut. v. 7),
and the first one which many prophets reproach to the Jewish
people (Amos ii. 4; Hos. ii. 4; Mic. i. 7; Jer. i. 16; Zeph. i. 4;
Baruch i. 22; Isa. lvii. 5; Ezek. vi. 1). Since the acknowledgement
of Yahweh as the sole God is the foundation of the whole morally good attitude of man, so one might see idolatry as the root

197

of all sin. That is why the Book of Wisdom describes how all kind of wretchedness derives from idolatry (Wisd. of Sol. xiv. 22-31), and Paul, imitating that passage in the New Testament, says that God delivers the heathens over to their impurity and mutual enmities on account of that idolatry. (Rom. i. 24 f., 28.) "For the worship of abominable idols is the cause, and the beginning and end of all evil." (Wisd. of Sol. xiv. 27.) In our present-day theology we often define sin as the act of turning away from God and towards the creature. In the bible it is rather a turning away from God towards the idols; on the other hand, conversion to the faith is a return. Later we hope to show that the positive element of sin, that towards which the sinner turns, is more exactly expressed in the biblical concept than in the usual definition. But now we are treating of the negative element in sin, the turning away from God. When the Book of Wisdom and Paul speak of the idolatry of the heathens, they mainly underline in that sin the denial of the real relation to the Creator. For the prophets, on the other hand, idolatry is especially a falling away from the God of the Covenant, a breaking of the alliance—adultery, misconduct towards Yahweh. That image may be found in almost all the texts we have just quoted, and in the prophets, starting with Hosea, Israel is often represented in its sinfulness as the adulterous woman; witness the two allegories of Ezekiel (chapters xvi and xxiii). Jesus will take over the language of the prophets about his fellow Jews when he speaks of a "wicked and adulterous generation." (Matt. xii. 39; xvi. 4; cf Hos. i. 2.)

As was already evident from our brief study of the use of words, the reference to God in sin is even more emphasized in the New Testament. Sin does not stand in opposition to the Law but in opposition to God's offer of grace, to God's demand, as they come to us in Christ. It is especially the Pharisees that Jesus really reproaches for their sins, the precise men who do not feel they need a physician because of their meticulous fidelity to the Law. (Mark ii. 17; viii. 12 f.; Luke iii. 31 f.) That is why the Pharisees deserve as their first reproach the denunciation, "But woe to you, scribes and Pharisees, hypocrites! because you shut the kingdom of heaven against men" (Matt. xxiii. 13); and why at the end of that discourse they are called the heirs of those who killed the prophets. (Matt. xxiii. 34-9.) The heaviest punishments threaten those who do not accept Christ and the kingdom of God: "But, whoever denies me before men, I also will deny before my Father who is in heaven." (Matt. x. 33; Luke xii. 9.) The cities which have not been converted by Christ's miracles may expect a harsher verdict on the day of judgement than Tyre, Sidon, and Sodom (Matt. xi. 20-24; Luke x. 12-15); and they will be condemned by the Ninevites and by the Queen of Sheba (Matt. xii. 38-42; Luke xi. 29-32). Finally, he who scandalizes the little ones, or, literally, who puts a stumbling-block ($\sigma\kappa\acute{\alpha}\nu\delta\alpha\lambda o\nu$) before their fath in Christ, deserves to be mercilessly thrown into the sea. (Matt. xviii. 6; Luke xvii. 2.) These are the greatest sins. All of them are some form of lack of faith in Christ; even he who does not love his fellow men and thus deserves the everlasting fire is punished that way because "you have not done it for me". (Matt. xxv. 41-6.) This lack of faith is a rejection of Christ not only in his human appearance but also in the divine mission and the power of the spirit with which he has come. Hence the difference between the forgivable sin against the Son of Man and the unforgivable sin against the Holy Spirit. (Mark iii. 28 f.; Matt. xii. 31 f.; Luke xii. 10.) The "sin against the Holy Spirit" is sin in its deepest malice. It is not explicitly identified with the $\dot{\alpha}\nu o\mu\acute{\iota}\alpha$ which we have just described. Yet the fact that the warning against this sin is directed to the same Pharisees whose "iniquity" Jesus stigmatizes afterwards (see Matt. xii. 34, and xxiii. 1, 13, 15, 23, 28), the fact especially that both are equated with a rejection of the Son of Man in his message and his work (see Mark iii. 22, 30; Matt. xii. 24, 30; xxiii. 13; Luke xii. 9) and that both end in eternal damnation (see Mark iii. 29; Matt. xii. 32; xxiii. 33; Luke xii. 10), entitles us to identify "iniquity" with the "sin against the Holy Spirit". Thus, in the Synoptic Gospels sin is presented mainly in its final outcome. Moreover, it is also faintly presented in its origin. As there is a hardening which goes beyond the transgression of the Law, so there is a hardening which gives rise to that transgression. We have already remarked that Jesus brings the Law to perfection by teaching how to accomplish it from the heart, by demanding the inner disposition and not merely the external observance. (Matt. v and vi.) In this way the interior sin comes naturally to the fore, especially the "misconduct of the heart". (Matt. v. 28.) That heart is the source of good and evil. (Matt. xii. 34 f.; Luke vi. 45; Mark vii. 6-14; Matt. xv. 8-20.) Even as conversion, which is the compunction of the heart, produces fruits corresponding to that compunction (καρπὸς ἄξιος τῆς μετανοίας: Matt. iii. 8; Luke iii. 8), so the person who is wicked in his heart is a bad tree producing bad fruit (Matt. xii. 33-5; Luke vi. 43-5).

We find this doctrine about the interior completion and the origin of the sinful action in the whole New Testament, especially in the writings of Paul and of John. For Paul's conception of hardening in sin it is enough to remind the reader of that which has been said about ἀνομία in his epistles, especially about the "man of iniquity" and "the mystery of iniquity", which he mentions also in his oral teaching (2 Thess. ii. 5). Especially worthy of notice is Paul's opinion that sin precedes the transgression of the Law and manifests it. Within the Old Testament we met that opinion, for instance in the description of the sin in the paradise story (Genesis iii), a story to which Paul makes several allusions; namely, in the Epistle to the Romans. We have already seen how in Romans v. 12-14 Paul describes the entrance of sin into the world, and its domination over man, even before the Law had been given:

> Law came in, to increase the trespass; but where sin increased, grace abounded all the more. [Rom. v. 20; cf. iv. 15; Gal. iii. 19]

so that the domination of sin is removed only when man is "not under the Law". (Rom. vi. 14.) This is thoroughly explained later on in the same Epistle. (Rom. vii. 7-13.) It seems that Paul borrows his opinion from the narration in Genesis iii, in which the snake, by presenting God's prohibition as a challenge, arouses in the first parents the wish to be like unto God. The only difference is that the apostle substitutes sin for the snake. This sin misuses the Law in order to take shape in transgressions:

> For sin, finding opportunity in the commandment, deceived me and by it killed me. So the law is holy, and the commandment is holy and just and good. Did that which is good, then, bring death to me? By no means! It was sin, working death in me through what is good, in order that sin might be shown to be

sin, and through the commandment might become sinful beyond measure. [Rom. vii. 11-13]

This is the apostle's strongest utterance not only about the Law
but also about sin. Let us not insist here upon the fact that,
according to Paul, this unmasking of sin by the Law ultimately
promotes salvation, because it arouses the need for a redeemer.
We simply remark how sin, as a situation or an attitude, is present in man even before turning into transgression of the Law,
and how, after becoming transgression, it leads into ἀνομία, when
man resists God and puts himself above him, so that he himself
may be god. (2 Thess. ii. 4.) In the Synoptic Gospels this hardening is equated with the sin against the Holy Spirit. Paul, on the
other hand, considers every sin as opposed to that Spirit. This
follows not only from a warning not to sadden the Holy Spirit
of God (Eph. iv. 30), but also from the fact that the Spirit leads
the children of God (Rom. viii. 14). Redeemed man is "spiritual",
nay, he himself is "spirit". On the other hand, he who still lives
in sin is "carnal" and "flesh". The concept "flesh" is the summary of what man *is* under sin, and sin, every sin, is a "work of
the flesh". (Gal. v. 19-21.)

We find the same elements again in John, with even more
emphasis upon eschatological hardening. In John's writings more
than in the other books of the New Testament, it is manifest
that the final times have already dawned. Hence, the choice for
or against Christ is a final decision; choosing against him means
choosing Hell:

He who believes in him is not condemned; he who
does not believe is condemned already, because he
has not believed in the name of the only Son of God.
[John iii. 18] He who believes in the Son has eternal
life; he who does not obey the Son shall not see life,
but the wrath of God rests upon him. [John iii. 36] I
told you that you would die in your sins, for you will
die in your sins unless you believe that I am he. [John
viii. 24]

The sin *par excellence*, the lack of faith in the Son of God, is
represented here as a lasting sin. We might identify it with ἀνομία
and consider these words about the permanence of sin as an

illustration of John's saying "sin is iniquity". (I John iii. 4.) This lasting sin should also be identified with the "sin against the Holy Spirit" mentioned by the Synoptic Gospels. The fact that this sin will be forgiven neither in the present nor in the future life is even more strongly emphasized by John, when he speaks of a "sin unto death"; he adds that one should not pray for him who commits this sin (I John v. 16); he relates that Jesus himself did not pray "for the world". (John xvii. 9.)

Hence John, more explicitly perhaps than any other sacred writer, speaks of a final hardening, a definitive turning away from the Son of God. But he is also aware that sin stands at the origin, that it precedes our meeting with Christ. For all the texts which we have quoted above about the permanence of sin presuppose that man *is* already in sin and that he can be saved from it only by God's Son. Paul's idea that a sinful situation precedes the meeting with the Law is not mentioned by John, who considers only the meeting with Christ. It is not sinful concupiscence which leads to transgression of the Law and to bad actions, but these evil actions lead away from Christ:

> And this is the judgment, that the light has come into the world, and men loved the darkness rather than light, because their deeds were evil. For every one who does evil hates the light, and does not come to the light, lest his deeds should be exposed. But he who does what is true comes to the light, that it may be clearly seen that his deeds have been wrought in God. [John iii. 19 f.]

Sin is infidelity, and also hatred, hatred against the light, which Christ himself is, hence hatred against the Son and the Father. (John xv. 18, 23-5.)

Sin is opposed to God and to Christ, to God as he meets us in Christ. But God is the Creator, who causes man to exist: he wishes to be a father for man. That is why he sends us his only begotten Son as a true fellow man. Hence, our relation to God does not exclude, but includes our relation to our fellow men. Even the Old Testament is aware of this, albeit not with the fullness and consistency of the New Testament. The prophets reproach those wealthy Jews who, while carefully peforming

202

the worship of Yahweh, oppress the poor. The prophets side with the poor; hence, Yahweh himself favours them. Thus the sin against one's fellow man is experienced and confessed mainly because Israel's God cares for that fellow man. When Nathan is sent to David after the latter's adultery, the prophet makes the King aware of his sin first by comparing it with an injustice among men, next by announcing how David has scorned Yahweh, to whom he owes everything. So David confesses, "I have sinned against Yahweh." (2 Sam. xiii. 13.) The *Miserere*, which is presented as "a psalm of David after the Prophet Nathan had come to him because he had sinned with Bethsabe" (Ps. li. 1 f.), sees that sin only as directed against God (1. 6, "tibi soli peccavi"). It is true that the teachings of the prophets have contributed to the social awareness of Deuteronomy, which is concerned not only with the weaker members of the Jewish nation, the "widows and the orphans", but also with the "alien within your gates". Yet the most consistent teaching of brotherly love comes from the incarnate Son of God.

We might summarize Jesus' teaching as recorded in the Synoptic Gospels in this respect under three headings: First, the commandment of loving one's neighbour is like unto the commandment of loving God. Hence, brotherly love is equal to love for God, although one's neighbour is, of course, not equal to God. (Mark xii. 28-34; Matt. xxii. 34-40; Luke x. 25-8.) Secondly, my neighbour is everybody who meets me, even my foe, so that here every conflict should be overlooked. (Luke x. 29-30; Matt. v. 43-8; Luke vi. 27-36.) Finally, the neighbour is not an "occasion for loving God". Quite the opposite is true: a favour done to the neighbour by him who does not know Christ is considered as done to Christ. (Matt. xxv. 31-46.) This doctrine is summarized in John as follows: love for one's neighbour means that man associates himself in the love which proceeds from the Father through Christ towards men. (John xiii. 34 f; I John iv. 7-12.) Through this revelation the Law loses all the arbitrariness which it might eventually possess in the vision of the Old Testament; it becomes an exigency deriving from God's relation to all of us, and likewise from our relation to each other. Sin becomes the offence against love for God and love for one's neighbour.

The fact that modern man feels that sin is first and foremost an offence against his fellow man constitutes a considerable progress compared with a conception in which God's commandments were presented mainly as extrinsic prescriptions and where his worship turned us away sometimes (frequently even, although not always) from the love of our fellow men. That development lies to some extent within the line of the New Testament, but on the condition that this orientation continues to acknowledge the God and Christ of the New Testament, or that it discovers them again in faith. For he who sins against man sins against a being who stands open to his Creator and for whom that Creator wishes to be a father in Christ.

### 3. Sin proceeds from our Freedom

When sin is defined as a transgression of God's law, we add that it is a *voluntary* transgression. In the Old Testament this is not always so evident. In the whole bible the interest for human activity is more religious than psychological; modern concepts such as "responsibility" and "conscience" seldom appear. "Freedom in the bible is a sociological rather than a psychological concept; it develops, therefore, into the "freedom of the children of God", not into a proper concept of "freedom of the will". In Israel's human legislation a difference is made between intentional and unintentional misdemeanours. (See the law on the cities of refuge: Exod. xxi. 13 f.; Deut. iv. 41-3; xix. 1-13.) Yet frequently even the crime committed out of ignorance draws a punishment, although a lighter one. (Cf Luke xii. 48.) For God, too, unintentional transgressions must be expiated with a sacrifice for sin (Lev. iv and v; Num. xv. 22-9), while at times Yahweh punishes without any mention of the question of guilt, as with Saul's sacrifice at Gilgal (I Sam. xiii. 7-14) and with Uzzah's touching the holy Ark (2 Sam. vi. 6 f.). Yet, in the Old Testament a principle is laid down, especially by the prophets, which will do away with these legalistic and magic conceptions. That principle states, "God looks into the heart." For the heart is the inner centre of the person, the seat not only of feelings but also, and mainly, of free will as the seat of good and evil. The prophets especially teach the supremacy of the heart in the Covenant with Yahweh as we mentioned above:

Piet J. Schoonenberg

The Lord sees not as man sees; man looks on the
outward appearance; but the Lord looks on the
heart. [I Sam. xvi. 7] He will punish his people, "because this people draw near with their mouth and
honour me with their lips, while their hearts are far
from me, and their fear of me is a commandment of
men learned by rote". [Isa. xxix. 13]

Circumcision itself, that sign of belonging to God's people, has
to yield to "the circumcision of the heart", and an uncircumcised
heart bespeaks the most thorough unfaithfulness to Yahweh.
(Lev. xxvi. 41; Deut. xxx. 6; Jer. iv. 4; ix. 25; Ezek. xliv. 7-9).
Hence, conversion from sin means compunction of a heart that
had first hardened into a stone. A heart which goes through such
a renovation is a sacrifice agreeable to the Lord (Ps. li. 19), but
it is, first and foremost, God's own creature and gift (Ps. li. 15;
Ezek. xi. 19; xxxvi. 26). Love for God must proceed from one's
"whole heart". (Deut. vi. 5.) Hence:

Keep your heart with all vigilance; for from it flow
the springs of life. [Prov. iv. 23] Every way of a
man is right in his own eyes, but the Lord weighs the
heart. [Prov. xxi. 2]

These words of Scripture provide us with the principle of that
which is good and evil in our activity, not according to outside
criteria, but religiously and morally speaking. That principle is
the heart, the centre of the person, the free decision. The concrete manner in which Scripture considers man rules out any
mention of sins or good actions which would be merely interior.
On the other hand, the conception of the heart as origin of sin
progressed to such a maturity that in the story of the sin in
paradise (Genesis iii) and in Job (xxxi) we discover a description
of sinful thoughts and desires. Sinful thoughts and wishes are
always a first step towards sinful actions.

That conception, which prevailed already in the Old Testament, rules unchallenged in the New Testament. Jesus observes
the Law of God, and he demands also that it be observed. (Matt.
v. 17-19.) But he wants it to be observed specifically as the Law
of God, assumed into the Covenant with God. He brings it to
greater perfection mainly by interiorizing it (Matt. v. 21-30) as

when he equates hatred and impure desires with murder and adultery. Negatively, this means that he rids the Law of the "traditions of men"; namely, in his discussion of eating with unwashed hands. (Mark vii. 1-23; Matt. xv. 1-20.) Thereby Jesus makes his own the word of Isaiah on the opposition between lips and heart; he declares that man is defiled not by what enters the mouth but by what comes out of the mouth, therefore from the heart:

> For from within, out of the heart of man, come evil thoughts, fornication, theft, murder, adultery, coveting, wickedness, deceit, licentiousness, envy, slander, pride, foolishness. All these evil things come from within, and they defile a man. [Mark vii. 21 f.]

Thus, we see Christ in his moral teaching as an heir of the prophets, as he completes their doctrine. In the final analysis he already does what Paul will explicitly formulate as follows: fulfilling the Law through love, through the two commandments of love, love for God and especially love for one's fellow man. (Mark xii. 28-31; Matt. xxii. 34-40; Luke x. 25-8.) This brings to the fore a new kind of sin: omitting to do for the least ones of his what love demands. (Matt. xxv. 41-6.) In this way Jesus clashes with the exterior cultivation of the law as practised by the Pharisees, and he reproaches them with a sin which is specifically a sin of the heart, hypocrisy (mainly Matt. vi and xxiii). We have already seen how this conflict discloses the deepest hardening of sin, the sin against the Holy Spirit and the ἀνομία. This consideration shows clearly how everywhere Jesus places man's heart before God, the heart as the root of virtue and of sin, or, in our terminology, the person's free decision as the foundation of religion and morality. It is evident that the writers of the New Testament continue to develop that doctrine. Suffice it to point to the primacy of love (cf I Cor. xiii; Gal. v. 14; vi. 2; John xv. 12) and to the doctrine of conscience as the inner norm of what is good and sinful for pagans, who have no law (Rom. ii. 12-15), and for Christians in connection with meat offered to the idols (I Cor. viii and x). Although Paul and John, as explained above, have emphasized the power of sin in man, they have not done away with the freedom of the will. That freedom is evident in Paul, not only from the passages treating of conscience but also from all his exhortations and warnings in the moral order. (Cf I Cor. vi. 18; Rom. vi. 19; Eph. vf.; Col. iii f.)

Hence, both Testaments clearly acknowledge that order of the heart, of freedom, in its peculiar moral and religious character. The specific nature of man's response becomes manifest within the Covenant with God, and also the free decision as origin of moral activity. The church will defend that development of the freedom of the will; for example, against Manichesism and astrology, against all denials of the *liberum arbitrium* in fallen man, or, finally, against a certain tutiorism which demands penance even for involuntary wrong actions. Free will as the basis of morality has also been discovered outside of revelation. But the remnants of dynamistic and magical ways of thinking and the menace of legalism which we meet in Scripture make it evident that the supernatural dialogue with God has had a very fecundating and liberating effect in bringing man to the discovery of his own freedom and responsibility. Within the realm of revelation the discovery of the living God historically precedes the discovery of the moral life, and the latter becomes explicit only in the reflections of the church, an unfolding helped among other things by Greek philosophy. It is the discovery of the heart, of the centre of the person, of the free decision for which man is responsible. What makes man good or bad before God is in truth not the qualities which can be noticed or measured, or the consequences of his actions, but the response of the free person which takes shape in these actions. To be sure, that outer and objective structure of his activity is important, very important, but the deepest value lies in the response of the heart. Herein the person expresses himself as such. As long as this is not the case, man acts like the merely material bodies of this world in the exterior elements of his activities and in reflex activity. These "activities of man" (actus hominis) differ profoundly from moral actions, actions of man as man, of the person as person, "human activities" (actus humani). The latter proceed from freedom, that specific feature of the person, the voluntarity (voluntareitas). Since human activities are performed upon this earth, where man can still choose even with regard to his final end, they derive especially from the power of free choice (the *liberum arbitrium*). How this inner derivation of good actions and of sins goes together with their outside manifestation will be discussed in the next paragraph.

### 4. Summarizing Description of Sin

Sin belongs, therefore, to the moral-religious order, that order of action and of self-utterance in which man realizes himself as a person. It is a negative reaction, a refusal and a resistance. Sin is a No of the human person, who shuts himself off and hardens himself when openness and self-donation are expected. As the bible puts it, it is the human heart turning into stone. That to which sin says No has already been illustrated from the bible. It is God, but likewise one's fellow man, nay, the whole of creation. Turning away from God necessarily alienates the sinner also from God's privileged creature, and the other way round. When sin is defined as "a turning away from God towards a creature" (aversio a Deo, conversio ad creaturam), that formula, with all the fine explanations it may receive, is, by itself, incorrect, and a source of harmful misunderstandings, even of an unchristian conception of asceticism. Sin is a *disordinate* turning towards a creature; that most important word should never be forgotten. Sin puts the creature towards which it turns outside of the ordination towards God. Hence it may be defined, in the spirit of the bible, as a turning away from God and towards an idol. It also puts the same creature outside of the intramundane order; by turning away from God it also in some manner or other turns away from the creature. That is why in Wisdom of Solomon xiv and in Romans i the idolatrous rejection of God is described as the source of all sins of men towards each other. As the same love goes out to God and creation, so sin, which is always a denial of love, is also directed against the whole reality of God and his creation, of the world and of its God.

Reality itself is supernatural, because God is for everybody a god of salvation. This affects the nature of sin. There are, of course, sins which directly offend the order of creation; for example murder. There are also sins which are directly against the supernatural relations which we have with God and with each other; for example, giving up the faith and the scandal which follows thereupon. In Scripture the latter kind of sin appears most frequently, since, in its extreme form, sin is directed against the Holy Spirit and even in the guise of a transgression of the law it goes against "Yahweh your God". This shows clearly that the whole order of creation is assumed with God in the covenant of grace. That is why the concrete sinner is either raised to the life of grace or at least destined to it. The person upon whom the life of grace has been bestowed may sin by rejecting it directly, by falling away from faith, by hardening his heart, and by a conscious resistance to God's invitation for a more intimate life with him. But even when he sins within the sphere of natural relations, this is ultimately assumed in the dialogue between God who bestowed and man who receives grace, so that man may lose the life of grace also through such a sin. It is obvious that this is possible not only within the church of Christ but wherever God grants his grace. Grace is proffered in some way to each man, since God wishes all men to be saved. At any rate, every man is assumed in the order of grace and destined to a supernatural end. That is why, in our world, sin always possesses a supernatural character; even when, on account of its content, sin might be called natural, it remains supernatural, inasmuch as it is a negative answer to a supernatural bestowal of grace. Should one wish to speculate about a merely possible (not real) creation without a supernatural end, the "natura pura", sin, despite all similarities, would have to be conceived quite differently. It would then constitute a No to God only insofar as the mere relation of creature to Creator may still be called a dialogue.

Actually, however, the sins which are directly opposed to the God of grace, stand against the theological virtues: faith, hope and love. But love, which embraces both God and one's neighbours, is also the soul, the "forma" of the moral virtues, which concern directly our intramundane relations. The same is true of the two other supernatural virtues, for love finds its light in faith and its strength in hope (even as, in their turn, faith and hope fully live only out of love). Faith, hope and love, the three of them, are present together in the moral virtues as their soul. They cannot be present in any other way but embodied in the moral virtues if we include among the latter the virtue of religion, whose object is prayer, worship, and the preaching of the divine truth. It follows that the sins against the supernatural virtues always take shape in an offence against religion or against the other moral virtues. Thus, lack of faith in the real God of salvation may manifest itself not only in idolatry, but also in persecutions, blasphemy, and negativism. And the refusal of love gives rise to all the sins against one's fellow man mentioned in Paul's catalogue of Romans i. On the level of religiosity as well as that of the other moral virtues, the No of sin shows itself in either of the two forms which always include each other: usurpation and refusal. Israel's No to the God of grace takes shape the very first time in the positive effort "to be like unto God" (Gen. iii. 5), to dispose autonomously, in magic and idolatry, of God's free gifts, of what belongs properly to God, of God himself. But afterwards the rejection of God's exigencies and gifts manifests itself also in the killing of the prophets by the idolatrous people and in the rejection of God's Son himself by those who called themselves just, who believed they needed no physician. Likewise appropriating one's neighbour and turning him into an object becomes perhaps most visible in the "degrading passions" which Paul sees as ruling idolatrous mankind of his time. (Rom. i. 26.) But it appears also in the repulsive and hateful shape of "wickedness, evil, covetousness, malice. Full of envy, murder, strife, deceit, malignity, they are gossips, slanderers, haters of God, insolent, haughty, boastful, inventors of evil, disobedient to parents, foolish, faithless, heartless, ruthless."

Thus sin is the violation of norms which apply to the concrete world of creation and Covenant, not of laws given to us only on stone tablets, or imposed in some other way from without. Sin is not against God's will *about* our nature, but against God's will and wisdom as expressed *in* our nature. Sin is not first and foremost an offence against so-called "positive laws", but against "essential laws" of natural and supernatural reality, and against positive laws insofar as they are justified by these essential laws. But even when we put it that way, there is a danger of misunderstanding, a danger of "essentialism". Man is not only placed in a reality to which he has to conform; he himself is the summit of that reality, and man carries within himself the task of "ruling the earth" (Gen. i. 28), that is, of building and moulding himself. Our free will is more than a power of welcoming; it is more also than the power of ruling what is outside of us. Free will is first of all the power of giving to ourselves an attitude and a definitive being. That is why we have not only to accept norms but to establish them. "Nature" does not contain any ready-made norms, but it contains the possibility of being meaningfully assumed in the personal relations which exist between human beings and which, in their turn, are assumed in the Covenant with God. Only the meaning which nature can have in that communication or which is bestowed upon nature by it is a moral norm. That is why sin is not only the unwillingness to accept ready-made norms but also the refusal to help in building and establishing norms, in the sense mentioned above. The "hardness of heart" (Mark x; Matt. xix. 8) which was among the Jews (and also among the heathens) an obstacle to the indissolubility of marriage, may serve as an example of the sin which opposes the emergence of a norm, even though, in accordance with the conception of his time, Jesus describes it as the giving up of a norm which existed already "in the beginning".

In this way sin is also opposed to the meaning of history, as an expansion of interiority, and certainly to the history of salvation. Sin, although standing in history, because it derives from freedom, is antihistorical. Although it is possible only within the history of salvation, it counteracts that history. It is not merely a modern existentialist conception, but a biblical and Christian doctrine which Bultmann presents when he repeatedly sees sinfulness as the "lapsedness" of the past and redemption as an openness for the future. From that point of view sin is a "resisting the Holy Spirit", who, through the prophets and in Christ, brings the history of salvation to its final fruition. (Acts vii. 52.) The ἁμαρτία or the sin against the Holy Spirit consists precisely in this: through his sin the individual pushes that aspect of sin to its extreme consequences in his own life, thus barring for himself every road to salvation.

If sin is opposed to God and to the world which has received grace from him in the history of salvation, it is by that very fact directed against Christ. As God's grace flows more and more abundantly, leading up to the incarnation of his Son, sin too drives more and more towards the rejection of Christ. Even historically the connection is visible between the idolatrous rejection of God, the killing of the prophets, and the crucifixion of Christ—

"The Jews answered him, we have a law and by that law he ought to die because he has made himself the Son of God." (I John xix. 7.) But sin is even more opposed to Christ, since glorified by his Spirit, he wishes to assume us in himself. Now every wasting of grace is, consciously or unconsciously, a refusal to be in him. "Hardened iniquity" especially rejects him. Hence we are used to calling that creature, in whom the apocalyptic writing of the New Testament see an embodiment of ἀνομία and ἄνομος par excellence, the "Antichrist". (2 Thess. ii. 8.) John declares that the Antichrist exists already and that everybody who refuses to acknowledge Christ is an Antichrist. (I John ii. 18; 2 John vii.) In the daily practice of the church that anti-Christian character of sin is experienced as the conviction that every sin which jeopardizes the life of grace makes the sinner unworthy of the Holy Eucharist. Paul noted this for the sins against brotherly love among the members of the church (I Cor. xi. 17-29); they clash most with the "Lord's Supper". But the intuition of the church rightly sees the same unworthiness when man harms his fellow man or treats him as a mere object, when he does not believe in God or resists him; in fine, whenever he refuses to imitate Christ's "loving unto the end" his Father and us. God's whole plan with the world and with us is to "unite all things in him, things in heaven and things on earth" (Eph. i. 10), and every sin is in some way a refusal to take part in this.

The impression may arise that this detailed description of that with which sin clashes puts all sins on the same level. Such a conclusion would agree with the moral earnest of the Stoics and of Pelagianism, and with the religious earnestness of the Reformation, which felt obliged to stigmatize the Catholic distinction between mortal and venial sin. But it does not take sufficiently into account the nuances of reality itself, which derive ultimately from God. Hence it is good to remember that sin comes from our heart, from the core of our personality, from our freedom, but that, on the other hand, our body and the world in which we live through it, constitute the domain in which that decision expresses itself and grows into a specific action. Holy Scripture knows of interior sins only as joined to exterior sins, for example, as desires of an exterior action, or as sins expressed in words, or, finally, as hypocrisy, where good external actions are performed for a wrong purpose, a purpose which may be recognized in other evil actions. All this shows that the outside manifests the inside, but that it may also camouflage it, because our body is the meeting place of that which is our own with that which is not us, of our ego and the surrounding world. In and through our body in the world we express our interior attitudes and give them a shape. Hence our exterior action, together with the content it derives from our corporeity and from our world, is a *sign* of our moral disposition. Normally the transgression of the Commandments cannot proceed from a good decision, nor their observance from a wrong decision. We say "normally". Since our interior reality can never express itself altogether, the signs which it uses both reveal it and veil it. That general rule applies also to our moral-religious attitudes. Moreover, the outward shape of our actions is never totally translucent for us. Thus it may happen that we perform with a good intention actions which are objectively or materially sinful, and it certainly happens that our objectively good actions are spoiled wholly or in part on account of a wrong intention, or are even used to camouflage our wrong attitude. Furthermore, because of that connection with exteriority, we can express our free decision more or less adequately in our external actions, and that decision itself is capable of further development. It follows that there exists a gradation in our sins and in our whole moral activity. It seems worth while to examine this gradation more thoroughly in order to have a closer look at the different degrees of sin, the difference between mortal sin and venial sin.

# Rudolf Schnackenburg

## 1914-

*Sacred Scripture is the very heart of the Christian tradition. Obviously it is not possible for Christians of any generation to develop a morality without a sound knowledge of the religious message of Jesus which necessarily serves as the foundation for Christian morality. Rudolf Schnackenburg, professor of New Testament literature at the University of Würzburg, was deeply committed to this thesis and attempted, in his work,* The Moral Teaching of the New Testament, *to clarify the foundations of Christ's moral teaching.*

*Schnackenburg looks upon Jesus' ethical teaching as religiously conservative, yet startlingly new, for it is difficult to distinguish the original ideas formulated by Christ and the Old Testament doctrines which he naturally incorporated into his message. Unlike the theologians of succeeding Christian centuries, Christ did not elaborate a system of moral theology. As he moved about from village to village, teaching and preaching, people sought his advice and asked for specific answers to specific questions. While responding to particular situations, Jesus taught fundamental principles that would hold true in any situation. His moral demands successfully pull together the concrete and the abstract.*

*Professor Schnackenburg very carefully separates the moral prescriptions that Christ received from the Old Law from those that He Himself established and gave to his followers. Further, Schnackenburg underlines that a third set of moral demands were established during the New Testament era by various preachers and writers. With this threefold classification of moral teachings as his framework, Schnackenburg examines the literature of the New Testament.*

*The commandment of love—love of God and love of neighbor—is the great commandment of the Christian worldview. It receives special attention in Professor Schanckenburg's study and is the portion of his book that we have reproduced below. What did Jesus do that was so unique? The commandments to love God and neighbor are present in the Old Testament. Basically, He linked the two commandments and put them into mutual relation. Further, He showed that the whole law could be reduced to the commandment of love. And He reinterpreted love of neighbor to mean love of the nearest person, an interpretation which gave love a universal meaning. This universal love, anchored in God's all-merciful love, permeated all the other teachings and the works of Jesus. It is this love alone that can guarantee the unselfishness which is lacking to almost all human love. It surpasses the love of friendship and meets others with goodwill, readiness to help, understanding and forgiveness. It extends even to the enemy.*

*At the present time, ethics has become a serious area of discussion, for professional philosophers and theologians as well as for the person who must make a specific decision at the level of everyday activities. It is not possible, within the Christian world to proceed with this discussion without a thorough knowledge of the New Testament teaching. Awareness of the original insights of the New Testament is essential if contemporary Christianity is to fulfill in our time the task of proclaiming the gospel of Jesus.*

# THE MORAL TEACHING OF THE NEW TESTAMENT

## CHAPTER THREE

### JESUS' DECISIVE ACTION: THE CONCENTRATION OF ALL RELIGIOUS MORAL PRECEPTS IN THE GREAT COMMANDMENT OF LOVE OF GOD AND THE NEIGHBOUR

### 9. *Jesus' Fundamental Pronouncement. Comparison with Judaism*

The early Church, and with it, Christianity throughout the centuries, was profoundly convinced that the greatest of Jesus' achievements in the moral sphere was the promulgation of the chief commandment of love of God and one's neighbour. The message of Christian *agape*, the model and highest expression of which is the mission of the Son to redeem the sinful human race, brought something new into the world, an idea and a reality so vast and incomprehensible as to be the highest revelation of God, and quite inconceivable apart from revelation. Yet realization of these facts was only possible after the death of Jesus and could only first be confirmed by the theology of early Christianity (see below sections 23 and 33). The foundation of this revelation was laid by Jesus himself, and furthermore he declared love to be the chief commandment of Christian morality. Our task here must be to examine this both within the framework of his moral teaching and in comparison with Jewish moral doctrine.

All three synoptic gospels record this great act of Jesus in an important pericope which, however, receives different formulation in the three evangelists. In Mark 12:28-34, it is a learned discussion with a well-disposed Scribe who is seeking God, approves Jesus' words, emphasizes the pre-eminence of love over external acts of worship, and is praised by Jesus for doing so. According to Matthew 22:34-40, a Pharisee lawyer tries to trap Jesus; the pericope—clearly the event was the same as that described by St. Mark—is given the form of a controversy. At Luke 10:25ff. the saying about the twofold commandment merely forms the introduction to the story of the good Samaritan, and, surprisingly, is uttered by the questioner himself. The whole passage has a practical aim. The teacher of the law wanted Jesus to tell him what he ought to do to inherit eternal life, and Jesus brought his parable of a merciful act of true neighbourly love to a climax with the words "Go and do likewise" (v. 37). Is it a different encounter of Jesus with a lawyer that is in question in Luke to the one in Mark and Matthew? In neither case are the indications of the situation, the setting, of decisive importance. In Mark and Matthew this is because the passage belongs to a section in which the early Church had brought together four fundamental questions on theological grounds and by reason of their content (Mark 12: 13-37). In Luke it is also the case because probably only the mention of the Samaritan in the parable led to the insertion of the passage in the Lucan "travel narrative". Of course two occurrences of a similar sort are not inconceivable. Jesus may several times have returned to this doctrine which he considered important. As regards the lawyer in Luke who enunciates of his own accord the summary of the two commandments of love, it would be possible to consider that he had already heard of this from Jesus' own discourses. It is preferable on grounds of the history of the tradition and for reasons of literary criticism, however, to regard one event as having provided the basis for the two differently narrated cases. Stylistically, and in the narrative, the Lucan pericope reveals the shaping hand of the evangelist. His chief concern was with the parable; he wanted to use the "great commandment" as an introduction to it, and constructed the pericope as a whole accordingly. That is also the simplest explanation why here the lawyer himself states the double commandment. "If in the Lucan text the lawyer himself designates the double commandment of love as the way of life indicated by the law, Jesus has only to insist on the actual accomplishment of this commandment, and to say how this must take place." In no event does the Lucan pericope oblige us to take the view that the summarizing of the two commandments is not to be attributed to Jesus but had already been taken over by him.

The repercussions of Jesus' chief commandment may be traced throughout the New Testament writings and especially in the life of the early Church. Was Christendom right in concluding that Jesus by it had done something of fundamental and unique importance for moral doctrine? This question has to be faced, because in recent times the originality of his pronouncement has frequently been challenged, and because in making it, Jesus did in fact do no more than link together two texts from the Old Testament.

Even in ancient Judaism attempts to reduce the many individual precepts of the Jewish law to a few basic principles had not been unknown. This is not difficult to understand when one recalls that in later times (in the second century A.D.) the commandments totalled 613, including 248 positive precepts and 365 prohibitions. Hillel (c. 20 B.C.) put forward the famous Golden Rule, but in the negative form, as the principle uniting the law (cf. Matt. 7:12 par.); Rabbi Akiba (d. c. A.D. 135) gave the commandment to love one's neighbour (Luke 19:8), and Rabbi Simlai (c. 250) named faith. The distinction between "small" (or light) and "great" (or heavy) commandments is also very old; but it was not uniformly made and did not correspond to what Jesus called the "first" (Mark) or "great" (Matt.) commandment. To Jesus, this was a twofold commandment; he put love of God and love of one's neighbour on an equal footing. On them all the law and the prophets "depend": that is, from them all other commandments can be derived (Matt. 22:40). In a similar way Bar Quappara (c. 220) said that all the chief things in the Torah could be hung from Proverbs 3:6, as from a hook.

Each of these two commandments which were to be found in different passages in the Old Testament enjoyed specially high esteem in Judaism. The commandment to love God (Deut: 6:5) belongs to the *Shema,* the old confession of monotheistic faith recited every morning and evening by the devout Jew and already customary in Jesus' time. There are striking examples of the seriousness with which Jews regarded this service of God.

In one ancient passage the Talmud (Baraitha) reports, "When Rabbi Akiba was being led away to death, it was the time for the recitation of the *Shema*. They raked off his flesh with iron combs and he took the yoke of the kingdom (reign) of heaven upon himself (that is, he recited the *Shema*). His disciples said to him, 'Master, enough?' He answered them, 'My whole life long I have been concerned regarding this verse 'with thy whole soul'; even if he takes away the soul (that is, life). I said, 'When will it be possible for me to fulfil it? And now, when it is possible for me, ought I not fulfil it?' " (*Berakh.* 61, b).

Neighbourly love was also accounted a primary duty. Rabbi Akiba summed up the whole of the Torah in this one commandment. For him it was just as much the great and universal foundation of the whole Torah, as the twofold commandment was for Jesus. This, moreover, was beyond all doubt the significance of the Golden Rule to Hillel. And so also in the Aristeas letter a Jewish sage puts the Golden Rule before the king of Egypt as a guiding principle for his government, and does so in both positive and negative form. It would, therefore, be wrong to claim superiority for Jesus on the basis of the occurrence of the positive form of the Golden Rule at Matt. 7:12 par. Both gifts made from love (almsdeeds) and services performed from love (personal acts of practical assistance) were held to be paramount "good works", through which one could ensure one's participation in the world to come.

What was it, then, that Jesus did? His action was threefold: he revealed the indissoluble interior bond between these two commandments; he showed clearly that the whole law could be reduced to this and only this chief and double commandment, and he reinterpreted "neighbourly love" as "love of the nearest person", that is he interpreted it in an absolutely universal sense.

If we are to understand Jesus' purpose in laying down the double commandment of love, we must realize that in it Jesus linked the two commandments and put them into mutual relation. According to Jesus' mind, love of God is to find expression and give practical proof of itself in the equally important brotherly love (Matt. 22:39) and, conversely, brotherly love receives as its foundation and support, the love of God. Detailed examination of the profound interrelation be-

220

tween religion and morality that this involves will be undertaken below (section 11); here it must suffice to point out that no Jewish teacher of the law ever attained such clarity. For ancient Judaism, indeed, there could be no worship without the fulfilment of moral obligations; but the very esteem in which the liturgical and ritual precepts were held and their equation with the purely moral commandments exerted a restrictive effect. Hence the teacher of the law was praised by Jesus (Mark 12:34) because he drew from Jesus' reply to his question the inference that the commandment to love is more important than any sacrifice. Judaism, then, was open to such ideas, but needed positive direction. And although the Jewish religion was certainly a moral monotheism to a degree that raised it above all other forms of religion then known, "justification by works" exposed it to the danger of seeing religious acts as moral "performances" and hence of emptying moral action of its intrinsic value by defective motivation. The work of clarification and purification undertaken by Jesus in regard to the Jewish law and legal practice must not be overlooked in his laying down the double commandment of love. With that Jesus simply set the seal of his work of promulgating the true will of God. With this reciprocal linking of the two commandments, he made a perfect unity of religion and morality and by doing so gave religious as well as moral values their full dignity.

Jesus' contemporary, the Jewish scholar of Alexandria, Philo, writes in one passage of his abundant writings that man's duty towards God is piety and holy service; and towards men, philanthropy and justice, describing these as the highest elements in the uncountable multitude of sayings and precepts. No similar summary resembling Jesus' twofold commandment is known from any Palestinian teacher of the law. But even if it were, Jesus' dictum would still not lose its importance, for any such saying would only be one among others; it would indeed show a better understanding of the law than was usual, but hardly a comprehension as fundamentally profound as that of Jesus, concerned entirely with the primordial will of God. His work is a unity in this respect. The new justice he demands expresses itself in love for God and the neighbour as he envisages it, boundless and issuing from the depth of the soul. His radical demands, going far beyond even the written Mosaic law, are also contained and implied in the commandment of love.

In the *Testament of the Twelve Patriarchs,* a work of exhortation dating apparently from the second century before Christ, love of God and of one's neighbour are linked together several times (*Test. Iss.* 5, 7; 7, 6; *Test. Dan* 5, 3). But here these two commandments are put together in a series with others and not set forward as the principle unifying the whole of moral activity. Furthermore, it is debatable how far this document, which we possess only in an edited form, has been subject to Christian influences.

At Leviticus 19:18 the commandment to love one's neighbour is made to relate only to the "children of thy people", and thus to those who belonged to the religious and national union of Israel. But a stranger, living among the Israelites, was to be thought of as a native: "You shall love him as yourselves" (Lev. 19:34). In later Judaism this commandment was interpreted as relating to the full proselyte, who had accepted circumcision and baptism. To extend it to all men whatsoever was very far from the thoughts of Jews in general. It was Ben Azzai (c. A.D. 110) who first recalled that all men are made in God's image and made this thought a motive for love. Acts of charity towards pagan fellow-citizens are demanded more than once in the Mishnah, but only "for the sake of peace" (and thus from social good sense). Hellenistic Judaism was more strongly imbued with the idea of universal philanthropy, for it was acquainted with the Stoic ideal of humanity. In a chapter "Concerning Philanthropy" (*de Virt.* 51 ff.), Philo seeks to show that this ideal is to be found in a perfect form in the Old Testament. According to him love should extend from one's fellow-citizens to one's enemies, and even to slaves, animals and plants. In the *Testament of the Twelve Patriarchs,* especially in the admonitions of Zabulon, on sympathy and mercy, and those of Gad, on love and hate, hatred is described as a satanic and destructive force, and love as the only attitude conformable to God. "Let every one of you love his neighbour and drive hatred out of your hearts; love one another in deed and word and sentiment!" (*Test. Gad* 6, 1). These are warm and generous words. But Jesus' demand that no limit be set on love of one's neighbour and that one stand by the sufferer with immediate practical help even when he is a national enemy (parable of the Good Samaritan) must still have been one that those listening to him realized they did not hear every day. It presupposes a universality of love that does not derive from noble humanity alone (as in Hellenism), nor venture hesitantly and reluctantly outside the circle of the chosen people (as in Judaism). The universality of love preached by Jesus was fired by God's all-embracing and all-merciful love. Thus his preaching of love was ultimately based on his preaching concerning God the Father and the advent of the hour of salvation.

## 10. *Closer Understanding of the Great Commandment from Jesus' Words and Deeds*

Apart from the great commandment Jesus nowhere spoke explicitly about loving God. But with the parallel commandment concerning brotherly love he indicated a broad field of action for that love. The close connection between the two commandments in the mind of Jesus is clear from Matt. 5:23f. Someone bringing his gift for sacrifice to God to the altar must first go and be reconciled with his brother. Love of God likewise obliges one to forgive. One can ask the heavenly Father for forgiveness of one's sins, if one has oneself forgiven one's debtors, so Jesus taught both in the Lord's Prayer (Matt. 6:12) and in a special admonition (Mark 11:25 par.). From this it is clear what Jesus meant by love of God: not a feeling, an emotional rapture, nor yet mystical bliss, but obedience and service. "Thus there can be no obedience towards God in a vacuum, as it were, no obedience apart from the concrete situation in which I stand as a human being among others."

It would, however, be wrong to equate love for God narrowly with the manifestation of love for one's neighbour. It is as all-embracing as the meaning of the saying about serving two masters (Matt. 6:24 par.). This practically requires one to leave oneself free for God by overcoming one's leaning towards Mammon. The following passage (6:25-34) requires us to free ourselves from the cares that bind us to the world. As it ends with the exhortation to seek first the kingdom of God and his justice (6:33), we can say that love for God, as Jesus understood it, above all means fulfilling in faith and obedience all the requirements that God has made known through Jesus as conditions for entering the kingdom of God. Thus we can say that everything we have already seen to be part of the content of the moral mission of Jesus is an expression of the love we owe to God, and that this love implies quite concrete guiding principles.

Religious acts properly so called also belong to this love of God. Matthew devotes two sections of the Sermon on the Mount to prayer (6:1-16; 7:7-11) and Luke a significiant part of his report of Jesus' journeyings (11:1-13). The Lord's Prayer (Matt. 6:9-13, and in a shorter form with a different rhythm, Luke 11:2-4) is unquestionably a prayer concerned with the kingdom of God; the petition for its coming is the central one. But it also shows clearly how Jesus' gospel of the Father and his proclamation of God's reign belong together. The most important intention is that God should exalt his name and, in his goodness and omnipotence, establish his kingdom. But Jesus' disciples who are still in this world, are permitted to entrust the anxieties of their earthly life to the Father, and they are also to implore him for protection against the powerful attacks and temptations of the Evil One. In prayer too, what is decisive is the interior disposition. So Jesus endeavours through a constant flow of new sayings, images and parables (Luke 11:5-8; 18:1-5, 7; cf. also Mark 11:24 par.), to awaken in his disciples a solid and unshakeable confidence in the heavenly Father. Prayer is especially important in the eschatological situation of struggle and temptation (Mark 14:38 par.). Confidence is essential to overcome not only anxiety but also terror in the storms of persecution (Matt. 10:26-33 par.). Love for God is very far, therefore, from being a weakly attitude; it engenders courage that even extends to fearless confession of faith and martyrdom. Jesus embodied this love which is obedience and readiness for death itself, in his own person, as his words in St. John's gospel make plain, "But that the world may know that I love the Father; and as the Father hath given me commandment, so do I" (14:31).

It is on the foundation of this utterly resolute love for God that love of the neighbour is built up. Hence unbounded and genuine, heart-felt forgiveness of our brethren is a primary duty. The parable of the merciless servant (Matt. 18:23-35) demonstrates that God's infinite mercy is given us in the expectation that we deal mercifully with our fellow men.

The metaphor of the remittance of debts applied here to forgiveness of spiritual guilt, is also used in the Lord's Prayer. The parable is part of the material found only in the gospel according to St. Matthew. Its connection with the exhortation to forgive repeatedly (v. 21f.) is secondary, for this feature is not prominent in the story and Luke has a parallel saying (17:14) not linked with the parable. In this parable the application intervenes several times in the narrative itself, for the total of the first servant's debt is unimaginably large, even if he is to be thought of as a steward, and he is incapable of ever paying it by his punishment at the end. Thus behind the king, God is to be seen, and behind the punishment, eternal damnation. This parable itself shows that our love for our human brethren is in fact only an answer to the love of God, a passing on of his mercy. It has learnt from the infinite love for sinners of God and Jesus.

Together with this "spiritual work of mercy", Jesus lays equal weight on the corporal works. The list of them is taken from the great picture of the judgement sketched by Jesus at Matthew 25:31-46 (more material peculiar to Matthew). This indicates a way in which the heathen, who do not know Jesus and yet must stand before the judgement seat of God, can win possession of the kingdom of God. If they have performed works of love towards those in need, the Son of man will reckon their actions as though they treated him in that way; for he looks upon the poor and needy as his "brethren". The duty of helpful love is absolutely binding on those who believe in him. Jesus holds in especially high esteem any act of charity done to those persecuted for his name's sake (cf. Matt. 10:42 = Mark 9:41). At Mark 9:37f. par. there is recorded another saying regarding "receiving" a "little one" ("these" little ones): in receiving a helpless child, one receives Jesus himself.

Although the interpretation is commonly made, it is debatable whether the guilt of the rich glutton (Luke 16:19ff.) rested on the fact that he paid no attention to poor Lazarus at his gate and did not help him. The introduction to this story simply describes the contrast between the two men, and Abraham answers Dives in torment in the underworld not with a reference to his lack of love, but merely by recalling the property he owned whilst he was alive (v. 25). Important with regard to the question of poverty as this parable undoubtedly is, (see below, section 13), it is also difficult to interpret, perhaps because it assumes familiarity on the part of its audience with a story in which the rich man was a sinner and the poor man just. Judaism frequently regarded the good fortune of the godless as a reward given for occasional good works, yet for their lawlessness, they were excluded from the future aeon. If Jesus had intended to indicate that the glutton was being punished for his lack of love, he would surely have said so more clearly.

Renunciation of worldly wealth and its distribution to the poor were required by Jesus not only of the disciples who wanted to follow him personally (Mark 10:21 par.), but also, to a lesser degree, of all (cf. Luke 12:33 - a Lucan supplement). If God is to give us his superabundant gifts of salvation, we too must give to those who ask (Luke 6:30 par.), and must lend without expecting anything in return (Luke 6:35 par.). And here too, as with forgiveness, the motive is "For with the same measure that you shall mete withal it shall be measured to you again".

It would, however, be wrong to interpret Jesus' exhortation to generous helpful love as though one saw in those in need only an opportunity for religious activity or to gain a heavenly reward. The good Samaritan (Luke 10:30-37) did not ask whether the injured man was a Jew, he had not got one eye on a reward, nor did he hesitate or say much. He simply helped, there and then, setting about it himself, sacrificing something that belonged to him, and was ready to do more than was absolutely necessary. Certainly brotherly love grows from the love of God, but just as certainly it aims at helping anyone in need, simply because he is a fellow human being. The more selfless the service to someone else, the purer the love. We should invite not friends, brethren, relations and neighbours, the poor, the crippled, the lame and the blind (Luke 14:12-14).

We should not give in order to receive (*do ut des*)! As in Judaism too, personal service is valued more highly than financial support. Anyone who loves is ready to give himself. Jesus himself provided the best example of this, by giving his life "for many" (Mark 10:45 par.). "I am in the midst of you as he that serveth" (Luke 22:27). According to John 13:4-15, Jesus humbled himself to perform the slave's duty of washing feet, and by so doing symbolized his love "unto the end" (13:1), that is, his sacrificial and atoning death. But he said to the disciples, " A new commandment I give unto you: That you love one another, as I have loved you" (13:34). John interpreted this as referring to Jesus' sublime love for his friends (John 15: 13) and as a summons to brotherly love (1 John 2:10; 3:14ff. etc). He saw this extreme example of laying down one's life for the brethren, not as a single pinnacle attained by the love of Jesus alone, but as an act binding us to do likewise (1 John 3:16).

This early Christian interpretation of the commandment to love makes it clear that the addition of the words "as thyself" to the commandment of neighbourly love is not intended to be taken as a limitation of its scope. Rather, the self-love that is spontaneously and essentially present in everyone should be an unforgettable reminder to us of how far our love for others ought to go. "This 'as thyself' cannot be twisted and explained away; judging with the severity of eternity, it pierces to the inmost hiding places of the love a man has for himself." That is what Jesus had in mind in the Golden Rule: "All things, therefore, whatsoever you would that men should do to you, do you also to them" (Matt. 7:12 par.).

Love of friends and love of enemies are only "two different forms of the Christian sentiment of love" (F. Tillmann). Love of the kind Jesus requires often demands painful self-conquest; in loving one's enemies, that is only too obvious. The step from loving one's friends in the right way to loving one's enemies, is not a big one. Not for nothing did Jesus make the symbol of the helpful man a Samaritan, a member of that half-pagan, half-breed nation with whom the Jews were at that time at particular enmity. But in the gospels, enemy primarily means personal opponent, as is also shown by the example at Matthew

5:39. Luke puts in one phrase, "Give to everyone that asketh of thee; and of him that taketh away thy goods, ask them not again" (6:30). The next step is to renounce revenge (Luke 6:29 par.), but loving one's enemies also involves positive action, "Love your enemies. Do good to them that hate you. Bless them that curse and pray for them that calumniate you" (6:27f.). Jesus was not concerned with the psychological difficulties that loving one's enemies might entail. It is enough that this is what God himself does, "who maketh his sun to rise upon the good and bad and raineth upon the just and the unjust" (Matt. 5:45), and imitation of God will make those who love God capable of a similar attitude.

The comparable utterances of the noble Stoics are well-known and are often quoted. Seneca, for example, said, "If you want to imitate the gods, do favours even to the ungrateful; for the sun rises even over the wicked, and the sea is open even to pirates" (De benef. VI, 26, 1, cf. also Marcus Aurelius, In sem., IX, 11). But in this pantheistic system there could be no question of a genuine imitation of God. Ultimately the philosophers were moved to make their statements, truly admirable as they are, by reason alone. Jesus demanded love of one's enemies as the highest expression yet necessary consequence of personal love for God and one's neighbour. Self-conquest was for him not a philosophical exercise, but profound love based on religion.

A practical application of love of this kind, operative both towards friend and foe, is avoidance of loveless condemnation. Here again the religious motive is evident, "Judge not, and you shall not be judged (by God). Condemn not, and you shall not be condemned. Forgive, and you shall be forgiven" (Luke 6:37 par.), and the wonderful saying about the mote or splinter in a brother's eye and the beam in one's own (Luke 6:41f. par.) makes the admonition unforgettable. It is astonishing how Jesus links bold and as it might seem superhuman demands with a very clear-sighted and realistic assessment of the limitations of human nature. He, however, has the right to call men in the name of God out of their narrowness up on to the heights of divine sanctity (cf. Matt. 5:48), for he not only preached this love, but lived it, not least in prayer for his enemies (Luke

23:34): a prayer which, at that moment on the cross and in its moving and incomparable form, is the worthiest testimony to his spirit.

## 11. *The Significance of the Great Commandment for Religion and Morality*

The linking together intrinsically of love of God and of one's neighbour, and the interpretation of this double commandment as the core and climax of the whole of moral doctrine, is a great gain for religion as well as morality, and this might perhaps be summarized more or less as follows.

Religion, the relationship of man with God, and its whole wealth of ideas, doctrines, emotions, endeavours and actions can no longer lead to a self-contained ceremonial piety. The Scribe of Mark 12:32f. had already drawn from the words of Jesus the conclusion that the love of God surpasses everything and that brotherly love is more than all the temple sacrifices. Early Christians understood this: "Religion clean and undefiled before God and the Father is this: to visit the fatherless and widows in their tribulation . . ." (Jas. 1:27). It can be a strong impetus to the life of the liturgy, worship itself (cf. the Agape, the fraternal feast), but especially to the influence of that life on the activities of the parish community and of individual Christians in the world. For believers in Christ the goal could not be the visionary mysticism which at that time exerted an immense power of attraction over not a few human beings (Hermeticism, the Mystery Religions, Gnosticism). It is not ecstatic visions that lead to communion with God, but love proved in action (cf. 1 John 4:12). At the same time, brotherly love affords genuine and powerful love for God a field of action. Love urges us to act; but God is invisible and afar off to human beings with their bodies and senses. Now, however, human beings can demonstrate their love for God through goodwill and acts of benevolence towards their brethren. The whole problem that people in modern times claim to find in loving God and in the commandment to love, consequently evaporates. Direct acts of worship of God are not thereby suppressed; but rather love makes possible true praise and thanksgiving, confidence and hope. Perfect love overcomes fear (1 John 4:18), but brotherly love can also help, for it assures us of our love for God, soothes our hearts when they condemn us and trouble us (1 John 3:19f.). Jesus also spoke sometimes about fear of God (Matt. 10:28), and his serious warnings about judgement could increase this; but in the great commandment he unmistakably proclaimed love as the decisive attitude. But anyone who asks how it is possible to express such love above all things for the all-holy God, is directed towards the simple path of brotherly love which the good Samaritan took.

These ideas are not a later glorification of Jesus' proclamation of the great commandment; at a very early date they had already been developed from his commandment of love. It is no accident that they are already to be found in the First Epistle of St. John. They are in accord with John's meditations on communion with God and were also called forth by the pseudomysticism and gnosis that John had to combat. Without setting out the theme as explicitly as has been done here, he, in fact, worked out the rich benefit the commandment of love affords for a healthy and profound piety (see also sections 33 and 34 below).

The value of the great commandment for morality is perhaps even more important. Unification and interiorization, a morality of intention and of action, love for the poorest and love for all have been extolled often enough; but often not enough account is taken of love of God as the basis of religion. This love alone guarantees the unselfishness which is lacking to almost all human love; it alone makes possible the self-conquest from which the most secret and powerful acts of love spring. Only this love grounded in God, becomes *agape,* which surpasses every natural *eros,* and the praise of which is sung at 1 Corinthians 13. It surpasses the love of friendship, for even without natural affinity it meets others with goodwill, readiness to help, understanding and forgiveness for the sake of God and Christ. In this Christian *agape* the urge towards union has quite receded in favour of pure benevolence and mercy. For that reason it can also extend to those who are not naturally worthy of love and even to an enemy. But where does it derive the stimulus to do so? Again only from love of God, by whom the Christian knows himself to be loved in this self-same way. This "completely different" love of God has been revealed to the Christian in the words of Jesus (Matt. 5:45), in Jesus' saving acts and finally in his death. Because Christian love of the neighbour is related to love of God, it impels the Christian, when it is correctly understood and taken to heart, to the utmost effort, to "perfection", as Jesus himself expressed it (Matt. 5:48).

This Christian perfection in love is different in kind from the Greek ideal of perfection. Its aim is not the attainment of a harmonious personality, morally faultless, self-contained, but of "holiness", as God is holy (cf. Lev. 19:2; 1 Pet. 1:16). In this context, that of loving one's enemies, and of the resolving of the antitheses of the Sermon on the Mount, holiness involves a love that completely surrenders the individual ego, and takes as its model God's incomprehensible love for mankind and for sinners. The expression "perfect" probably derives from Matthew, who is the only evangelist to use it again, in 19:21. In Luke 6:36, the words of the Sermon on the Mount read, "Be ye therefore merciful as your Father also is merciful", and that must have been the original wording, because in the Old Testament the predicate "perfect" is never applied to God (though it is to his actions, Deuteronomy 32:4, his law, Psalm 18:8, and to the way in which he guides), but the predicate "merciful" often is. By his expression Matthew has wished, in accordance with the sense, to bring out and condense for his Jewish Christian readers, the morality demanded by Jesus, which exceeds all previous "righteousness" (5:20), and which concerns the whole man and claims him wholly. Consequently, in Matthew, Jesus also says to the rich young man, when he is asking the hardest of him, "If thou wilt be perfect, go sell what thou hast" (19:21). On the basis of Hebrew thought "perfect" (tamim) really means "intact", "faultless", "sound" (often used in this sense of sacrificial animals) and the noun (tom) also means "innocence", "purity". The idea is not of a perfecting by stages, but of the integrity of the whole person who belongs to God. In Judaism too we meet with the exhortation, "As God is called merciful and gracious, so be thou also merciful and gracious, and give to every man without reward", but here it is closely linked with other attributes of God that are to be imitated. The command to be perfect and to walk before Yahweh, was already given to Abraham (Gen. 17:1). But to Jesus perfection as he demands it at the climax of the Sermon on the Mount is more, it is in fact the highest peak of love, final renunciation of self and utter devotion to God and fellow men.

By this a goal is set for the moral striving of men, which goes far beyond the range of vision of any philosophical system of ethics and every purely human ideal of perfection, a goal beyond the reach of purely human powers, but not unattainable with the help of God's grace. This moral task set before the Christian, although consisting primarily in the attainment of salvation and of all the blessings of salvation promised by Jesus, is also a source of true happiness and lasting peace in the earthly life of men with one another.

# John Lawrence McKenzie
## 1910-

*During the past century, biblical studies have undergone a kind of scholarly revolution. Sophisticated techniques in archaeology, as well as the Form Criticism approach to biblical texts, have provided new insights on the gospel message. Naturally the ethical teachings of the Bible have been re-examined along with the doctrinal.*

*One of the outstanding American contributors to contemporary biblical studies is John L. McKenzie. For well over a quarter of a century he has been considered a leader in Catholic circles of biblical criticism and interpretation. His* Dictionary of the Bible *is highly respected both for its completeness and practicality. His books on the Old and New Testaments, respectively,* The Two Edged Sword *and* The Power and the Wisdom *are designed to make available to the average Catholic the best results of recent biblical scholarship. McKenzie, who presently teaches at DePaul University in Chicago, has a vivid and stimulating approach to the Bible. His books are challenging to the person who seeks new and rich insights into the biblical foundations of Christianity.*

*The selection below, a chapter from* The Power and the Wisdom, *is entitled "The Christian Moral Revoluion." McKenzie leads up to his study of the moral overtones of the New Testa-*

*ment by exploring the world of the New Testament, the concept of the gospel, the reign of God and the saving mystery of Jesus.*

*His chapter on the moral revolution begins with the observation that, though many Christians can accept the creation of a new life notionally, it often seems impossible to reduce the notion to practice. Yet, Jesus was serious about his teaching and certainly invited no one to become an unfinished Christian. Jesus and the apostolic church rejected the conventional morality of the first century of the Christian era. This morality was contained particularly in the Jewish Law and the Greek Stoic philosophy. In their place the gospel proposes a morality founded on the mystery of Jesus. It is a morality of personal dignity and of life in community. Within the Christian morality, detailed prescriptions are superfluous; the transformed person has no need of them.*

*Love is central to the moral revolution. In fact, love is the entire Christian moral code. One wonders whether this radical concept of Christian love has been adequately grasped throughout the twenty centuries of Christian history. The complex and legalistic moral systems developed at various times by the Church suggests that it was not. McKenzie closes his chapter on a rather disturbing note. In the face of love, "the central theme of New Testament morality, one is depressed by a feeling of despair—despair of one's fellowman and of oneself. Is it possible? Is it practical?" The contemporary Christian is confronted with an inevitable decision—follow the standards of the day's morality which has no room for love, or live by the Christian message of love and revolt against the accepted morality. One cannot have both; it is either one or the other. The decision is in the hands of the person.*

## A Christian Manner of Life

I n the preceding chapter we saw that freedom from the Law was one of the ideas which was elaborated in the controversy over Judaism. Law and freedom deserve closer study; for the gospel in this respect initiated a moral revolution which has not yet worked itself out. That Christianity creates a new life is one of the truths of the gospel which Christians have found difficult to grasp in its totality. Or, if the creation of a new life is accepted notionally, it often seems impossible to reduce the notion to a manner of life which can be practiced. At times the desire to fulfill the demands of the new life has led to deviations which ended in some form of withdrawal from the world and from human society. Other ways of fulfilling the new life which are deviations by secular standards are approved by the Church as safe ways of leading a Christian life. Such are the monastic and other orders which profess a life according to a rule taken under vow. The rule is intended to institute a form of life in community which is called "evangelical," that is, according to the gospel. The essential features of the religious life are poverty, chastity, and obedience; the differences between one order and another are variations on the essential obligations. This is called the life of the counsels in contradistinction to the life of the precepts, to which all members of the Church are obliged.

## An Evangelical Manner of Life

The traditional terminology here is not entirely fortunate. The difference between the life of the counsels and the life of the precepts is not intended to imply that the life of the precepts is not evangelical. If all Christians do not live according to the gospel, then Christ did not affect the moral life of man in general at all. Furthermore, the distinction between counsel and precept is not too securely founded in the Gospels. The usual base for this distinction is the story of the rich young man (Mt 19:16-30 = Mk 10:17-31 = Lk 18:18-30). This episode does not suggest an option between the life of the precepts and the life of the counsels. Jesus puts before the inquirer the Law and the gospel; and when the inquirer chooses the Law, Jesus does not invite him to an intermediate phase between discipleship and the life of the precepts. He observes that those who refuse the gospel will not enter the Reign of God. The primitive community of Jerusalem, which Luke idealized, urged candidates for baptism to renounce their wealth (Acts 2:44-45; 4:32-35; 5:1-11). They may have misunderstood the teaching of Jesus; and their practice did not endure in the Church. Before we say they misunderstood him we must look carefully to see whether it was not rather a failure to find a practical way of executing an idea which they understood very well.

The reader of the New Testament is not left with the impression that either Jesus or the apostolic Church conceived the plan of creating a spiritual elite within the Church. Even the apostolic college is not described as a spiritual elite. Jesus makes no distinction between the moral level of the apostolic college and the moral level of all who become his disciples. The epistles of Paul were written for the members of the churches he founded without distinction between members. There is only one gospel, as there is only one Lord, one faith, one baptism. We have seen in the preceding chapter that the Church could not tolerate a division into a Jewish church and a Gentile church. She can no more easily tolerate a division into one church for the spiritual elite and one for the spiritually mediocre. No such division has occurred, of course; but one may ask whether the Church has here reached the perfect unity which is her destiny. And one may certainly ask whether all her members desire this unity, or whether all of them even think it is possible. Some wit has said, not without cynicism, that in modern times it is impossible to be canonized unless one is a bishop or a member of a religious community. The cynicism is unpleasant; but it points

to the fact that the Church needs in modern times some recognized saints who were married and had children. On the
records of canonization, most of the laity have to be judged
as spiritually mediocre. Obviously we need another standard
of judgment. We shall have it if we recall that in the New
Testament the fullness of the Christian life is not a matter of
option. Jesus invited no one to become an unfinished Christian.

## The Morality of the Law

Let us try to assess the Christian moral revolution. One
may begin by pointing out that Jesus and the apostolic Church
rejected the conventional morality of the world in which the
incarnation occurred. The conventional morality of the day can
be summed up in two systems of law: the Jewish Law and the
natural law of Stoic philosophy. Of these the first is by far
more prominent in the New Testament. We have already had
more than one occasion to refer to the place which the Law
had in Judaism and to the attitude of Jesus and St. Paul toward
it. The attitude is summed up in the statements of Paul that the
Law is inefficacious for salvation. The Gentile may not observe
the Law, the Jew need not observe it. Neither Jesus nor the
apostolic Church proposed another law to replace the Torah.
To speak of the gospel as "the new law" is a misleading expression. It is the new law in the sense that it displaces the old law,
but not in the sense that it is another and better law. That it
is not a law at all will, I hope, emerge from this discussion.

## The Morality of Stoicism

The second moral system in question is the natural law of
Stoicism (see Chapter I). This is certainly not mentioned in
the Gospels; and the allusions in the epistles are so few and
fleeting that some scholars question whether it is mentioned
there at all. I am convinced that it is. Stoicism was the dominant
moral system of the Hellenistic world; it was so well known that
it is difficult to see how Paul could have been unaware of it. If
he knew anything about it, he knew that it was something
which the gospel had to displace; he could not have left it alone.
A review of Stoic morality will show that it was not an ignoble
system. It was the morality of most of the more admirable

figures of Hellenistic and Roman history, and it produced some men of greater than average stature. Marcus Aurelius, known vaguely to most people as one of the ten persecuting emperors if he is known at all, left a journal of his meditations which is a monument to an honest and fair-minded man who was fully aware of his duties and responsibilities. Stoicism was the best moral system of the Hellenistic world; one can guess that men who were convinced of it would be slow to believe that the gospel offered a better way of life.

### A Morality of Reason and Nature

The morality of Stoicism was a morality of reason and nature. It integrated its cosmology and its ethics better than any other philosophical system of its time; and it had an attractive simplicity which made it comprehensible even to the unlearned. The universe itself is governed by law; and the law which governs the moral life of man is patterned after the natural law of the cosmos. The universe in Stoicism is logical; it is governed by a creative and unifying principle called Fire, Spirit, or Reason (Logos). This principle is the one true divine being; it can also be called Nature or God. It is the soul and the principle of the life of the universe; it does in the universe what reason does in man. Therefore the universe is governed by intelligence and providence. The good of reason is the moral good, and therefore moral good is prior in the universe, whence it is participated to man. The good life for man is to live "conformably," or "conformably to nature," or "conformably to the experience of the events of nature"; the Stoics had some trouble finding the best phrase to express this norm of morality. Nature, both of the individual and of the universe, is the common law, the right reason pervading all things. This law is above any human law; human law is valid only in so far as it is in harmony with the law of the universe. Justice is established by nature, not by ordinance; and the law of nature is eternal, immutable, and invariable. Local laws are necessary for most men because they do not participate sufficiently in Reason. The wise man does not need human law, for his own reason is the only rule which he needs and the only rule which he can accept with dignity. He is self-sufficient and has all he needs to live a happy life. No evil can disturb him, for the only true good is the moral good, which he can preserve.

## Stoic Virtues

The Stoics insisted on the four cardinal virtues: prudence, justice, temperance, and fortitude. Their understanding of these virtues was sound; the system did not admit immorality in the common sense of the term. The Stoic conception of the brotherhood of man was quite unusual in the ancient world. The system arose in the Hellenistic period, when, as we have seen (Chapter I), political allegiance had been relaxed. In the Stoic system the world was one great city (cosmopolis), and all men were its citizens. The slave could be a wise man, and if he was wise he was free; for only the wise man is free.

## Stoic Faults

There were soft spots in the Stoic system. The self-sufficiency of the sage is hard to distinguish from pride and arrogance. The ideal of apathy led to disengagement; the rise of the Hellenistic kingdoms and empires destroyed the ancient freedom of the Greek citizen, and the Stoic was inclined to accept the world passively. He could create his own little island of serenity; but to do this he had to be detached from the affairs of his fellow man. It recommended suicide, we noticed (Chapter I), as an honorable escape.

This was, as we have called it, a morality of reason and nature; and it is obvious that to the apostolic community it was a morality of reason without revelation for man without regeneration. It is hard to see how St. Paul could have been more sympathetic to the natural law of Stoicism than he was to the revealed law of Judaism. The law of Judaism was at least the revealed will of God. St. Paul, as we have seen, gives Stoicism little attention. He could not have used the word "law" of the norm of Stoic morality; for him there was only one law, and that was the Law of Moses. Anything else is called a law in a transferred sense. Hence he does not take the trouble to reject the law of Stoicism. He may have given the question no thought at all; or he may have thought that his rejection of the Law of Moses was enough of a rejection of law in principle to need no explicit extension to the law of Stoicism. If he thought this, it must be noticed that many of his interpreters have not. The suggestion that the gospel may reject the law in principle is challenging; and an examination is in order to see whether this is a tenable interpretation of what the New Testament says about law.

## Nature Without Regeneration

The Stoic natural law is based on nature as it is known by reason. Nature as it is known by reason is an unreality in the world of biblical thought. Man is not an abstract essence but a historical existent. As historical he is under judgment, the slave of sin and of his own demonic impulses. He lacks precisely what Stoicism boasted it gave, the self-sufficiency by which he can lead a happy life. He is incapable by his own resources of achieving moral good; he is desperate without the salvation which Jesus Christ alone brings. Whatever is deduced from nature as a code of conduct is deduced from the nature of this fallen lump of clay, who is a reasonable animal only when he chooses to be. The deductions are made by other fallen lumps whose limited vision is obscured by personal desires. Paul does not give man, enslaved to sin and death, any possibility of escaping his slavery by his wits. In the first chapter of Romans he has written a moral analysis of the Hellenistic world of his day, and his appraisal of this world is dismal. This recital of the vices of the world is Paul's estimate of the moral capacity of man led by reason and nature.

## Reason Without Revelation

As a Jewish Christian Paul believed that the most important events in history were the revelation of God's word to Israel fulfilled in Jesus Christ. The Stoic system is innocent of any revelation. Man acquires wisdom by reason which he shares from the reason of the cosmos. He is his own master; indeed he cannot be truly wise until he is his own master, for the sage must be self-sufficient. What would Paul think of a system which expressly declared that we really do not need God's revelation of himself to devise an adequate code of conduct? He did not think it deserved mention. The only true wisdom is the knowledge of

240

God which is acquired by the self-revelation of God. In biblical terms any other alleged wisdom is folly. To assert the self-sufficiency of reason is to deny man's dependence on God. To the Stoic claims on behalf of reason Paul could well have responded with the story of how man sought the knowledge of good and evil by eating of the tree of knowledge, and discovered only that he is naked.

## Law and Obligation

Morality considered as a system of law imposes obligation. This is the only effect of law and it is the only motive for the observance of the law. This fits well into Paul's conception of the Law as made for man under sin. Other philosophies such as Platonism did not consider obligation as the motive for doing the good. The good is to be chosen because it is good and is intellectually apprehended as good; if the object of one's act is good, no other motivation for the act is either necessary or possible. Law and obligation make it unnecessary for the agent to apprehend the good. The agent is moved not by goodness recognized but by the threat of some external evil which is attached to failure to meet the obligation. This is the moral level of children: if you are not home by a certain hour, you will not be allowed to attend the party on Saturday. The only evil attached to tardiness is the loss of the party; whether tardiness is good or bad independently of the party is not known and is not important. For law does not look to motivation but simply to observance, which it does not reward, and to nonobservance, which it punishes. Is motivation important? Not to law, for the integration of personal life is not the purpose of law. The integration of personal life is the object of the gospel; for the gospel is directed to the creation of the new man who lives in Christ and in whom Christ lives. And it would be unfair to Stoicism to say that it did not have the integration of personal life within its purpose. The wise man is integrated with nature; strangely, neither Stoicism nor any other morality of reason and nature has been able to tell precisely what such a person is.

241

## Morality of Duty

The morality of law is by definition minimal and negative. It is minimal because it is a morality of duty; and duty is that which is owed. It is unreasonable to go beyond your duty, and it can be annoying to others. The morality of law seeks not the good but the lawful; and the lawful is the permissible. The morality of law tends to look less at the observance of the law and more at the violation; and this morality easily becomes an ideal of moral goodness which is achieved not by doing what is good, but by abstaining from what is wrong. If one could list all the ways in which law is violated, one would have a model of perfection in reverse; one would know everything which one should not do.

## Atomization of Conduct

The morality of law leads to the atomization of moral conduct into a multiplicity of individual acts; and each act becomes a case in itself. Acts are performed in concrete reality. The act in the casuistry of law is abstracted from living reality and analyzed as an isolated fragment hanging in the air dissociated from the person who performs it. Yet each individual act is a part of a continuous chain of one human life with relations to other individual human lives. The act arises from a living individual person with his own defined personality formed by his experience and his associations. It is his response to a concrete situation and to certain persons. It is a personal decision which forms his personality further. In a true sense each individual act is unique; it will not be repeated either by the same person or by another. No individual act is understood unless it is recognized that X did it in situation Y. This does not imply that each individual act creates its own moral standards by which it is judged; but it does imply that the moral judgment of the concrete act which abstracts the act from its situation in life can be notably distorted. When the act is considered in abstraction from the inner personal principles from which the act flows, one can recognize that it is wrong; but one cannot see what makes it good.

242

## Chastity

The atomization of the individual act can be illustrated from an area which is notably more emphasized in modern moral philosophy than it is in the New Testament; I mean the virtue of chastity. The student finds the treatment of this virtue in the New Testament rather casual; in contrast, the morality of sex receives more treatment in modern literature than any other moral question. He may be tempted to ask himself whether chastity has not displaced charity as the basic Christian virtue. The difference in emphasis is hardly due to a deterioration of the moral situation from what it was in the Hellenistic world; no one who is acquainted with the history of Hellenistic culture could think that chastity needed less attention then than it does now. Corinth, where St. Paul founded a church to which he wrote at least two letters, had a reputation which can be checked in the Greek lexicon. In Greek "Corinthian girl" means prostitute, "Corinthian merchant" means procurer, and "to act like a Corinthian" means to visit a house of prostitution. The temple of Aphrodite at Acrocorinth had a staff of a thousand temple prostitutes. One would never deduce from 1 and 2 Corinthians that chastity was a particular problem in Corinth, and in a sense it was not; for chastity as a virtue was esteemed nowhere in the Hellenistic world. Paul had an excellent opportunity to write a flaming sermon on the subject to the Corinthians; instead he wrote the hymn to love (1 Corinthians 13). May one conclude that Paul considered that chastity would be a product of Christian love which needed no special attention? And may one ask whether he would have thought that it was possible to attend to chastity as if it were an end in itself, possible of achievement in some other way than as a product of charity?

In the Christian scheme chastity is not a way of life but a component of a way of life; and the consideration of chastity in a morality of reason and nature fails to present it as a part of a way of life. Chastity is found both in the celibate state and in the matrimonial state. The usual presentation of chastity describes it as a virtue which is achieved by not doing something.

The Christian, if he takes the time and trouble, can be very sure what are the wrong things to do; he is less certain that by not doing them he has done the right thing. The use of sex is a fulfillment of the human person; concentration on single acts as permissible or prohibited has little or no reference to the fulfillment of the human person, and abstention from the use of sex without further qualification seems to be no more than a denial of fulfillment. That so many Christians, married and celibate, have found a positive understanding of their way of life is not due to the morality of reason, nature, and law. It is due to the movement of the Spirit which reveals the nature of Christian love even when love is obscured by a thorough study of actual and possible sexual deviations.

## Fragmentation of Society

Law is a social phenomenon; yet a morality of reason, nature, and law tends to fragmentate the moral and social structure. For the isolated act is performed by an isolated person; and morality, when it is the morality of an isolated person, becomes self-centered. This is illustrated very well in the moral system of Stoicism. The end of Stoic morality was the perfection of the individual wise man; his success involved the success of no one else, and he was not concerned with the failure of anyone else. To become involved would disturb his serenity. Law is more a principle of regulation in society than a principle of morality; and morality reduced to law does not achieve much more than regulation. Where the Christian moral revolution has penetrated least is in the morality of society. It took some centuries for Christians to realize that one man cannot own another. Christians have not realized yet that what men may not do as individuals they may not do when enough of them are gathered in large numbers to form a political society. To tolerate and use a moral jungle in social relations while one strives to "save one's soul" in what private life is left is more or less the ideal of Stoicism.

## Law and Responsibility

Law is an external regulating agency. It cannot possibly cover all contingencies; but in any contingency the law is there

244

as a norm. The law is an abstraction, and it can often fail to touch reality. It is a general direction which must be rendered particular in each concrete action. But because law offers a certain security that what we are doing is right just because it is the law, we prefer not to incur the risk which a flexible interpretation of the law entails. Law offers a set of prefabricated decisions for every concrete situation up to a point. No reflection on the good or the better is necessary. One need feel no personal responsibility; for one has transferred all personal responsibility to the law. One has only to consult one's mental card file of the permissible and the prohibited and the decision comes out. It is all very simple up to a point, as I have said. The point of limitation is the point where a few crises occur. These crises, of course, are what make or break a person. What is to be expected from one who has trained himself not to make his own decisions but to look for the prefabricated decision? Anything can be expected, even the right thing; but the right thing will be done for the wrong reasons.

## Reason and the Gospel

I have presented what I think are the implications of the principles of a morality of law based on reason and nature. The picture has not been altogether favorable, and I do not think it needs to be; were such a morality the supreme morality of man, the gospel need not have included a moral revolution. Our question was whether the moral revolution of the gospel is a rejection of the morality of reason and nature in principle. The answer will not be entirely clear until we have set forth the Christian revolution, if indeed it becomes clear then; but I think it is safe to say, at least as a hypothesis, that the gospel rejects those principles involved in a morality of reason and nature which have been set forth above. We shall find a direct antithesis between the gospel and these features of rational morality. One will, of course, ask whether rational morality can be rejected any more than one can refuse to have a head. Admitted that the gospel is a moral revolution, the revolution must be worked out by the personal decision of each Christian, as I have insisted. The gospel does not give specific directions for each situation either; and the Christian can make his moral decisions only by the intelligent use of Christian moral principles applied to particulars—which is a morality of reason.

With this there can be no quarrel. But Christian morality must be primarily Christian. Moral thinking cannot be based on an abstraction of what is convenient to human nature; it must think of historic man, fallen and redeemed. This means that man's potential is reduced by his fall and that fallen man is inevitably a moral failure. Redeemed man, on the other hand, is endowed with moral powers which he does not possess by natural endowment. Christian morality will consider what man can and cannot do; its conclusions will not be those of reason and nature. The moral ideal of the Christian is known by the revelation of God in Jesus Christ. The means by which the Christian can attain this ideal are the gift of grace known through the revelation of God. When reason considers nature and abstracts from these things, reason is not considering reality. This should seem obvious; yet solutions to moral problems are often alleged which are devised as if the incarnation had not occurred.

## The Morality of Secular Goods

The Christian moral revolution overturns so many accepted ethical values that it is difficult to see how much of a rational structure of law based on nature could be left. Rational morality is the code by which man used the goods of self and of this world in a way suitable to man living in society. The gospel does not so much reject secular goods as ignore them. The words of Jesus on wealth scarcely allow any room for a morality of the use of these goods. I have already noticed that the primitive community took him seriously. Does their failure to find a practical way to follow his teaching excuse other Christians from looking for a way? It is not without design that Matthew begins his account of the teaching of Jesus with the words, "Blessed are the poor in spirit"—a phrase nicely mistranslated for hundreds of years. It means those who are poor of spirit, who have not much spirit, the helpless of the world who have no power to resist. The gospel was proclaimed to the poor whose masses constituted the vast majority of the population of the Hellenistic world, and it was proclaimed by one of them. He did not offer riches but congratulated them on their poverty.

Both Matthew (6:25-34) and Luke (12:22-31) preserve the sayings in which Jesus scoffs at concern for such basic needs as food and clothing. This saying is so stunning that it has been simply ignored except by a few who were regarded as fanatics. In the story of the rich young man (Mt 19:16-30; Mk 10:17-31; Lk 18:18-30) Jesus concluded the dialogue by saying that it is very hard for a rich man to enter the Reign, about as hard as it is for a camel to pass through the eye of a needle. The history of the efforts to interpret this as something else than what it means is pathetic. The disciples understood Jesus better; they gave the obvious retort, "Who, then, can be saved?" This was the opportunity for Jesus to explain that the camel was really a rope and the needle's eye one of the gates of Jerusalem, or that he was using Oriental metaphor which is so popular in Oriental speech and need not be taken seriously. Instead he observed that what is impossible with men is possible with God—suggesting that resources were available to achieve the impossible. Luke alone (14:33) has preserved the saying that one must renounce all his possessions to become a disciple of Jesus. The saying is not out of character with other sayings; and one finds it easier to understand how the Jerusalem community did not treat poverty as an option in the Christian vocation. One has a little difficulty in seeing how it is treated as an option.

In any case, the attitude of Jesus toward the use of wealth even in the sense of the minimum material possessions is such that it renders all the ethical treatises on ownership, theft, transfer of ownership, contracts, etc. simply so much abstract speculation for the Christian. When Paul appealed to the Corinthians for contributions for the poor in Jerusalem, he gave the example of Jesus Christ, who impoverished himself for us although he was rich (2 Cor 8:9). Paul's churches did not practice the communism of Jerusalem as far as we know; but his teaching was that the abundance of one should counterbalance the need of another so that equality should result (2 Cor 8:13-15). Paul was no more sympathetic to wealth than Jesus. The parable of Dives and Lazarus (Lk 16:19-31) does not recommend Christian communism; but it describes a man who is damned for doing nothing.

## The Morality of Personal Dignity

The gospel focuses its attack on secular values against material goods because the need for them is so obvious and because they are so easy to justify. One hears it said that Jesus had rich friends, although the enumeration stops at Joseph of Arimathea; and it is conveniently forgotten that if Joseph joined the Jerusalem community he ceased to be rich. But the gospel attacks other secular goods with no less vigor. Jesus congratulates the poor on their poverty and his disciples for being reviled and persecuted (Mt 5:11; Lk 6:32). Jesus promises them no better treatment than he himself received (Mt 10:24; Jn 15:20). The disciple must take up his cross and deny himself (Mt 16:24; Mk 8:34; Lk 9:23). The sentence deserves scrutiny. In modern speech we can paraphrase the taking up of the cross only by some such phrase as "You have to become a gallowsbird." To deny oneself is to assert that one is not; it is to remove the self from the list of values. Whatever Jesus meant by hating one's self or life and thus saving it (Mt 16:25; Mk 8:35; Lk 9:24), he certainly meant a declaration against the ethics of survival which dominate the systems of rational morality. But much more than that is intended. The goods of the person are as unimportant in Christian morality as the good of wealth. The Christian can expect revilement and persecution for no other reason than his Christianity. Discipleship is not a way to honor and esteem; it is as certain a way as one can find to their opposites. Christians have found this as difficult as the sayings about wealth. They wish to be esteemed because esteem of them is an esteem of Christianity; and external honor paid to the Church and her prelates and members reflects honor on the Church. Jesus seemed to have expected something else. We can conclude that by these declarations ethical thought on the goods of the person is rendered otiose. The Christian needs no ethics on the use of the goods of the person because he will not have them to use. Against this background efforts to make the Church or her individual members honorable figures by secular standards seem dubious.

## The Morality of Life in Community

The moral revolution of the gospel restores unity to isolated acts and to isolated persons. The moral life of the Christian is lived in and through the Church. Moral life is life not merely life in a community, but life which is fulfilled by means of the community. Salvation for Christians is a common effort. The members of the body in Paul's figure need one another; the life they share is shared fully by one when it is shared fully by all. When moral life is viewed as social and ecclesial, the decisive step is taken which removes the tendency of rational morality to be self-centered. The Christian does not look for his own fulfillment alone, nor does he think that fulfillment is possible alone. The self-sufficiency of the Stoic is foreign to Christian morality. What is impossible with men is possible with God; and it is through the Church that this divine power is meditated to the Christian.

## Integral Personal Morality

The moral revolution of the gospel is directed toward an integral moral life. This we found lacking in ethical systems of reason and nature. One could if one wished compile a catalog of moral precepts and prohibitions from the New Testament; it has rarely been attempted because such a catalog would so evidently omit the central features of gospel morality. The gospel shows no interest in detailed directions, in cases and their solutions. Persons will live the gospel because of a revolutionary change in their personal life, their values, their habits, their attitudes. Once this change has been worked, detailed prescriptions become unnecessary; they could even inhibit the full development of the Christian life, well intentioned as they might be. We observed that each concrete individual act is a part of a vital chain; the gospel conceives a person's acts in this way, and it is concerned with the person who performs the acts. Given the personal qualities, the proper acts will follow. A good tree produces good fruit. The personal change is not conceived as the acquisition of habits of virtue; it goes deeper.

The New Testament frequently describes this personal transformation as putting on Christ, as living in Christ, as

Christ living in the Christian, as the life of the Spirit in contrast to the life of the flesh. What Christ has done the Christian can do because he is a member of the body of Christ. He has the power of the Spirit which enables him to live in Christ. The language expresses a mystery which can never be fully comprehended; but the mystery is not penetrated more deeply by reducing union with Christ to the acquisition of good moral habits. In one passage (Phil 2:5) Paul calls it having the same mind among yourselves which you have in Christ Jesus. This verse is followed by the famous hymn in which Jesus is said to have emptied himself. We should notice that the mind of Christ is given to the Philippians as a guide to the way in which they should deal with each other. Their mutual relations should be governed by the personal transformation which has brought them to think like Christ, whose true mind is grasped in his emptying of self and his humiliation and obedience to death. This is the way in which the Philippians should attend to the interest of others. One can think like Christ because in the Church one is incorporated into Christ.

## Imitation of Christ

The imitation of Christ is a form of Christian spirituality which rests on long tradition. Some recent writers have questioned whether the imitation as it has usually been presented is a correct interpretation of the New Testament. A mechanical imitation of Jesus is impossible, and where he exercises the unique power which he possessed it is scarcely conceivable. Actually the imitation of Christ is mentioned only twice in the New Testament (1 Cor 11:1; 1 Thes 1:6). One could say that the New Testament more frequently tells us that the Christian should be Christ than that the Christian should imitate Christ. And the passages where imitation is mentioned should be read against the passages in which living in Christ is stated as the Christian ideal. One lives in Christ not by aping him, but in the manner described in Philippians 2:5-7. The Christian lives Christ when he shares in Christ's passion and death in the way in which God commits this share to him. Imitation could be again a question of isolated acts; identification with Christ touches the root of the acts, the principles by which one habitually judges and decides. When he becomes a disciple, the Christian denies that he is anything; and after this denial no future decision can ever be what it would be in rational ethics. There can simply be no morality of self-interest, enlightened or unenlightened.

## The Centrality of Love

The personal transformation of the Christian is a mystery which cannot be pierced; but the effects of the transformation are set forth clearly—with such clarity, in fact, that Christians have sometimes tried to make them more obscure than they are. The pivot of the Christian moral revolution is love. This is the entirely new and unique feature of Christian moral teaching; it is not the center of a moral structure, it is the entire structure. No one questions the centrality of love in New Testament morality; it is questionable whether Christians have always grasped how different it is and how total it is. I venture to state the difference by saying that it is not only a love which is known solely by Christian revelation, but it is a love of which only a Christian is capable. I venture to state its totality by saying that in the New Testament an act which is not an act of love has no moral value at all.

There are New Testament sayings which express the centrality and the totality of love. The first is a saying of Jesus found in the Synoptic Gospels with some variations: the saying about the greatest and the first commandment (Mt 22:34-40; Mk 12:28-31; Lk 10:25-28). The commandment of the love of God is called the greatest (Matthew) or the first (Mark) or the commandment by which one obtains eternal life (Luke). The commandment is named by Jesus (Mark and Matthew) or by the inquirer (Luke). The second is the commandment of the love of the neighbor. Matthew adds that the entire Law and the prophets (that is, the entire revelation made to Israel) depend on these two commandments. Luke adds to the discussion the parable of the Good Samaritan in answer to the question who is meant by neighbor. The answer, which mentions the group most hated by Jews, is altogether inclusive. The second saying is found in Romans 13:8-10. Here Paul says that one has no duty toward his neighbor except to love him, that all the commandments are summed up in the commandment to love one's neighbor, and that love of the neighbor is the fulfillment of the Law.

## Love and the Moral Code

These passages, I think, support the statement that there is no moral action in Christian life except the act of love. It is necessary to add that the New Testament does not conceive the love mentioned in the two commandments as two loves but as one. What is done to one's neighbor is done to Christ (Mt 25:40, 45). John observes that one's love of God can be proved only by his love of his brother (1 Jn 4:20). We have noticed (Chapter VI) that John draws a paradoxical conclusion in 1 Jn 4:11: "If God has so loved us, we also ought to love one another," where rigorous logic would lead one to expect "If God has so loved us, we ought to love God." But it is paradoxical only by ethical standards; John knew what is so clear in the New Testament, that when one loves one's neighbor one loves God. Matthew 25:31-46 contains a parable of an assembly of all men before the Son of Man, who divides them into two groups according to their merits. The sole question on which they are divided is the rendering of service to others. I suppose one would go too far in saying that this is the only point on which men are judged, but one would scarcely go too far in saying it is the chief point; for love is the fulfillment of the law.

The commandment of love, then, is the entire Christian moral code. The commandments such as those which prohibit murder, theft, and adultery are not voided; but it is fairly well assured that one who loves his neighbor will not commit these crimes. One who loves his neighbor with the fullness of Christian love is as assured against sin as it is possible for man to be. He may make errors of judgment and mistake love for something else. This is a risk which cannot be avoided; but Jesus apparently was willing to trust the mistakes of love more than the mistakes of reason. It would take a rather bold moral philosopher to say that his system assures infallibly against errors in moral judgment; and his errors will not be the mistakes of love. Justice under law is compatible with hatred.

# John Lawrence McKenzie

## Uniquely Christian Love

This is the centrality and the totality of love; the difference between this love and any other moral attitude I have said can be seen in the fact that only the Christian is capable of this kind of love. It is the love of God for man revealed in Christ Jesus, altogether other-directed with no return asked or expected and no limits placed on the demands it makes. Should love of the neighbor carry the Christian as far as Jesus' love of man carried him, the Christian has a better assurance that it is love and not something else which motivates him. It is always a help to re-read Matthew 5, perhaps the best statement of the paradoxical folly of Christian love in practice in the entire New Testament. John said that the Christian cannot prove his love of God except by his love of man; Matthew makes it very clear that it is not really proved unless the person we love is an enemy. The Christian can be the object of enmity, but not its subject; one who is loved ceases to be an enemy. "Love of one's enemy" is a contradiction in terms; and Christians who think they are doing well when they love their enemies are often quite careful to make it clear that they remain enemies. The Christian loves his enemies as Christ loved man hostile to God. He is an agent of reconciliation, and a persevering agent. God has revealed to the Christian a value in his fellow lumps of clay which they do not have by their nature. Reason demands moderation in love as in all things; faith destroys moderation here. Faith tolerates a moderate love of one's fellow man no more than it tolerates a moderate love between God and man.

Among the condescending remarks which Europeans like to make about Americans is the statement that Americans like to be loved. One who is skilled in Mr. Stephen Potter's games-manship recognizes that this is a true ploy, to say that Americans like to be loved has as much point as saying that Americans have two feet. The Christian who begins to grasp the moral revolution of love begins to dream of a world, or at least a community, in which mutual love glows like the bright warm sunshine. Love returned is its own reward. It was necessary for Jesus to say explicitly that Christian love does not care whether it is its own reward or not; one should reread 1 Corinthians 13 for the classic statement of this principle. The Christian knows that his love is the active presence of God in the world; if he lacks it, he takes away God's presence from the only place where he can put it. He has come between his neighbor and the saving love of Jesus Christ. But if he is true to his Christian love, it may kill him, impoverish him, or disgrace him. In any hypothesis he is sure to lose at least some of those goods of this world or of the person which Jesus took some trouble to point out are of no importance.

### Encounter of Reason and Gospel

We can now return to our question: Does the gospel reject a morality of law based on reason and nature? If the above exposition is based on the New Testament, it is difficult to see where there is room for it. If such a morality necessarily includes such elements as a morality centered on self, the atomization of the human community into isolated persons and of the moral life of the person into isolated acts, the minimal and negative morality of the permitted and the prohibited, and the partial or even total abdication of personal responsibility, then one must say that the gospel rejects any system which implies these things. Reason has its place in Christian morality in finding ways to fulfill these difficult and "unreal" commandments of love, not to evade them and substitute something else far more natural and practical and therefore just as good; at least no Christian has yet dared to say in so many words that rational morality is better.

But when one reviews the central theme of New Testament morality, one is depressed by a feeling of despair—despair of one's fellowman and of oneself. Is it possible? Is it practical? And one knows that one is asking God why he does not change the world into a community of love where it would not be so awfully hard to love one's neighbor as oneself. And one further realizes that the operation of this change is the mission God has committed to the Christian in that part of the world which is under the control of the individual person.

# Vatican II
## 1966

*"A sense of the dignity of the human person has been impressing itself more and more deeply on the consciousness of contemporary man." These are the opening words of the Second Vatican Council's* Declaration on Religious Freedom. *Accompanying this sense of dignity is the demand that men should act on their own judgment, enjoying and making use of a responsible freedom.*

*Freedom is one of the major concerns of contemporary man. As a concept, it is central to the intellectual tradition that supports Christianity. As a reality, it appears to be highly elusive. Wars have been fought in its name, political movements have been launched under its banner, countless millions of individuals long for a taste of it. Whether or not mankind will ever be truly free is a question that may know no answer.*

*The Fathers of the Second Vatican Council, aware of contemporary man's thirst for freedom, turned their attention to this theme and, in their effort to clarify the foundation of true freedom, gave to the world an unusual example of freedom in action. Their debate on freedom, and particularly religious freedom, was heated, emotional, truthful and free. Because the concept of freedom leads naturally enough into that of the development of doctrine, the document produced by their debates and discussions was the most controversial of the Council.*

*The two chapters of the declaration treat the general principle of religious freedom and religious freedom in the light of revelation.*

*The document clearly states that in matters religious no one is to be forced to act in a manner contrary to his beliefs, nor to be restrained from acting in accordance with his beliefs. Though this is not a new principle of religious freedom, it is certainly a step forward for Catholic documents, insofar as it puts to rest forever any suggestion that the religion professed by a majority of the people in a given country should be or must be practiced by everyone. The principle protects the minority, as well as the individual. Further it protects all mankind from political structures that would refuse the practice of religion to citizens.*

*Freedom is rightly founded on the dignity of the human person. Of course this assumes a healthy understanding of the person as the meeting point of individuality and communality and as the being who, endowed with reason and will, is capable of assuming responsibility. It also assumes that men will enjoy immunity from external coercion as well as psychological freedom.*

*In an era that is experiencing great confusion around the concept of freedom and tends to encourage immature individualism and socialism, this document is most welcome. Nations, cultures and religions are intermingling today more than ever. It is essential that this process be accompanied by a deep sensitivity to the human drive for freedom and a respect for all individuals and societies that want to be free. Then only will a new world be created in which everyone will enjoy the freedom of the children of God.*

# DECLARATION ON
# RELIGIOUS FREEDOM

ON THE RIGHT OF THE PERSON AND OF COMMUNITIES
TO SOCIAL AND CIVIL FREEDOM IN MATTERS RELIGIONS

A sense of the dignity of the human person has been impressing itself more and more deeply on the consciousness of contemporary man. And the demand is increasingly made that men should act on their own judgment, enjoying and making use of a responsible freedom, not driven by coercion but motivated by a sense of duty. The demand is also made that constitutional limits should be set to the powers of government, in order that there may be no encroachment on the rightful freedom of the person and of associations.

This demand for freedom in human society chiefly regards the quest for the values proper to the human spirit. It regards, in the first place, the free exercise of religion in society.

This Vatican Synod takes careful note of these desires in the minds of men. It proposes to declare them to be greatly in accord with truth and justice. To this end, it searches into the sacred tradition and doctrine of the Church—the treasury out of which the Church continually brings forth new things that are in harmony with the things that are old.

First, this sacred Synod professes its belief that God himself has made known to mankind the way in which men are to serve Him, and thus be saved in Christ and come to blessedness. We believe that this one true religion subsists in the catholic and apostolic Church, to which the Lord Jesus committed the duty of spreading it abroad among all men. Thus He spoke to the apostles: "Go, therefore, and make disciples of all nations, baptizing them in the name of the Father, and of the Son, and of the Holy Spirit, teaching them to observe all that I have commanded you" (Mt. 28:19-20). On their part, all men are bound to seek the truth, especially in what concerns God and

His Church, and to embrace the truth they come to know, and to hold fast to it.

This sacred Synod likewise professes its belief that it is upon the human conscience that these obligations fall and exert their binding force. The truth cannot impose itself except by virtue of its own truth, as it makes its entrance into the mind at once quietly and with power. Religious freedom, in turn, which men demand as necessary to fulfill their duty to worship God, has to do with immunity from coercion in civil society. Therefore, it leaves untouched traditional Catholic doctrine on the moral duty of men and societies toward the true religion and toward the one Church of Christ.

Over and above all this, in taking up the matter of religious freedom this sacred Synod intends to develop the doctrine of recent Popes on the inviolable rights of the human person and on the constitutional order of society.

## CHAPTER I

### GENERAL PRINCIPLE OF RELIGIOUS FREEDOM

This Vatican Synod declares that the human person has a right to religious freedom. This freedom means that all men are to be immune from coercion on the part of individuals or of social groups and of any human power, in such wise that in matters religious no one is to be forced to act in a manner contrary to his own beliefs. Nor is anyone to be restrained from acting in accordance with his own beliefs, whether privately or publicly, whether alone or in association with others, within due limits.

The Synod further declares that the right to religious freedom has its foundation in the very dignity of the human person, as this dignity is known through the revealed Word of God and by reason itself. This right of the human person to religious freedom is to be recognized in the constitutional law whereby society is governed. Thus it is to become a civil right.

It is in accordance with their dignity as person—that is, beings endowed with reason and free will and therefore privileged to bear personal responsibility—that all men should be at once impelled by nature and also bound by a moral obligation to seek the truth, especially religious truth. They are also bound to adhere to the truth, once it is known, and to order their whole lives in accord with the demands of truth.

However, men cannot discharge these obligations in a manner in keeping with their own nature unless they enjoy immunity from external coercion as well as psychological freedom. Therefore, the right to religious freedom has its foundation, not in the subjective disposition of the person, but in his very nature. In consequence, the right to this immunity continues to exist even in those who do not live up to their obligation of seeking the truth and adhering to it. Nor is the exercise of this right to be impeded, provided that the just requirements of public order are observed.

Further light is shed on the subject if one considers that the highest norm of human life is the divine law—eternal, objective, and universal—whereby God orders, directs, and governs the entire universe and all the ways of the human community, by a plan conceived in wisdom and love. Man has been made by God to participate in this law, with the result that, under the gentle disposition of divine Providence, he can come to perceive ever increasingly the unchanging truth. Hence every man has the duty, and therefore the right, to seek the truth in matters religious, in order that he may with prudence form for himself right and true judgments of conscience, with the use of all suitable means.

Truth, however, is to be sought after in a manner proper to the dignity of the human person and his social nature. The inquiry is to be free, carried on with the aid of teaching or instruction, communication, and dialogue. In the course of these, men explain to one another the truth they have discovered, or think they have discovered, in order thus to assist one another in the quest for truth. Moreover, as the truth is discovered, it is by a personal assent that men are to adhere to it.

On his part, man perceives and acknowledges the imperatives of the divine law through the mediation of conscience. In all his activity a man is bound to follow his conscience faithfully, in order that he may come to God, for whom he was created. It follows that he is not to be forced to act in a manner contrary to his conscience. Nor, on the other hand, is he to be restrained from acting in accordance with his conscience, especially in matters religious.

For, of its very nature, the exercise of religion consists before all else in those internal, voluntary, and free acts whereby man sets the course of his life directly toward God. No merely human power can either command or prohibit acts of this kind.

However, the social nature of man itself requires that he should give external expression to his internal acts of religion; that he should participate with others in matters religious; that he should profess his religion in community. Injury, therefore, is done to the human person and to the very order established by God for human life, if the free exercise of religion is denied in society when the just requirements of public order do not so require.

There is a further consideration. The religious acts whereby men, in private and in public and out of a sense of personal conviction, direct their lives to God transcend by their very nature the order of terrestrial and temporal affairs. Government, therefore, ought indeed to take account of the religious life of the people and show it favor, since the function of government is to make provision for the common welfare. However, it would clearly transgress the limits set to its power were it to presume to direct or inhibit acts that are religious.

The freedom or immunity from coercion in matters religious which is the endowment of persons as individuals is also to be recognized as their right when they act in community. Religious bodies are a requirement of the social nature both of man and of religion itself.

Provided the just requirements of public order are observed, religious bodies rightfully claim freedom in order that they may govern themselves according to their own norms, honor the Supreme Being in public worship, assist their members in the practice of the religious life, strengthen them by instruction, and promote institutions in which they may join together for the purpose of ordering their own lives in accordance with their religious principles.

Religious bodies also have the right not to be hindered, either by legal measures or by administrative action on the part of government, in the selection, training, appointment, and transferral of their own ministers, in communicating with religious authorities and communities abroad, in erecting buildings for religious purposes, and in the acquisition and use of suitable funds or properties.

Religious bodies also have the right not to be hindered in their public teaching and witness to their faith, whether by the spoken or by the written word. However, in spreading religious faith and in introducing religious practices, everyone ought at all times to refrain from any manner of action which might seem to carry a hint of coercion or of a kind of persuasion that would be dishonorable or unworthy, especially when dealing with poor or uneducated people. Such a manner of action would have to be considered an abuse of one's own right and a violation of the right of others.

In addition, it comes within the meaning of religious freedom that religious bodies should not be prohibited from freely undertaking to show the special value of their doctrine in what concerns the organization of society and the inspiration of the whole of human activity. Finally, the social nature of man and the very nature of religion afford the foundation of the right of men freely to hold meetings and to establish educational, cultural, charitable, and social organizations, under the impulse of their own religious sense.

Since the family is a society in its own original right, it has the right freely to live its own domestic religious life under the guidance of parents. Parents, moreover, have the right to determine, in accordance with their own religious beliefs, the kind of religious education that their children are to receive.

Government, in consequence, must acknowledge the right of parents to make a genuinely free choice of schools and of other means of education. The use of this freedom of choice is not to be made a reason for imposing unjust burdens on parents, whether directly or indirectly. Besides, the rights of parents are violated if their children are forced to attend lessons or instruction which are not in agreement with their religious beliefs. The same is true if a single system of education, from which all religious formation is excluded, is imposed upon all.

The common welfare of society consists in the entirety of those conditions of social life under which men enjoy the

possibility of achieving their own perfection in a certain fullness of measure and also with some relative ease. Hence this
welfare consists chiefly in the protection of the rights, and in
the performance of the duties, of the human person. Therefore,
the care of the right to religious freedom devolves upon the
peoples as a whole, upon social groups, upon government, and
upon the Church and other religious Communities, in virtue of
the duty of all toward the common welfare, and in the manner
proper to each.

The protection and promotion of the inviolable rights of
man ranks among the essential duties of government. Therefore,
government is to assume the safeguard of the religious freedom
of all its citizens, in an effective manner, by just laws and by
other appropriate means. Government is also to help create conditions favorable to the fostering of religious life, in order that
the people may be truly enabled to exercise their religious
rights and to fulfill their religious duties, and also in order that
society itself may profit by the moral qualities of justice and
peace which have their origin in men's faithfulness to God and
to His holy will.

If, in view of peculiar circumstances obtaining among certain peoples, special legal recognition is given in the constitutional order of society to one religious body, it is at the same
time imperative that the right of all citizens and religious bodies
to religious freedom should be recognized and made effective
in practice.

Finally, government is to see to it that the equality of citizens before the law, which is itself an element of the common
welfare, is never violated for religious reasons whether openly or
covertly. Nor is there to be discrimination among citizens.

It follows that a wrong is done when government imposes
upon its people, by force or fear or other means, the profession
or repudiation of any religion, or when it hinders men from
joining or leaving a religious body. All the more is it a violation
of the will of God and of the sacred rights of the person and the
family of nations, when force is brought to bear in any way in
order to destroy or repress religion, either in the whole of mankind or in a particular country or in a specific community.

The right to religious freedom is exercised in human society; hence its exercise is subject to certain regulatory norms. In the use of all freedoms, the moral principle of personal and social responsibility is to be observed. In the exercise of their rights, individual men and social groups are bound by the moral law to have respect both for the rights of others and for their own duties toward others and for the common welfare of all. Men are to deal with their fellows in justice and civility.

Furthermore, society has the right to defend itself against possible abuses committed on pretext of freedom of religion. It is the special duty of government to provide this protection. However, government is not to act in arbitrary fashion or in an unfair spirit of partisanship. Its action is to be controlled by juridical norms which are in conformity with the objective moral order.

These norms arise out of the need for effective safeguard of the rights of all citizens and for peaceful settlement of conflicts of rights. They flow from the need for an adequate care of genuine public peace, which comes about when men live together in good order and in true justice. They come, finally, out of the need for a proper guardianship of public morality. These matters constitute the basic components of the common welfare: they are what is meant by public order.

For the rest, the usages of society are to be the usages of freedom in their full range. These require that the freedom of man be respected as far as possible, and curtailed only when and in so far as necessary.

Many pressures are brought to bear upon men of our day, to the point where the danger arises lest they lose the possibility of acting on their own judgment. On the other hand, not a few can be found who seem inclined to use the name of freedom as the pretext for refusing to submit to authority and for making light of the duty of obedience.

Therefore, this Vatican Synod urges everyone, especially those who are charged with the task of educating others, to do their utmost to form men who will respect the moral order and be obedient to lawful authority. Let them form men too who will be lovers of true freedom—men, in other words, who will come to decisions on their own judgment and in the light of truth, govern their activities with a sense of responsibility, and strive after what is true and right, willing always to join with others in cooperative effort.

Religious freedom, therefore, ought to have this further purpose and aim, namely, that men may come to act with greater responsibility in fulfilling their duties in community life.

## CHAPTER II

### RELIGIOUS FREEDOM IN THE LIGHT OF REVELATION

The declaration of this Vatican Synod on the right of man to religious freedom has its foundation in the dignity of the person. The requirements of this dignity have come to be more adequately known to human reason through centuries of experience. What is more, this doctrine of freedom has roots in divine revelation, and for this reason Christians are bound to respect it all the more conscientiously.

Revelation does not indeed affirm in so many words the right of man to immunity from external coercion in matters religious. It does, however, disclose the dignity of the human person in its full dimensions. It gives evidence of the respect which Christ showed toward the freedom with which man is to fulfill his duty of belief in the Word of God. It gives us lessons too in the spirit which disciples of such a Master ought to make their own and to follow in every situation.

Thus further light is cast on the general principles upon which the doctrine of this Declaration on Religious Freedom is based. In particular, religious freedom in society is entirely consonant with the freedom of the act of Christian faith.

It is one of the major tenets of Catholic doctrine that man's response to God in faith must be free. Therefore no one is to be forced to embrace the Christian faith against his own will. This doctrine is contained in the Word of God and it was constantly proclaimed by the Fathers of the Church. The act of faith is of its very nature a free act. Man, redeemed by Christ the Savior and through Christ Jesus called to be God's adopted son, cannot give his adherence to God revealing Himself unless the Father draw him to offer to God the reasonable and free submission of faith.

It is therefore completely in accord with the nature of faith that in matters religious every manner of coercion on the part of men should be excluded. In consequence, the principle of religious freedom makes no small contribution to the creation of an environment in which men can without hindrance be invited to Christian faith, and embrace it of their own free will, and profess it effectively in their whole manner of life.

God calls men to serve Him in spirit and in truth. Hence they are bound in conscience but they stand under no complusion. God has regard for the dignity of the human person whom He Himself created; man is to be guided by his own judgment and he is to enjoy freedom.

This truth appears at its height in Christ Jesus, in whom God perfectly manifested Himself and His ways with men. Christ is our Master and our Lord. He is also meek and humble of heart. And in attracting and inviting His disciples He acted patiently. He wrought miracles to shed light on His teaching and to establish its truth. But His intention was to rouse faith in His hearers and to confirm them in faith, not to exert coercion upon them.

He did indeed denounce the unbelief of some who listened to Him; but He left vengeance to God in expectation of the day of judgment. When He sent His apostles into the world, He said to them: "He who believes and is baptized shall be saved, but he who does not believe shall be condemned" (Mk. 16:16); but He Himself, noting that cockle had been sown amid the wheat, gave orders that both should be allowed to grow until the harvest time, which will come at the end of the world.

He refused to be a political Messiah, ruling by force; He preferred to call Himself the Son of Man, who came to serve and to give his life as a ransom for many" (Mk. 10:45). He showed Himself the perfect Servant of God; "a bruised reed he will not break, and a smoking wick he will not quench" (Mt. 12:20).

He acknowledged the power of government and its rights, when He commanded that tribute be given to Caesar. But He gave clear warning that the higher rights of God are to be kept inviolate: "Render, therefore, to Caesar the things that are Caesar's, and to God the things that are God's" (Mt. 22:21).

In the end, when He completed on the cross the work of redemption whereby He achieved salvation and true freedom for men, He also brought His revelation to completion. He bore witness to the truth, but He refused to impose the truth by force on those who spoke against it. Not by force of blows does His rule assert its claims. Rather, it is established by witnessing to the truth and by hearing the truth, and it extends its dominion by the love whereby Christ, lifted up on the cross, draws all men to Himself.

Taught by the word and example of Christ, the apostles followed the same way. From the very origins of the Church the disciples of Christ strove to convert men to faith in Christ as the Lord—not, however, by the use of coercion or by devices unworthy of the gospel, but by the power, above all, of the Word of God. Steadfastly they proclaimed to all the plan of God our Savior, "who wishes all men to be saved and to come to the knowledge of the truth" (1 Tim. 2:4). At the same time, however, they showed respect for weaker souls even though these persons were in error. Thus they made it plain that "every one of us will render an account of himself to God" (Rom. 14:12), and for this reason is bound to obey his conscience.

Like Christ Himself, the apostles were unceasingly bent upon bearing witness to the truth of God. They showed special courage in speaking "the word of God with boldness" (Acts 4:31) before the people and their rulers. With a firm faith they held that the gospel is indeed the power of God unto salvation for all who believe. Therefore they rejected all "carnal weapons. They followed the example of the gentleness and respectfulness of Christ. And they preached the Word of God in the full confidence that there was resident in this Word itself a divine power able to destroy all the forces arrayed against God and to bring men to faith in Christ and to His service. As the Master, so too the apostles recognized legitimate civil authority. "For there exists no authority except from God," the Apostle teaches, and therefore commands: "Let everyone be subject to the higher authorities . . . : he who resists the authority resists the ordinance of God" (Rom. 13:1-2).

At the same time, however, they did not hesitate to speak out against governing powers which set themselves in opposition to the holy will of God: "We must obey God rather than men" (Acts 5:29). This is the way along which countless martyrs and other believers have walked through all ages and over all the earth.

The Church therefore is being faithful to the truth of the gospel, and is following the way of Christ and the apostles when she recognizes, and gives support to, the principle of religious freedom as befitting the dignity of man and as being in accord with divine revelation. Throughout the ages, the Church has kept safe and handed on the doctrine received from the Master and from the apostles. In the life of the People of God as it has made its pilgrim way through the vicissitudes of human history, there have at times appeared ways of acting which were less in accord with the spirit of the gospel and even opposed to it. Nevertheless, the doctrine of the Church that no one is to be coerced into faith has always stood firm.

Thus the leaven of the gospel has long been about its quiet work in the minds of men. To it is due in great measure the fact that in the course of time men have come more widely to recognize their dignity as persons, and the conviction has grown stronger that in religious matters the person in society is to be kept free from all manner of human coercion.

Among the things which concern the good of the Church and indeed the welfare of society here on earth—things therefore which are always and everywhere to be kept secure and defended against all injury—this certainly is preeminent, namely, that the Church should enjoy that full measure of freedom which her care for the salvation of men requires. This freedom is sacred, because the only-begotten Son endowed with it the Church which He purchased with His blood. It is so much the property of the Church that to act against it is to act against the will of God. The freedom of the Church is the fundamental principle in what concerns the relations between the Church and governments and the whole civil order.

In human society and in the face of government, the Church claims freedom for herself in her character as a spiritual authority, established by Christ the Lord. Upon this authority there rests, by divine mandate, the duty of going out into the whole world and preaching the gospel to every creature. The Church also claims freedom for herself in her character as a society of men who have the right to live in society in accordance with the precepts of Christian faith.

In turn, where the principle of religious freedom is not only proclaimed in words or simply incorporated in law but also given sincere and practical application, there the Church succeeds in achieving a stable situation of right as well as of fact and the independence which is necessary for the fulfillment of her divine mission. This independence is precisely what the authorities of the Church claim in society.

At the same time, the Christian faithful, in common with all other men, possess the civil right not to be hindered in leading their lives in accordance with their conscience. Therefore, a harmony exists between the freedom of the Church and the religious freedom which is to be recognized as the right of all men and communities and sanctioned by constitutional law.

In order to be faithful to the divine command, "Make disciples of all nations" (Mt. 28:19), the Catholic Church must work with all urgency and concern "that the Word of God may run and be glorified" (2 Th. 3:1). Hence the Church earnestly begs of her children that, first of all, "supplications, prayers, intercessions, and thanksgivings be made for all men. . . . For this is good and agreeable in the sight of God our Savior, who wishes all men to be saved and to come to the knowledge of the truth" (1 Tim. 2:1-4).

In the formation of their consciences, the Christian faithful ought carefully to attend to the sacred and certain doctrine of the Church. The Church is, by the will of Christ, the teacher of the truth. It is her duty to give utterance to, and authoritatively to teach, that Truth which is Christ Himself, and also to declare and confirm by her authority those principles of the moral order which have their origin in human nature itself. Furthermore, let Christians walk in wisdom in the face of those outside, "in the Holy Spirit, in unaffected love, in the word of truth" (2 Cor. 6:6-7). Let them be about their task of spreading the light of life with all confidence and apostolic courage, even to the shedding of their blood.

The disciple is bound by a grave obligation toward Christ his Master ever more adequately to understand the truth received from Him, faithfully to proclaim it, and vigorously to defend it, never—be it understood—having recourse to means that are incompatible with the spirit of the gospel. At the same time, the charity of Christ urges him to act lovingly, prudently and patiently in his dealings with those who are in error or in ignorance with regard to the faith. All is to be taken into account—the Christian duty to Christ, the life-giving Word which must be proclaimed, the rights of the human person, and the measure of grace granted by God through Christ to men, who are invited freely to accept and profess the faith.

The fact is that men of the present day want to be able freely to profess their religion in private and in public. Religious freedom has already been declared to be a civil right in most constitutions, and it is solemnly recognized in international documents. The further fact is that forms of government still exist under which, even though freedom of religious worship receives constitutional recognition, the powers of government are engaged in the effort to deter citizens from the profession of religion and to make life difficult and dangerous for religious Communities.

This sacred Synod greets with joy the first of these two facts, as among the signs of the times. With sorrow, however, it denounces the other fact, as only to be deplored. The Synod exhorts Catholics, and it directs a plea to all men, most carefully to consider how greatly necessary religious freedom is, especially in the present condition of the human family.

All nations are coming into even closer unity. Men of different cultures and religions are being brought together in closer relationships. There is a growing consciousness of the personal responsibility that weighs upon every man. All this is evident.

Consequently, in order that relationships of peace and harmony may be established and maintained within the whole of mankind, it is necessary that religious freedom be everywhere provided with an effective constitutional guarantee, and that respect be shown for the high duty and right of man freely to lead his religious life in society.

May the God and Father of all grant that the human family, through careful observance of the principle of religious freedom in society, may be brought by the grace of Christ and the power of the Holy Spirit to the sublime and unending "freedom of the glory of the sons of God" (Rom. 8:21).

Each and every one of the things set forth in this Declaration has won the consent of the Fathers of this most sacred Council. We too, by the apostolic authority conferred on us by Christ, join with the Venerable Fathers in approving, decreeing, and establishing these things in the Holy Spirit, and we direct that what has thus been enacted in synod be published to God's glory.

Rome, at St. Peter's, December 7, 1965

I, Paul, Bishop of the Catholic Church

# Paul Hanly Furfey
## 1896-

The Respectable Murderers *is a disturbing book, for it faces squarely the perversities either committed or condoned by decent Christians throughout the world: American Negro slavery, the slaughter of European Jews, the bombing of non-combatants, the injustice of extreme poverty in the United States. The author of this book is a most unusual man, for at the age of 82, he retains a sense of outrage that has driven him on as a critique of social evils since he was a young man.*

*Monsignor Paul Hanly Furfey has been associated with The Catholic University of America for more than sixty years, mostly as a professor. His lectures and writings have been an incessant prod to Catholics, laity, clergy and hierarchy. Though primarily concerned with the social issues that paralyze the world today, he is quite aware that change requires the true ethical commitment of individual Christians to the revolutionary message of Jesus.*

*In the preface to* The Respectable Murderers, *he observes that the people Christ denounced were the rich and the powerful, the respectable members of the upper classes. And He earned their hatred. Furfey knows that it is almost impossible to repudiate the respectable. The very word is an obstacle. Yet he insists that this is the task of the Christian.*

*We have selected two chapters from the book, "Respect-ability is not enough" and "The Ethic of Christian Love." In the first, Furfey discusses the ethic of respectability. He argues that the person who lives by this ethic cannot be said to be moral. Rather he is quite amoral. This is the ethic that protects the established order and the members of the dominant classes go to great pain to force everyone to observe it. To challenge this ethic is to challenge the privileges of the privileged. Too often organized religions, at least tacitly, lend their support to the ethic of respectability. Furfey suggests that it is the ethic of respectability that made it possible for America to condemn the Nazi policy of genocide while carrying out its own policy of bombing non-combatants. And he predicts that the future will be filled out with even greater horror stories of mass slaughter, persecution, and exploitation of the weak, unless our society can get rid of the ethic of respectability and replace it with a much healthier one.*

*The Ethic of Christian Love? It could change history, but its seeming simplicity is an obstacle to most people who call themselves Chrsitians. They don't understand the most basic and essential teaching of Christ. It is easy to talk about love of God and neighbor; to live it is something else, for it requires, all too often, brave disobedience, refusal to conform, or public protest.*

*Whether the world is yet ready for the Christian ethic of love remains the question. If the Christian hesitates, he can at least retain his respectability.*

# THE RESPECTABLE MURDERERS

## CHAPTER 6

### RESPECTABILITY IS NOT ENOUGH

T he preceding chapters have summarized "case studies" of a highly disturbing phenomenon. Vast and cruel injustice can exist with the active cooperation, or at least with the passive acquiescence, of decent citizens. How this can be is hard to determine precisely. It is difficult enough for the criminologist to understand why common criminals revolt against the moral and civil law. It is much more difficult to understand why respectable citizens aid and abet monstrous social crimes.

In our first chapter we attempted to give some reasons. The community insists on certain customary types of action—the mores. Citizens are coerced to follow these mores by various sanctions, ranging from social disapproval to the death penalty. In a paramoral society certain of the mores are contrary to the moral law, so that the citizen who realizes this fact must either act against his conscience or suffer certain unpleasant consequences; or he may, as a third alternative, stifle his conscience and act immorally. In any case, what usually happens in a paramoral society is that the citizens as a whole, including the decent and the respectable, will accept the mores, whether they are right or wrong.

This explanation is doubtless valid as far as it goes, but it leaves unanswered a more fundamental question. Why do the mores, with their attached sanctions, exist in the first place? Why does the organized community set up these standards of conduct, formal or informal, and why is there such great social pressure that they be observed? Why do the mores have so much prestige that in a paramoral society they take precedence even over the moral law itself?

The answer is not far to seek. The mores are essentially important because the social order could not be maintained without them. There could not be an organized community unless its members had agreed to follow certain standards, unless, for example, they had agreed to drive on the right-hand side of the road, to pay their just debts, to send their children to school, and to obey a thousand other rules and customs. Some of these are obviously arbitrary; we could, for instance, agree to drive on the left instead of the right. Some are based on the moral law; one must, in justice, pay one's debts. However, the essential fact is that all citizens must accept these standards, at least the principal ones and at least most of the time. Unless they did so, there could be no society; there could be only chaos, until a new set of mores was developed.

Loyalty to the mores, then, is simply loyalty to one's community. He who follows them strengthens existing society and earns the respect of his fellow citizens. He is respectable. In a moral society there is no conflict between morals and mores; one can be respectable and virtuous at the same time. However, in a paramoral society there are vast areas of conflict, and citizens are faced again and again with an unavoidable choice between the mores and the dictates of conscience. It is a choice between two ways of life. If a man decides to disregard his conscience and follow the mores habitually, whether right or wrong, he is actually following a perverted, though real, system of ethics which we have here been calling the ethic of respectability. This is a code of conduct as well as a philosophy of life. However, indefensible as it may be in the light of reason or religious teaching, the ethic of respectability does nevertheless provide a definite guide to behavior.

But a man who lives by the ethic of respectability cannot be said to be moral. His deepest motive of conduct is not the moral law or any religious principle. His ultimate loyalty is directed towards society-as-it-is. He lives to stabilize this society and thus gain the applause of like-minded men. He may appear virtuous because he is a very regular church member, pays his debts promptly, and is faithful to his wife. Really, however, he acts in this manner because it is regarded as respectable. The man is actually quite amoral.

It is not surprising that those most loyal to the established order are likely to be those who profit most from it. It is they, too, who are likely to follow the ethic of respectability most meticulously. Thus the most esteemed citizens will be those who control money, political power, and prestige, those men and their followers who profit by being connected with them. On the other hand, citizens with only a small stake in the established order have less reason to be loyal to it. The poor, the unemployed, members of minority groups, have small reason to feel constrained by the ethic of respectability.

The respectable members of the dominant classes go to great lengths to force their fellow citizens to observe the ethic of respectability. This is understandable. To attack the ethic of respectability is to attack the established order, and to do that is to attack the privileges of the privileged.

A striking example of the social significance of the mores and of the ethic of respectability which supports the mores is furnished by the slaveholding society of the Old South. The whole economic system of the region rested on the plantation with its slave labor. The gracious and charming life of the upper class was possible because obsequious slaves were available as house servants. Fundamental to the class system was the rule that every white person was accounted socially superior to every colored person; the poorest of the poor whites could bolster his ego with this thought. Not only the southern apologists for slavery, but even northern moderates, believed that the abolition of slavery would bring complete chaos, complete anarchy, to an entire region.

The bitter injustice of American Negro slavery was as obvious as any evil in history. Yet this clear fact could not be admitted, and fierce measures were used to suppress it. For example, a Louisiana law prescribed the death penalty for using "language in any public discourse, from the bar, the bench, the stage, the pulpit, or in any place whatsoever," that might cause "insubordination among the slaves." Literally interpreted this would mean that a clergyman who denounced the immorality of slavery could be dragged from his pulpit and hanged. The punishment was threatened on no abstract ground of ethics. It was threatened simply and solely because the denunciation of slavery would undermine the region's socio-economic system.

The imposition of false moral standards by force is, of course, not at all uncommon. On the contrary, it is a regular feature of paramoral societies. Anyone in Cuba who should dare to denounce the evils of Castroism would not for long have his freedom. The persecution of the Jews was commendable by the ethic of respectability prevalent in Nazi Germany; to brand the persecution as immoral was to court disaster. A grim proof of this was the fate of Dompropst Lichtenberg who, after daring to pray openly for Jews in the Berlin Cathedral, was sent to prison for two years, and then died on his way to a concentration camp. Hitler was equally successful in coercing citizens to fight in his obviously unjust wars. After exhaustive investigation, Gordon Zahn could find among Catholics only seven who openly refused military service; of these, six were executed.

There are methods more subtle than crude persecution to coerce public opinion into accepting the evil mores of a paramoral society. One is to obtain the approval, at least the tacit approval, of organized religion. To do this requires a certain moral dexterity, but it is far from being impossible.

In a normal, moral society, the cooperation of church and state is a natural requisite of the peace and well-being of the people. The state has the high function of "guiding its members to their greatest perfection in the material and temporal order." Ideally, therefore, church and state should work together not only for such immediate goals as the preservation of public order with the suppression of theft and violence, but also for more comprehensive goals, such as the establishment of a socio-economic structure which conduces to the welfare of all citizens. It is thus understandable that statesmen and religious leaders should develop strong mutual respect and should become accustomed to cooperate readily in the pursuit of their common objectives.

But this condition can be disturbed if paramoral elements are introduced into government programs. Often this will take place, not openly, but silently and deceptively, so that religious leaders may find themselves facing a moral aberration which is an accomplished fact. They then must decide when and with what emphasis they should repudiate the state's unjustifiable policies. The whole situation can be complicated, as it was in Nazi Germany, by false propaganda, counter-accusations, and a generally intensified emotional atmosphere.

When Hitler came to power, he seemed to do so legally enough and there appeared to be no reason for the German citizens to refuse him the obedience due to a lawfully constituted authority. Pius XI concluded a concordat with the Third Reich which Hitler covertly began to violate almost immediately. He soon started to persecute the Jews, to develop a quasi-religious cult of the state, and to introduce other immoral policies. However, when the Second World War began, Hitler could as chief of the government demand the loyalty of all citizens in the defense of their fatherland. In this new situation, which engendered agonizing problems of conscience, there seemed to be little that the individual citizen could do. Although he might protest openly he would as a consequence be shot or sent to a concentration camp, so that such a protest seemed futile. If he conspired to thwart Hitler's war aims he would be tormented by the thought that he was betraying his country. The usual result was inaction, both on the part of Catholics and of members of other religious groups. There was little sustained and effective protest. Thus, much against their wills, religious leaders were placed in the embarrassing position of seeming to give a certain tacit approval to Hitler's paramoral society.

It must be admitted, of course, that religious leaders are not always merely trapped by circumstances. History knows only too many instances of spiritual leaders who were too cowardly to protest against an evil government or who voluntarily cooperated with it for their own selfish ends. The public profession of religious principles does not automatically make one virtuous. The Pharisees were not the only prominent churchmen who set themselves up as models of devotion and yet "left undone the weightier matters of the Law, right judgment and mercy and faithfulness."

A paramoral society can obscure its perverse policies in an atmosphere of respectability by manipulating the machinery of law making and law enforcement. The law has naturally a certain majesty, since it exists for the application to specific situations of the abstract principles of right and wrong. And the law makes such application very theatrically. Anyone who has ever been present while sentence was being pronounced in a criminal court will realize this. The defendant stands manacled between guards; the judge sits at a raised desk, wearing robes which symbolize the impersonality of his office; the courtroom is hushed as the sentence is pronounced. It is a dramatic repudiation of the evil-doer by organized society, and a concrete manifestation of the public conscience. The distinction between right and wrong is presumably spelled out with the utmost clarity.

In a paramoral society, when evil laws are enforced by the courts it is very hard for the spectator to realize that the above situation has been completely reversed. The manacled defendant represents justice and the judge in his robes represents evil. Certainly, under the Third Reich it must have required an unusual clarity of thought and an unusual independence of judgment to grasp the fact that the prisoner at the bar might be standing there simply because he was courageous enough to resist the outrageous anti-Semitism of the state. It must have been hard for the average citizen to realize that the elaborate machinery normally associated with the maintenance of justice was being used to support the most infamous injustices. For even when the law is evil, it remains majestic; and its majesty remains impressive.

After the war, the major leaders of the Third Reich were put on trial for waging aggressive war and for "crimes against humanity." It is surely a laudable principle that those responsible for the conduct of a war should be held accountable for their actions; however, it is more than regrettable that in this instance the defendants should have been chosen exclusively from among the victors. For representatives of the Allies to have acted as judges would seem to have been a violation of the elementary principle that a judge should not be involved, either personally or as a member of some corporate entity, in the issues to be tried before him. It was particularly ironic that representatives of the cruel and despotic government of Stalinist Russia should have been selected to judge the "crimes against humanity" committed by others.

One thing the war-crimes trials achieved brilliantly: they dramatized the respectability of the Allies. That was perhaps their chief, though unadmitted—perhaps even unconscious—

purpose. Possibly the British and American members of the tribunals may have felt an occasional scruple as they picked their way through the rubble of German cities where their bombers had so relentlessly slaughtered tens of thousands of noncombatants; but once in the courtroom their equanimity was doubtless restored. They cloaked themselves in the majesty of the law. Day after day, week after week, the evil deeds of the Germans were discussed in detail while the representatives of the Allies passed judgment on their enemies. It was not enough to win the war; the moral superiority of the victors had to be demonstrated.

Respectability consists in conformity to the mores. The existence of a set of mores presupposes the existence of a society which imposes those mores and supports those who conform to them. As long as the Third Reich prospered, prominent Nazi officials enjoyed great prestige. With the aid of swarms of subordinates, they implemented public policy, they received honors, they lived in comfort, even during the widespread poverty of the period. By Third Reich standards, they were eminently respectable patriots. When the Third Reich vanished, their respectability vanished with it. During the war-crimes trials they stood at the bar in the shabby clothing of common criminals. Stripped of the insignia of respectability, they could be seen for what they really were, dishonorable, immoral, craven men.

But during the trials it was impossible to overlook entirely certain parallels between the wartime conduct of the victors and of the vanquished. An interesting incident took place when the so-called "Einsatzgruppen Case" was being heard before a Nuremberg Military Tribunal. Technically, this was an international court because it had been set up under the authority of a four-power charter; but the arrangements were entirely in American hands and the personnel of the court was American. The twenty-three defendants had been associated with the mobile killing units which followed the German armies in their invasion of the U.S.S.R. in the summer of 1941 and which, as we have remarked, were responsible for the death of some 1,400,000 Jews. The trial has been rightly called the greatest murder trial in history.

The most important defendant was the Gruppenfuehrer (Major General) Otto Ohlendorf, an intellectual with a doctorate in jurisprudence and a former research director in the Institute for World Economy and Maritime Transport at Kiel. He had early joined the Nazi party and during the war he was put in charge of Einsatzgruppe D, a mobile unit which, by his own admission, had killed 90,000 Polish Jews. He was found guilty by the court and was executed in 1951.

During cross-examination Ohlendorf was asked whether it was the policy to kill Jewish children as well as adults. He replied that such was indeed the policy, although he personally had never seen children put to death. Then he added, in reference to obliteration bombing as practiced by the Allies, "I cannot imaine that those planes which systematically covered a city that was a fortified city, square meter for square meter, with incendiaries and explosive bombs and again with phosphorus bombs, and this done from block to block, and then as I have seen it in Dresden likewise the squares where the civilian population had fled to—that these men could possibly hope not to kill any civilian population, and no children. And when you then read the announcement of the Allied leaders on this—and we are quite willing to submit them as document—you will read that these killings were accepted quite knowingly because one believed that only through this terror, as it was described, the people could be demoralized and under such blows the military power of the Germans would then also break down."

The Einsatzgruppe commanded by Ohlendorf followed the invading armies of the Third Reich into enemy territory, rounded up Jews, and slaughtered them. The planes of the U.S. Army Air Forces slaughtered the civilian inhabitants of enemy cities by bombing. In both cases the victims belonged in the same category; in both cases they were noncombatant enemy civilians, men, women, and children. The Einsatzgruppen killed those who happened to be Jews; the Army Air Forces killed those who happened to be in a certain city at a certain date. Apart from the overwhelming perverseness of genocide as such, from the moral standpoint the instances offer a number of tragic parallels. The moral responsibility of the participants was quite comparable in the two cases. As the Nuremberg Military Tribunal correctly pointed out, the duty of obedience does not excuse a subordinate who carries out the immoral orders of his superior. There is no question that Ohlendorf should have refused to slaughter the Polish Jews, just as the American airmen should have refused to slaughter the civilian inhabitants of cities. However, it is more than naive to expect military men in the heat of warfare to display a greater moral sensitivity than leaders of public opinion at home who can examine the morality of national policy in a less emotional atmosphere.

Certainly, the crew of the B-59 which set out from Tinian early in the morning of August 6, 1945, to bomb Hiroshima and the crews of the observation planes which accompanied it were not encouraged to question the morality of their act. In fact, before taking off, they attended "religious services." Then, having implored God's blessing, they rose from their knees, these pious young men, and proceeded to perpetrate what Pope Paul IV was later to call "an infernal massacre." One may wonder whether the bomb crews felt any scruples during their long trip back to Tinian. Did they think of the tens of thousands they had slaughtered? Of the sufferings of the survivors? If they did, reassurance awaited them. As the crews alighted, General Carl A. Spaatz greeted them, presenting the commanding officer with the Distinguished Service Cross and the others in the crew with appropriate medals.

From the standpoint of abstract morality it is clear that the deeds of Ohlendorf and his Einsatzgruppe D and the deeds of the 393d Bombardment Squadron are parallel, in that in both cases noncombatant enemy civilians were slaughtered. It is true that the Nazi policy was in itself much more evil than the Allied policy of bombing noncombatants both because the former was responsible for the slaughter of millions whereas the victims of the latter were numbered merely in the hundreds of thousands, and because the Nazi policy was clearly genocidal in intent. It is true also that the action of the American bombardier was impersonal; he pressed a button and did not even see his victims. And such impersonal action does not convey the same horror to the imagination as the action of the Nazi who shot his victim face to face and watched him die in agony. However, these differences are accidental. The essential fact is that both Ohlendorf's men and the men of the 393d Bombardment Squadron killed without justification—they were literally murderers. The parallel is inescapable.

Why, then, do Americans in general judge so differently the slaughter of the Jews by the Nazis and the slaughter of non-combatants by the Allies? Why is the usual judgment of the two men ultimately responsible for these slaughters so different? The memory of Hitler is detested; he is thought of as an almost sub-human savage. On the other hand, Truman remains a respected citizen. The minions of Hitler were condemned as common criminals. The more prominent among their leaders were tried at Nuremberg and put to death. Yet the members of the 393d Bombardment Squadron are treated as the honorable veterans of a great war. At their reunions they discuss their deed at Hiroshima without embarrassment with newspaper reporters and pose for photographs.

If Americans in general judge so radically differently the Nazi policy of genocide and the American policy of bombing noncombatants, there can be only one possible explanation. Their moral judgments are based on something other than sound ethics or moral theology. They are based either on emotions or on sophisms which conceal the truth; they are based, in the terminology of the present chapter, on the ethic of respectability. This is a fact to fill one with the utmost horror; for unless man can learn to guide his societal life by some higher principle, one can predict with certainty that the history of the future will be filled with stories of mass slaughter, persecution, and the exploitation of the weak. Against such evils, the development of a sound social ethic is the only defense.

## CHAPTER 7

### THE ETHIC OF CHRISTIAN LOVE

We have shown examples of certain immoral social mores, how these mores had the tacit or explicit approval of the mass of respectable citizens of their time and place, and the consequences of abiding by these mores. However, calling these mores evil implied some criterion. Our criterion has been the Christian law of charity, which we will now discuss explicitly and at length.

Possibly the chief obstacle to the understanding of Christian charity is its seeming simplicity. To say that man's supreme duty is to love God and his neighbor may sound too pat to be convincing. Yet the reality is not obvious; not the greatest contemplative saints could boast of understanding it fully. To obtain even an elementary insight into the nature of Christian love requires long and intense consideration.

There is no better way to begin than with the well-known words of Christ Himself as recounted in the tenth chapter of St. Luke's Gospel. A certain lawyer, that is, an expert in the Jewish Law, put a question to our Lord, "Master, what must I do to obtain eternal life?"

Christ returned the question to the lawyer, "What is written in the Law? How does it read?"

The lawyer answered, "Love the Lord your God with your whole heart and with your whole soul, and with your whole strength, and with your whole mind; and your neighbor as yourself."

Christ approved. "Your answer is correct," he said. "Do this and you will live."

It is interesting to note that the lawyer quoted from the Old Testament and that Christ approved the quotation as a rule of life for Christianity. It was in this sense that He came not to abolish the Law or the Prophets, but to fulfill them. It is therefore important not to exaggerate the contrast between Judaism and Christianity. Both have preached, as man's most basic obligation, the duty of universal love.

But to return to the lawyer—he was finding the situation somewhat embarrassing; for it was now apparent that he had known the answer to the question all along and that he had not asked it in good faith. So he quickly shifted to another question, "And who is my neighbor?" Our Lord's answer was the extraordinary parable of the Good Samaritan.

There are several often overlooked points to be noted about this parable. It is important to realize, first of all, that it illustrates the minimum standard, not the ideal. The question was about what one *must* do to obtain eternal life, and the answer was that one *must* practice charity according to the example of the Good Samaritan. Whoever fails to meet this minimum standard cannot hope for heaven. Charity is not a work of supererogation. It is the very essence of the Christian life. If the question had been about perfection instead of about the minimum standard, doubtless our Lord would have answered with what He said to the rich young man. "If you want to be perfect, go, sell your property and give to the poor, and you will have treasure in heaven; then come, follow me." A second frequently overlooked point is that the Samaritan proved his love genuine not primarily by *feeling* something but by *doing* something. It is true that love is quite usually accompanied by emotion; but emotion is not of its essence and proves very little. Genuine love resides in the will and is directed towards the well-being of the beloved; genuine love must therefore show its quality by active efforts towards this goal. The priest and the Levite could have helped the wounded man, but did not; certainly, then, they could not be said to love him. The Samaritan loved and *therefore* acted.

Finally, the Samaritan loved across an ethic barrier. The enmity of the Jews for his people was traditional. Two centuries earlier, the Son of Sirach had written:

> My soul loathes two nations
>> and the third is not even a people:
> Those who live in Seir and the Philistines
>> and the foolish folk who dwell in Sichem.

Thus the author hated the Samaritans of Sichem as he hated the Edomites and Philistines. In the time of Christ the same feeling prevailed. "Jews have no dealings with Samaritans." This enmity had a long history. After the fall of Israel in 722 B.C., Sargon of Assyria had exiled some of the Jews living there and had replaced the deportees with a mixture of captives from various pagan nations. The Jews and the new arrivals gradually intermarried, and their cults, too, became mixed. The Jews of our Lord's day looked down upon the Samaritans with contempt as a mongrel-ized people who had degraded the pure worship of God and the pure blood of Israel with a pagan admixture—a contempt very similar to that displayed by Hitler's genocidal underlings and white southern racists today. The Good Samaritan knew this, of course, but he acted nevertheless.

The lesson of the parable of the Good Samaritan is clear, simple, and direct. To attain "salvation," we must not merely love God, but we must love our neighbor with a love that expresses itself in deeds. We must be willing to make sacrifices, to take trouble and incure expense, to promote our neighbor's well-being. Finally, we must love *all* our neighbors, regardless of their origins or personal characteristics.

The passages just quoted leave one obvious question unanswered. Religion is essentially the loving service of almighty God; how, then, does it also involve the loving service of one's neighbor? The two duties seem to be considered in some sense identical, and it is not immediately clear why this is the case.

Some light is thrown on the question by the description of the Last Judgment in the twenty-fifth chapter of St. Matthew's Gospel. It is a highly dramatic description. The Son of man, attended by all the angels, will seat Himself on the throne of judgment. Before Him, all nations will be assembled. He will separate them into two groups "just as a shepherd separates the sheep from the goats." He will say to those on the right: "Come, O blessed of my Father. Take possession of the kingdom prepared for you from the foundation of the world; for I was hungry and you gave me to eat, I was thirsty and you gave me to drink, I was a stranger and you received me as a guest, I was without clothes and you clothed me, I was sick and you visited me, I was in prison and you came to see me."

To this the just will reply with questions: "Lord when did we see you hungry and feed you, or thirsty and give you to drink? When did we see you a stranger and receive you as a guest, or see you without clothes and clothe you? When did we see you sick or in prison and come to visit you?"

Then the King will answer: "I tell you truly, inasmuch as you did it to one of these least of my brethren, you did it to me."

The wicked will be judged by the application of the same principle. They showed no love for their neighbors in need and thus they proved that they had no real love for Christ. "Inasmuch as you did not do it to one of these least ones, neither did you do it to me."

Here, then, is the answer to the question posed above about the relation between the loving service of God and the loving service of neighbor. Surprisingly enough, the relation turns out to be an identity. Serving one's neighbor *is* serving God in men who are His images. To give food or drink or clothing to the poor is to give them to Christ. This is true even of service to prisoners. A man in jail does not seem to be a very good representative of our Lord. He is, nevertheless, inasmuch as his character as an image of God is ineradicable. Note that the statement is not limited to prisoners who happen to be, in fact, guiltless. It is quite general. One must be prepared to see Christ in *all* men. Charity must be universal or it is not charity.

The two Gospel passages which we have quoted define the dimensions of Christian charity. We must, as a minimum, love all men without distinction, we must show our love by helping them in practical ways in their day-by-day necessities, and we must be motivated by the realization that our love for the humblest of our neighbors is the measure of our love for Christ. This duty is not presented as an ideal for rare heroic souls. It is the simple duty of the everyday Christian.

Charity is the *essential* Christian virtue; it is the only virtue necessary for salvation. It is easy to see why this is so. He who has charity loves God and therefore will not sin against God; he loves his neighbor and therefore will not sin against his neighbor; he loves himself supernaturally and therefore will not degrade himself by sin. Moreover, since charity is a single virtue, he who acts charitably in one way, say, by helping his neighbor, proves that he is willing to practice charity in other ways when the occasion arises. Thus St. Paul could write, "He who loves his neighor has fulfilled the Law." Thus, too, it is easy to understand why in the twenty-fifth chapter of St. Matthew men are judged solely on their willingness to practice the corporal works of mercy. By these deeds they proved that they possessed charity; and that was enough to merit heaven.

The Christian social ideal is simply a society controlled by the law of charity, the ethic of Christian love. This is the premise of all the Church's social teaching. This is presupposed by all the social encyclicals. This is illustrated very excellently in the lives of the saints.

One cannot but be struck by a clear contrast between the Christian life as it is presented theoretically in many books of asceticism and as it is illustrated practically by the way the saints lived. The ascetical literature emphasizes prayer and penance. The saints also emphasized prayer and penance in their lives; but to this they added a third element, the practice of the works of mercy. Even the cloistered saints shared this concern for their neighbor's welfare, and they prayed unceasingly for him. Service of one's neighbor has an extraordinarily sanctifying effect. This is true not only in the case of the saints, but also in the case of ordinary Catholics. Wherever people gather together to serve the poor in a direct personal way, at the cost of self-sacrifice, they find holiness. This is evident in the Catholic Worker and Friendship House groups in New York and elsewhere and in Washington's Fides House with which the present writer was long associated. The way to be a good Christian is simply to serve one's neighbor in need.

If charity is beautiful, then lack of charity is correspondingly abominable. Not only hatred, but even a careless disregard of one's neighbor and his necessities is enough to deserve damnation. Those condemned to hell in that terrible twenty-fifth chapter of St. Matthew did not, apparently, really hate their needy neighbors. They were simply too busy with their own selfish lives to care about them. Obviously, then, a mere lack of concern for human suffering is itself damnable.

It is very hard to find an excuse for those who call themselves Christians and who yet consistently refuse to face realistically the problems of the subproletariat. It is almost impossible to imagine the muffling of conscience in a man who votes against a fair-housing law or who refuses to hire a worker on account of race; it is almost impossible to imagine how he can reconcile his conduct with the exigent law of Christian love. The middle-class American who talks glibly about the "shiftlessness" and the "immorality" of slum dwellers and who opposes adequate relief budgets for them would seem to express clearly the attitudes of those who will hear on Judgment Day the words, "Inasmuch as you did not do it to one of these least ones, neither did you do it to me."

But if a mere callousness towards one's neighbor is damnable, what can be said of those who actively hate others and who persecute and destroy them? This is a degree of evil which is simply diabolical; yet it is a degree of evil which frequently controls national policy with the cooperation of the respectable. This fact is illustrated by examples discussed in this book; but these are merely examples; it would be very easy to multiply instances of the callous exploitation or cruel persecution of the defenseless by the respectable holders of power.

Of course, it is extremely unfair to judge the personal guilt of any individual who may have acted in what he misguidedly thinks to be good faith. Indeed, there is reason to believe, for example, that many slaveholders actually did live with clear consciences. What is shocking is not the personal guilt of those responsible for the major crimes of society; for that is something we cannot know. What is shocking is the objective evil of their policies and of the systematic long-term erosion of conscience which tolerated them.

It ought to be a subject of endless meditation from the bishops down to the ordinary laymen that Catholics participated in the formation and execution of the national policies criticized in this book, policies which were—objectively speaking—the very antithesis of Christian charity. Catholics, lay persons, priests, religious, and bishops held slaves and defended slavery in the United States. Catholics supported Hitler's war, and the slaughter of the Jews was part of his war policy. Catholics were as active as their fellow Americans in the massacre of noncombatants during the Second World War.

One fact emerges very clearly from the foregoing discussion. To be charitable, one must often be disobedient. To acquiesce in slavery or genocide or—worse still—to take an active part in the execution of such policies is certainly to sin very greviously against charity; it is to be un-Christian to the uttermost. Disobedience is the necessary alternative. The good Christian cannot conform to the mores of a paramoral society. He must make it clear by both words and actions that he rejects these mores. By doing so, of course, he will exclude himself from the ranks of those who are considered "respectable." He may become an outcast. In some instances his opposition may cost him his liberty or even his life.

The supreme example of a refusal to conform to evil mores and of the personal cost of that refusal is given by our Lord Himself. He attacked the respectable classes of the time for their vices and thus earned their bitter hatred. When the danger of this position became evident, He did not relent. On the contrary,

He continued the attack. The crucifixion was the final result of the power structure's hatred for Him.

Thus, Christ attacked the rich. "How hard it will be," He remarked one day, "for those who have riches to enter the kingdom of God." This indictment of the most respectable segment of society struck His hearers as shocking. "The disciples were dumbfounded at his words." However, instead of modifying the statement, Christ reinforced it. "It is easier for a camel to get through the eye of a needle than for a rich man to enter the kingdom of God." There are, indeed, exceptions. Joseph of Arimathea and Zaccheus are explicitly called "rich," yet they were virtuous men. This, however, must be ascribed to the special grace of God with whom "all things are possible"—even the salvation of the wealthy. What our Lord was condemning in the passage quoted—and what is condemned elsewhere in the New Testament—seems to be not so much the mere possession of wealth as the obsessive pursuit of gain. Some passages give information about the financial background of those spoken of as "rich." They seem to have been merchants, farmer-capitalists, and those who might roughly be called financiers, that is, persons such as bankers or tax collectors who dealt directly with money. All were actively seeking financial success.

Christ did not hesitate to show disdain for civil authorities when they deserved it. On being told tht Herod Antipas wanted to kill Him, He referred to this powerful ruler as "that fox." The word implies a knavish craftiness and is the only example of "unmitigated *contempt* (as distinguished from rebuke and scorn) recorded among the utterances of Christ." Later, when brought before Herod in the course of the Passion, He further showed contempt by refusing even to speak to him.

The bitter denunciation of the scribes and Pharisees by our Lord must have created a profound sensation. These men were not only powerful; but they passed as models of righteousness. If any group in the country was looked up to as eminently respectable, surely it was this group. Yet Christ's language in reference to them was extreme. To realize just how much so, one has only to reread the twenty-third chapter of St. Matthew's Gospel, where these representatives of the power structure are called "hypocrites," "blind guides," "blind fools," "serpents," "brood of vipers." They are denounced as obstacles to the spread of the Kingdom, as petty casuists who pervert the moral law, as murderers of God's envoys. Outwardly, in the eyes of men, they appear righteous, but within they are full of iniquity. "How," Christ demanded of them, "can you escape being sentenced to hell?"

Certainly, on one, and most probably on two occasions Christ drove a group of respectable businessmen out of the Temple. Apparently, there were quite a few of them. Some were merchants who offered for sale the sheep and oxen needed for sacrifice. Others sold doves to be used as offerings by the poor. Other were money-changers who furnished the shekels needed for the temple tax in exchange for foreign coins.

If Jesus had merely denounced these practices, that itself would have been very dramatic. However, He went beyond words. "He made a lash out of cords," St. John tells us, "and drove all the men out of the Temple, the sheep, too, and the oxen; and he scattered the coin of the money-changers and over-turned their tables." This physical violence, this public humilia-tion must have infuriated the merchants. It also infuriated "the chief priests and the scribes." By invading the Temple precincts, Christ had trespassed on their prerogatives. St. Mark, in his account of the incident, states that these latter then plotted to kill Him. However, they had to restrain their anger because the crowd was on his side.

Quite clearly, Christ was threatening the privileges of the respectable classes, the rich, the influential, the religious leaders. He did not stop at words. He made scenes; that is, like many civil-rights advocates today He "demonstrated." He had, more-over, a popular following, which, if it were allowed to increase, might cause a social upheaval in which the respectable would be unmasked. The obvious thing to do—as has been done in the South today—was to put the "radical" to death. However, His enemies had to bide their time. They had to plan carefully. Fi-nally, however, the propitious moment came and they struck. Christ was dragged before Pilate.

It is illuminating to examine the immediate causes of the crucifixion. It was, in the first instance, the judicial murder of one who had earned the hatred of the privileged classes; and so it is not surprising that the indictment which was brought forward when Christ stood before Pilate emphasized the fact that He was an agitator.

We have found this man perverting our nation
and forbidding the payment of taxes to the emperor,
and claiming to be Christ, a king.

Of course, these charges were false and misleading; Christ certainly did not oppose the payment of taxes. But His messiahship was made to appear as implying the seizure of civil power. However, the charge of "perverting our nation" betrays the fact that the accusers were worried about the effect of Christ's social teaching. When Pilate remained unimpressed by these charges, the accusers renewed their indictment.

He stirs up the people, teaching throughout all
Judea, from Galilee even to this place.

To stir up is to agitate and demonstrate. Christ was a social agitator for what today would be called "human rights." He threatened the existing state of affairs. To the privileged classes, this was intolerable.

Christ's denunciation of the privileged classes illustrates the contrast between the ethic of respectability and the ethic of Christian love; but it does more. It shows that charity can be denunciatory and violent as well as gentle and meek. Christ showed charity towards the woman taken in adultery by being very kind and tactful with her. However, His denunciation of the scribes and Pharisees was also an act of charity—and this because, first, the only hope of making these hypocrites realize their true condition was to jolt their consciences by strong and candid language; and secondly—and more importantly—because these false teachers were corrupting the people by their perversion of the moral law, and the only way to lessen their pernicious influence was to expose them. This was an act of charity towards His hearers. Acts of fraternal charity, viewed externally, differ vastly among themselves. What unifies them is the fact that they are all directed towards the well-being of one's neighbor.

It is a mistake to overemphasize Christian meekness as it has, in high and low places, often been overemphasized. It even happens that a false and degenerate Christian art will picture Christ as weak and effeminate—which is, of course blasphemy in the strict theological sense. It is true that Christ told His followers to turn the other cheek; but He also proclaimed that He came not to bring peace, but the sword. Meekness is only one Christian virtue; perfection consists in the combination of all the virtues in harmony.

Charity can be defined alternatively as the following of Christ. Thus not only His words, but also His deeds, constitute a lesson for mankind. His way of acting under various circumstances shows man how he too should act when similar circumstances arise in his own life. Of course, one imitates Christ by living quietly and unobtrusively as He did at Nazareth, by quietly facing the duties of each successive day and performing them to the best of one's ability, by living modestly and temperately as a good Christian citizen.

There are times, however, when the follower of Christ must go beyond these everyday duties. If he lives in a paramoral society, if he sees his fellow human being deceived or exploited or enslaved or massacred, then love of neighbor must manifest itself by public protest or by a brave disobedience to unjust laws, when the occasion arises. Under such circumstances, it is un-Christian to hold one's tongue for fear of being thought eccentric or to refrain from action for fear of punishment. "Christ himself suffered for you, leaving you an example so that you might follow his footsteps."

# Daniel Callahan
## 1930-

Traditionally theological writing and reflection are considered the domain of the clergy. Far too few are the numbers of laymen who have gone through the academic formation that is necessary to enter the field of theology and make serious contributions. This is an unfortunate aspect of Catholicism for, as had become quite evident in recent years, there are many laypersons who can offer excellent and significant insights to the process of theology. Among contemporary Catholic laymen, the name of Daniel Callahan is well known. He has written several books on the present status of the church, as well as dozens of articles on topics of interest and importance to Catholics in America.

His book, The New Church: Essays in Catholic Reform, is a collection of some of the articles that Callahan wrote between 1959 and 1965. As Callahan points out in his introduction, the articles reveal the concerns, dilemmas and uncertainties experienced by many American Catholics just previous to and during the years of the Second Vatican Council. They also represent one way of coming to grips with some of the most difficult questions that contemporary Christians must face.

We have selected two of the articles in this collection for the reading below. The first deals with the quest for honesty. To be honest is a kind of in-thing at present. Callahan observes *that since the Second World War the idea of honesty has been a critical one. Everyone claims it; writers are particularly extolled for it. Exactly what it is, however, is not easy to say. It can take on a variety of meanings according to situations and circumstances. In the church, the idea of honesty remains fresh, but one wonders how long it can remain that way. To proclaim honesty is simple enough; to live it is altogether something else.*

*The second article below is on birth control and the theologian. Note that it was written in 1964. Callahan likens the atmosphere in the church concerning birth control to a difficult drama. The play is constantly being rewritten, the critics are not much help, the audience is confused. Contemporary social and theological revolutions have not been correctly understood and worked into the script. The effort to hold to a traditional middle way is, for some reason, preventing the drama from developing properly. The time has come for theologians to enrich their perspectives and to take a firm stand on solid, contemporary scholarship. Callahan seemed to sense that not enough theologians and church authorities were preparing themselves adequately for the climax of the drama. They were not sufficiently attuned to the actual world in which we live. The latent tragedy of the drama came out into the open four years after this article was written, when Pope Paul VI issued* Humanae Vitae, *the encyclical which put to the test the radical honesty of millions of Catholics throughout the world.*

# THE NEW CHURCH

## CHAPTER THIRTEEN

### THE QUEST FOR HONESTY

While it would probably smack of irreverence, there are times when I wish it were possible to feed into an advanced computer some knotty problems of religion. At the moment there are two I would give it. The first, a general question: How long does it now take for an idea which originates in the secular world to make its appearance in religious writing? The second is more specific: How long does it take before problems which agitate Protestant minds begin to agitate Catholic minds?

The questions are not as idly speculative as they may sound. For surely a competent computer, with the aid of a few historians, social observers, and literary men feeding it raw data, could have predicted some years ago that Catholics would eventually take up the cry for "honesty" in the Church. The idea of "honesty" has been, after all, a critical one in the post-war secular mind: writers are extolled for their honesty, their sincerity; political scientists are forever "candidly" speaking their mind about political myths; psychotherapists have been telling us how much we lie to ourselves; someone or other is always condemning us for lacking the courage to tear away at the falsehoods in our society. When one hears Catholics finally talking this kind of language, whether it be for "honest" reporting in the Church, for "honest" talk about Catholics and family planning, for "honest" admissions that the Church needs reform—one can only say: "aha, it's come."

The odd thing is that however quickly Catholics pick these things out of the air, Protestants have often been there first. Again, a computer could probably have predicted that just as Catholics would begin tentatively talking of honesty, many Protestants would be in the midst of a full-scale debate on the same point. The most prominent sign of this is that prodigious Protestant best-seller, *Honest to God* (Westminster Press, 1964), written by the Anglican Bishop of Woolrich, England, John A. T. Robinson. Less noticed, but in much the same vein, is *Objections to Christian Belief* (Lippincott, 1964), a set of lectures by four Anglican theologians at Cambridge. The point of both books is to take a hard look at "traditional" Christianity, subjecting both creed and morality to unflinching examination. In particular, the various theologians aim to set forth their doubts and worries, not in order to destroy Christianity but rather to achieve some sort of harmony between what the modern world takes for granted about reality and what, by contrast, they think Christian theology says about it. There is also an implicit consensus among the authors that Christians today do not, in fact, give as much credence to traditional thought as they themselves think; and that this is the source of considerable dishonesty.

The Catholic quest for honesty, if I interpret the clues correctly, has now reached a point at which many are discovering that what bothers them is not this or that specific problem, but more: that it is so hard to speak openly in the Church. Difficulties seem concealed altogether or buried beneath carefully laid layers of sanctimonious optimism. John Cogley put it well recently when he wrote that he would like to see the "layman feel free to express his convictions, doubts, and dissents without fear of 'violating orthodoxy' or seeming to be brash. . . ." Yet it would be a mistake to identify too closely the Protestant and Catholic quest.

No Catholics, so far as I know, are suggesting, as does Bishop Robinson, that a lack of honesty in the Church is keeping them from expressing radical doubts on the "mythological" world-view of the Scripture writers, on the very idea of "supernaturalism," or on relevance of "religion" to Christianity. Yet is is precisely this kind of "honesty" which Bishop Robinson wants. If not, there will be, he believes, "an increasing alienation, both within the ranks of the church and outside it, between those whose recipe is the mixture as before (however revitalized) and those who feel compelled to be honest *wherever* it may lead them." "We are being called," he thinks, ". . . to far more than a restating of traditional orthodoxy in modern terms. Indeed, if our defense of the Faith is limited to this, we shall find in all likelihood that we have lost out to all but a tiny religious remnant." What, practically, does this mean; "We have to be prepared for *everything* to go into the melting . . . even our most cherished religious catagories and moral absolutes. And the first thing we must be ready to let go is our image of God himself."

Honesty, however, can cover a multitude of sins and virtues. Understood one way, it can simply mean the opposite of hypocrisy, which is a concealing of one's true beliefs beneath a veneer of conformity. Understood another way, it can mean a radical willingness to take nothing as too sacred for searching examination, a willingness to pay whatever price is required to get to the bottom of things. Bishop Robinson seems to use the word in both senses. On the one hand, he thinks many Christians do not in fact believe in certain elements of traditional Christianity nearly so strongly as they pretend to. On the other, he thinks that Christians lack the courage to face their own irrelevance and so are prevented from taking the steps necessary to confront modern man.

All of this may sound vaguely familiar to Catholics, as if an amplification from another room of the debates centering around the Council. The similarity is there, but the differences are pronounced. One difference is Bishop Robinson's belief that even the best kind of revitalization of old Christian doctrines will not do any longer. Another is that he has been influenced by those elements of recent Protestant thought which have remained outside the mainstream of Protestant-Catholic ecumenism. From Rudolf Bultmann he has taken his criticism of a continuing Christian dependence on the three-layered "mythological" imagery of the Bible; from Paul Tillich his rejection of traditional theism; from Dietrich Bonhoeffer his critique of what Bonhoeffer called the "religious premise," i.e., that there exists a "supernatural" sphere over against the "secular."

There is still another difference, one best expressed perhaps in A. R. Vidler's introduction to *Objections to Christian Belief*. There Dr. Vidler asserts that "the objections are likely to be perceived and felt even more keenly by people who, maybe for years, have been living with one foot in Christian belief and the other resolutely planted in the radical unbelief of the contemporary world, so that they are, as it were, torn between the two." Clearly Bishop Robinson is such a man, as are the contributors to *Objections*. Yet I daresay there are few Catholics who would care to describe their tensions in this way (however suitable such a description might be). For the most part, Catholics approach unbelief as something which exists *outside* of the Church and *outside* of the believer. The possibility that unbelief may exist within the Church, even among the solid "faithful," seems rarely to cross the minds of most Catholic writers. The merit of Bishop Robinson's book and the authors of *Objections* is that they take this coexistence of belief and unbelief within the heart of the believer with full seriousness.

It is worth noting a certain oddity here. While it could be expected that many conservative Anglicans would react violently against the ideas expressed by Bishop Robinson and his Protestant mentors, the sharpest attacks have come from some non-Christian philosophers. The English philosopher Alasdair MacIntyre, for instance, said of *Honest to God* in an *Encounter* review: "This book testifies to the existence of a whole group of theologies which have retained a theistic vocabulary but acquired an atheistic substance." Of Paul Tillich's work Sidney Hook has commented that "I am not fully persuaded that Tillich's ambiguities can get the idol-worshippers out of the temple; there is some evidence that his ideas provide the rationalizations for those to remain who otherwise would have left." The same attitude is prominent in Walter Kaufmann's *Faith of a Heretic*. For these men, the new "honesty" is in fact the worst kind of dishonesty.

One of the few points I can see with any clarity here is that "honesty" is a classic example of a weasel-word, the use of which depends almost entirely upon one's starting point. In the case of Bishop Robinson, much of what he rejects in "traditional" Christianity is in fact not traditional at all. Instead, it is what the popular mind thinks Christianity is, quite a different matter. The unfortunate thing is that the Bishop himself only half-realizes this; thus many straw men are destroyed in the name of honesty. Again and again he distorts traditional theology. How honest a procedure is that?

In any case, I am reasonably certain that Catholics cannot long remain out of the fray. Bishop Robinson's book is a harbinger of more to come. Sooner or later our own quest for honesty will probably take some to that "radical questioning" which Bishop Robinson calls for. What is surprising is that the Hooks, the MacIntyres, and the Kaufmanns have managed so far to overlook the Catholic efforts at renewal initiated by Pope John. Surely they could find something to say about the twists and turns of the conciliar debates, especially about the "new insights," "deeper understanding," and "expanded horizons" of the progressive majority. For it is a fairly good rule-of-thumb that whatever appears suspect to the conservative theologian will be just as suspect in the eyes of some non-believers. Each will accuse the innovator of selling out, however different the grounds for their objections may be. That this is so makes everyone's task that much the harder. When everyone begins shouting for honesty, and all condemn self-deception, one can only expect confusion.

So far, thankfully, we haven't reached that point in the Church. The idea of honesty still remains a fresh one. But can we keep it that way? Much will depend upon our ability to be both thorough and creative in our honesty. The way to be thorough is, in the very first instance, to realize how honesty itself can be a form of self-deceit. (The most common example of this in our day is the homage paid to self-confessed egoists: they are at least credited for being "sincere"; the rest of us are hypocrites.) Creativity is even more important. Unless we ruthlessly explore our own motives, biases, and hidden impulses, searching in every nook and cranny of our mind and emotions, we are likely to fool ourselves as much as ever.

The best example of creative honesty I have run across recently is a passage in Father Karl Rahner's translated collection of essays, *Nature and Grace* (Sheed & Ward, 1964). After singling our Modernism as one form of "hidden heresy" he goes on to point to another: "[But] much more frequent (although difficult to pin down) is an attitude of mistrust and resentment against the Church's magisterium, a widespread feeling of being suspiciously and narrowly controlled by it in research and teaching, the feeling that 'one can't say what one thinks' (but one is nevertheless justified in thinking it in 'good' conscience). Doesn't one come across the feeling that one can say more (at least among friends) than one can write? Or the attitude that one should be glad that this and that has been said by Protestant theologians outside the Church, and one has to go to them to read it because one could not say it without risk oneself? . . . Isn't there here something like an esoteric teaching which is spread only by word of mouth? Isn't there unformulated heresy which avoids clear exposition in print and works by omissions and one-sided perspectives . . . ?"

That, I say, is honesty; and it hurts. Nor is the pain appreciably lessened when Father Rahner goes on to say that a rigid conservatism can also be a form of heresy: "This freezing of the form in which the truth of the Gospel is expressed is in fact a dangerous symptom of indifference . . . to the truth." One way or another, I fear, Father Rahner's insights on heresy will leave most of us "honest" folks feeling like the emperor when he discovered he was naked.

But it won't do to escape from our nakedness by half-hearted attempts at humor. There is something funny here, but the joke may be on us. Is it in fact possible for Catholics to be wholly honest? I, for one, am not certain. I doubt that the Church is now prepared to accept those who would, willy-nilly, undertake the kind of "radical questioning" which Bishop Robinson has urged upon his fellow Anglicans. Even a serious and solemn attempt would run into a barrage of criticism, if not gaining for its author summary excommunication should he refuse to recant. But the incapacity of the Church to stand this kind of "honesty" is not necessarily a mark against it. The Church teaches with authority. This it could hardly do if it was compelled to put its most central truths up for total debate every time someone felt that honesty compelled him to question them. At the same time, of course, it would be well for the Church, so far as is possible (and that may be much further than we think), to be patient toward its interrogators. Before it dismisses them, let it put some charitable questions to them. Let it take their questions seriously. We desperately need such openness. That way both honesty and truth can be served.

Such encounters will, for the time being, probably be rare. Of greater immediate relevance is the question whether the Church can be honest enough to carry through the renewal sought by the Council. The signs are both good and bad. They are good insofar as there is in practice (if not yet in theory) considerably more freedom for the individual Catholic to speak his mind directly on controverted questions. Many are still fearful of doing so, but it is becoming clear that those who do so do not always encounter the criticism and censure their imagination often conjures up before they take their stand. More than one would-be martyr for honesty has found that, instead of the stake, he gets praise, honor, and money.

There are many bad signs, however. Among the worst can be found in some speeches praising the work of the Council. Of course the Council condemned anti-Semitism; the Church has always opposed anti-Semitism. Of course the Church favored religious liberty; it has always been a champion of a free conscience, of a "free Church in a free society." Of course the Council stood for a free press and free speech; only the misinformed could think otherwise. Each of these statements contains a grain of truth and a grain of falsehood, in about equal mixture. But the way statements of this sort have been bandied about, as the whole truth, is sufficient evidence that we still have a way to go to reach even an approximation of honesty.

In fact, however, the situations just mentioned touch only a few of the different occasions in which questions of Catholic honesty could arise. They can arise when there is discrepancy between theory and practice; when there are unvoiced difficulties about living up to a moral teaching of the Church; when some or many people find a particular argument employed by the Church obscure or unconvincing; when doubts exist that a principle is being properly applied; when many believe that a given teaching, tradition, or custom needs reform; when a general feeling arises that a new scientific, historical, or sociological discovery calls for a fresh look at an old, well-established belief; when there is evidence that an ancient Church law has become outmoded; and so on. The possibilities seem almost infinite.

One problem is that different kinds of self-deception (individual or communal) can come into play in different situations, calling, in turn, for different kinds of honesty. Thus the very fact that the Church's teaching on the immorality of contraceptives is a difficult teaching will mean that it will be just that much harder to be honest with oneself about it. The very fact that one might be willing to admit with all candor that it is difficult might, by the very same token, lead one to escapist doubts about the cogency of that position. Is it not likely that someone caught in a desperate conflict of family planning would be the most prone to believe that the Church's teaching *could* change? Or that it *must* be wrong? Or that it is all the fault of the celibate clergy? To go to the other extreme, would not the person who honestly believed the Church's position is irreformable be the one most likely to be dishonest about the kinds of difficulties which can arise (by shaping facts to fit principles)? It is as if, in both cases, sheer honesty about one side of a problem paves the way for dishonesty about another.

If nothing else, then, one should be wary about where one judges honesty to be required, and what kind is needed. It is easy enough to say "everywhere." But it is rarely going to be that easy. It is one thing to be honest about, say, what one thinks the Church teaches. It is still another to be honest about whether one in fact accepts this teaching. And it is something else again to be honest about how one feels about this teaching even while accepting it.

The secular experience with the idea of honesty, to which we should be indebted, ought to be a warning. As Peter Berger has well put it, "There are, after all, far more sincere liars than cynical ones, if only because self-deception is psychologically easier than Machiavellianism." To this I would add that much in Catholicism offers an enticement to sincere self-deception. Since authority counts heavily in the Church, and the Church makes strong claims, there is every inducement to convince oneself that one is convinced. At the same time, since the Church is authoritiarian those who attempt to exercise their freedom can easily come to believe that the forces of repression are inexorably weighted against them. It thus often happens that those who do have the courage to speak out are far more liable to dote on the rebuffs they receive than the praise. It is as if they can only confirm their freedom by dwelling on the price they have to pay for it. Of course since the price *is* sometimes high, their emphasis may not be misplaced.

Well, then, where are we? The banner of "honesty" has been raised. It is a good banner, just as long as the staff on which it is raised does not have worm holes. That means we must be honest about our honesty; and honest about our honesty about our honesty. . . .

## CHAPTER FOURTEEN

### BIRTH CONTROL AND THE THEOLOGIAN

The argument over family limitation in the church today may be likened to a drama, but one so rich in rhetoric and sub-themes that it is increasingly difficult for the audience to follow the plot. They are not to be blamed for their confusion. The play is constantly being rewritten, new scenes are added with increasing rapidity, and no one has yet been able to devise a satisfactory ending. The critics have not been helpful either. Some see only an old-fashioned morality play: faithful Catholics standing firm against the secularist hordes and their Catholic fellow-travellers. Others see it as a courtroom drama: the people vs. the minions of the law. Still others see it as a tragedy (though they are not always clear who the tragic hero is).

Well, of course all these elements are present on the stage, so each of the critics has a point. But I would like to suggest that the development of the play to date has gradually uncovered what may be the real and lasting issue at stake here: how authority in the Church is to be understood, interpreted, and developed. For that is the one issue which seems most to determine the lines spoken by the actors. Whatever he may privately think, the layman is only likely to speak those lines which he believes are assigned him in the Church. Exactly the same thing can be said of the theologian. Now and then, of course, an errant line escapes from someone's lips (more today

303

than ever); and some of the lines have a double-meaning. Even so, the stage curtain of authority hangs over everything: as a source of confidence for some, anxiety for others, and perhaps as a puzzle for most.

A convenient way to grasp the unfolding of this play is to begin with those changes which have marked the past decade or so. Up until about the middle of the fifties there was a remarkable harmony among the ideals of the magisterium, the theologians, and the married laity. The large family was accepted as the norm of a Catholic marriage, even though it was formally recognized that medical, economic, or other "indications" could justify, for "serious reasons," recourse to rhythm or abstinence. But these indications were clearly thought of as exceptions. All of this brought comparatively few objections from the laity, at least those who might be accounted "zealous" Catholics, or "nuclear" Catholics. Indeed, we are sometimes prone to forget today how the ideal of a large family was once seen by many to go hand-in-hand with the liturgical movement, social justice, and contemporary spirituality.

Social realities, which arrived in a variety of forms, soon unbalanced this equilibrium. Catholics finally realized how much the Protestant consensus had changed, so much so that now family limitation (by the most efficient means) is taken to be a Christian duty. Then the population explosion began to be noticed by demographers, and the early efforts to dismiss their work as secularist propaganda made less and less sense. Of more immediate concern to Catholic parents, it turned out that American society is simply not geared for very large families; that fifteen-room Victorian houses are in short supply; that a family of six, eight, or ten children requires an income well above the average; and that such an ideal, even if physically possible, takes little account of the emotional needs of the husband and wife, much less those of their children. A new perception of the importance of education, of the necessity that a wife be something more than a mother, and that a husband be something more than a breadwinner, helped to round out the change of perspective. Here lies one revolution.

No less important was the revolution beginning to gather speed in the Church. Manual scholasticism, with its baggage of

304

apodictic certainties, showed signs of an impending death. Personalism, existentialism, and the thought of the Church Fathers began to make more sense and to speak a more meaningful language. The Bible came into its own, not just as a book to be praised in the abstract, but as a living source of concepts, perspectives, and spiritual animation. It too speaks a different language, a language which makes the old books of moral theology appear dangerously inadequate, if not altogether misleading. The Second Vatican Council pushed the revolution forward. To an extent which still remains undetermined, it has called into question many episodes in the Church's past. More importantly, it has cast doubt on many traditional ways of thinking about Catholic doctrine. It shattered old certainties. It showed that Catholics could think unthinkable thoughts (even if it has not made clear how far this can go). It brought the beginning of freedom in the Church—freedom of conscience, not just that old-time Catholic freedom, the freedom of perfect submission to every iota of the law.

All of this amounts to a theological revolution, of which only the barest hint has shown itself in the Council. Yet all the while this revolution was in the making those I will call the "Center Party" moral theologians have remained firmly imbedded in the atmosphere of the past. In America, probably the finest fruit of the work of this party is *Contemporary Moral Theology,* Vol. 2: *Marriage Questions* (Newman, 1964) by Fathers John C. Ford, S. J. and Gerald Kelly, S. J. Their work over many years, of which this and an earlier volume are the outcome, has provided American theologians with detailed and probing surveys of the whole spectrum of moral problems, both practical and theoretical. On the whole, they have steered a middle course between the arch-reactionaries and the pioneers (and thus have been attacked from both sides). For that reason, Fathers Ford and Kelly could be said to personify the center, and *Marriage Questions* to epitomize the thrust of its thinking.

The range of problems covered in *Marriage Questions* is broad, the treatment of them marked with precision and sublety, and the criticism of those with whom they disagree eminently charitable and fair. Among other things, they sketch the development of Protestant thought on marriage, detail the problems posed for traditional theology by the emergence of a school of personalist theologians, present their own *via media* between the personalists and the canonists, and argue their own theory of the ends of marriage. Throughout the first half of their book Fathers Ford and Kelly are preoccupied (in a very illuminating way) with the relationship of the "primary" and the "secondary" ends of marriage. In the second half, they deal with more concrete problems: contraception, sterilization, "the pill," periodic continence, and other matters. On the crucial question (at least in the popular mind) whether the Church can or is likely to change its teaching on the immorality of contraceptives they are forthright. "The Church," they write, "is so completely committed to the doctrine that contraception is intrinsically and gravely immoral that no substantial change in this teaching is possible. It is *irrevocable*." Moreover, they think it "very likely" that the Church has taught this doctrine infallibly (a judgment, of course, disputed by other theologians).

When seen in the light of the double revolution noted above, certain characteristics of Fathers Ford and Kelly's methods are at once apparent. One searches in vain for a heavy use of biblical texts (or even a light use). The primary proof-texts which they employ are papal encyclicals and allocutions and the comments and decisions of other organs of the magisterium. Next in importance are the writings of other moral theologians. The philosophical presuppositions and concepts (which loom large) are drawn almost exclusively from traditional scholastic terminology and that of the canon lawyers. There is only the barest hint that Fathers Ford and Kelly have been much swayed by the theological revolution in the Church.

At the same time, it is important to note, they are sensitive to the kinds of difficulties which confront married couples today. That they do not speak the ordinary language of the laity should by no means be held against them. There is much evidence implicit in the book that they understand this language, and, more than that, that they have heard their share (far more than most laymen) of the anguished cries of couples caught in acute moral dilemmas. That they do not speak in the vernacular themselves is beside the point: they were not writing sermons or popular manuals, but instead write as professional theologians for a professional audience.

In many ways, then, *Marriage Questions* is a model book, once care is taken to note the purposes, methods, and presuppositions of the authors.

It is also a book which, like the theological tradition it represents, is years behind the revolution now in progress. Here lies the tension inherent in the book itself, a tension particularly visible in the author's fear that a substantial change of Catholic teaching on licit methods of family limitation would have disastrous consequences for the Church's claim to teach with authority. It is this sense that the Church's fidelity to its position takes on a symbolic value which goes far beyond the particular doctrines in question. If the Church changes here, then nothing is safe: that is the unveiled fear which Fathers Ford and Kelly (not to mention many others) cannot help but concede. If there is a theological revolution in progress in the Church generally, then this is one of those critical issues which, in the eyes of many, will mark the difference between doctrinal development and chaos. Fathers Ford and Kelly are wary of the former and abhor (rightly) the latter.

Hardly less important as a source of tension is the way they seem to conceive of their tasks as theologians. The best analogy that comes to mind is that of government civil servants. There is, for one thing, little indulgence in personality in their book. Their tone is that of proper functionaries, ever shy of the first person, self-effacing to the point of psychological obliteration, and totally awed in the face of what they take to be authoritative documents or pronouncements.

Now there is of course nothing traditionally wrong in such a stance. Seen in a less harsh light all of these characteristics bespeak genuine humility and wholly dedicated service to the magisterium of the Church. In other respects, however, it is far more difficult to adopt such a perspective. For it is one mark of the civil servant that he tries to cover up, or gloss over the weaknesses in the position laid down by the high command. He puts, in short, the best face on things he can, keeping as far as possible from the public eye the gaps, the inconsistencies, and the uncertainties of the official policy. This he can do by skirting the hard questions put him, or, if he is a loyally creative civil servant, by inventing ingenious *ad hoc* arguments to cover all eventualities. Still another part played is that of devising a new rationale for an established policy when it has become clear that the old arguments in its favor are no longer adequate.

All of these tendencies are present in *Marriage Questions,* but are most prominent when the authors try to show the reasons behind the Church's rejection of contraception. They are, for instance, aware that the traditional natural law arguments no longer persuade many Catholics. To meet this situation, however, they do not wonder whether the position is defective, but instead conclude that better arguments have to be devised, and that it is the task of the theologian to devise them. Yet since they are also aware that the Church has rested in case heavily on the natural law, they have an inherent difficulty on their hands: how can the position be assumed correct if the reasons once taken to demonstrate it are now seen to be inadequate or incomplete? Their answer is not one to shed luster on the theological profession: "When the Church asserts that a truth is of natural law, she does not *ipso facto* become responsible for providing a convincing demonstration of the truth based on arguments derived solely from reason." It is, they say, "the task of the theologians to elaborate these points." As for the embarrassment inherent in a recognition that the natural law arguments do not persuade, their response is to say that this perception shows the "moral necessity of a religious authority for an adequate knowledge of the natural law." As fast as one prop collapses, then, a new one is devised to take its place. And what are the married laity to do while this work of reconstruction goes forward? Hold fast, naturally, since "for Catholic living . . . internal conviction and external conformity is enough; it is not necessary to know why the Church teaches that contraception is intrinsically immoral." (Fair enough, if that is the way things must be: but if the theologians cannot demonstrate the cogency of the doctrine, why are they and the magisterium so certain that it is correct, much less "irreformable"? One is reminded here of the English philosopher who described the demise of an old philosophical doctrine as the result of a "death by a thousand qualifications.")

At this point, let me say I am aware how harsh this way of approaching *Marriage Questions* and the work of Fathers Ford and Kelly sounds. Any portrayal of obviously dedicated, obviously committed, and obviously sincere theologians as akin to loyal civil servants or faithful party workers is bound to appear offensive. It also has the effect of minimizing unduly their valuable insights. For that I am sorry. Yet it is helpful to take such a special vantage point, for it assists in explaining why the birth control question is such an unusually troubling one for the theory of authority in the Church. It has been urged, for instance, that dialogue between the theologians and the laity is essential. Indeed it is, but what good will that dialogue do if at the very outset the theologian conceives his task as that of defending, developing, and rationalizing an "irreformable" doctrine?

How can the layman possibly trust the theologian if he suspects that the latter never speaks personally but always as the representative of higher authority? Who delimits the lines uttered by the theologian: his own Christian reason and his informed conscience or those he supports as an obedient, loyal servant? There is just no way of knowing. This is particularly true of published works by moral theologians since one knows that to win publication, they had to run a gauntlet of censors. It is also true, however, of face to face confrontations with theologians. There is nothing more painful than to watch a theologian think twice before he answers a direct question; to listen to him carefully and haltingly frame a precise answer which will not put him or the Church in an embarrassing position; to see him twitch and squirm while defending publicly a position which he (and everyone else) knows to be a weak one, or while devising a jerry-built "answer" to a pointed objection. To bring the pain to a fine point, one need only ask of the theologian: What do *you* think? There is little in his role as docile servant which prepares him to confront, much less bare in public, his personal beliefs. For him, they do not count. He is prone to camouflage his private opinions, his attitudes, his way of thinking. In extreme cases, he tries to act as if he does not even exist, or as if his mind is perfectly interchangeable with that of the magisterium. I conform; therefore I am. (Unfair? Yes, but not very.)

I would not want to suggest that such a self-image is incompatible with the creation of genuine theological advances. On the contrary, the numerous Center Party theologians have been responsible for much of the development of doctrine which has marked recent decades: the shift away from the large family norm, the taking seriously of the "secondary" ends of marriage, and the rejection of a purely legalistic approach to family limitation. But it is a self-image incompatible with some essential requirements in the present situation. It is, first of all, vital that the theologian understand not just where his predecessors went wrong, but why. Was it not, for example, a partially false conception of authority which led so many theologians for so many centuries never to wholly reject a tradition which saw any use of sex apart from procreation as dangerous if not sinful? It is just not enough to pass off the rejection of this position as the unfolding of "new insights" or a normal doctrinal development. For centuries a serious mistake was made, one which misled many people. Why? If the theologian sees himself only as a docile servant of an established doctrine, how can he avoid making the kinds of mistakes his predecessors have often made? He must, secondly, therefore, explore afresh his relationship to the magisterium, asking himself and the magisterium whether his role has been so conceived as to endanger the possibility of unbiased scholarship.

Third, it must be possible for the individual theologian to take, in public, a position counter to that of established teaching if his Catholic conscience and his scholarship so dictate. Otherwise, the layman will never have full confidence in the integrity of the theologian. So, too, the magisterium must allow this liberty to the theologian. Otherwise, it could never have confidence that he was not simply fawning on authority or that a purported theological consensus was the real one. Finally, the whole atmosphere supporting the enterprise of moral theology must encourage the theologian to be candid with himself, candid with his colleagues, candid with non-theologians, and candid with the magisterium.

The birth control question is, above all, a test case for the Church's understanding of itself and especially of its understanding of the development of doctrine. That means it is a test case for the contemporary renewal of the Church. Its importance lies in the direct confrontation of the theological methods and inclinations of another generation with those now emerging. The reason, for instance, why the natural law arguments against contraception are so unpersuasive today does not stem from some suddenly undiscovered fallacy in one step of the argument. Nor does it stem only from a rejection of the premises of the argument. Significant changes rarely take place in this way (though detailed critiques of old arguments normally accompany such changes and are necessary to help them along). They come about, rather, because of a radical shift of perspective, the development of a new group consciousness, the shaping of new conceptual and linguistic tools, and the impact of history and social circumstances. All of these forces are present within the Church today and present within that world of ours in which the Church exists. They are more than just "present": they are operating with a positive fury.

If there is a tragedy latent in this drama, then it lies in the desperation of good people trying to use old tools to cope with new material. It lies also in the desperation of married couples trying to relate old certainties to new uncertainties, holding on by their fingertips to a sandstone ledge they had been assured was made of granite. In each case, the natural inclination is to panic. That is a sensible response, but not the only one possible. A better one would be for the Church, in its teaching authority and in its members, to immerse itself in the present. No theologian today can be expected to be understood if he continues to argue that the primacy of the species takes precedence over the personal good of individuals. He will not be understood if he argues that biological values take precedence over personalist values. He will not be understood if he says that one must accept a doctrine or a law on the basis of authority alone. The problem is not that these things are necessarily wrong. They are incomprehensible, flying in the face of everything contemporary man has learned about himself, about his conscience, about nature, and about value. They have been taught him by the Church as much as by the world. If the concept of a "living magisterium" has any meaning at all, then it must at least mean this: one way to remain faithful to the past is to affirm the present. That is the demand which our life here today has directed to the Church's exercise of its authority. That is the cutting edge of renewal.

# Marc Oraison
## 1914-

Marc Oraison, a French surgeon, psychoanalyst, philosopher, writer and priest, caught the attention of moral theologians
in 1953 with his startling book, Christian Life and Problems of
Sexuality. *Since that time he has not ceased to be not only a
controversial personality, but a prime force in bringing about
the renewal of Christian moral thinking. In the book, Oraison
interpreted moral theology in the light of modern medicine and
Freudian psychology. Oraison had been spurred on by his own
unfortunate experiences with courses in moral theology which
he judged to be cut off from vital sources and in grave need of
radical revision.*

*Because of his approach to morality, Oraison came upon
hard times. Ultra-conservative church authorities terminated
his work in the seminaries of France. Undaunted he went to
Paris where he started working with juvenile delinquents. In
France he is well known as a public lecturer and author. He has
built his life work around a rich personal Christology and has
chosen to carry out that work within the structures of the
Church. Through translations of several of his books, his influence
has become world-wide.*

*The selection below is taken from* Morality for Our Time.
*In the introduction to the book, Oraison enters into a frank
discussion of the breakdown in dialogue between moralists and*

*psychologists. He is obviously speaking of the moralist who is closed to contemporary psychology and looks upon it as a destruction of religion. He sides with the psychologists who "since they reject constraint, are looking for some criterion more in line with their clinical findings." Oraison describes the present state of morality as one of shock, but he is convinced that it is a healthy one. Christian morality, he says, will emerge from the debate lucid and alive—but only on condition that it returns to being truly Christian.*

*The reader will quickly sense the richness of Oraison's insight. He is steeped in an existential mood and writes about real human beings, men and women who are struggling to resolve the questions of their own identities and of their relationships with other humans. He knows how a person can be tortured by a rigid, legalistic moral structure that calmly and coldly declares: "You have sinned." Rejecting this as both unhealthy and un-Christian, he pushes on to the concept of personal relationships anchored in love as the foundation of all morality.*

*One might be tempted to criticize Oraison for his near-glorification of modern psychology. Yet, within the context of the tradition of moral theology in which he was trained, his extreme reaction is comprehensible. Whether one accepts or rejects his theses, it must be admitted that his work has played a key role in opening up the thinking of moral theologians. The Church needs this kind of writer and should be most grateful that he has spoken so courageously in behalf of his fellow man.*

# MORALITY FOR OUR TIME

## CHAPTER ONE

### WHAT IS MORALITY?

*Morality is Dynamic*

U ltimate achievement for any philosophy is found in a theory of morality. A philosophy that disregards the dynamics of human behavior in its conception of the world is patently deficient. For morality does more than add the final intellectual fillip to a particular philosophical enterprise; it implements it concretely and brings about its practical effect. This perhaps explains why we tend to judge the sagacity of a philosopher on the strength of his moral preachments. It is at once the summation of his thought and its crowning achievement.

Morality is, and has always been, the most crucial element in human life. Therefore it is all the more disconcerting to see how much uncertainty persists despite man's continued preoccupation with disclosing practical norms by which to order his conduct. A number of basic intuitions are common to most civilizations and philosophical systems—respect for life, a sense of propriety and justice, a concern for social order to preserve human existence—but they always assume a variety of peculiar forms. Sometimes in fact the basic intuition is barely recognizable within certain doctrinal systems. Even something so basic as the respect for human life with its associate inalienable rights rarely appears outside a discriminating context. Pagan civilizations denied the human dignity of slaves and barbarians; capitalistic cultures implicitly impugn the human dignity of proletarians, while Marxists do just the opposite.

Man has always been concerned with his predicament; he is preoccupied with comprehending the significance of the world and his human presence within it. Of the numerous definitions of morality that have been advanced, I would choose the one formulated by Antonin Sertillanges: "Morality is the science of what man ought to be by reason of what he is."

Morality is first of all a science, though obviously not in the mathematical sense and not in the sense of the "exact (natural) sciences." Living as we do in a world dominated by the physical sciences, our notion of "science" has become somewhat limited, and perhaps unavoidably so. But for our present context we would have science understood as the aggregate of all conscious and established knowledge. Thus for instance when I go to the trouble of informing myself about the life, personality and peculiar habits of Napoleon, I feel I have acquired a science, though admittedly neither my term "science" nor my method have anything to do with the physical sciences. I note that this undertaking helps me to know Napoleon and to know myself at the same time, if only by the instinctive process of imagining myself in his place or in the position of the underling whose ear he pinched.

Every step in knowledge is simultaneously a step in the knowledge of oneself; each new confrontation with what is not myself represents and implies a personal meeting and an attitude that only I could know exists. This attitude could very well end in a refusal to confront myself any longer or in flight from existential engagement. In this event I can take refuge in universal and abstract ideas which permit me the reassuring comfort of a broad logic. A rationalistic or idealistic attitude of this sort involves far less personal jeopardy. It is less dangerous to sit at one's desk making logical deductions about volcanoes than exploring them firsthand. But even if I choose the less precarious pastime, someone still must leave his armchair and eventually tell me about his experiences. For all science is one. Even if the theoretician in his study should reject and hold in contempt the enlightened man who went in search of experience, he is totally dependent upon him. That is why I feel it anything but useless to keep recalling these two aspects of the scientific attitude: it involves a progression in the knowledge of oneself, and it affirms the fundamental primacy of human intercommunication.

Morality is a science. It is necessary knowledge. Paradoxically, we can define a man by means of the experience he has of himself. In his relations with others man has the need to know. Without knowledge he does not exist at all; he disappears from the face of the earth. It is quite likely that man requires knowledge more than food. With an animal it is just the opposite. It has no need of knowing or, rather, of comprehending; everything happens as if it were known beforehand. Its behavior is wholly directed by what we call instinct. There is no distance at all between the animal and the world of which he is a part and an expression. He is one of the rhythms written into nature. Having no need to confront nature, he need not know himself. Self-consciousness and growth in understanding, which are inseparable, are basically two expressions of the uncertain and uncomfortable human situation. Therefore, there is no question of morality on the animal level. But for human beings totally disarmed upon arrival in the world, with poor reflexes of adaptation, restrained and so powerless, it is imperative to learn, to grasp and to understand, and thus to engage ourselves, which is the same thing.

But just as certainly the universal importance of morality stems precisely from the fact that it is not and cannot be an intellectual science; it is at its very core a "living science"— we cannot live without it.

Sertillanges calls it "the science of what man ought to be." We are projected irresistibly toward a future not yet fully realized. I am not yet fully myself, since there is a tomorrow and I do not know what or whom I will see; I am not sure I am going to wake up tomorrow in good spirits nor am I sure the day will be a pleasant one. Certainly I can foresee a number of things, but I do not know today how I will be tomorrow. I do not know quite who I will be tomorrow—myself to be sure, but a self I have still to discover.

It belongs to me to be me. Tomorrow's confrontation is bound to be new, even if it happens to appear monotonous. The same bus driver I meet each day on the way to the office will not be quite the same. His wife might have given birth to a son last evening or he might be angry with his best friend. Who will I be when I meet this man who is the same and yet not the same? This constantly new adaptation cannot be arranged in advance, or by habit. There always remains a margin of the unforseen to guarantee that I always have the initiative in my personal attitude and comportment. I can rely on a mechanical set of gestures, words and practiced reactions to protect myself to some measure against the unknown, that is to say against life. But only to a degree. Life, complex and rich as it is, make fresh demands on me each succeeding day, in spite of all appearances to the contrary. When "I" respond I will already have lived today and yesterday and the day before. I will already possess a certain experience of the world and of myself. For me, tomorrow will be entirely new and yet not new at all. And how am I going to respond? This is a question I have to ask myself at the very outset.

Obviously I can walk away from it or retreat into myself. I can dismiss the question of tomorrow's world or, for that matter, even today's. If I take the bus to my office, I can pretend to respond, without actually consenting to "be there." No one can act my part for me. If tomorrow I refuse to be what the day demands, I am the one who is going to suffer. I will have the bitter feeling of being less than myself; I will have failed to be myself to the extent I was not present to the world that interrogates me by its very presence. The imperative dictating what each person should be is not of some obscure order; it is at once the individual, irresistible appeal of the world and an exigency of my own proper existence. It is a call to constant discovery and progression; it requires movement, not stagnation.

"The science of what man ought to be by reason of what he is." First of all we must know who we ourselves are. This knowledge should be as accurate as possible so as not to unfavorably prejudice our knowing progressively more about ourselves in the future. If we devise or deduce things about ourselves on the basis of insufficient or false evidence, we are only inviting disaster.

### Determining Authentic Moral Norms

It should be clear from the beginning that we are investigating the problem in Christian perspective. We take for granted a world where someone other than ourselves knows the final word, who in revealing his own intimate secrets makes us known to ourselves. This divine revelation by no means dispenses us from personal reflection and quest. On the contrary, we might say it actually invites us to use our own initiative.

Now, aside from revelation the two ways of knowing ourselves and the world are science and philosophy; they represent the human spirit acting under its own power. And it is on this level that an authentic twentieth-century revolution is in progress.

The roots of the uprising can be traced far into the past, but particularly to the eighteenth century when for the first time man developed an authentic scientific attitude. There were of course prior attempts; we need only mention the contributions of the first Greek philosophers, Aristotle and the revival of research in the twelfth and sixteenth centuries. But it is only rather recently that we learned to disengage ourselves sufficiently from a "magical" mentality to the point where we are to make rapid progress in scientific knowledge of the world. Despite this advance, quite obviously we have neglected to investigate man himself in a similarly scientific manner. There has been unequal development in man's knowledge of the material universe on the one hand and what might be called a scientific knowledge of man-by-himself on the other. Symptomatic of that failure is the current unrest in the field of medicine.

It is certainly true that this relatively recent enterprise is more difficult than anything that preceded it, but then self-reflection was never very assuring. Science has progressed outward rather than inward, indicating that perhaps we are afraid of what we might discover about ourselves under sharp, methodical scrutiny. It has all the indications of terror in face of the inexplicable.

On the other hand, in the last ten years we have initiated an era of extraordinary development within the human sciences with the aid of Freud's radical transformation of psychology. It is not unlike the stimulus given biology by the discoveries of Pasteur. Formerly, psychology was looked upon as a part of philosophical or literary empirical knowledge. But now it has become a methodical and rigorous science, solidly established and rich in promise.

But while we have made a considerable leap forward in methodical reflection upon ourselves as personal and social subjects, psychology and psychosociology require us to pursue our reflection further. It is now a question of scrutinizing our own intimate selves, myself, you, our parents and our close friends.

At first glance this might be disconcerting or even frightful to some. But by virtue of the elementary principle that the revelation of God does not fail and that certain knowledge cannot be contradictory, these developments can only herald a better understanding of what God is telling us.

Along with psychology contemporary philosophy has also taken a new turn. The philosophical man of the twentieth century senses—sometimes vaguely, sometimes profoundly—that he is a captive of ready-made ideas and intellectual constructs whose foundations are no longer intelligible. He feels compelled to relive personally the reflection on life and the world, but first he must understand what is going on within himself. This does not imply that the intellectual constructs are devaluated in any way or, worse, that they must be destroyed—even if it may sometimes appear that way. The phenomenologist simply insists upon an experience of the world which is at once existential, lived and reflexive. His attitude precludes passing over thorny questions about a very complex reality that a philosopher of another bent might miss for love of correct but deceptive abstraction. There is a profound need better to understand what *exists*. We have to end the game played with purely intellectual concepts and cease contenting ourselves with philosophical questions that have no answers. I believe that in our concrete world of concrete realities this phenomenological endeavor is making an effort to arrive at the same clear verification as modern psychological research. The two disciplines have many points in common.

By way of summary, there are two ways of knowing what we are in order to become ourselves: the word of God and the actual state of our self-reflection (anthropology).

## 1. *Revelation*

Christianity is no more a philosophy than it is a morality. It is a religion. For man's part it represents the acceptance and integration of a living relationship with someone else (God). It is not at all simply knowing of his existence intellectually, but knowing him in reciprocal *engagement,* that is to say in dialogue.

If I am in someone's office in his absence, I can certainly discover something about him: I know he exists; I can ascertain what tobacco he smokes, what books he reads, his main line of works, his tastes, and perhaps even his height, age and manners. But I still cannot say that I know him until he enters the room and speaks to me. He first has to initiate a dialogue and solicit my response. This image expresses the difference between philosophical reflection about God and true religion.

A personal meeting which dispenses with abstract ideas (however correct they may be) is obviously going to change our perspective radically. It will singularly enlighten me and complete my knowledge of the person, of the room, of the inexpressible things about our lives, of myself and what takes place between us. In other words, to transpose the image, the incursion of God into our world by his direct word will precipitate profound reverberations in human reflection (philosophy) and in the behavior of men (morality). But nonetheless the very essence of Christianity—and we cannot stress this enough—is the real historical encounter.

A second comparison might help. The moment a man meets the woman he is to marry, he is somehow altered, yet retains the same identity as before. He is at once more free and more constrained. In the beckoning glance of the other he discovers his own personal meaning. And through a new, dynamic reflection he transforms his behavior for her sake and for the sake of their new relationship. Through an interplay of intellectual and existential knowledge the relationship assumes a distinct form. When the other is not physically present he is present in thought and his existence is taken into account. From what his partner already knows she attempts to deduce a deeper and more exact knowledge of herself, her beloved, and their mutual relationship. But once they are in each other's presence, this petty game of deductions gives way to more profound and literally unutterable truth. Ideas and words no longer suffice; the signs and symbols have evoked a mutual existential need.

Our living relationship with God, which is to say our religion, unfolds in an analogous manner: God was once present to us visibly in his historical incarnation, and now he is visible in the Church, but no longer in the manner of ordinary human beings. Therefore the sacraments as signs must be able to signify God and actually contain the real power of his presence.

It is an historical fact that mankind actually encountered God living and speaking, in the same concrete fashion as the couple we just mentioned. In fact the bible, and especially the prophet Ezekiel, uses the image of lover and beloved to illustrate its message. The entire history of the world is viewed as an ongoing dialogue. Abraham, Christ and the Church are accessible references in a comprehensive historical reality.

Seen in this same light the human situation is that of man being called by another to cooperate in accomplishing an exalted work. This is the significance of the first two chapters of Genesis. In the quintessential act of creation the Word called forth the human couple as a response. It was unlike any response that preceded it. Up until that moment the Word "commanded" things to exist; it was a world of inert matter, vegetation and animal life. The Word did not address himself to it. But the Word *spoke* to the human couple: "Be fruitful and multiply, and fill the earth and subdue it." In other words: Now it is your turn to act; we have something to do together. I am not speaking as a potter to a vase, nor as a woodsman to a tree, but to my son, my very own issue.

The human race is called by infinite love to a role of response; in fact it is an exigency of his very existence. Hence within the human race itself there must be mutual and intersubjective call and response.

Creation can be described as the first harmony of consciences; and it is at this moment that God made his initial call. The human race faced itself, lost interior contact with the presence of God and thereby transformed the harmony of the first morning to cacophony. This is the mystery of dissociation. Notwithstanding, God pursued the dialogue along other lines so magnificiently described in the Son of Solomon. And what is the whole of Hebrew history if not a witness to God's continual intrusion into ongoing events so as to make himself more intimately known? The definitive encounter is achieved finally in Christ. Henceforth the human race succeeds in finding itself in him and through him at the very moment of his apparent failure. This is a much more profound harmony, since it involves a unique call that actually alters our very form.

Thus God (himself a threefold subject) addresses individual men of all races as so many subjects by means of an infinite exchange of love across time. First and foremost the Christian is a resurrected person. He is conscious and ongoing. Whatever he does he will not refuse or oppose God.

Consequently the moral law is simply an indicator; it reveals (to use St. Paul's phrase) a sense of our own drama, namely the necessity to love.

## 2. *Anthropology*

Anthropology has made significant advances in the last sixty years. We have become less and less preoccupied with man in the abstract and have learned to direct our investigations towards man as he really exists. At long last we are subjecting the human presence in the world (as both individual and collective) to the rigors of scientific study. And not without effect. Several broad lines are already converging, as if inviting us to draw some proper distinctions and to attempt an initial exposition.

As propitious as the occasion might be, the task is still a difficult one. We have to deal with dimensions and perspectives of truly novel character, and our vocabularies offer us no appreciable assistance in giving expression to what we see. If we want to avoid the technical jargon that is unintelligible to non-specialists, all we have left at our disposal are words that already have been used to describe other things and, consequently, are tainted with alien cultural significance. Anyone bent on studying modern anthropology goes into the field like an explorer trekking uncharted terrain. There are only hints of paths, and settlements are few and far between.

One of the fundamental affirmations of this new discipline is the psychosomatic unity of the individual human subject and his ultimate uniqueness. There is no "body" or "soul" to serve as container and contents. Psychic life at all its stages is expressed on the somatic register as much as in self-consciousness. In fact the impact of affectivity on the biological mechanism appears much more crucial than the reverse process. Just as it is arbitrary and false to dissociate the sun from its rays, it is unpermissible to *separate* the body from the soul—something quite different from distinguishing between them. While this observation is based on clinical evidence and methodical investigation, even Thomas Aquinas, who only had philosophical reasoning at his disposal, was able to arrive at an identical conclusion regarding the unity of the human person. There is not "my soul" and "my body"; there is only myself. Unfortunately, however, our entire vocabulary gravitates around the dualistic notion that anthropology no longer finds acceptable.

When Francis of Assisi referred to the source of his bodily deficiencies as "my brother ass," he was unable to express in other terms what he actually meant. And today his image has no contemporary significance, except perhaps as a vestige of an outmoded mentality. When we say an ascetic has become the "master of his body" (and I grant this might involve pathological aberrations), we are not particularly concerned with his body as such, but rather with certain affective forces which are expressed bodily and emotionally. When St. Paul speaks of the "flesh," we are not supposed to understand the body in the organic sense as opposed to some more-or-less ethereal "spirit." The dualistic notion is dangerous insofar as it distorts the profound sense of God's inspired message and effects a regression to an archaic, pagan mentality. If we want to do justice to the integral context of Pauline thought, the "flesh" has to be understood as the "carnal condition" involving the mysterious contradiction of sin. And sin is an attitude of man's spirit, not his physiological organism.

But if the human condition characteristically involves an indissociable psychosomatic world then each individual reality, each concrete personality, is absolutely unique; it cannot be identified with any other personality, and in a sense it is *alone,* sometimes dramatically so. The contemporary theater (Ionesco, for instance) provides evidence to this effect in a paradoxical and tragicomic form; sometimes it is so charged with anguish that we mask it under a flood of pseudo-language and conventional conversation.

There is no need to belabor the clarification modern psychology gives of this attitude. The individual personality sets and elaborates itself from birth—if not earlier—in living relationships with the concrete personalities of its immediate surroundings. There is, for example, the "Oedipal" confrontation that occupies a moment of this long and obscure personal history. But the child does not enter relationships with an abstract mother and father, but with particular individuals, who are themselves the product of their own personal histories.

No two human beings have an identical history. Though a family gives every guarantee of stability, no two children will have lived the same moments of this stability, since it something in constant flux and always liable to be put in question. Ideal maturity can be described as the full assumption of one's personal solitude, "solitude" being understood here as a personal awareness that I am totally autonomous and distinct. This is man's sole mode of being: to live at a distance from others. Otherwise dialogue is impossible and, hence, existence itself. Up until a short while ago the notion of the "human person" was something purely metaphysical. Now it is being reevaluated in a new light: it is a unique and subjective existential reality that can only exist in an authentic sense when it enters into relationships with other individuals.

At this point I would like to cite an eminent psychoanalyst, Dr. Hesnard, one of the pioneers of modern psychology in France. He concludes the introduction to his book *Psychanalyse du lien interhumain* (Editions Presses Universitaires de France) with the following lines:

> The human person is not ... construed as mechanism or spirit. It is a being of flesh that is total and individual and cannot be understood except through the *bond* which unites it to its interhuman milieu. ...

When this being integrates the organic or biological activities that maintain its existence, and the bond itself, with its biological milieu, it is called *body*. When it integrates, along with organic activities, its activities of need or affectivity, thus identifying itself with the objects of its vital interests and *binding* itself to other living human beings, it is called an individual. When it integrates, along with its organic and instinctive activities, activities of a complex structure, thus identifying itself as a self and with others like itself as a spiritual projection of some ideal, thereby becoming a value-conscious being, a being of rights and obligations that becomes more related to other men in its moral intimacy as it acquires autonomy and liberty, it is called a *person*.

After reading a statement like this one could hardly maintain that psychoanalysts deny or suppress human liberty! In the same introduction Dr. Hesnard continues:

We also ascertain among civilized peoples the existence of a profound socialization that exerts its energy on natural intersubjectivity for the purpose of human communion as this collective bond is further evolved.

This is not a purely philosophical gloss. Dr. Hesnard's theoretical reflections are the product of long years of clinical experience. For the first time in human history man is investigating himself methodically; he is no longer dependent upon introspective intuition alone. He is taking note of the fact that he exists only by and for love, and he is prepared to use this ascertainment as a new basis for philosophical and religious reflection.

The human person in the reality of his existence does not engage in relationships with principles or with a law. He rather binds himself to other *persons*. This constitutes the affirmation of the self as subject of intersubjectivity. This can occur at different levels; the clinical experience of the interhuman stage (whether it be preconscious or conscious) does not of itself exclude the existence of other stages.

To say "I" is to respond to another because that person by his "word" (and here we do not restrict the term to articulated language) posits me as subject. The child discovers himself as a subject in his relations to the parents who wanted him (or *accepted* him, which comes to the same thing). This self-discovery is very primitive; it is like seeing oneself in a mirror for the first time. One day through my parents' concern for me I came to understand that *I* was existing, and I laughed with joy. By the same token, one day through the concern shown me by the incarnate Word, I came to see that *I* was existing even more than I had thought, and death took on meaning.

It is no wonder that the dynamic character of the person that is cultivated in contemporary science has replaced the old, abstract notion of a static metaphysical entity. The human person is constantly on the go, encountering until death a variety of complex situations and individuals without ever being able to say his own structurization is complete. This constant forward movement is oriented toward effecting increasingly more successful encounters. As present-day psychological science sees it, man's natural destiny is to achieve that communion of which Hesnard speaks. If I may quote him again:

> Social psychology obliges us to characterize peoples and nations by an analysis of the psychic bond that draws men together into collectivities, large or small, open or closed. *Without this natural bond none of these groups could aspire—except very seldom—to universality, since they would certainly fail to realize it even in perfunctory fashion.*

## The Drama of Human Behavior

The italicized portion of Hesnard's last remarks are of singular importance. It is not only replete with meaning but it poses some important questions as well. Here Hesnard is introducing an aspect of anthropology that is extremely difficult to express and even more difficult to accept. It is what I would readily characterize as the "dramatic" aspect.

The history of any human being is in reality a tension, a fundamental dynamism of opening himself in order to recognize others and to be recognized by them in return—without his ever being entirely successful. Here some classical images are to the point: Man is chained to freedom and he eventually succeeds in realizing that the chains are deep within himself, so deep in fact that they elude his reach. This bears out the evidence of anthropology. Psychoanalysts understand only too well that even in an optimal case the best they can hope for is a *clinical* cure for the sick person. They only hope they can allow him to live in a more autonomous fashion relative to his own personal drama, the deepest sources of which remain inaccessible. Perhaps it is right here that psychoanalytic discoveries have precipitated the greatest shock. A rational and scientific—or, if you will, conformist—world is incapable of enduring such a revelation of the real mysteries of the human soul. It is never very agreeable to recall that we are not masterpieces that the maker has succeeded in forging to his own image and likeness. In fact some people react against the unpleasant reminder in a particularly violent manner. These are people who are couched in the false security that an inflexible way of thinking provides. It is not a matter of chance that medical doctors, ecclesiastics and mathematicians, to name but a few, reject the contributions of dynamic psychology with a vehemence closely akin to despair.

It goes without saying that their opposition should not keep us from articulating our recognition of man's drama and attempting to fathom certain of its aspects. At best the enlightenment proffered by modern psychology will only further underline the inaccessibility of a definitive explanation. Even if we do disclose certain aspects of the how of things, we are still left with a disturbing silence about the ultimate why, a silence that is the fault of none other than man himself.

The only value that develops without limit toward the infinite—a value that coincides with the person—is the encounter and communication between individual consciences. Everyday experience indicates that *authentic* encounters are rare and limited. *Total* intercommunication is impossible; I cannot communicate totally with another person because I am never totally *distinct* or *different* from him. In every encounter which engages me ever so minimally, I bring along my "interior world," a large part of which is unconscious. Practically speaking, it cannot be otherwise. Perfectly balanced as I may be, there are in me inaccessible balances of all my earliest affective experiences. Even before initiating a conversation with another, I have an "image" of him, a ready-made representation which is not a function of him at all, but rather of me. If this image remains in the background and interferes only marginally with the encounter, it will do no more than limit an otherwise fruitful dialogue. But if my preconceived image were unknowingly to take the upper hand, then dialogue would be impossible.

To clarify this admittedly oversimplified aspect of things, I would say that this "image of the other " exists simultaneously on two planes, only one of which is directly accessible to our consciousness.

At the outset there is what we could call the imaginative level. For example, I arrange a business meeting with a prospective client. I do not as yet know him; I have never seen him and know very little about him. Looking forward to the meeting, I "prepare" what I am going to say beforehand. But what invariably happens is that I *imagine* my client, his way of reacting, his bearing and his personality. I decide: "I will say this to him; and if he answers thus and so, I'll retort. . . ." This goes on and on, as a kind of rehearsal. This imaginary dialogue takes place in *me*, with a person I carry about inside me, after a manner, and whom I project. This imaginary man is created as a function of the person I happen to be, since I do not know my visitor sufficiently well to have even an approximate idea of him. I create *what I need him to be like*, either to obtain what I am after or to manifest some sort of aggression. When I face him in person, he is always completely different than I imagined he would be. If I let myself be duped by my imagination I run a risk of deceiving myself; we would begin our conversation badly, thereby jeopardizing any positive results that may have been forthcoming. But this is so common to one degree or another that all we can do is try to avoid the pitfall as much as possible.

This is rooted in an unconscious zone of our physic apparatus that is the vital residue of our earliest affective experiences. From infancy the child creates progressively clearer notions of himself and others through his association with people who share his environment. The earliest encounters with the "non-self" are portals to our conscious reflections later on. If our affective development was normal, the unconscious interior world of "notions of the non-self" will not prejudice our adult relationships with reality. But there will always be a certain amount of inability to communicate: what I carry in me of my earliest experience is too subjective and too inaccessible to exploration to integrate it into my actual adult situation; it simply cannot be *verbalized*.

It often happens that in our encounters with other persons we try to reduce them to this primitive "vision of the world" which we carry about within us and which we find awakened in times of emotional stress. Some psychoanalysts regard this vision of the unconscious world as a "world of phantasms" in order to distinguish it from simple imaginary projections. In its extreme form it arouses a feeling of fear in the one so conceived, for it is a genuine menace to his unique existence. No doubt this explains the profound discomfort we feel in the company of "strangers" since, down deep, we sense that we "do not truly exist" for them. We experience authentic anguish when we are deprived of being ourselves.

Of course this is the pathological side of the situation. But it helps us grasp what takes place in various lesser degrees in every human situation. And if we take time to reflect, it will become apparent just how frequently this "world of phantasms" intervenes in human relationships to the detriment of all dialogue. It is precisely the insufficient perspective obtaining between two persons in each other's presence that prevents them from being wholly themselves. This is even true on the physical level. If I am too close to someone, I actually do not see him—the pores of his skin perhaps, but not *him*. And if I am too far away it goes without saying that I do not see him either.

Psychoanalysts who speak of the "world of phantasms" regard it as a fundamental tendency in all human encounters—even successful ones—unconsciously to view the other person in a thoroughly narcissistic manner. Mysteriously and primordially we identify him with ourselves, and by refusing to separate him from us we find that we are unable to locate and identify him. If we could resolve this enigma we would know liberation:

to know the other precisely as other would be to accept the fact that we are indeed separate beings. But the enigma is an insoluble one; the ultimate "separation" which would permit us to be *integrally* ourselves in any encounter with the other is in all probability only realized in death.

Within this web of confusion obscuring every personal encounter, "law" intrudes as an ambivalent imperative. Law obviously indicates how I ought to behave if I am to establish successful relationships with myself and with others. But the primitive emotional factors involved in the moral entreaty can arouse my instinctive fear. "Law" always tends to wedge itself between the other person and myself (and between me and myself) in order to assist me in finding something I have lost. Consequently I run the constant risk of using other persons to relocate that primordial part of myself from which I really ought to dissociate myself. Herein lies the impasse and illusion of legalism, at once so complete and despairing. It is in this sense that St. Paul speaks of the "killing" power of the "law" (Rom. 7).

## The Divine Perspective

In light of what we have seen of modern anthropology I think it would at this point be profitable to recall rather succinctly several aspects of Judeo-Christian revelation.

What crowns and dominates this revelation is the God who makes himself known as the *trinitarian mystery*, that is, as three subjects so infinitely distinct and distant from one another that they are infinitely one. Christ let this be known to his apostles when he said: "If I do not leave the Spirit cannot come." For love to establish itself in eternal perspective, the resurrected Christ had to distance himself from sensible and temporal experience.

The existence of the universe, whose essentially dynamic, evolutionary character has been established by modern science, is the response to a call. As St. John relates in the preface to his Gospel, the spoken Word summoned the universe into existence and continues to sustain it. At the end of an enormous succession of created life, man, or rather the human couple, appeared at the apex of creation to empower that creation to actually *answer* God's call and not simply to obey it as had hitherto been the case. However, as a self-conscious creature man turned toward himself; he listened to himself and became deaf to the call of love. We might say that this reaction was typically "natural" for the human race in its first stage of self-consciousness, and now a new intervention became imperative to unify the race as well as to integrate each individual. At the first stage man was only beginning to establish interpersonal relationships. Due to its insufficiency the relationship was crude and still quite illusory. So God intervened in human history. A woman well schooled in her cultural heritage became so completely attentive to the divine call that the historical event actually took place inside her: the Word-made-flesh was conceived within her human *flesh* (in the integral, psychosomatic sense we were speaking of before).

He also came to break the bonds of death that had been established by the deadening of human conscience. The entirety of human history could now be unraveled in its full significance; the call of God went forth and brought into being its unique answer. Christ said: "He who believes in me has life . . . and I will raise him up on the last day." But, and this is clearly implied, we can *refuse* to believe in him; we can refuse to *see* him; we can refuse his word. There is no affirmation, I think, so strong and so concrete regarding human freedom. It is easy to understand why some people find the thought frightening: nothing is at once so simple and so difficult as to say Yes to someone.

Finally, using numerous images, the most frequent of which is the wedding banquet, Christ announced the kingdom of heaven as the perfected world he came to create. This is the network of interpersonal relationships established in perfect *communion* without the least trace of reticence. This is the vision that is able to dispel the somewhat bitter nostalgia we can sense in the writings of Dr. Hesnard.

It is worthwhile to recall St. John's mention of the "sin which leads to death" (1 Jn. 16): the personal rejection of the personal salvation that Christ earned for us by his blood. According to the transcendental logic of revelation, the refusal to be loved is what actually kills.

## The Point At Issue

Everything I have indicated up to now has been by way of introduction. I now want to address myself to the crucial issue.

Through the centuries the word of God—that other who is love—has been confused with elements of natural knowledge, natural reflection, natural expression. But at this particular stage of the revolution when man is becoming acutely aware of himself and his own drama, the rationalists' articulation of the word of God is ridiculous and tragic in its insufficiency. Now as in other great periods of the Church's history, theologians who want to transmit the word rather than to study in libraries have a grave obligation to remain faithful—or better, to deepen their fidelity—to the word of life. Since this will require illumination, no one in the twentieth century can afford to be satisfied with an oil lamp when he has electricity at his disposal.

Before we return to Sertillanges' definition of morality it is legitimate to ask whether or not a genuine moral revolution is in progress. And by this I mean a revolution in the way morality has been traditionally articulated. By now I think the reader is aware that my answer is an emphatic Yes. And if I were asked to describe quickly the nature of the revolution, I would say it entails a process of purgation. Traditional notions have congealed and become static and stultifying; consequently we are currently making every attempt to restore dynamism to moral thinking and to resuscitate our moribund conceptions of the world and man's relation to it. The only thing that might be surprising about the revolution is that it should come only now.

But when did it actually begin? What were some of its causes? I tend to think that the confusion in the post-Constantinian era between the earthly city and the kingdom of God is far from insignificant in this regard. I think we fail to appreciate the terrible slackening of spirit that was introduced by the theocratic government of the period. But then again neither is the tendency to revert back to that theocratic notion of political society about to disappear, since it represents a highly archaic regression toward the mentality of the primitive tribe passing from nomadic life to a stable society. But whatever the precise cause or causes, one thing is certain: the rise of moralism progressively obscured, paralyzed and falsified the Christian dynamics of behavior. Moral speculation gradually dissociated itself from the context of human acts and began to be bandied about by a closed group of professionals. In due time this led to the impasse modern psychology demonstrates to be intolerable.

Modern man is fundamentally dissatisfied with abstract principles that are rigorously deduced one from the other. Their inexorable character befits a Prometheus or Greek philosophy, but certainly not the message of the Gospel. The rationalistic structure in its entirety must be interrogated by the modern human sciences.

Any formulation of morality that is supposed to have a profound effect on our way of thinking has to be the result of a second, more perceptive look at the word of God and the true nature of human reality. It might well require several decades of concerted effort, but we have no choice. We either expend the energy and find collaborators or we suffer an irreparable loss. Now is the time to ask whether what we generally call "Christian morality" is in fact truly Christian; whether the "values of Christian civilization" that some people are prepared to defend to the death—without ever explaining what it is precisely that they understand by the phrase, I may add—are actually derived from Christ, or whether perhaps they are vestiges of an ancient Stoicism, or whether an adamant fidelity to certain traditions is not tantamount to betraying authentic Tradition, that is to say the life of the Spirit in the Church.

Among the many reflections by competent psychologists on the central problem of morality, I would like to single out for special mention a work by Dr. Berge, entitled *Les Maladies de la vertu* (Grasset, 1960). It poses the same question we do at the moment. And while admittedly it does not treat the problem in its theological context, it does provide a wealth of clinical evidence that we cannot afford to ignore. He writes: "We must all the same ask ourselves the question whether morality is made for man or man is made for morality." In effect he is asking whether we have understood that man has been created to achieve complete happiness (the very foundation of morality according to Aquinas) and not to be sacrificed to a body of drastically depersonalized teachings. Dr. Berge goes on: "A moralizing morality has made all morality suspect." As we see, psychologists are crying out against this obvious form of inhumanity. It is now up to theologians to examine whether our pretense at morality is not in effect the ultimate subtle refuge of a pride that actually misconstrues the existential relationship of man to God, the creator and savior.

# John Giles Milhaven
## 1927-

*Little did Catholic theologians realize what challenges and responsibilities would be theirs as a result of the Second Vatican Council. Once the atmosphere was cleared for dialogue and questioning, it became necessary to nourish the newly discovered freedom to think and search while at the same time offering the Catholic world sufficient guidelines by which everyday life could be lived. Though some theologians balked at the challenge and saw their responsibility as one of keeping control of things, a great number responded vigorously and creatively with an effort to make available a theology that could blend in with the modern world.*

*John G. Milhaven, an American theologian, is one of the latter group. His book,* Toward a New Catholic Morality, *is recognized as a major contribution to postconciliar moral theology. He believes that Christians are at a turning point in the history of the Church. In response to the innumerable questions with which the Christian of today must deal, Milhaven seeks new answers which are not totally discontinuous with the old. The book is a statement of the new direction that he sees the Church taking in the area of Christian ethics or moral theology.*

*The topics of several of the chapters quickly reveal that Milhaven wants to discuss some of the most important issues in moral theology today, issues that touch the lives of Christian* men and women, for example, homosexuality and love, abortion, adultery, pre-marital sex, contraception, dissent in the Church, and authority. His chapter, "No Absolutes" clarifies what he means by the new morality. Far from being an invitation to lawless anarchy, it is a challenge to live responsibly, creatively and maturely.

In the passage below, Milhaven takes up the questions of loyal opposition in the Church, responsible dissent, and the importance of being a Roman Catholic. For Milhaven, obedient responsibility and responsible disobedience are marks of the mature Christian. As a fact, loyal opposition is a tradition in the Church. One need only recall such great personalities as Catherine of Siena, Ignatius Loyola, or John Henry Newman. This is obviously a very delicate area of life. How does a member of the Church decide whether the pronouncements of an authority are right or wrong? How does one arrive at the most loyal response, whether that be silence or public opposition?

There are no easy answers to these and the many other questions that must be faced by contemporary Christians. Milhaven is highly sensitive to the anxiety and despair that has entered the lives of many Catholics in recent years. His reflection on being a Catholic can be of great service to anyone who has thought of leaving the Church or asked whether there is any value in Catholicism.

It is wonderful to be free. But human freedom requires great strength and courage. It calls for men and women of integrity and truthfulness. The opportunity to be a free people is available to the Church today. It is a slow, difficult and demanding business. The Church and her people will be free only if they assume responsibility for the human.

# TOWARD A NEW
# CATHOLIC MORALITY

## CHAPTER 11

### LOYAL OPPOSITION IN THE CHURCH

I n the preceding chapters, we scrutinized the new Christian morality as it deals with ethical questions common to believer and nonbeliever, concerning student freedom, homosexuality, abortion, etc. For the remainder of the book, I will try to present the new morality as it deals with ethical questions peculiar to Christians, concerning aspects of Church life.

We are in one of the periods in the history of the Church when the rhythm of its development gathers speed like a galloping horse. At such a time, a Christian is exhilarated by the new prospects to which the Spirit is leading the Church. But the rapid pace of change also exacerbates tensions. One form of aggravated tension arises in the matter of the Christian's obedience. The direction of changes already made seem to an individual Christian to indicate where a further change should take place. Or perhaps a change may appear hasty and misdirected and call for a change back to the old way. In either case, however, those who hold authority in the Church may see things differently. The authorities may not only oppose the desired change for the moment; they may explicitly reject it once and for all. Tension mounts. And thus in a time like our own, when changes multiply around us, so do the tensions.

An obvious example is the birth control question. As everyone knows, a growing number of Catholics today—including theologians, philosophers, psychologists and doctors—cannot, despite honest effort on their part, understand the position taken by the ecclesiastical authorities on birth control. They have grown increasingly convinced that the official stand is neither infallible nor irrevocable, but badly in need of revision.

In the present chapter, I am not inquiring whether this and similar dissident opinions are well-grounded or not. I am simply taking as given the case, widespread today, of the Catholic who has arrived at convictions contrary to those of authority. Whatever worth his convictions may possess, he now holds them and finds he cannot change them. He asks himself: "What can I do? What should I do?"

Some repond by simply disobeying. If the point in question is birth control, they buy contraceptives and employ them. They encourage others to do the same. They justify themselves simply with their belief that the official Church position is wrong, inhuman and unChristian. Conscientious disobedience, they say, is the only responsible practice. Such a response by the individual Christian not only is actual disobedience but reveals as well a remarkable ignorance of what Christian obedience is.

On the other hand, one can find the opposite extreme among Christians who, like those just mentioned, cannot alter their interior conviction that the offical stand could and should be revised. Such persons completely collapse. In the question of birth control, they do not merely refrain from any use of contraception and any encouragement to its use. True to their concept of obedience, they also abandon all effort to see that the Church—the whole Church "teaching" and "taught"—might come to the view they hold to be more true, human and Christian. In particular, they do not feel free to work toward changing the mind of the ecclesiastical authorities. Such a response by the individual Christian not only is not true obedience; it also reveals a remarkable ignorance of what Christian obedience is.

In brief, both reactions are too simplistic and childlike to be the mature, sophisticated, demanding thing that Christian obedience really is. More precisely, neither of these reactions recognizes that, for a Christian, obedience and responsibility go hand in hand. The first reaction proceeds as if responsibility dispensed a man from obedience. The second as if obedience dispensed him from responsibility. Of Christians choosing to react in these ways, one might well repeat the exasperated cry Robert Bolt put on the lips of Thomas More: "O sweet Jesus, these plain, simple men!" The Christian dedicated enough to be sophisticated sees as possible choices rather obedient responsibility and responsible disobedience. In the present chapter, I will discuss the former; in the following chapter, the latter. Both are traditionally Christian possibilities, and in endorsing them, the new morality is not doing anything new.

In the case we are considering, where the Christian cannot help favoring changes that the authorities oppose, obedient responsiblity can mean loyal opposition. There is a long tradition of loyal opposition in the Church. Few of the changes that eventually took place in the Church during its nineteen centuries sprang full-grown from some bishop's head. Many of the changes, when first proposed, met official disapproval and rejection. But often, at these times, leaders arose in the Church, men and women of tenacity and purpose who, while obeying carefully and completely, still maintained their conviction that the authorities were wrong. They labored persistently and ingeniously—but not disobediently—to bring about the changes. One thinks of Catherine of Siena or Ignatius Loyola or John Henry Newman.

We need not look so far back into the past. In our own time we have been privileged to know those whom *America* recently called the "giants of *aggiornamento.*" Now that their work is bearing fruit, we should not forget their spirit and conduct as they endured decades of waiting. No authoritative declaration of policy could weaken their convictions that certain things must be brought up to date—e.g., the liturgy and biblical studies. They complied with each order, whether it was by general decree or by direct restriction of their personal activity. But to the extent to which obedience still left them free to discuss and write and experiment, these men of the Church worked to prepare the way for an eventual change in the mind both of those in authority and of the whole Church. Fortunate were those who came to know these "giants," to converse with them at table or consult them in private. One could see in them the marks of interior suffering and self discipline. But much more, one admired and rejoiced in their loyalty to the Church, their integrity, their serene confidence in the Spirit leading the Church.

Having known these men, a Catholic could be proud of the Church. What they were doing in loyal opposition, the Church was doing. For what the Church does is by no means restricted to what the authorities do. The Church is the people of God—all of them. It is the Lord's whole congregation. The human beings in authority are no more and no less the Church than are their subjects. If it is correct to say that the Church sent Fr. Daniel Berrigan to Mexico, it is equally correct to say that the Church bought an ad in *The New York Times* to protest the sending. This is quite independent of whether or not the religious superior who sent Fr. Berrigan was right in so doing, or if those who signed the ad were right—or both, or neither. It in no way denies the fact that the Christians in authority have the right to receive obedience just as the Christains who are subject have the right to receive respect and concern from their superiors. The point is that neither superiors nor subjects are the Church in the sense of either being alone the whole Church. And both are the Church in the sense that together they make up the Church and each have their individual responsibility.

There is thus no reason to deny the perennial tension in the Church between those who on a given point would replace the old with the new and those who would retain the old. Nor to deny that authority may for a time take the side that eventually shows itself to be wrong or less preferable. It is a tension, and therefore neither comfortable nor relaxing, but it is a healthy tension, a tension that goes with life.

Incidentally, there is no reason, either, to insinuate that one pole of the tension is *a priori* better than the other. Is it more genuinely Christian to be bringing forth the new? Or upholding the old? Jansenism was something new, advanced by sincere Christians. The best biblical scholarship looks for something old, the original meaning of the sacred text. The point is rather that the tension between new and old is simply part of the continuing life of the whole Church. And it gives rise to an equally organic tension between obedience and responsibility, where obedient responsibility can at times mean only loyal and obedient opposition. This, too, is a vital role within the Church.

# John Giles Milhaven

It may be of use to list some key aspects of that role:

1. Take our Christian at the present time who claims to be obedient, yet interiorly disagrees with a position taken by authority. He can be called obedient only if he has tried hard to agree. Only if sincere effort to see the point of the official position has failed and the opposing evidence stands up under critical examination, can the loyalty to truth of the obedient man command interior disagreement. This is not as difficult as it may sound. Three or four years ago, the ordinary experience of an educator, reinforced by the growing consensus of other Catholic educators, could easily convince him that the Church law on prohibited books (the "Index") needed revision. Few would criticize as disobedient or intellectually presumptuous the interior opposition before the rescinding of the law.

2. The Christian of the loyal opposition recognizes his obligation to obey. He recognizes those of the people of God whose role is to command, and he respects their role. Even when he disagrees, he can obey, and obey with the peaceful interior recognition that it is good for him to do so.

3. May the Christian who obeys, but disagrees with the policy and views of authority, express his disagreement publicly in the Church? May he try to win other Christians to his dissident views? Here there seems to be no single, simple answer. In certain circumstances he unquestionably may. One cannot blame for disobedience those who ten years ago began to criticize publicly the existent liturgy and in the face of various pro-Latin declarations of authority still urged the vernacular. Nor those today who protest that the new liturgical changes are doing more harm than good. One may disagree strongly with one or the other group and still recognize that both are exercising their Christian responsibility in a way completely consonant with obedience. If such public criticism of Church law and official pronouncements is expressed appropriately (perhaps, for example, not from the pulpit, but in a journal of opinion), it is a form of Church life that can be of great use to those in authority and to the Church as a whole.

But on certain questions, Church authorities may directly forbid any public expression of dissident views. It seems clear that the Holy Father has, at least for a time, forbidden a Catholic to defend publicly the opposite of the official position on birth control. An American bishop might forbid his priests to protest the war in Vietnam. A European bishop might forbid them to defend it. One bishop may silence any espousal of racial integration; another, of segregation.

Once more, the loyal opposition recognizes the obligation to obey, though obedience is more costly here. It is silent to the extent—though no further—that authority has commanded it to be silent. In the following chapter we will ask whether, in a given case, a Christian might be free, even obligated, to say publicly what authority has forbidden? Church lawyers traditionally hold that the force of positive law can be outweighed by other values, such as justice and charity. We are fond of reminding German Catholics who lived under the Nazis that no prescription of human authority, whether ecclesiastical or civil, dispenses a man from intrinsic moral obligations. Nevertheless, the case where a Christian would be justified in directly violating a command of silence seems so rare and exceptional, a last resort of desperation, that it need not be considered in studying that activity of the loyal opposition which is essential to the life of the Church. The loyal opposition is ready, when commanded, to be silent.

> To set oneself up as misunderstood seems ridiculous and conceited. And yet, in truth (without, I think, the least touch of conceit), I do not believe that I can see something, and I would like that something to be seen. You can't imagine what intensity of desire I sometimes feel in this connection, and what impotence. What keeps me calm is my complete confidence that if there is a ray of light in "my gospel", somehow or other that ray will shine forth. At the worst—of this I'm sure—it will reappear in another heart—all the richer, I hope, for having been faithfully guarded in me.—The only wise and Christian attitude is obviously to wait in all loyalty for God's own hour—if it is to come. I am counting more than ever on the influence of your prayers that I may never fail the light.

Thus Teilhard de Chardin wrote in a letter from the front, at the close of World War I. Did he dimly suspect the forty years of virtually uninterrupted silence that would be imposed upon him? In any case, he was ready.

4. But the loyal opposition—obedient even, if need be, to the point of silence—can still do great things for its cause in the Church. It can, for example, turn to history. It can write a historical study of the Church's position on birth control or on the relationship between Church and State, of the liturgical practices in the early Church or of the theological views of certain Fathers of the Church, of the political evolution of Vietnam. History often inspires a requestioning of contemporary attitudes. "If these are the arguments that originally motivated the prohibition of contraceptives, are there any better ones today?" Whether the requestioning leads to a revision of the present official position or to its confirmation, the loyal opposition serves by bringing new light and perspective.

Similarly, a journalist might conduct and publish a survey indicating some negative effects of the new liturgical changes. A psychiatrist might criticize the argument of certain theologians that the marital act loses force as an expression of love when contraceptives are used. A sociologist could advance statistics on the harmful consequences of integrated schools.

Such studies are invaluable. At times, they eventually win authority over to their view. More often they do not. In any case, they are likely to stimulate the whole Church to a more critical, balanced, nuanced attitude. They should not be resented or feared. They play a part in the growth in truth of the people of God.

The above examples illustrate rather what a specialist of the loyal opposition can do. But the ordinary layman also wields power. For instance, without generalizing he can report facts. Without commentary, he can tell his pastor how individual Negroes have reacted to their reception, or rather, non-reception, in the parish. He can tell his old professor how meaningless his philosophy course now seems to this alumnus. Especially in the day of the thoughtful, articulate layman, such testimony has been having great influence on specialists. The

345

growing number of theologians and philosophers who oppose the official position on birth control is due less to speculative objections than to the simple testimony of men and women to the harm wrought in their married life by the practice of rhythm or complete continence. The present revision of religious education in the Catholic schools was inspired in part by the comments of discontented students. The students were right in their criticisms, and their children will profit from the obedient opposition their parents once gave to authority.

Down the nineteen centuries of its history, the Church has been a wonderful thing. It has been built of nothing but living stones—the people of God, both superiors and subjects. History shows their life to have been tumultuous, confused, sinful and generally fallible. History also shows it to have been a life of faith in Christ, docile to the Spirit, always moving forward to grow in the truth and charity of God. The forward movement has grown naturally and fruitfully out of the interaction of position and opposition. Let those take heart whom responsibility compels on a given question to stand obedient, but in the opposition. They are serving the Church. They are the Church.

## CHAPTER 12

### RESPONSIBLE DISOBEDIENCE IN THE CHURCH

One does not have to look far for a possible paradigm of the responsible disobedience that we have been discussing. The public expression of opposition within the Church to the encyclical *Humanae Vitae* was as short-lived as it was violent. Aside from a salvo here and there, it has died away. The opposition to the encyclical has not. Instead of being preached, it is being quietly practiced by millions of Catholics. They do not form an opposition that disagrees, but obeys. They form an opposition that disobeys and claims to do so responsibly. What merits has their claim?

Opposition to the encyclical began as soon as it was published. On July 30, 1968, the day after the Vatican made the text public, Norris Clarke, speaking in a symposium at Fordham University, could already assure representatives of the press, television and radio that the large number of theologians

346

# John Giles Milhaven

openly disagreeing with the encyclical made it a unique, historic moment for the Church. Despite pleas and remonstrances of the Holy Father and other authorities of the Church, public opposition continued during the rest of 1968.

The encyclical incurred criticism on various counts, but the central thrust of the opposition was a simple, practical one: Catholics were justified in disobeying the encyclical and in practicing contraception. This is undoubtedly why the opponents of the encyclical have become silent in 1969. Their chief point was practical, they made it vocally to their own satisfaction, and those convinced of it are now putting it into practice. As a subject for debate, opposition to the encyclical is a dead issue.

But in passing from theory to practice, the opposition became a current part of life in the Catholic Church and is having widening and deepening repercussions in Catholic faith and life. It scandalizes Catholics who see obedience as the only possible response to the encyclical. They ask how one can be a Catholic and disobey the highest authority. They wonder what the Catholic Church really is, when open disobedience is tolerated. Catholics living in contradiction to the encyclical ask themselves similar questions. They wonder whether they are, in effect, still Catholics. And what should the Catholic Church mean for them if they are free to ignore its teaching?

The reactions reveal a need to clarify the grounds of the disobedience, or, if one prefers, its conditions of responsibility. This is the purpose of the present chapter. It is not an attempt to prove that the disobedience is in fact justified, nor to present completely any proof that has been offered. It is an attempt to outline the rationale of the disobedience and to show how it is, in principle, consonant with what the Church is and with what it means to be a Catholic, and how it therefore illustrates the true relationship of the individual Catholic to the whole Church. One could therefore agree with the chapter that all this is true *in principle* of the disobedience to the encyclical, and still doubt or deny that it is so *in fact*.

No one contests, of course, that every Catholic ultimately has to follow his own conscience. The bishops of the United States affirmed:

> Responsible parenthood, as the Church understands it, places on the properly formed conscience of spouses *all* the judgments, options and choices which add up to the awesome decision to give, postpone or decline life.

The bishops of England and Wales insist: "Neither this encyclical nor any other document takes away from us our right and duty to follow our conscience." The reason is a simple, traditional one. Conscience, as the American bishops point out by invoking Thomas Aquinas, is "the practical judgment or dictate of reason by which we judge what here and now is to be done as being good, or to be avoided as evil." Only the individual can make the judgment. Even God cannot do it for him. Consequently, whether his judgment be true or false, he has nothing else to follow. Traditional moral theology recognizes that when a man comes in good faith to have an erroneous conscience, he incurs no subjective guilt in following it, indeed would be subjectively at fault not to do so. This is why the American bishops underline that *"Humanae Vitae* does not discuss the question of the good faith of those who make practical decisions against what the Church considers a divine law and the will of God. The encyclical does not undertake to judge the consciences of individuals . . ."

Thus the possibility of a *subjectively* good conscience is not disputed. But many in the Church, including a good number in authority, maintain that it is the most one can say for disobedience to the encyclical, just as one could say it for the misguided assassination of a great, national leader, or for other objectively immoral behavior. Those disobeying naturally deny this and claim valid, *objective* grounds for their action. This is the issue in general.

One unusual element of the present situation is that not only do a large number of competent theologians agree with the claim of the opposition, but certain national hierarchies have given it encouragement. The French and Dutch hierarchies go the furthest; their statements clearly recognize that disobedience to the encyclical can, in fact, be objectively justified. In the early, provisional statement of the Dutch bishops, the authority of the encyclical is seen as only one ". . . many factors that determine the individual conscience in regard to the conjugal act . . . for example, mutual love, relations in the family and social circumstances." Implied is that the other factors can objectively outweigh the authority. The same implication is in the motion submitted by the nine Dutch bishops to the national Pastoral Council, cited below.

Although the reasoning offered by the French bishops is, in my experience, not typical of the opposition to the encyclical, they conclude to an unequivocal justification of disobedience. They concede: "Contraception can never be a good. It is always a disorder, but this disorder is not always guilty. It occurs in fact that spouses consider themselves to be confronted by a true conflict of duty." Because they "believe themselves in conscience bound to avoid a new birth or postpone it to a little later, and are deprived of resorting to biological rhythm," the couples have to choose between two evils, to practice contraception or "to renounce for the present a physical expression of their love" and thus see "the stability of their home being threatened." The bishops "simply recall the constant teaching of morality: When one faces a choice of duties, where one cannot avoid an evil whatever be the decision taken, traditional wisdom requires that one seek before God to find which is the greater duty. The spouses will decide after a joint reflection, with all the care that it calls for by the grandeur of their conjugal vocation."

Although only the Dutch and French hierarchies clearly recognize objective justification for opposition, a good number of other hierarchies have notably refrained from adopting the contrary position, that disobedience *cannot* be objectively justified. Four have gone so far as to state that loyal, well-informed, thoughtful Catholics could find reasons to dissent and disobey. This would imply that here is not merely the usual possibility of an erroneous, but subjectively good conscience, but that in the objective order there are grounds for opposition that, whether or not they are truly adequate, at least are serious enough to compel the minds of sincere and competent Catholics.

Most explicit are the Canadian bishops:

It is a fact that a certain number of Catholics, although admittedly subject to the teaching of the encyclical, find it either extremely difficult or even impossible to make their own all elements of this doctrine. . . .

\* \* \*

Since they are not denying any point of divine and Catholic faith nor rejecting the teaching authority of the Church, these Catholics should not be considered, or consider themselves, shut off from the body of the faithful. But they should remember that their good faith will be dependent on a sincere self-examination to determine the true motives and grounds for such suspension of assent and on continued effort to understand and deepen their knowledge of the teaching of the Church.

\* \* \*

In the situation we described earlier in this statement [the one just cited in this excerpt] the confessor or counsellor must show sympathetic understanding and reverence for the sincere good faith of those who fail in their effort to accept some point of the encyclical.

Counsellors may meet others who, accepting the teaching of the Holy Father, find that because of particular circumstances they are involved in what seems to them a clear conflict of duties, e.g., the reconciling of conjugal love and responsible parenthood with the education of children already born or with the health of the mother. In accord with the accepted principles of moral theology, if these persons have tried sincerely but without success to pursue a line of conduct in keeping with the given directives, they may be safely assured that whoever honestly chooses that course which seems right to him does so in good conscience.

The Scandinavian bishops imply the same possibility of honest, thoughtful, informed Catholics coming to disobey the encyclical:

> . . . it is self-evident that no one should doubt the content of the encyclical without entering into its way of thinking and intention thoroughly, honestly and with consciousness of his responsibility before God.
>
> However, if someone, from weighty and well-considered reason, cannot become convinced by the argumentation of the encyclical, it has always been conceded that he is allowed to have a different view from that presented in a non-infallible statement of the Church. No one should be considered a bad Catholic because he is of such a dissenting opinion.
>
> Everyone who, after conscientious consideration, believes himself entitled not to accept this teaching and considers himself not bound to obey it in practice, must be responsible before God for his attitude and way of acting.

The Austrian and Belgian bishops express a similar view, although they seem to be speaking of dissidents whose knowledgeability in the matter is more than the average Catholic possesses.

> Since the encyclical does not contain an infallible dogma, it is conceivable that someone feels unable to accept the judgment of the teaching authority of the Church. The answer to this is: if someone has experience in the field and has reached a divergent conviction after serious conviction, free of emotional haste, he may for the time being follow it. He does not err, if he is willing to continue his examination and otherwise affords respect and fidelity to the Church.
>
> Someone, however, who is competent in the matter under consideration and capable of forming

a personal and well-founded opinion—which necessarily presupposes a sufficient amount of knowledge—may, after a serious examination before God, come to other conclusions on certain points. In such a case he has the right to follow his convictions provided that he remains sincerely disposed to continue his enquiry.

Highly unusual is the explicit acknowledgment by the four hierarchies of the possibility of sincere and well-informed dissent and disobedience to the teaching of the encyclical, as well as their abstention from criticizing the dissent and disobedience on objective grounds. Equally significant is the positive encouragement: a dissident "may be safely assured that whoever honestly chooses the course which seems right to him does so in good conscience," "may for the time being follow his divergent conviction," "has the right to follow his convictions," should not "be considered a bad Catholic," but himself "must be responsible before God for his attitude and way of acting."

The bishops evidently feel that at least a good enough case can be made for disobedience to convince a fair number of sincere, well-informed, mature Catholics. It would follow that the grounds for disobedience are not purely subjective, but have a certain objective weight, whether or not they are fully adequate. This conclusion, which the rest of the present essay would explicate, may seem curious. What sense is it to speak of grounds for disobedience that are "objective," though they may not be "fully adequate." If one were trying to decide whether or not personally to disobey the encyclical, it would make little sense. But it makes excellent sense if one is trying to understand how the disobedience, in principle, fits in with being a Catholic, a loyal member of the Church. It is not only the Holy Father who speaks fallibly; so, too, do those who disagree with him. To recognize their stance as authentically ecclesial one does not have to hold that they are right. It is enough to see that the grounds they adduce are objectively serious in the context of the Church.

The point at issue is not whether the encyclical contains authoritative teaching of the Pope in his office as supreme teacher of the Church. Isolated voices have denied him the authority to speak on matters of natural morality, and, therefore, on contraception. But, on the whole, the liberal positions, whether of national hierarchies or of theologians, take into account the authority of the encyclical. There are good theological reasons for this. But it might suffice to note that no one has challenged the right of the Pope to speak out on nuclear warfare, peace, racism, starvation, etc.

Correspondingly, the point at issue is not whether the individual Catholic owes respect to the authority possessed by the encyclical. As the Dutch bishops expressed it, "A Catholic owes respect to the authority and the word of the Pope. The individual conscience cannot ignore such an authoritative declaration as this encyclical." The Scandinavian bishops, who, like the Dutch, offered one of the more liberal statements, recalled approvingly the teaching of the Second Vatican Council that

> religious submission of will and mind must be shown
> in a special way to the authentic teaching authority
> of the Roman Pontiff even when he is not speaking
> *ex cathedra* (as the supreme teacher in an infallible
> manner).

The point at issue, therefore, can be narrowed down. Is the respect due the authority of the encyclical such that a properly informed, objectively true conscience has no choice but to obey? Many in the Church, including Pope Paul VI, maintain the affirmative.

> In the encyclical the Holy Father has given us the
> principles according to which Catholics are to form
> their consciences in this matter. The obligation of a
> Catholic to accept the teaching of the Church on any
> grave moral problem can never justifiably be regarded
> as an offense against the freedom of his conscience.
> Rather, the free acceptance of that particular obliga-
> tion is implicit in the free decision, already made and
> still continuing, to accept the claim of the Catholic
> Church to speak with the authority of Christ.

Those who maintain the negative, namely, that Catholics can respect the authority of the encyclical and still find objective grounds justifying their disobedience, premise, first of all, that the encyclical is not proposed as an infallible declaration of doctrine. No one contests the premise. As Msgr. Fernando Lambruschini observed when he presented that text at a Vatican press conference,

> Attentive reading of the encyclical *Humanae Vitae* does not suggest the theological note of infallibility; this is also shown by a simple comparison with the "Profession of Faith" proclaimed on June 30, during the solemn rite in St. Peter's Square.

He does not hesitate to affirm simply, "It is not infallible . . ."

To say the encyclical is not infallible is to admit the possibility of its being in error. It is logical, therefore, as well as traditional, that a Catholic can legitimately come to disagree with such teaching. Of an authoritative, but not infallible declaration of the Supreme Pontiff,

> . . . one need not say: the Holy Spirit will never permit that this decree be published with erroneous content. . . . The presumption that it contains no error stands as long as the presumption is not brought down by a weighty reason to the contrary. Its authority demands a religious assent to the truth of its contents. The assent is, therefore, interpretatively conditioned, i.e., given with the tacit condition: "unless grave suspicion arise that the presumption is not verified."

Not all those who insist on unconditional obedience to the encyclical have taken into consideration this traditional right of dissent from authoritative teaching. But no one of theological competence nor any national hierarchy has denied it. The conservative statement of the American hierarchy provides a clear vindication of it:

> There exists in the Church a lawful freedom of inquiry and of thought, and also general norms of licit dissent. This is particularly true in the area of legitimate theological speculation and research. When

conclusions reached by such professional theological work prompt a scholar to dissent from noninfallible received teaching, the norms of licit dissent come into play.

One sentence of the American bishops could well constitute the major premise of the reasoning of the present chapter:

> The expression of theological dissent from the magisterium is in order only if the reasons are serious and well-founded, if the manner of the dissent does not question or impugn the teaching authority of the Church and is such as not to give scandal.

The rest of this chapter can be seen as an attempt to establish the minor premise of the syllogism: the expression of theological dissent from *Humanae Vitae* dissent not theoretical, but justifying contrary practice fulfills the conditions laid down by the American hierarchy.

As the first of their "serious and well-founded reasons," the dissenters submit that the argumentation offered in the encyclical is not convincing. It is easy to pinpoint the argumentation which the opposition finds unconvincing since the encyclical repeatedly grounds the prohibition of contraception on one basic premise. Only in number seventeen of the encyclical does Pope Paul adduce other arguments against contraception. "Upright men can even better convince themselves of the solid grounds on which the teaching of the Church in this field is based, if they care to reflect upon the consequences of methods of artificial birth control." But the first two consequences are not developed (in the English translation, less than 150 words for the two together), nor are they presented as decisively proving the immorality of all contraception. The third and final consequence is developed a bit (about 230 words), but appears to presuppose and merely confirm the one basic premise that runs through the encyclical:

> And such limits cannot be determined otherwise than by the respect owed to the integrity of the human organism and its functions, according to the principles recalled above and according to the correct under-

standing of the principle of totality illustrated by our predecessor Pius XII.

It is rather this integrity of organism and functions that constitutes the one basic premise of the argumentation of *Humanae Vitae*:

> God has wisely disposed natural laws and rhythms of fertility that, of themselves, cause a separation in the succession of birth. None the less, the Church, calling men back to the observance of the norms of the natural law, as interpreted by her constant doctrine, teaches that each and every marriage act must remain open to the transmission of life.
>
> That teaching, often set forth by the magisterium, is founded upon the inseparable connection, willed by God and unable to be broken by man on his own initiative, between the two significations of the conjugal act: the unitive meaning and the procreative meaning.

* * *

> Hence one who reflects well must also recognize that an act of mutual love that prejudices the openness to transmission of life that God the Creator, according to particular laws inserted therein, is in contradiction with the design constitutive of marriage, and with the will of the author of life. To use this divine gift, destroying, even if only paritally, its meaning and its purpose, is to contradict the nature both of man and of woman and of their most intimate relationship, and therefore it is to contradict also the plan of God and His will.

This argumentation, the fulcrum of the reasoning of the encyclical, is the chief target of the opposition, e.g., in the motion submitted by the nine bishops of the Netherlands and overwhelmingly adopted by the representative assembly of the Dutch Church:

356

The plenary assembly considers the absolute rejection by the encyclical *Humanae Vitae* of the artificial means of birth control not convincing, on the basis of the argumentation given. The well-considered personal decision of conscience of married people should be respected.

The operative principle of the encyclical, therefore, is that natural reason can see in the very nature of marriage and the conjugal act that God has willed that the act always be left open to the transmission of life. What the opposition finds unconvincing lies behind the word "always." The teaching of the Church is based on, and the Holy Father is appealing to, evidence not derived from revelation, but found in the "natural law," accessible, therefore, to natural human understanding. Such evidence is said to show what is *always* God's intention, i.e., for every single conjugal act regardless of consequences for the particular spouses and children and regardless of the general procreative tenor that their acts as a whole may have.

To justify conjugal acts made intentionally infertile one cannot invoke as valid reasons the lesser evil, or the fact that such acts would constitute a whole, together with the fertile acts already performed or to follow later, and hence would share in one and the same moral goodness.

God's intention, found in nature, makes every single act of contraception "intrinsically disordered and hence unworthy of the human person." Those who share the contemporary understanding of man's responsibility before God cannot see how it is evident to human reason that such a divine intention governs every single act. They experience the opposite of what Pope Paul believed, "that men of our day are particularly capable of seizing the deeply reasonable and human character of this fundamental principle." It is noteworthy that the encyclical makes no attempt to present this evidence that the divine intention bears on every single conjugal act without exception.

Obviously, the mere fact that one does not find convincing the argumentation of an encyclical does not justify disobedience or even disagreement. The authority of Church teaching is independent of its effectiveness in persuading or convincing by the reasons it gives. One of the purposes of the magisterium is to bring members of the Church to accept truths that for one reason or another they cannot come to by themselves, even after listening respectfully to the teaching. An example could be the authoritative teaching of the immorality of racial segregation. Consequently, to outweigh the authority of *Humanae Vitae,* powerful, positive reasons must be found showing it to be in error.

The positive reasons offered to this effect vary, but have, I believe, a common drift. Married people have indeed the responsibility, given them by God, of transmitting life. But it is their married life as a whole, and not necessarily each single conjugal act, that need meet the responsibility. Moreover, the responsibility of transmitting life must be coordinated with other responsibilities, such as those of rearing children or of their own mutual love and assistance. In regard to the procreative responsibility, the moral question is: have they over the years been generous in bringing life into the world? That every conjugal act be left open to procreation not only does not follow from this responsibility; it often runs counter to other responsibilities of the couple, such as bringing their children up well. In an ethics of responsibility, contraception can be of obligation for a married couple.

Convincing as the argument may be, an individual Catholic would be presumptuous to pit his own reasoning alone against the supreme teaching authority of the Church. But the exceptional character of the present situation is seen in the large number of Catholics, living actively their faith, educated in Catholic matters, and having competence in the matter in question, who have followed similar reasoning to similar firm conclusions concerning the legitimacy of contraception: theologians, philosophers, doctors, demographers, historians, sociologists, priests in pastoral ministry, and, last but not least, married couples. Typical were the 172 American theologians who by August 1, 1968 had signed a statement criticizing the encyclical and concluding "that spouses may responsibly decide according to their conscience that artificial contraception in some circumstances is permissible and indeed necessary to

preserve and foster the values and sacredness of marriage."
Typical, too, were the six American lay members of the Papal
Commission; within a week of the publication of the encyclical, all six were quoted in the press criticizing it. Names like
Donald Campion, editor of *America*, Bernard Häring, Karl
Rahner, Richard McCormick, Avery Dulles and Walter Burghardt
made it clear that the opposition was not simply a reaction of
the far out left. So, too, did the encouragement, mentioned
above, given by certain national hierarchies to conscientious
dissent and disobedience. Essential to the grounds of disobedience are these numerous respected voices, indicating in one way
or another that the other grounds have objective weight.

The wide extent of open dissent has further force because
it arises organically from the nature of the Church. Contrary
to the use of the word "Church" in the encyclical, the Church
is not to be identified simply with its teaching authority, but
includes the whole people of God in their various roles. The
witness of theologians, pastors and laymen, therefore, constitutes ecclesial evidence for truths about Christian faith and life.
Karl Rahner has expressed well what is new in the present
development in the Church and what is perfectly traditional,
revealing the true nature of the Church.

What a Catholic and a theologian experience
today in our question is really nothing absolutely
new, for in the course of the history of the Church,
there obviously have always arisen developments of
doctrine as well as situations in which such a development was still open and one could not clearly predict its future history. The only thing new is that
such developments of doctrine and such situations
proceed or change more rapidly and thus force themselves more sharply on the individual, short-lived
human being. New, too, is that this question affects
more immediately the concrete life of countless men
than other dogmatic questions. Whatever it may have
been psychologically with the consciousness of the
average Catholic in his relation to the Church, above
all, in the last hundred years, it is not true that the
Catholic Church has understood, or understands,

itself as a Church in which everything important is always clear in advance and is held with absolute certainty, and in which every discovery of truth takes place uniquely and alone through the utterance of its supreme teaching office. The teaching authority in the Catholic Chruch—and especially when it gives no definitive declaration (and in many cases it is not even capable of doing it)—is an important, indispensable factor for the discovery of truth or the development of doctrine in the Church. But it is not a factor that alone, independently in every respect of other realities in the Church, determines totally this discovery of truth or development of doctrine. Even *ex cathedra* decisions of the Pope or the Councils were really always something like an underlining of a development that had been borne along by factors quite distinct from the teaching office and its formal authority. The authority of the teaching office in the Church and the respect due to it do not, therefore, demand that one so act in the Church as if all theological views in the Church were only the obedient repetition of a declaration of the teaching office. Properly understood, there is also in the Catholic Church an open "system," in which most diverse factors (the "sense" of the faithful, new acquisitions of knowledge by individual Christians and theologians, new situations of the time with new posing of questions, and many other things) work together to clarify the Church's consciousness of its faith and toward a development of doctrine. Nor would this total, open "system," in which the teaching office has its own proper and necessary place, be comprehensively and totally taken over and manipulated by this teaching office itself.

Further ground for the opposition, according to some, would be signs that, in historical fact, the Church is nearing the end of a development of doctrine such as Rahner describes, and that therefore ecclesiastical authority will soon abandon the older position. Most of the theologians defending the encyc-

lical, it is claimed, are about sixty years of age or older. Few of
the younger theologians defend it. Moreover, many of those
demanding absolute obedience to the encyclical do so exclusively because of its authoritative force; some of them admit
privately that the natural law reasoning on which the encyclical
is based would not convince them by itself. If this be true, it
would seem likely that in a few years the vast majority of
theological advisors to the Pope and the bishops will be critical
of the present official position.

A sign pointing, by way of analogy, to this likelihood of
change of the official position is the development that took
place within the Papal Birth Control Commission after it was
enlarged in June, 1964.

> The papal commission now stood at about
> sixty-five members; all the human probabilities, as
> far as the composition of the group permitted, were
> that the result of discussions would be a basic con-
> firmation of *Casti Connubii*—possibly with significant
> changes in the pastoral approach. At the start, only
> about three or four of the theologians were in favor
> of a new theological approach; the rest were known
> for their faithfulness to *Casti Connubii*. . . .

* * *

> However, developments in the Council, the absolute
> honesty of thought in the commission, and especially
> the presence of lay people, who were now assured
> that they could think and speak frankly, changed
> the situation, especially toward the end of the Coun-
> cil and right after it was over.

Is it not likely that the similar honesty of thought and frank
speaking and thinking now present in the Church will lead to
an outcome similar to that of the commission?

> The overwhelming majority of the commission of
> theologians and lay people and a sufficient majority
> of the bishops commission approved the majority
> report, which argued that the choice of methods of

birth regulation be left to the discretion of the married couple, within the guidelines given in the *Constitution on the Church in the Modern World.*

The convergence of all the above grounds for opposition suffices, in the eyes of some, to justify not only disagreement, but also disobedience. If the teaching is shown to be erroneous, what obligation remains for carrying it into practice? Others feel, however, that the encyclical does not merely teach, but also commands. Consequently, though evidently in error, it still possesses an authority analogous to that of positive ecclesiastical law. To justify disobedience, therefore, the individual married couple must be able to go a step further and find evidence (analogous to the "causes" that "excuse" from positive law) that obedience in their case would work proportionately grave harm to themselves and their family.

The disagreement on the necessity of establishing this further ground for opposition may be academic rather than important practically. Those who insist on the necessity admit that in the light of the other grounds for opposition the "proportionately grave harm" need not be very grave. And all those who oppose the encyclical recognize that the harm obedience could bring about for married couples is a principal motive for their opposition, regardless of the way in which they integrate it into rational argumentation.

The grounds of disobedience are various: against the authority of *Humanae Vitae* it is held that the encyclical is not infallible; that its argumentation is unconvincing; that an ethics of responsibility leads to a contrary conclusion; that many in the Church, having varied competence and experience, support contrary action; that in their support they are exercising their roles in the Church; that from an historical point of view there is evidence pointing to an imminent change in the official teaching and that obedience to the encyclical can concretely work grave harm to individual families. The case rests. Since the disobedience is well known, the individual Catholic has to give his verdict. Do the grounds of the disobedience fit in, in principle, with the reality of the Catholic Church in which he believes? Whatever his answer may be, he will be judging not only disobedience to the encyclical, but the Church and himself.

## CHAPTER 13

### THE IMPORTANCE OF BEING ROMAN CATHOLIC

American Catholics in the 1970s are experiencing thickening anxiety and discouragement, even despair. The mood is produced by the changes going on in the Church but, ironically enough, in two opposing ways. For some Catholics, the changes are going too far and too fast and look like they will go farther and faster. For other Catholics, the changes are too little and too late and there is no hope of stepping up the tempo.

The anxiety and despair engendered by either point of view can lead a Catholic to think of leaving the Church. He may think of it consciously and envision a departure that would have a certain punctuation and flourish. Or, on a practical, half-aware level, he may just gradually stop bothering about what has hitherto made up his Catholic practice. More commonly, the anxiety and despair induced by the changes tempt a Catholic, not to leave the Church or to give up his practice, but to mutter an embittered or confused "What's the use?" and to stop putting himself on the line and giving himself wholeheartedly to the life of the Church.

The question comes up painfully, "What is the importance of being Roman Catholic? What is its necessity, its value?" The question is all the more painful because the answer no longer comes easily. If a genuine theological question arises out of the lived experience of the Catholic people so, too must the answer. The answer comes in understanding the experienced life of the faith of the people. The trouble is that in regard to the importance of being Roman Catholic (as in regard to many other things), the lived experience of the American Roman Catholic is in the process of hurtling transformation. The old theological answers are no longer pertinent. The new experience demands new theological understanding, new answers.

I would like to try to identify certain aspects of the new experience before offering a theological understanding of it.

It already seems to have been in some dim, distant past that evermounting statistics of conversions and headlines about Clare Booth Luce and Thomas Merton and other famous converts symbolized wonderfully for us the value of Catholicism. What has happened since then is not so much that we have become less successful in converting (though that seems to be true, too), but that we are getting less and less interested in it. The entry of Tennessee Williams into the Church causes hardly a ripple and seems somehow anachronistic.

Even missionaries are caught up in the trend. At their gatherings, when they return temporarily to the States, they talk more and more of giving witness to Christ's love and improving the human condition of the people, and less and less of the number of conversions. A Fordham theology professor remarked prophetically a few years ago: "Francis Xavier no longer serves us as a symbol." That is obviously true today: as our Catholic experience has changed, it needs a symbol other than that of a man hastening about the world to save souls from hellfire.

For some centuries now, educated Catholics could explain why it was necessary to belong to the Church and still possible to be saved without being a member. But regardless of explanations, the day a Catholic stops being interested in conversions, something has happened. Something has gone from his concrete, lived understanding of his Church. This is why he is no longer satisfied with his old answer to the question, "Why is it important for me to be a Catholic?" The teaching authority of the Church has sensed the need to elaborate new answers.

> A more recent example [of the Church reversing its teaching] would be Vatican II. In all honesty it is not possible to say that Vatican II speaks about the other Churches, the other religions, or religious liberty in the same way as earlier popes and councils had spoken. The ancient doctrine, "Outside the Church no salvation," has been so drastically reinterpreted by Vatican II that the meaning is almost the opposite of what the words seem to say. Modern Catholics take a very different view of this matter than their ancestors in the middle ages.

# John Giles Milhaven

In a document released by the Vatican Secretariat for Promoting Christian Unity, one reads:

> Relations between Christians and Jews have for the most part been no more than a monologue. A true dialogue must now be established. The condition of dialogue is respect for the other as he is, for his faith and religious convictions. All intent of proselytizing and conversion is excluded.

The growing loss of interest in converting is one aspect of the change we are noting in American Catholic experience. Another aspect is seen in a new phase of ecumenical dialogue. Several times in recent months, I have heard ecumenical groups ask, "Why is the excitement going out of ecumenism?" I think the reason is simple. Catholics, Protestants and Jews are getting to know each other. That's why. They are no longer acquaintances courteously respectful of each other; they are friends. When you get to know a man and his faith, not as it is outlined in propositions, even by himself, but as it is part of the man you have come to like and admire, then the differences between his faith and yours seem not less, but less important. The drama of men of different faiths getting together fades. Instead one realizes more keenly the sobering common task of religious men today.

I disagree, for example, with theses of Martin Luther concerning divine grace and fallen human nature. But when I lunch with my Lutheran colleague on the faculty and discuss, as I have many times in the past, religious matters of common interest, his Christian life and mine, it is simply impossible for me to say to myself interiorly, "Well, he's obviously sincere and invincibly ignorant, and God does not hold it against him, but of course, I, being Roman Catholic, have a better understanding of God and Christ and man than he does." If nothing else, my sense of humor prevents me from thinking this way. It might be that all the theses I hold are true, and that some of his are false, but now that I know the man, I cannot say that, objectively speaking, Christ is less understood and appreciated and lived by him than by me. The evidence arising out of our friendship is clearly the contrary.

One might object that the point is not to compare individuals, but Churches. But Vatican II has reminded us that the Church is nothing but the people of God, the living individuals who make it up. If coming to know certain Lutherans, I begin to suspect that all the individual Lutherans living in the United States understand and appreciate and love and live Christ more or less as well as all the individual Roman Catholics, I face anew the old question, "What is the importance of being Roman Catholic?" And I have to look for a new answer.

I believe that those of us who have come to know the personal faith of Jewish believers experience the same thing. That this rabbi is in error concerning Jesus Christ, and I am right— yes, I can hold that. But that he understands what God is basically doing with men less profoundly and perceptively than I do—this I could hold only until I got to know Rabbi X.

A third aspect of the change in Catholic experience that I am talking about could be identified by the now familiar label, "the anonymous Christian." The theology of the anonymous Christian is not new. It was worked out during the Second World War by thinkers as diverse as Karl Rahner, Jean Mouroux and Jacques Maritain. But only recently has the anonymous Christian become part of general Catholic experience, our imagination and feeling and apperceptive background. The incredible communication media have helped to bring about our increasing awareness of the rest of mankind on this dwindling earth, and therefore a keener sense of ourselves, the professed Christians, as a minority group. Then, too, we have come to know of men like U Thant and Albert Camus. We have left the ghetto and come to work side by side with agnostics, searching for truth with them, laboring with them for racial justice or peace or food for the starving. We have worked with them in Appalachia or some inner city or campaign headquarters or Peace Corps or theology department. And there is something in the air of our times—I do not know what it is—that makes it a little absurd for us to imagine that Christ is present in our minority group in a fuller, realer way than in the vast millions that press around us or in these men with whom we have shared ideals and labored to realize them.

Rather we cannot help seeing Christ working in all men so that all that is true (was it Saint Ambrose who first said it?) is said by the Holy Spirit, so that Christ (as Saint Justin insisted) is the light that enlightens *every* man that comes into the world, and that He is the light in which all human light is. The theological analyses of Rahner and Maritain and Schillebeeckx help us to understand how it is possible for these men to believe in Christ, to be enlightened by him, to be energized by him, and yet not know it. But the new vision contained in Catholic experience does not appear to depend on subtle theories. In fact, as far as theories go, the popularity of the synthesis of Teilhard may well be due to his expressing the new experience more faithfully than the neo-Scholastic analyses of Maritain and Rahner do.

In any case, our religious imagination now has Christ working in full redemptive efficacy in all men of good will. We are starting to talk of the Roman Catholic Church as the extraordinary means of salvation. As a vision of the world, it offers no practical problems to see Christ implicitly recognized and at work everywhere where men become more human, more loving. But it does pose in a new way the problem of the Church. What then is the Church doing? What is the value of being Roman Catholic? The old solutions no longer fit our experience.

And so, if my description is accurate, there is today in the onrushing transformation of American Catholic experience one current that can be discerned among the many. It shows itself in progressive disinterest in conversion, in high regard for the faith and wisdom of our Protestant and Jewish brothers, in a deepening sense of Christ's anonymously enlightening all men and fructifying all human endeavor, in a growing suspicion that those who have left the Church to marry a wife had honorable and good reasons for doing so. The core of the new experience is a dawning realization that Christ can be present as fully outside the institution of the Roman Catholic Church as within. The American Catholic has always realized that Christ can and presumably does save good people outside the visible structure of the Church. What he is now coming to realize is that Christ, His saving presence and gracious love, can be and presumably is *as fully* at work outside the visible Church as within. Consequently, he needs a new answer to the question of the importance of being Roman Catholic.

There are, I believe, at least two answers one might give. The first would be to explore what the Second Vatican Council proposed as the role of the Church in the world. The Church, as sacrament for all men, can be understood to communicate sacramentally God's saving grace even to non-believers. Although I may hold that Christ is as fully and effectively present outside the Church as within, I can still rejoice in belonging to this visible community which is the efficacious sign of all his presence, i.e., which, by signifying union with Him, effects it in all men of good will. The answer is probably a good one and reputable theologians today endorse it. But it has difficulties. How can the Church be a sacrament for those who do not see it as a sign of anything real? And does not the concept of an inexperienced instrumental efficacy follow only from scholastic metaphysics?

Without rejecting the above answer, I would like to suggest another reason that makes it important to be Roman Catholic, even in the problematic we have been discussing. It may be that other men have found their way to Christ as well or better than I, and their way was separated from Rome or was only implicitly Christian. It still remains true that *for me,* the way of finding Christ is in the Roman Catholic Church. It is *my* ordinary means of salvation.

I advance the thesis for human, pragmatic, empirical reasons, for I believe it is only in a human, pragmatic, empirical way that Christ comes to me and I go to Christ. This means that I meet Him in my personal human history and in my personal, human community. I also happen to believe it is the same visible community He founded 2000 years ago, but that is not key here. Christ undoubtedly speaks to the Lutheran in many concrete, human ways, and the Lutheran undoubtedly finds Him there, and in his reponse of faith and love, is enlightened and strengthened by His grace. But I have no reason to think it would be equally true for me, if I entered the Lutheran community. Christ speaks to me, not by mystical inspiration, not by injecting new ontological acts into my potencies, but through the events of my history and the contacts of my community. I cannot, like Descartes, reject my past and the human contacts I have had and have, and start all over again. Neither could Descartes, for that matter. You can't go home again, but you can't leave it either. H. Richard Neibuhr said that he was a Christian because he was fated to be one. The historical forces under which he had been placed had irrevocably made him that way. I would say the same of my Roman Catholicism, adding only that I see the "fating" as God's free choice to give me a Roman Catholic history and community instead of a Lutheran or Jewish or Buddhist one.

For example, I can, if so inclined, indulge in the contemporary fun-game of criticizing the nuns who taught me. The fact remains that their teaching is part of me (including, incidentally, many true and beautiful things about God and man) and will always be. Despite whatever flaws the teaching may have had, or whatever flaws my reception may have had, it remains within me in memory and imagination and habits of thought and feeling. It is one broadway where Christ speaks to me. Not mystically or ontologically. Not because of any authority of the nuns. But empirically, practically, Christ speaks to me through those human beings. Through them he gives me insights, feelings, impulses of action that mirror Him and His love. Much that He gives me through them is not what they intended to give. Often it is rather something that arises from my reaction to them, a reaction often negative. But part of my ongoing dialogue with Christ will always be in terms of my experience in grammar school under the Sisters.

That is only an example. One could speak of parental faith, liturgy, ways of private prayer, long conversations with friends, declarations of the hierarchy, apostolic enterprises, etc., etc. The point is that even if the hierarchy had made all the mistakes we subjects ascribe to them, even if the state of the liturgy were as regrettable as the worst critics claim, even if the visible Roman Catholic Church had all the defects of which its members have accused it—and the presuppositions cannot be true, since much of the criticism is mutually contradictory—it still would be true that Christ is speaking to me through this hierarchy, this liturgy, this Catholic Church.

He is speaking, as He has always done, through the human beings that make it up. Sometimes I find His Word in listening and receiving what they say and do. Sometimes I find it in reacting negatively and trying to change things. But this is where I find Him. And the fact that my Lutheran colleague finds Him as fully in his Lutheran faith, and my atheist friend finds Him implicitly in his lack of faith, is of little use to me. I do not doubt that men, like Charles Davis, were not only following their conscience in leaving the Church, but may well have found a more human life, greater maturity and therefore greater peace of soul, and therefore found Christ more fully on some implicit level. But I find it hard to believe that for men who have taken such a step, Christ remains, at least on the explicit, conscious level, as much the center and fullness of life as before. I say this partly because of my understanding of man as made up by *his* history and *his* community; there he finds himself and others and, consequently, Christ. But I say it also because of my acquaintance with individuals who have left the Catholic Church on the grounds that Christ was not lived there purely enough, not taken seriously enough. My experience is limited, and it is a hard thing to appraise. But I have the definite impression that the reality of Christ has subsequently paled and moved to the periphery of the lives of these individuals, for all their sincerity.

Most of us American Catholics do not face the dilemma of having to choose between active participation in the life of our Church and an adequately human life. A good number, however, as I mentioned in the beginning, are tempted presently to anxiety or discouragement. I would suggest that the reflections just offered on the importance of being Roman Catholic could counteract the temptation by revealing to us "the freedom of the Roman Catholic."

When Martin Luther vaunted "the freedom of the Christian man," he spoke of a freedom from anxiety and discouragement. When he looked at his persistent failings, anxiety and despair gripped him. But when he looked to Christ, he heard that God had chosen to love him, to accept him despite his weaknesses. And looking to Christ, he chose to believe His love for him, accept his acceptance, and thus he experienced the peace and joy that belongs to the Christian man. Since he had all that matters—God's love—he was at peace. And being at peace, with nothing to fear or worry about, he was free, too, to give to others, to love unreservedly. In fact, knowing now what Christ was for him, he spontaneously chose to be a Christ for others.

The freedom of the Christian man, described profoundly and eloquently by Luther, is also the freedom of the Roman Catholic of the last third of the twentieth century. It just takes a different concrete form. The anxiety and despair Luther and his contemporaries felt and from which Christ freed them arose from an oppressive experience of their humanness The humanness that oppressed them was their personal sinfulness, their personal failure to love. The anxiety and despair American Catholics feel in 1969 arise, too, from an oppressive experience of their humanness. The humanness that oppresses them is the humanness of the whole Church (not excluding themselves), seen in the confusion wrought by the ongoing changes. The anxiety and despair, of both conservatives and liberals, come from their impotence to control the changes and an inability to see where they are going. The confusion makes it impossible at the moment to see how the Church is, and is going to be, an effective community of God's love.

What Karl Rahner wrote recently of the evolution of theology concerning birth control applies to many another current evolution in Catholic theology and life and experience. It is by no means new in the history of the Church that there be such evolution. What is unprecedented is the rapidity of the change. One suspects that 1975 may belong to as different an historical era from 1965 as the mid-sixteenth century did from the mid-fifteenth. In any case, it is the rapidity of the changes that has multiplied the confusion for the Catholic in 1969 and leaves him with a persistent tightening of the stomach along with a feeling of helplessness. One can imagine that the bark of Peter has run into stormier weather than this; what unsettles is that stars, compass and landmarks have disappeared and the old ship is rushing headlong into darkness.

The American Catholic today must remind himself of the freedom of the Christian man that is his as a Roman Catholic in this time and place. The only thing that matters is that God loves me and I have that. I believe and accept God's love as it comes to me concretely, i.e., through my history and my community, above all, through my Church today, the given individuals that make up this people of God, parents, colleagues, friends, old teachers, writers, superiors, Terence, Archbishop of New York, Paul, Bishop of Rome and Pope of my Church, etc., etc. However God's light and love may come to others, it is through these individuals around me and our interacting life that it comes to me, despite their limitations, and despite my limitations. If I look to the limitations, I am drawn to anxiety and despair. If I look to Christ, loving me through the history and community that make me what I am, through my Roman Catholic Church, then I am at peace, and free from fear and discouragement, and free to labor in love with Him, to try to be a Christ for others in this Church.

Indeed, the fact that the humanness of the situation presses down on me and limits all my endeavors can intensify my freedom as a Catholic. Sartre meant something analogous: "We were never so free as under the Nazis." The limitations and frustrations imposed by the Occupation threw him back on what was the only thing that mattered, his inner freedom, his self-affirmation, the creative autonomy of his choice to be and do. Unlike Sartre, I believe myself not to be alone. The limitations and frustrations imposed by the situation in the Roman Catholic Church today, the night into which the bark of Peter is careening, throws me back on the only thing that matters, that through this human, sinful, confused Church God is loving me and I accept His love. Never have I been so free.

# Charles E. Curran
## 1934-

When New Perspectives in Moral Theology *appeared in 1974, it was immediately recognized as an important and valuable contribution to the contemporary literature on morality. As Father Charles E. Curran, the author, observes, the changes that had taken place in the Catholic Church during the 1960s were abrupt and caught most people unprepared. The resulting atmosphere was one of confusion and unsteadiness. Catholics were not used to open and public discussion on issues such as abortion, sterilization and divorce; nor were they at ease with the thought that there were no simple, clear-cut answers to these and similar issues. Given the rapidity with which problems and questions in moral theology were arising, theologians could not possibly come up with a finalized statement that could serve as a guideline in moral matters. Apparently for a long time to come theology will once again be in the state of tentative beginnings.*

*Curran's book is a clear and concise statement of the state of contemporary Catholic moral theology. As the title indicates, the purpose of the book is to give the perspectives existing today in moral theology. And that it does. Curran introduces the reader to the most recent thinking on themes such as the radical Catholic, the social mission of the Church, the legal and moral aspects of abortion, an evaluation of past teaching on steriliza-*

*tion, and Catholic theory and practice in the United States concerning divorce.*

*We have selected Curran's general survey on moral theology for the following reading. The author's purpose is to present today's Catholic moral theology as it exists in the context of a dialogue with various forms of Protestant ethics. Surprisingly there was no noticeable dialogue between Catholic and Protestant scholars before 1960. Yet by 1970 it was unimaginable that a serious scholar within either tradition would not be familiar with the thinking of the other tradition. Recognizing that this dialogue has had a tremendous impact on Catholics, Curran discusses three topics of significance, viz., natural law, authoritarianism, and theological presuppositions. Under each topic he shows where Catholic and Protestant scholars agree or disagree. One point that comes through quite clearly is that there is no such thing as the Catholic position on specific, complex moral questions.*

*Father Curran is a man highly sensitive to the tremendous gap between the actual state of Catholic moral theology and the understanding of the Catholic in the street. Much of this is due to the suddenness and radicalness of recent changes. Curran invites the Catholic community to put aside its fears of subjectivity, relativism and individualism, and to participate willingly and enthusiastically in the educational process that is essential if Catholic moral theology, in our time, is to be mature and relevant.*

# NEW PERSPECTIVES
# IN MORAL THEOLOGY

## CHAPTER 1

### CATHOLIC MORAL THEOLOGY TODAY

The changes that have transpired in the Roman Catholic Church and in Roman Catholic theology in the last decade are enormous. The purpose of this first chapter is to consider the present self-identity of Roman Catholic moral theology especially as it exists in the context of a dialogue with various forms of Protestant ethics. Dialogue with Protestant thought has played an important role in the development of Roman Catholic moral theology in our time, but it is far from the only factor in the developing self-identity of moral theology. Both Roman Catholic and Protestant ethics alike have been involved with an even wider dialogue—an interface with the rapidly changing moral questions of our day and with all forms of philosophical and humanist approaches to these questions. However, this chapter will concentrate on the identity and self-consciousness of Roman Catholic moral theology today as seen in terms of its dialogue with Protestant ethics.

The very existence of dialogue between Protestant and Catholic ethicians is comparatively recent. In 1963 Franz Böckle began a very perceptive series of lectures with the remark that encumenical discussion is strikingly faint and insignificant in the area of Christian ethics. In the United States one can witness the same growth in ecumenical discussions about Christian ethics. The very influential "Notes on Moral Theology," which have regularly appeared in *Theological Studies,* indicate little or no reference to Protestant ethics in the years before 1966. One moral survey appearing in 1965 did not contain any footnote references to Protestant literature. The history of the American Society of Christian Ethics illustrates the same fact, for it was only in 1965 that Roman Catholics began to participate actively in this society.

The rapid changes which have occurred within such a short time are astounding. In 1963 Böckle indicated some of the practical differences existing between Roman Catholic and Protestant life—Sunday obligation, days of fast and abstinence, contraception, divorce. These practical differences, so pronounced less than ten years ago, have now either been done away with or seriously questioned by Catholic scholars. The dialogue has reached such a level of exchange that no reputable scholar within either tradition can afford to be unaware of the literature and thinking existing in the other tradition.

In the light of these rapid changes of the past few years, what is the self-identity of Roman Catholic moral theology in terms of the dialogue with Protestant ethics? A recent book on the subject by Roger Mehl indicates both convergences and persistent divergences. I fundamentally agree with the insistence on the convergences arising from the common source (amounting to a return on the part of Catholic thought) of the Scriptures and also arising from the fact that both traditions are facing new and unprecedented changes in our social life. Mehl also notes persistent divergences in the following areas: nature and supernature—the anthropological problem; natural law and natural morality; the meaning of secularization; soul and body.

## General Comments

In general I deny both the extent and the intensity of the persistent divergences mentioned by Mehl. Three general considerations have apparently influenced the different conclusions reached on this point by Mehl and myself. Although *Catholic Ethics and Protestant Ethics* was published in French in 1970 and in English in 1971, the material was originally presented as the Warfield Lectures at Princeton Theological Seminary in 1968. Obviously there have been many developments since that time, which have indicated that the differences are somewhat disappearing. However, even in 1968 it seems that there were changes already occurring that are not that prominent in Mehl's consideration. Böckle in Germany and Gustafson in this country were well aware that there were developments then in Catholic ethics which were lessening the persistent differences with Protestant ethics.

Secondly, Mehl assumes that Catholic ethics is still a monolothic moral theology, which he frequently refers to as Thomistic ethics. This insistence fails to appreciate the incipient pluralism which was present in Catholic thinking even in 1968. Too often Mehl illustrates his points by quotations of older papal documents (e.g. Pius IX, Leo XIII) which most Catholics even in 1968 realized were somewhat dated.

Thirdly, I believe that the ecumenical dialogue between Protestant and Catholic ethicians has proceeded at a more rapid rate in this country than in Europe. One has to be careful of a hidden chauvinism in such a judgment, but the facts seem to bear out such a conclusion. Catholic and Protestant ethicians in this country have been meeting together more than in European countries. The literature of Catholic ethicians in this country shows a greater ongoing dialogue with Protestant thought.

Perhaps too the conditions for dialogue were more conducive in this country. In Europe the dialogue often exists on a very speculative level, and the Protestant partner in the dialogue frequently belongs to an Orthodox or Neo-Orthodox persuasion so that theological differences appear to stand out. In the United States there has been a greater working together on practical moral issues such as civil rights, peace, and also the dialogue has not been only with Neo-Orthodoxy. Thus the climate in the United States seems to have facilitated the possibility of a better dialogue and exchange between Protestants and Catholics. A recent article by the influential German Jesuit Joseph Fuchs, who teaches at the Gregorian University in Rome, lends some support to this view. In writing on the absoluteness of moral norms Fuchs very frequently refers to the American literature which indicates his appreciation of its significance.

This essay will consider the persistent divergences mentioned by Mehl and others as existing between Protestant and Catholic ethics. Obviously one cannot speak about Protestant ethics as a monolithic ethical system, since under the umbrella of Protestant ethical thought there are many different methodologies. In the course of the present discussion a somewhat similar pluralism should also become evident in contemporary Catholic moral theology. The questions generally raised in Protestant ethics about Roman Catholic theological ethics can readily be summarized under three headings—natural law, authoritarianism and theological presuppositions.

## Natural Law

The category of natural law will include the philosophical questions of methodology, the meaning of nature, the place of law in ethics and the role of norms or principles in the solution of practical questions. This consideration prescinds from the more theological questions connected with natural law such as the relationship of nature-grace, the role of sin, the connection between the order of creation and the order of redemption. These topics will be discussed under theological presuppositions.

In general the critiques against natural law presuppose a monolithic philosophical system based on a "non-temporal and imperceptible nature" and a "reason that is incorrectly postulated not to have a history." "Catholic moral theology seeks a foundation in an original and ontological given, which seems difficult to grasp. It is also led to call certain exigencies eternal, which in fact are relative and sociologically conditioned."

Catholic theology itself in the last decade has been involved in a serious critique and revision of the natural law theory as found in the manuals of moral theology and incorporated into the hierarchical magisterium's pronouncements, especially the papal encyclicals. In this ongoing discussion there are some who reject any change in the methodology or the practical conclusions of the manuals of moral theology. The vast majority of Catholic ethicians today refuse to accept the natural law approach of the manuals. Some have abandoned the concept of natural law altogether and adopted newer and different methodologies; while others, retaining the concept of natural law, have tried to show how the manuals departed from the true natural law approach of the past as seen now in a better appreciation of the exact position adopted by Aquinas and not the one espoused by later scholastics. The concept of natural law as a deductive methodology based on eternal and immutable essences and resulting in specific absolute norms is no longer acceptable to the majority of Catholic moral theologians writing today.

Charles E. Curran

J. M. Aubert stands out as an example of the approach which seeks a revision of the natural law more in accord with its understanding in Saint Thomas and not the conception developed by a later scholasticism. The major problem with the concept of natural law as found in the manuals of moral theology and in papal pronouncements stems from the failure to recognize and employ the Thomistic distinction between *lex naturalis* and *jus naturale*. *Lex naturalis* for Thomas is human reason seeking to regulate the total human reality (body and soul); whereas the *jus naturale* comprises the basic human tendencies and inclinations which need to be studied empirically and then regulated and directed by reason.

According to Aubert the textbooks reduced natural law just to the given aspects of *jus naturale* and thereby downplayed the creative and regulative role of reason as well as the function of empirical discovery. Modern natural law theoreticians have concentrated almost exclusively on the naturalist and the *a priori* aspects of human existence; whereas Thomas stressed the rational aspect and an open and changing understanding of the basic human tendencies and inclinations. Aubert thus shows that Thomas did not advocate the physicalism which has characterized so much of Catholic moral theology until the present time. Scholastic thinking after Thomas considered nature in a universal and closed way; whereas for Thomas man as a spiritual being cannot be understood as a simple nature closed and formed once for all, since a spiritual being transcends his given order and is challenged to grow and develop. Personally I believe Aubert is somewhat one-sided, for he fails to appreciate that Thomas did employ Ulpian's understanding of natural law as that which is common to man and all the animals.

Aubert also criticizes a legalistic, voluntaristic interpretation which sees natural law as a source of obligation and restraint rather than a rational guide for the free development of man's existence. A further critique concerns a dehumanization of natural law resulting from the triumph of purely metaphysical and abstract concepts of natural law thus ignoring the historical and cultural conditioning of the existence of man in this world.

In the light of these inadequacies and misunderstandings of the true Thomist concept of natural law, Aubert proposes a

379

more functional understanding of natural law. Natural law should express the being of man, but the being of man is more complex, open and changing than was admitted by an essentialist view of man. The reflexive and transcendental aspects of man emphasize the subject more than the object so that human nature is conceived as always deeper and more vast. The empirical and existential character of natural law must become more evident. All these different aspects will bring about a pluralism in our understanding of man so that there can no longer be a monolithic view of human reality. Different interpretations of human and social reality in the more theoretical realm will result in a growing diversity on the level of conclusions and opinions about a particular moral question.

Such a view of natural law obviously responds to many of the critiques proposed by Mehl and others. Aubert's theory of natural law, which he claims to be based on the true interpretation of Thomas, relies on a historical, inductive and empirical understanding of man. As mentioned above, I do not completely accept Aubert's interpretation of Aquinas.

The emphasis on the empirical element in natural law is also found in the natural law theory proposed by Germain Grisez, who has vigorously defended traditional Catholic teaching on artificial contraception, abortion, and generally been a severe critic of newer approaches in moral theology. Grisez acknowledges the first prescription of practical reason as enunciating that good should be pursued. But towards what definite goods should practical reason direct human action? To determine the goods that man should seek, one must examine all the basic tendencies and inclinations of man. Grisez thus admits that man is endowed with basic tendencies prior to acculturation and free choice of his own, but only empirical inquiry can determine what these inclinations are. Grisez's theory illustrates the fact that the empirical has a much greater place in contemporary revisions of natural law theory even among Catholics who have generally opposed newer developments and changes in moral theology.

Other Catholic theologians have discarded the concept of natural law and proposed other moral methodologies which do not claim to be revisions of the natural law. Although these approaches implicitly or explicitly reject natural law, they share natural law's insistence on the capacity of human reason to arrive at ethical truth. Differences do appear about the ontological and metaphysical underpinings of ethics and also about the general ethical models proposed.

At the present time these newer theories are somewhat sketchy and tentative which obviously reflects the fact that they are the first efforts on the part of Catholic theologians to develop newer ethical approaches in the light of the dissatisfactions with the past approach and the rapidly changing historical and cultural circumstances of our contemporary human existence. Many of these newer approaches have appeared in books which are not truly systematic studies but rather collections of essays (e.g., Johann, Milhaven, Antoine), a fact which again underscores the incipient and fledgling state of such developments. However, the basic fact is very clear—there is now existing in Roman Catholic ethics a plurality of ethical theories and methodologies which will only expand and become more numerous in the future.

A quick survey reveals the diversity already existing. Robert Johann employs a more relational moral model rather than the teleological model of Thomism and acknowledges a strong dependence on American pragmatism. A different philosophical approach emphasizes a transcendental method which has become popular in Catholic theology through the works of Rahner, Lonergan and Coreth. The transcendental method begins not with the object, but with the human knowing subject and the process by which man experiences, understands, judges and decides. Rahner's development of the discernment of the Spirit in decision making corresponds with his transcendental philosophy.

John Giles Milhaven has proposed and developed a love ethic based on a proper empirical evaluation of the consequences of our actions in the light of love. Milhaven recognizes a close relationship between his theory and that proposed by Joseph Fletcher, who also acknowledges that Milhaven is in basic agreement with Fletcher's own approach. Herbert McCabe has argued against both a love-centered, situation ethic derived from empirical consequences and a natural law theory based on the under-

THE CATHOLIC TRADITION: Personal Ethics

standing of man as a member of the human community. McCabe
views ethics as language and communication which sees meaning
in terms of ways of entering into social life and ways of being
with each other. A more phenomenological basis marks the
Christian ethics proposed more than five years ago by William
van der Marck. Enda McDonagh has recently outlined a moral
theology built upon reflection on the experience of the moral
call in the human situation which has interpersonal, social and
historical dimensions. McDonagh likewise rejects the teleological
approach as well as the ontology which undergirded the manu-
alist teaching on natural law, for moral obligation is discovered
in experience. McDonagh goes from the experience of the
"ought" to the "is" and not the other way around.

The radical departure from the natural law theory of the
manuals is well illustrated in the theory proposed by Pierre
Antoine, S.J., which he negatively describes as a "morality without anthropology" and positively as "praxeology" or "a pragmatic calculus." Morality today cannot be based on anthropology because we cannot develop a model of man or vision of the
world which is applicable. The dimensions of our understanding
of man today include artificiality rather than nature, the experimental state of man rather than the fixed essence, relational
rather than substantialist understandings. These new emphases
do not call for newer applications of older methodologies and
principles, but they call for a more radical change in the methodology itself. No *a priori* models of man can exist today. Morality
concerns practical reason which involves a pragmatic calculus.
Antoine denies the existence of a hierarchy of values and prefers to view morality under the controlling rubric of cost.

This survey has indicated various newer approaches and
methodologies which have been emerging in Catholic moral
theology in the last few years. In general I agree with the
strictures made against the approaches of the past, but it is important to develop some critical stance in the light of the plurality of approaches now being sketched and discussed in Catholic
moral theology. Chapter Two attempts to develop a basic stance
for Christian ethics. One important critical point of reference
concerns the importance of considering all the elements which
must enter into a theory. Especially in developing newer ap-

proaches and at the beginning stage of development, one is acutely conscious of the danger of failing to consider the complexity of the moral reality and all the elements which must enter into moral theology. For example, some approaches based on a transcendental method fail to give enough importance to the societal and political aspects of reality. Theories based on interpersonal relationships occasionally do not give enough importance to societal elements as is evident in discussions of particular questions such as sexuality.

I have also criticized some approaches because of their consequentialism, but in the light of ongoing dialogue I can try to express better my basic concerns and correct some inadequate argumentation. John G. Milhaven has developed more extensively than any other Catholic theologian in this country a moral methodology based on love as known through the consequences of our actions. At times I have felt that such an approach too easily identifies the moral judgment with the findings of empirical and human sciences. Such an approach seems to me to deny the creative and transcendent aspects of any truly human and Christian moral theory. It is not enough just to know the consequences as indicated by the empirical sciences, but one must also have a creative and practical intelligence to direct things to a better future than is now existing. All human morality needs this transcendent and creative aspect which is stressed in transcendental approaches. From a Christian perspective the limitations and sinfulness of the present call for us to work in the direction of an eschatological future which must transcend the present. Take a practical example. One who is planning the future of our cities must have not only the relevant sociological data but also a creative intelligence which can attempt to form new ways for men to live together in cities.

A consequentialist model—especially when it depends so heavily or almost exclusively on the findings of the behavioral sciences—seems to be too similar to a technological view of man. Today people are rightly reacting against such a model of human existence. There is also the danger in such a view of seeing man primarily in terms of his productivity and contributions to life and to society. I believe these are important considerations, but they are not the ultimate reasons for the values we give to human existence. Too often our society wants to treat man only in terms of his ability to contribute and be productive for our society. One has only to think of recent welfare proposals and the facile distinctions between the deserving and the undeserving poor.

The ultimate ethical model for a consequentialist approach is a teleological model, which H. Richard Niebuhr has referred to as the model of man-the-maker. Perhaps because of the somewhat pejorative description proposed by Niebuhr and in light of the obvious analogies with a technological view of man, I tend to reject a teleological model as the ultimate model in theological ethics. Man, despite all the control which he does have over his life and future today, nonetheless does not have the same control over his life that the artisan has over the raw material out of which he is fashioning his product. The limit situation of death too often becomes glossed over in such a concept of man. This model as mentioned does not seem to express enough the aspects of creativity and transcendence. From the Christian perspective it does not seem to do justice to the Christian realities of suffering, death and resurrection, and the hope which always transcends the limits of the present situation.

Rather than the teleological model of man-the-maker or the deontological model I would opt with Niebuhr for the relational-responsibility model as more fundamental in describing the Christian life—if only because it allows one to incorporate the best elements of the other models. In practical matters the relationality model would share the same diffidence towards absolute norms because one can not absolutize what exists in terms of relationships. Nor would such a model accept a static hierarchy of values because of the multiple and changing relationships seen within a more historical perspective. Such a model realizes the importance of both empirical data and the creative and transcendent aspects of human existence even though these can never exist in a vacuum or merely in the abstract.

Perhaps some forms of consequentialism do not necessarily involve all the negative aspects I have seen in consequentialism. John G. Milhaven has recently insisted that human experience must include affective and creative aspects which correspond to the aesthetic judgment. There seems to me to be a difference between the scientific and the aesthetic judgment which roughly corresponds to the greater emphasis on creativity and transcendence in the aesthetic judgment. Moreover, I have some difficulties with the way in which Milhaven develops his insistence on experience.

Milhaven rightly implies that we have often been insensitive to moral problems because we have not experienced these things ourselves. I personally realize my lack of sensitivities at times because I have not experienced racial discrimination, war, poverty, or hunger. However as a limited human being I cannot experience all these realities. Sometimes experience of only one side of a question will definitely prejudice my understanding of the total human situation with which I am confronted. Actual experience of reality is helpful and important, but it is not sufficient. There is the need for a creative sensitivity and moral sense which does not have to actually experience something before it can morally react. The insistence on actual experience seems again to be an indication of the lack of creativity and transcendence in the theological method employed. Especially in the midst of the great complexity existing today and the impossibility of actual experience, the ethician and the individual person must develop a creative moral sensitivity which enables him to go beyond the boundaries of his own limited actual experience. Today we can perhaps accuse our predecessors of white racism, but what will our successors rightly accuse us of?

Perhaps part of the disagreement arises from two different perspectives. Milhaven originally was concentrating primarily on the question of absolute norms in moral theology and denies such norms on the basis of his appeal to the ultimate importance of consequences in determining our actions in these cases. The perspective I have outlined considers rather a very basic posture for our total moral life and thus does not want to reduce our total ethical posture to the model of consequences or of man-the-maker. On particular questions involving the existence of absolute norms, I too would agree on the need to evaluate and weigh all the elements involved in the light of my relational vision of human existence. A relational understanding of reality incorporates the historical and changing aspects while denying any eternal, static hierarchy of relational values. Obviously in particular situations one determines what is good in terms of what will promote his understanding of relational values. In this light I must point out some inadequacies in my own somewhat unnuanced argument against consequentialism based on the inability to know all the consequences of my actions.

Richard McCormick has recently acknowledged the decisive role of consequences in moral theology, but he realizes the importance of Christian intentionalities and ethos in the light of which consequences are weighed and evaluated. In this way he avoids some of the problems I have with other types of consequentialism, although at least part of the problem may result from the different perspectives mentioned above.

This type of dialogue, discussion and disagreement among Catholic moralists on methodological issues will continue to grow and increase. One must expect to find continuing diversity in the search for more adequate moral theologies. The thrust of this brief survey is to show the diversity of moral methodologies already existing among Catholic moral theologians.

Perhaps the most frequent complaint of Protestant ethicians against Catholic moral theology has been the charge of legalism. The last few years have seen Catholics themselves make the same charge about their own theological tradition, or at least the tradition as it was interpreted in the manuals of moral theology. The discussion has developed from a context of positive law to the context of natural law. Are there certain actions which are always and everywhere wrong?

In the context of the situation ethics debate in the 1960's Catholic theologians have reexamined the role and place of absolute norms in moral theology. I agree with an increasing number of Catholic theologians who deny the existence of negative moral absolutes; that is, actions described solely in terms of the physical structure of the act (a material piece of behavior) which are said to be always and everywhere wrong. There are a variety of reasons for such a denial including both a reexamination of the teaching of the past which does not appear to be as absolute as presented in the manuals and newer methodological approaches to meet our changing understandings of man and reality. Obviously such a denial stems from a more inductive, relational and empirical approach to moral problems. Milhaven, followed now by Crotty, would understand moral norms as empirical generalizations. Note here how Catholic theologians are departing from the ontological foundations upon which the theology of the manuals was based. Others, however, such as McCabe would deny the fact that absolute moral norms are just empirical generalizations.

Perhaps one of the most important principles in the older Catholic moral theology was the principle of the double effect, which decided conflict situations in which an action would have both good and bad effects. As generally understood in the manuals, the differentiation between direct and indirect was based on the physical structure of the act itself as illustrated in such descriptions of the direct effect as the *finis operis* of the act or the act which by its very nature does this particular thing. The literature on the question has been growing in the past five years with more and more Catholics disagreeing with the older understanding of direct and indirect.

The newer approaches call for a weighing and comparison of all the values involved so that I perform the action which brings about the greatest possible good. Note the obvious consequentialist calculus in such a determination but also the fact that the relative importance attached to the different values involved transcends the present limited situation and can be verified only in the context of the fullness of the Christian experience. Richard McCormick has recently suggested that such an understanding of the principle of the double effect based on the proportional weighing of all the consequences of my action also serves as the ultimate basis for the understanding of the principle of totality and also the principle of discrimination in the just war theory.

On more specific ethical questions there is already an ever growing divergence of opinions among Catholic moral theologians. In many ways the criticism of the older teaching on contraception marked just a beginning. The arguments proposed against the teaching on contraception presupposed different theological methodologies which would also lead to different opinions on other complex, specific moral problems. These differences are illustrated in that contemporary literature. On the question of abortion there is now existing among Catholics a plurality of opinions even though the gamut of these opinions at the present time does not seem to be as broad as the spectrum of opinions existing among the population at large. Chapter Six will consider in detail the question of abortion.

Catholic theologians frequently deny the existing teaching of the hierarchical magisterium on such issues as contraception, sterilization, artificial insemination, masturbation, the generic gravity of sexual sins. Newer approaches have recently been taken to the question of homosexuality. Some Catholic theologians have argued against the moral norm condemning all sexual relationships outside marriage. In this particular area, there is not a great number of theologians proposing such views nor is there the range of opinions which exists among the population at large, but there is divergence from the heretofore accepted norm. Another absolute norm in Catholic moral teaching that has been questioned is the absolute prohibition of euthanasia in all cases as distinguished from the traditional teaching on the need to employ only ordinary means to sustain human life. All these questions in the area of medical and sexual morality are being questioned today because some theologians believe that the absolute prohibitions define the forbidden action in terms of the physical structure of the act seen in itself apart from the context, the existing relationships or the consequences.

The plurality of opinions also exists in other questions where previously there was *the* Catholic opinion. Contemporary theologians are calling for a rethinking of the absolute prohibition against divorce and openly favoring a more benign moral and pastoral attitude to people who are divorced so that they are not excluded from the sacramental life of the Church. Chapter Seven will discuss in detail the teaching and practice of the Church on divorce and advocate a change. In questions of social and political morality there is also a divergence of opinions among Catholic theologians. On the question of war, actual Catholic opinions include pacifism, nuclear pacifism and just war theory. Recent historical research indicates that there has been a just war tradition with different theories even within that tradition. Thus again historical research shows a greater flexibility within the tradition, although contemporary discussions range even beyond the traditional approaches.

The conclusion of this brief overview is evident. Within the context of Roman Catholic moral theology there is not only a growing plurality of ethical methodologies but also an ever more noticeable divergence on particular moral questions. There is a connection between the two statements, for the newer methodologies obviously lead to different conclusions especially in complex issues which are not as simple as they were once thought to be. Recently an American bishop has recognized the fact of this growing pluralism although his reaction to the fact is much different from the generally approving tone of this essay. Thus the myth of a monolithic Roman Catholic moral theology with *the* Catholic opinion on specific, complex matters is exploded.

### Authoritarianism

A second source of critical concern for Protestant ethicians has been the authoritarian intervention of the Roman Catholic Church in moral matters to direct and even bind the consciences of her members. The Catholic Church has claimed a unique competency to interpret authoritatively even the natural law for its adherents and thus supply a sure and reliable guide for conscience in moral matters.

Here again both a reexamination of the tradition and contemporary theological opinions have joined forces to change quite radically the understanding of the role of the teaching authority of the Church in matters of morality. Today there is also emerging within the Catholic Church a proper discussion about the meaning of infallibility as it pertains to the Church and to the papal office, but our discussion can neatly dodge the present furor over infallibility. In my judgment there has never been an infallible, *ex cathedra* pronouncement or an infallible teaching of the ordinary magisterium on a specific moral matter. Our concern is with the so-called authentic or authoritative, noninfallible hierarchical magisterium.

This expression—the authoritative, noninfallible teaching authority—apparently first appears about the time of the famous letter of Pope Pius IX to the archbishop of Munich in 1863 on the occasion of the conference of intellectuals held under the leadership of Döllinger with the intention of bringing Catholic thought into dialogue with the philosophy and science of the modern world.

The theologians of the time developed this teaching on the authoritative, noninfallible teaching authority and the consent that was required to such teaching on the part of Catholics. The faithful owed to this teaching an internal religious assent of intellect and will as distinguished from the absolute assent of faith which Catholics must give to infallible Church teaching. The 19th and 20th century theologians generally admitted that this assent was conditioned even though they were rather general in describing the conditions. Thus in general the theologians admit the possibility of error in such teaching and even point to historical precedents for error in the teaching function of the popes—e.g., Liberius, Vigilius, Honorius, as well as Celestine III and the heralded Galileo case. Lercher admits at least the possibility of the Church correcting the Pope. Thus the theologians who wrote the theological manuals of the day admit the possibility of error in the papal teaching with the corresponding possibility of nonacceptance on the part of the faithful.

The twentieth century witnessed a growing entrenchment of an overly juridical and authoritative understanding of the Church and of the hierarchical magisterium ever since the insistence in the nineteenth century against a real dialogue with the modern world. The encyclical *Humani Generis* in 1950 was an attempt to clamp down on the "New Theology" and to reassert the papal teaching authority as a means of controlling theological speculation. In this letter Pope Pius XII applies to the ordinary papal teaching authority as found in encyclicals the biblical words—he who hears you hears Me. If the Pope goes out of his way to deliberately speak on a controverted subject, the subject can no longer be regarded as a matter for free debate among theologians.

Changes occurring in the intervening years are reflected in the teaching of Vatican II and its differences with the teaching of *Humani Generis*. It is interesting to note that conservative opposition to some of the teaching of *Mater et Magistra* brought momentarily to the surface the right of Catholics to dissent from the authoritative, noninfallible teaching of the Pope. The first draft of the Constitution on the Church of Vatican II did contain the teaching of *Humani Generis* mentioned above. The final version of the Constitution purposely left out the teaching of *Humani Generis*. The final document employs the terminology of the manuals in distinguishing the religious assent owed to noninfallible teaching from the assent of faith and describes this religious assent in terms of a religious submission of intellect and will. That the section is to be interpreted in the light of the teaching of the manuals is evident from the response given by the doctrinal commission to the query about an educated person who for solid reasons cannot give internal assent to a noninfallible teaching. The commission responded simply: "For this case approved theological explanations should be consulted."

The ensuing development of this teaching has some interesting aspects. In 1967 the American bishops issued a collective pastoral letter, "The Church in Our Day." One section is devoted to religious assent, but the matter is presented in a confused and an inaccurate manner. This document speaks of religious assent as owed to both infallible and noninfallible teaching, but in the first case the religious assent is definitive, while in the second case such assent is required but not definitively. "A Catholic abides not only by the extraordinary decisions of the Church but by its ordinary life as well where faith and discipline are concerned." Such an assent includes questions touching on dogma, "but it is also required for certain decisions bound up with the good ordering of the Church." In addition to the novel use of religious assent and the confusion between faith and discipline, there is no explicit mention of the possibility of dissent.

On September 22, 1967, the German bishops issued a pastoral letter, which also took up the question of the assent due to noninfallible papal teaching. "To protect individuals and ultimately the substance of faith, the Church must make doctrinal pronouncements which are binding to a limited degree, despite the danger or error in particular matters. Since these are not definitions of faith, they are to some extent provisional and entail the possibility of error. . . . In this kind of situation the individual Christian and indeed the Church as a whole is like a man who has to follow the decision of an expert whom he knows is not infallible." Thus the German bishops rightly interpret the authoritative, noninfallible teaching as provisional.

Before the issuance of Pope Paul's *Humanae Vitae* in 1968, theologians had been developing the possibility of dissent from such authoritative, noninfallible papal teaching. Theologians such as Donlon, Rahner and Schueller explicitly affirmed the right of public dissent which had not been found in the earlier manualists. Perhaps the most perceptive discussion of the moral magisterium was by Daniel Maguire, who realized that the very nature of the search for moral truth argues for the possibility of dissent from papal moral teaching on specific issues. Maguire pointed out that the hierarchical magisterium could not continue to function in an overly juridical and legalistic style and constructively suggested ways for the hierarchical magisterium to proceed in carrying out its function in the changed theological understandings of the post Vatican II Church.

The negative reaction of theologians and even bishops to the papal encyclical on artificial contraception issued in the summer of 1968 brought to the attention of all Catholics, perhaps for the first time, the right to dissent from authoritative, noninfallible papal teaching when there are solid reasons for so doing. This same reality can and must be understood in a somewhat broader context and in a more positive manner. Even when the hierarchical magisterium has spoken on a particular issue, there can still be a pluralism of Catholic thinking on this issue. Thus from the viewpoint of a proper understanding of the moral teaching office of the hierarchical magisterium it will be impossible to speak about *the* Roman Catholic position on a particular moral issue as if there could not be any other possible position.

One must understand the reason for such a pluralism not only in methodology but also concerning practical questions. The basic reason for such a pluralism is the complexity of moral issues and the need for relational and empirical considerations which involve many aspects and afford the possibility of arriving at different ethical judgments. In the past when forbidden actions were described in terms of the physical structure of the act, then it was possible to speak about certain actions which were always and everywhere wrong. A relational understanding of morality or an empirical calculus cannot admit such absoluteness. In the midst of all the circumstances which must be considered in complex questions one must admit a possible diversity of concrete, ethical judgments.

The fundamental reason for this possible diversity—the many elements to be considered in the final decision and the complexity of the situation itself—had been acknowledged in the past by Thomas Aquinas himself. Thomas admitted that although the first principles of the natural law were always the same, the proper conclusions of these principles can admit of exceptions because of the complexity of the situation and the diverse elements entering into the final decision. The more one descends into particulars, the greater is the possibility of exceptions because of the complexity of the situation.

## Theological Presuppositions

Theological presuppositions of Protestant and Catholic ethics do seem to be a source of divergences in the two traditions, but even here the differences are much less today than in the past, and in some cases are negligible so that there really are no outstanding, pertinent theological differences between some Protestant and some Catholic ethicians. Unfortunately Mehl reflects more of the past divergences rather than the present convergences in his assessment.

The question often referred to as the nature-supernature question is of paramount significance in this area. Catholic theology has generally accepted the goodness of man, a continuity between nature and grace as well as between creation and redemption, and the possibility of going from man to God which has been the basis for a natural theology and a natural law. An earlier section has considered the philosophical aspects of the question of natural law, which included the precise understanding of man and nature with the different operative methodologies developed as a result of such understandings. From the theological perspective the natural law theory has asserted that the Christian can arrive at true ethical wisdom and knowledge through his reason and his understanding of man. Some forms of Protestant theology especially in the Orthodox and neo-Orthodox traditions have denied or denigrated the place of reason and the natural in Christian ethical consideration although often some substitute has been proposed. Chapter Two will consider in greater detail some aspects of these differences.

Mehl rejects the Catholic position which he describes as seeing man under two aspects—man as natural being and man as a being with a supernatural vocation. In such a system there seem to be two separate ethics for man—a purely human one and a supernatural one. Although there will continue to be differences in this area between some Catholic and some Protestant theologians, there have emerged some developments in Catholic thinking which can and do bridge the former gap at least with some Protestants.

Catholic theology today willingly admits the impossibility of proposing two ethics—an ethic of natural law for those living in the world and an ethic of evangelical perfection for those who choose to enter the religious life. Contemporary Catholic theology recalls that all Christians are called by God in Christ to change their hearts and follow him.

One can notice even in the documents of the hierarchical magisterium a real move away from the notion of an existing natural order to which the supernatural is then added. The Pastoral Constitution on the Church in the Modern World is most instructive in this area—the phrase natural law appears only three times. The anthropology described in this document marks a definite advance over the older anthropologies. The essential nature of man, the same in all possible states of human existence, is not the fundamental concept to which the supernatural order is added. Man is described in terms of the history of salvation which sees man and reality in terms of the work of creation, the reality of sin, the redemptive work of Jesus and final resurrection destiny. I personally have some difficulties with this particular presentation. The older concept of the two separate spheres of the natural and the supernatural is overcome, but the tension and ambiguity of our present existence in the light of the full Christian horizon do not appear. Some chapters of Part One (specifically: 1, 2, and 4) fail to give enough importance to the eschatological future and the discontinuity existing between now and the future. The eschatology of this document has too much emphasis on realization now that Jesus has come. Correlatively, not enough importance is given to sin and its effects on human life.

Even in the document itself, but especially in the light of my personal critique, one can understand the nature-supernature question or the Christ and culture question in terms of H. Richard Niebuhr's classification of Christ transforming culture or of grace transforming nature rather than the Christ above culture model which characterized Catholic thought in the past. My personal criticism is that this Constitution and the encyclical of Paul VI *Populorum Progressio* do not stress enough the transforming aspect, because sin and the eschatological future as somewhat discontinuous with the present do not receive enough attention. The fact that nature-supernature can be understood in terms of a conversionist or transformationist model in Catholic thought obviously indicates a broad area of agreement with many Protestants. The stance for moral theology to be developed in Chapter Two is most compatible with a transformationist motif.

The ramifications of a transformationist motif have appeared in an interesting way in a study of human sexuality by J. M. Pohier. Pohier rightly acknowledges the unfortunately negative understanding of sexuality in the Catholic tradition, which apparently comes from too easily equating sin with sexuality. Christians should understand sexuality the same way they understand justice, truth, and love. The eschatological future does not call for one to deny these realities or to die to them but rather to transform them. A reconsideration of sexuality calls for a reconsideration of some basic understandings of the Christian faith, especially the resurrection.

In this light Pohier denies the fact that man is by nature immortal. To believe in the resurrection is to believe that God will do to us as his gracious gift what he has done in Jesus. This is entirely different from asserting the natural immortality of man or the soul. These different understandings of immortality affect our understanding of sexuality. If man is by nature immortal, if death is punishment, if recovery of immortality demands that man willingly accept and inflict upon himself the penalty of death, the repression or abolition of sexuality signifies and realizes par excellence this recovery of immortality. If, on the contrary, the resurrection is the work of God, if it is a property of the love of God and not a property of the nature of man, and if it implies a change of man, then sexuality is neither more nor less than all the other dimensions of the present existence of man and the object of this future change.

Certainly it is part of the Catholic theological tradition to uphold a basic goodness present in man, the power of human reason to arrive at some speculative and practical truths, and some continuity between man and grace. Thus Mehl correctly asserts that the Catholic tradition would not accept a total opposition between *agape* and *eros*. There is some continuity between human love and divine love which both transforms and perfects human love. For the same reasons the Catholic theological tradition would have some problems with the theological presuppositions of Paul Ramsey's ethic, such as obedient love, the stress on fidelity with no attention to some notion of fulfillment, and his very basic insistence on order because of the prevailing presence of sin. Today Catholic theologians must correct some of the overemphases of the recent past by realizing also the discontinuity between nature and grace and some discontinuity between the present and the eschatological future. Such an insistence makes it easier to adopt a transformationist or conversionist model.

Intimately connected with the nature-grace question is the importance given to the reality of sin. There is no doubt that Protestant theology has generally placed much more emphasis on sin than the Catholic tradition has. The insistence on order in some Protestant social ethics is derived from their understanding of the pervading power of sin. Catholic theology can legitimately be criticized for not giving enough importance in the past to the reality of sin, although such a consideration was not always lacking in Catholic thought. Thomas Aquinas, for example, acknowledged the existence of the right to own private property not on the basis of the dignity and needs of the human person as was done by later Popes, but because of human sinfulness. Peace, order and the care of goods would be better provided for if each person owns his own property even though all property retains a relationship for all mankind so that one's use of his right to private property is limited by this communal consideration.

Today Catholic theologians are trying to develop a better understanding of the reality and moral significance of sin. Böckle here presents a more adequate picture of the developments in Catholic theology than does Mehl, who is obviously writing from within a different theological tradition. Catholic theology has learned especially in dialogue with Protestant theology to place more emphasis on sin and the sinner rather than on sins. Relying heavily on biblical theology and more personalist and existential themes, as well as a revival of older Thomistic notions, contemporary theology has developed the reality of sin in terms of the fundamental option. Catholic theology has also tried to recover a way in which it can accept and incorporate the insights of the *simul justus et peccator* concept of the reformation with the corresponding call for continual conversion on the part of the Christian. Likewise, the natural order does not continue to exist as if it were unaffected by sin but rather the very fact that sin has not destroyed man and the human is the work of God's gracious love.

The effect of sin in the moral life of man is seen in the attempts by some Catholic theologians to come to grips with conflict situations in the light of the presence of sin. The overly rationalist approach of the manuals according to Nicholas Crotty denied the very existence of the possibility of a conflict of values in moral decision making. In the older approach there could be no conflict of values because there is a perfectly ordered plan for the world in which all things are arranged in proper relationships and order, and reason can perceive this order. In all situations including those which apparently involve conflicts there is an objectively valid moral decision which can simply be called good. Moral duties can never really conflict.

Crotty points out that some Catholic theologians deny such a view of reality because there are true conflict situations which are brought about by the presence of sin. Some might still object that these are not real moral evils but only physical evils or pre-moral evils. In some cases I would readily agree that the evil is pre-moral (e.g. contraception), but in other cases the social dimension of sin so affects reality that there is the necessity of recognizing that the conflict arises because of the presence of sin. Strictly speaking, the evil here is not moral in the sense of intended by one of the persons involved, but it results from the presence of sin incarnated in the structures of human existence and not just from human finitude and limitation. Crotty sees the Christian as weighing the good and the evil consequences of his action with the realization that his action will bring about some evil which must be recognized and deplored in true Christian repentance. It seems to me that those who deny this fact or say the values involved in all cases are only pre-moral have too individualistic a view of sin and repentance. Above all in these days we must understand the very real existence of corporate guilt and repentance. Theories of this type in Catholic theology obviously owe much to the ongoing dialogue with Protestant ethicians.

Justification and sanctification have been a perennial source of debate among Catholics and Protestants, and different approaches to those theological questions can have important repercussions in the area of Christian ethics. Differing opinions about the possibility of growth or development in the Christian life depend upon one's understanding of the reality of justification and sanctification. Recent Catholic scholarship has tried to show that there may not be that much difference on the question of justification between Protestant and Catholic position.

In moral areas Catholic thought has underscored the importance of works, and the danger of pelagianism is ever present and sometimes succumbed to, at least in practice. The tendency in Protestantism is to highlight faith, and quietism and passivity have threatened such an approach. Some Protestant and Catholic theologians seem to be more aware of the dichotomies in their older approaches to these questions and are now trying to do justice to both faith and the rightful place of works in the Christian life.

Another important theological difference between Protestant and Catholic thought centers on the concept of freedom. A few years ago it was a commonplace in the incipient ecumenical dialogue to show that Catholic thought exaggerated order at the expense of freedom, whereas Protestant thought

398

overlooked order in their insistence on freedom. There is obviously truth in this assertion, but there have also been some attempts to overcome such dichotomies.

Protestant theology highlights the transcendence and graciousness of God, who in his freedom has chosen to act in human history. God in his freedom acts in concrete ways with individual men which can never be totally determined in advance by any human calculations or laws, since the freedom of God is sovereign. Catholic theology traditionally understands God's acting with man through different mediations; whereas Protestant theology has insisted often on the immediate character of God's relationship with man. Catholic theology has developed these mediations of the divine action in terms of the Church, the sacraments, Church order and natural law. Some Protestant ethicians understand the divine transcendence, the freedom of God and the concreteness of his way of acting with man in the context of a soteriology which places an unbridgeable chasm between Christian ethics and any form of human or philosophical ethics. This type of approach is quite foreign to the Catholic tradition with its acceptance of mediation and the role of the natural. Catholic theology, however, is beginning to recognize the importance of the transcendence and freedom of God as practically reflected in the whole dispute about absolute norms in the moral life.

Correlatively, Protestant ethics recognizes the fundamental importance of the freedom of the believer, whereas Catholic theology has traditionally had difficulty with the concept of freedom. Catholic insistence on the objective and on the ordered structure of human existence left little room for creative freedom and the subjective. Recall the tortuous development in Catholic thinking on the question of religious liberty. The recent change of emphasis is evident in a development in Pope John's teaching. In 1963 he insisted that a just and Christian social order should be based on truth, justice, charity and freedom, but two years earlier in *Mater et Magistra* he had not mentioned freedom. Today some Catholics are calling for a morality based on freedom with the consequent importance of responsibility which fits in with the move away from an understanding of an essential structure of man and human community as presupposed in the older natural law approach.

## Implications

This chapter has attempted to survey the present state of Roman Catholic theology under the limited perspective of the ongoing dialogue with Protestant ethics. There still do exist some differences based primarily on theological presuppositions which are especially evident in discussions with Orthodox and neo-Orthodox Protestants. In general there has been a remarkable breaking down of the barriers and differences between Catholic and Protestant ethics so that often there is agreement across denominational lines on both methodological and content questions. The factor contributing the most to this change is the breakdown of a monolithic, Roman Catholic moral theology. Whatever value judgments one might want to make about the present situation, the fact seems to be that there is no monolithic, Catholic moral theology and no such thing as *the* Catholic position on specific, complex moral questions.

What are the implications of this description of the factual situation of Catholic moral theology today? I think that many Catholic moral theologians actively working in the field and teaching today would be in general accord with the situation of pluralism as described here. However, the rapidity of the change and the somewhat radical nature of the change have contributed to the fact that the vast majority of people outside the field of Catholic moral theology are unaware of this new situation. Obviously this situation with so many possibilities for tension and misunderstanding is difficult. The Catholic moral theologian has the responsibility of making other interested people aware of the actual situation in his field as it exists today, even though there would be a number of Catholic ethicians, perhaps a minority, who would not agree with this description. The Catholic theologian has a responsibility to communicate this situation to many publics, but this discussion will just concentrate on three different groups.

First, Protestant ethicians. As exemplified in the case of Mehl the rapidity of the changing situation in Catholic ethics has caught some Protestant theologians unaware. Many Protestant ethicians are quite familiar with the present state of Catholic moral theology, probably more so in this country than elsewhere. A realization of the breakup of a monolithic methodology or a detailed monolithic code will prevent Protestants from speaking about *the* Roman Catholic ethics or *the* Roman Catholic solution to a particular problem without further nuances.

Secondly, the Catholic community generally. Roman Catholics on the whole are unaware of the present state of Roman Catholic theology. In any science there is always an educational lag between what the theoreticians are saying and what the ordinary person knows. This gap is even more pronounced now because of the suddenness and the radicalness of the change. Such a change has obviously been very difficult and traumatic for people who were in the field of moral theology. One of the many problems with Catholic moral theology in this country and even abroad today is the fact that most of the people actively engaged in the field today have been in the field for less than 15 years.

The gap between the actual state of Catholic moral theology and the understanding of the Catholic in the street is enormous. There is need for a real educational effort on the part of all, including theologians. Fears of subjectivity, relativism and individualism must be put aside. Likewise such people also have to be shown how the discipline arrived at the present state and continuities as well as the discontinuities with the past teaching. One can appreciate the anxiety and fears of many Catholics, but this only underlines the need for education.

Thirdly, the bishops and the hierarchical teaching office in the Church. The Catholic Church has experienced many painful shocks in the last few years. The easiest solution at times is to blame the Pope and the bishops. As an ethician who believes in the theoretical and practical importance of complexity, I tend to reject overly simplistic solutions which really fail to respond to the realities of the situation. The Pope and the bishops have enormous concerns and many groups asking for their attention and consideration. More than anyone else, they experience and know the tensions of the rapid changes which have taken place in Catholic life and theology in the past few years.

There has not been a relationship of dialogue and trust between bishops and theologians in the past few years. This is true not only of the United States but also exists in countries such as Germany. Obviously there is fault on both sides contributing to this lack of dialogue.

However, the simple fact of the matter is that the bishops of the Roman Catholic Church in general and the bishops of the United States in particular are unwilling to admit the present state of Roman Catholic moral theology and apparently feel unable to enter into dialogue about this. Again I realize that different perspectives exist between theologians and bishops and that there will always be such a tension between them; but the existing differences are actually quite destructive for the life of the Church as a whole. Nor would I merely reduce the teaching office of the bishops to repeating a theological consensus, but there must be increased dialogue and understanding.

In a sense the bishops were forced by the quality and quantity of the dissent to *Humanae Vitae* to try to live with such a reality. However, they obviously thought that it was an isolated phenomenon which would quickly disappear or that would be forgotten about if they just stayed around long enough. What they have not realized is that the dissent to *Humanae Vitae* was symptomatic of changes occurring in moral theology and these symptoms are bound to appear ever more increasingly. Much more was involved than just speculative dissent from one specific teaching of the hierarchical magisterium. This historical episode signified a new understanding of Catholic moral theology and the way in which the hierarchical magisterium should carry out its teaching function in the area of morality.

Perhaps the most blatant sign of the gap between bishops and theologians was the issuance by the bishops of the United States of "The Ethical and Religious Directives for Catholic Health Facilities," which was approved by the American bishops at their November 1971 meeting by an overwhelming vote. This document in the words of the chairman of the bishops "Committee on Doctrine" amounts to a mere updating of the 1955 directives. In such things there can never be essential changes but only accidental changes.

# Charles E. Curran

In the light of the present state of Roman Catholic moral theology, especially the discussions on absolute norms and medical ethics, it seems preposterous that the American bishops could issue medical directives substantially the same as those issued in 1955. The bishops by their action show that they do not understand the present state of Catholic moral theology and consequently are trying to exercise their teaching function in a way that is totally incompatible with the concept of our search for moral truth.

The preamble of these directives speaks about the prohibited procedures as recognized to be clearly wrong according to present knowledge. The document goes on to talk about the basic moral absolutes in a way that completely ignores the developments of the past few years. The reference to Catholic moral teaching is to a "code," although it is precisely such an approach that is questioned by many Catholic theologians today. This document fails to recognize three important realities stressed in this paper: the pluralism of ethical methodologies in Roman Catholic moral theology; the possibility of dissent on specific questions and the more positive formulation admitting of some pluralism; the particular moral conclusions which have been seriously questioned by Catholic scholarship in the last few years.

I personally and many other Catholic theologians would object to the following specifics of this code: the condemnations of contraception, direct sterilization, masturbation for seminal analysis, artificial insemination with the husband's seed; some aspects of the teaching on abortion and euthanasia; the processes forbidden in the handling of extrauterine pregnancies; the distinction between direct and indirect which is stated in terms of the physical structure of the act itself ("Any deliberate medical procedure, the purpose of which is to deprive a fetus or an embryo of its life"; "Every procedure whose sole immediate effect is the termination of pregnancy before viability is an abortion."—Notice here the failure to adopt the traditional terminology of direct and indirect abortion and the effort to redefine abortion in terms of direct abortion so that the absoluteness of the prohibition may be strengthened); the solution of conflict situations involving life by the application of the principle of double effect.

Perhaps even more disturbing is the attitude proposed by one bishop who was influential in the work of the directives because of his position as chairman of the "Committee on Doctrine" of the American bishops. In a commentary on the proposed hospital directives the bishop took up the question of possible dissent from the norms of such a code.

> All this is risky business—this following of personal conscience in any issue on which the moral law holds otherwise. It is possible to find these days a Catholic writer on speculative moral theology advancing in nearly every subject a theory contrary to traditional Catholic doctrine. You cannot "follow" him, because he is not an authorized leader of the People of God. Accept his theories and you are on your own, crossing Niagara Falls on a tightrope with the abyss beneath, rather than using the bridge which the Church has constructed for your safety and direction in reaching the opposite shore.

This paragraph contains a very poor and I believe harmfully erroneous notion of the teaching authority in the Church and how it is exercised. The bishop acknowledges there is existing a plurality of theological opinions in nearly every subject. In the midst of this moral complexity the problem can be solved in a juridical and authoritarian way by the teaching authority of the Church. This is the worst kind of juridical and voluntaristic notion of a true teacher. Perhaps some of the problem arises from the too frequent juxtaposition in the Catholic tradition of those two words—teaching authority. The teaching office thus easily becomes understood in a juridical and authoritative way. The possibility and the right to dissent are not specified in a way that a true teacher should explain these realities. One sees in these hospital directives and in this interpretation that monolithic natural law theory based on the nature of things, a legalistic code approach to complex specific questions, and an authoritarianism which are the precise points of contention and dispute in contemporary Catholic moral theology.

Obviously we are living in changing and confusing times. The American bishops felt many pressures urging them to give some hospital directives. There are good points contained in these directives as well as in the older directives. I am not sure how I would proceed in trying to draw up such directives in the light of the changing theological scene, the possibility and even the right to dissent acknowledged to exist in the Church, the changing understanding of the Catholic health facility in terms of its funding and its service, the principle of religious liberty and the rights of people to act in accord with their conscience provided public order and the rights of other innocent people are not disproportionately affected. The problem is very complex, and no perfect solution can ever be arrived at; but the directives as issued by the American bishops are in my judgment theologically inaccurate and pastorally harmful in the long run.

The issuance of the hospital directives by the American bishops is just another indication of the tension existing in the Roman Catholic Church today. Obviously one does not want to exacerbate such tensions, but at times it is necessary to speak forthrightly in the hope of bringing about greater good. Obviously theologians are also at fault for not having done more in this area. If Catholic theologians had taken the initiative and come out with their own set of directives, perhaps they could have avoided some problems.

The implications of the state of Catholic moral theology have thus far concentrated only on the present. What are the implications for the future? This essay has in general followed an approach showing the importance of both continuity and discontinuity in moral theology. A revision and restudy of past teachings has brought about almost radical reinterpretations. At the same time newer approaches have also greatly contributed to the changing reality of moral theology. Any valid approach in the future must appreciate the significance of both continuity and discontinuity, but it seems that discontinuity will need a greater emphasis both because of the rapidly changing conditions of human existence and also because of the fact that an artificial, monolithic approach backed by an overly juridical teaching authority was able to preserve in existence what was really an historically and culturally limited reality.

405

The future development of Catholic moral theology can well profit from some of the traditional emphases—the ability of human reason to arrive at good ethical decisions, a basic goodness in man which despite sinfulness remains in some continuity, as well as some discontinuity, with grace and redemption. Likewise the traditional Catholic emphasis on the structure of man and human existence can be of help if interpreted in a way to appreciate the web of relationships in which man finds himself so that he cannot be defined primarily in terms of an unrestricted freedom which does not take into account the relationships which both limit and perfect him.

However, the future will continue to develop the discontinuities especially in terms of the understanding of man and the ethical methodologies proposed for decision-making. The incipient pluralism described above will only become more evident in the years to come. Dialogue with contemporary scientific and philosophical approaches will result in newer approaches in Catholic moral theology. In the area of personal ethics, if one can make a distinction between personal and social ethics, this dialogue has already begun. But in the area of social ethics Catholic theology must begin to develop different approaches. The natural law approach of the papal encyclicals of the past is no longer sufficient. A suitable methodology must be constructed which will incorporate a critical dialogue with the sciences in trying to deal with questions of social morality. One can notice the lack of any such methodology among Roman Catholic ethicians at the present time. The great social problems of our day obviously involve the question of means to bring about the values to be incorporated into our society. Perhaps in the area of social ethics there is the greatest need for newer approaches and methodologies.

The fact that there will be discontinuities with the past and perhaps very noticeable discontinuities in the area of approaches to social ethics should not be discomforting to one who deeply appreciates the Catholic tradition. The greatness of Thomas Aquinas comes from his boldness and creativity in trying to express the Christian message in the thought patterns which were then current in his world. Thomas was not content merely to cite the authorities of the past, but rather he creatively attempted to express the Christian message in terms of the Aristotelian thought which was then coming into the University world of Europe. The Catholic tradition with its rightful appreciation of human reason must always be willing to enter into rational dialogue and discover newer approaches and understandings.

Ironically, Thomas Aquinas in the last two centuries has been used by the hierarchical magisterium for the exact opposite purpose of what he tried to accomplish in his own times. The hierarchical magisterium has employed Thomas as a means of prohibiting any dialogue with the modern world and of preserving a monolithic philosophical system often referred to as the perennial philosophy. If Catholic theology had been allowed to develop normally in the last two centuries there would not be the traumatic experience of so abrupt and sudden a change as the Roman Catholic Church is experiencing today. Future developments will only accent and bring to the fullest development the changes already mentioned as occurring in Roman Catholic moral theology. But the willingness to accept the ability of man to arrive at moral truth, together with an historical world view, implies the need for a continuing dialogue ever incorporating contemporary human wisdom with the critical realization that such wisdom must always be put to the test.

Obviously the present state of Catholic moral theology and my understanding of its future development will also create problems for the discipline of moral theology as well as for the life of the Catholic Church. I have expressed my personal disagreement with some aspects of these new developments although I generally favor such a pluralistic understanding. However, whether one likes it or not, it will be impossible to change the present directions in Catholic moral theology.